GunDigest BOOK OF
.22 RIMFIRE

─── 2ND EDITION ───

Published by

Gun Digest® Books, an imprint of F+W Media, Inc.
Krause Publications • 700 East State Street • Iola, WI 54990-0001
715-445-2214 • 888-457-2873
www.krausebooks.com

To order books or other products call toll-free 1-800-258-0929
or visit us online at www.gundigeststore.com

ISBN-13: 978-1-4402-4659-3
ISBN-10: 1-4402-4659-9

Cover Design by Kevin Ulrich
Designed by Jana Tappa
Edited by Corrina Peterson

Printed in the United States of America

10 9 8 7 6 5 4 3 2 1

Related Titles from Gun Digest

Customize the Ruger 10/22

Gun Digest Book of Rimfire Rifles Assembly/Disassembly

Gun Digest Book of Exploded Gun Drawings

Standard Catalog of Ruger Firearms

Gunsmithing Pistols & Revolvers

Gunsmithing Rifles

Visit GunDigestStore.com for these titles and more.

CONTENTS

PREFACE

SLIGHTLY MORE THAN A DECADE has passed since the first edition of this book was published. In the interim, there have been an enormous number of changes in the rimfire shooting sports. Perhaps the most notable has been the introduction of the .17 Winchester Super Magnum (WSM). Also noteworthy is the virtual passing of the .17 Mach 2 and .17 Aguila, both good cartridges, but unable to compete with the .17 HMR.

It is also interesting to note that major manufacturers who produced rimfire rifles no longer do so. Coming to mind in that context are Winchester and Kimber. Since the publication of the first edition of this book, many rimfire rifles and handguns have gone out of production and many others have been introduced. As a result of the many changes in the rimfire scene, a second edition of the *Gun Digest Book of .22 Rimfire Rifles, Pistols, and Ammunition* is warranted to reflect the current status of the field.

As with the first edition of this book, the emphasis in this edition is placed on the equipment and ammunition to a greater extent than telling about shots made. However, with the enormous number of models of firearms and the sometimes numerous number of variants of them, it is impossible to catalog every species of rifle or handgun. As a result, descriptions are given of general models of numerous types. With the rapidity of the introduction of new models and discontinuing of others, any book on rimfires is almost a snapshot in time of a field that changes rapidly. Therefore, it is the attempt of the author to provide thorough discussions of types of ammunition, ballistics, and firearms that will be of long-term use to the rimfire shooter. It is also to be hoped that the material will be of sufficient breadth and depth that the book will serve as a useful reference to a large number of shooters.

Preparation of a book such as this involves the help and cooperation of many individuals. The author wishes to express his gratitude to many people in no particular order. Anthony Imperato (Henry Repeating Arms), Ken Jorgenson (Ruger), Beth McAllister (Ruger), Dino Longueira (Majestic Arms), Scott Volquartsen (Volquartsen Custom Limited), Amy Shaw (Tactical Solutions), Herman Tom (Hornet Products), Jason Morton (CZ USA), Sheryl Gallup (Magnum Research), Rachel VandeVoort (Kimber), Chris Ellis (Timney Triggers), John Vehr (Timney Triggers), and Ron Herman (Hogue, Inc.) have helped in many ways. A special thank you is accorded to Ron Darnall of Darnall's Gun Works and Ranges who not only handled numerous firearm transfers, but also ordered several items for the author.

Numerous friends and family members have made available equipment for testing and it is a pleasure to acknowledge the assistance of Keith A. House, Ronald K. House, Larry W. House, and David Duley.

The author would like to express his gratitude to the following for supplying photographs for the gallery section of this book: Browning Arms, CZ USA, Henry Repeating Arms, Keith House, Kimber, Remington, Ruger, Savage Arms, Smith & Wesson, and Winchester.

Working with Corrina Peterson at Krause Publications has been a pleasant and rewarding experience. She has been supportive, accommodating, and thorough, and to her goes a hearty thank you.

It is with a debt of deep gratitude that the author acknowledges the immense help of his wife, Kathleen A. House, in producing this book. She not only helped with testing the equipment, but also read the complete manuscript, which resulted in numerous corrections and modifications. Her thorough knowledge of virtually all aspects of shooting sports made her a sounding board for ways to treat many topics. She is a good marksman and a shooting buddy par excellence.

CHAPTER 1

DEVELOPMENT OF RIMFIRE AMMUNITION

FOR THE LAST FEW YEARS, rimfire ammunition has been in short supply. If the rimfire section of the ammunition counter in a sporting goods store is well stocked, you will see stacks of boxes labeled .22 Long Rifle (LR), .22 Winchester Magnum Rimfire (WMR), .17 Hornady Magnum Rimfire (HMR), and .17 Winchester Super Magnum (WSM). If the store has a comprehensive line of ammunition, you may also see a few boxes of .17 Mach 2, .22 Short, .22 Long or perhaps those dinosaurs known as the .22 CB Short and .22 CB Long that live on for some reason. It is possible that you may also see a box or two of .22 Winchester Rim Fire (WRF), a cartridge that was introduced in 1890 along with the Winchester Model 90 pump rifle that was chambered for the cartridge.

If this list of approximately 10 cartridges makes it seem as if there are many choices in rimfire calibers, look again. The .22 Short, Long, Long Rifle and the two CB rounds may all be fired in a .22 LR chamber. The .22 WMR is a separate caliber, as are the .17 HMR and .17 Mach 2. We can ignore the .22 WRF for the moment, but it can be fired in a .22 WMR. What we have is really a short list of rimfire cartridges, most of which can be used in firearms of one caliber, but as we shall see it has not always been so. In this chapter, we will provide a brief history of rimfire ammunition and a description of some of the most significant obsolete and current rimfire cartridges.

Rimfire ammunition spans the range from the .22 Short to the .17 WSM.

Cartridge Development

One should not lose sight of the fact that developments in different areas of science and technology are interrelated. For example, it would not be possible to build a long-range rocket without developments in rocket fuel (which is a problem in chemical science). It was not possible to produce the atomic bomb until methods of enriching uranium were developed. The high performance of cartridges today is in great measure the result of improvements in propellants and metallurgy. Some of the basic principles involved in cartridge performance will be described in Chapter 8.

A cartridge consists of a primer, propellant, projectile, and a case to contain these components. In order to ignite a propellant, some substance that explodes is needed. The cause of the explosion is actually percussion (crushing the primer), which is the result of a spring-loaded striker (hammer or firing pin) changing positions at the time of firing. In order to have shot-to-shot uniformity (which is required for accuracy), it is necessary to have the same amount of explosive (primer) ignited in the same way for each shot and to have the same amount of propellant in each cartridge.

Early developments in muzzle loading firearms include ignition systems known as the flintlock and the cap lock, which used a percussion cap. In the flintlock, the primer consisted of a small amount of fast burning black powder of fine granulation (FFFFg) that could be easily ignited by the sparks produced when a piece of flint struck a piece of steel, which is known as the *frizzen*. The priming charge was held in the flash pan, which had a hole that led downward into the barrel where the main propellant charge was held. The gas resulting from the burning powder in the main charge provided the driving force to move the bullet down the bore.

As firearm technology developed, so did the chemistry of explosives. It was discovered that mercury fulminate exploded violently when it was struck. Therefore, percussion caps were produced that consisted of a small amount of mercury fulminate contained in a small copper cup that fitted over a hollow nipple. When the hammer fell and struck the cap, the mercury fulminate in the percussion cap exploded, which in turn ignited the powder charge as fire was directed from the primer into the barrel breech. The percussion cap was introduced in the early 1800s, and its use in muzzle loading rifles continues to the present time.

Cap lock rifles of yesterday and today are relatively reliable devices. This author has fired many rounds through his muzzle loading rifles with only a few instances of misfiring or delayed firing (known as a hang fire). Loading a cap lock rifle is a slow process because the powder charge must be measured and poured into the barrel and a projectile loaded on top of the charge. The process is slightly faster if the projectile is a "bullet" rather than a lead ball that is used with a lubricated cloth patch. New developments in muzzle loading make use of propellant that is compressed into pellets of known weight. One or more of these pellets can be dropped down the barrel and projectile loaded on this charge. Over time, it became apparent that producing a single unit containing the primer, propellant, and projectile that could be loaded in one operation would be a great convenience. That is exactly the impetus that led to the development of so-called metallic cartridges. However, there still remained the problem of where to place the primer in the cartridge and how to cause it to explode reliably so it could ignite the powder charge. Attempts to solve that problem led to several early designs in metallic cartridge ammunition.

Black powder had been in general use in muzzle loading firearms for many years so it was the propellant utilized in early metallic cartridges. Black powder consists of a mixture of potassium nitrate (saltpeter), charcoal (carbon), and sulfur in the approximate percentages 75, 15, and 10, respectively. Burning rate of the propellant, which is designated by an "F" system, is controlled by the particle size. A granulation known as FFFFg (very fine, often referred to as "4F") is a very fast burning form, whereas a coarse granulation designated as Fg is comparatively slow burning. Black powder used most often in rifles is FFg (medium) although FFFg (fine) is used in handguns or rifles of small caliber.

One of the early designs for a self-contained cartridge is known as the pin fire, and it dates from about 1830 when it was invented in Paris by Monsieur Casimir Le Facheux. The cartridge contained a bullet, propellant (black powder), and a primer. However, the blow of the hammer was transmitted to the primer by means of a pin that stuck out of the side of the case at the rear. This meant that the cartridge had to be oriented in the chamber in such a way that the hammer would strike the pin to push it into the case to crush the primer. Although placing the cartridges in the firearm in the correct orientation made loading slow by today's standards, it was still rapid compared to loading a muzzle loader. With pin fire cartridges, there was also the possibility that the protruding pin could be struck accidentally, which could force it into the case causing the cartridge to fire. From the standpoint of safety, the pin fire left a lot to be desired. However, cartridges of this type were fairly popular in Europe and some shotguns employed this type of cartridge.

Teat fire cartridges were developed in the 1800s before rim fire cartridges were introduced.

Pin fire cartridges were produced in several calibers including shotgun rounds.

Another cartridge design consisted of a closed tube that contained the bullet and propellant with the primer being contained in a small protruding portion at the rear end of the tube. This type of cartridge, known as the Moore teat fire, was loaded into the front of the cylinder of a revolver with the teat at the rear where it could be struck by the hammer. The front end of the cartridge was flared to form a retaining flange that fit against the front of the cylinder. Cartridges of this design were produced in the mid-1800s. Because the protrusion that held the primer was located in the center of the cartridge head, it was actually a center fire design rather than a true rim fire.

Each of the early cartridge designs described above contained a primer that was sensitive to shock. Subsequent designs would also rely on shock or percussion to cause the primer to explode, but the primer would be located differently in the cartridge. In 1845, a man named Louis N. Flobert in France loaded a round ball in a percussion cap and produced a very small cartridge known as the .22-caliber BB (bulleted breech) cap. Power was the result of the primer because no powder was used. Some American versions of this cartridge employed a conical bullet (hence these were known as CB caps) that was loaded over a small powder charge. In 1851 at an exhibition in London, Horace Smith and Daniel B. Wesson became convinced that this cartridge design could be refined.

The rimfire cartridge was developed by producing a cartridge case with a flange or rim of larger diameter than the body by folding the rear of the case over on itself. The rim was hollow, which allowed the priming mixture to be contained in the rim. The priming mixture was placed in the case while wet and spinning the case caused the mixture to fill the void in the hollow rim. When the primer was dried, it then became sensitive to shock. Crushing the rim by a forward blow of the firing pin caused the primer contained within it to explode, which in turn ignited the powder charge.

A short. self-contained .22-caliber cartridge called the Number One Cartridge (essentially identical to the .22 Short of today except for primer and propellant) was introduced in 1854 by Smith & Wesson for use in a small

The Smith & Wesson No. 1 First Issue was the first revolver chambered for the .22 Short black powder cartridge. Shown here is a No. 1, Second Issue model.

The frame of the Smith & Wesson opened at the bottom and was hinged at the top.

The .41 Swiss (left) and .22 Short (right) illustrate the range of cartridges that were eventually produced in rimfire calibers.

revolver. The revolver was designated as the Smith & Wesson Model 1 First Issue, which was produced from 1857 to 1860. It was followed by the Model 1 Second Issue that was produced from 1860 to 1868 and the Third Issue from 1868-1881. All issues of the Model 1 had a hinge that connected the barrel to the top of the frame at the front end. It was opened by means of a latch at the bottom of the front edge of the frame, which allowed the barrel to be tipped up so that the cylinder could be removed for loading and unloading. The cartridge employed a 29-grain bullet that was propelled by 3-4 grains of black powder contained in a case that was slightly longer than that of the BB cap. A patent was granted on August 8, 1854 for the rimfire cartridge, and it became the precursor of the .22 Short. Although it is certainly no powerhouse, the .22 Short has been used as a target load for many years in firearms designed specifically for that cartridge. As strange as it may seem, the .22 Short was originally viewed as a self defense load that could be fired in a small handgun! In modern times, small semiautomatic pistols chambered for the .22 Short have been produced for concealed carry and self defense. Fired from a rifle, the 29-grain bullet from the .22 Short high velocity load has a velocity of approximately 1,095 ft/sec whereas the 27-grain hollow point bullet has a velocity that is a slightly higher.

The four approaches to firing metallic cartridges are illustrated here. The cartridges illustrate (left to right) teat fire, pin fire, rimfire, and centerfire types.

Introduced in 1887, the .22 Long Rifle (LR) is by far the most popular rimfire cartridge. However, another .22 rimfire cartridge appeared in the 30-year interval between the introduction of the Short and the Long Rifle cartridges. That cartridge, the .22 Long, was introduced in 1871 and made use of a 29-grain bullet propelled by a charge of five grains of black powder. As with other .22 rimfires, the .22 Long eventually became loaded with smokeless powder. The current .22 Long cartridge has an advertised muzzle velocity that is about the same as that of the .22 Short. Any difference in power is more imagined than real, and there is no logical reason for the .22 Long to survive. Most of the ammunition companies have ceased production of the .22 Long.

When we come to the .22 LR we arrive at a cartridge that is the most popular and widely used metallic cartridge that exists. It is used throughout the world for recreation, competition, and hunting. The original load consisted of a 40-grain bullet and a five-grain charge of black powder. Ammunition in .22 LR caliber is loaded in many parts of the world and in some instances to the highest level of technical perfection. The accuracy capability built into a competition rifle chambered for the .22 LR is matched by several types of ammunition that are specifically designed for competition at the highest level. Such ammunition is a far cry from the old black powder loads with corrosive priming that appeared in the 1880s. In later chapters, some of the characteristics of the modern "high tech" .22 LR loads will be described. The .22 LR uses a bullet of 0.223-inch diameter that has a short section that is smaller in diameter (the heel), which fits inside the case. The lubricated portion of the bullet is outside the case.

Although the target shooter has special ammunition available, the hunter of small game and pests has not been left out. The .22 LR high speed solid uses a 40-grain bullet that has a muzzle velocity of approximately 1,235 ft/sec whereas the 36-38-grain hollow points are about 40-50 ft/sec faster. Other specialty loads will be described elsewhere in this chapter and in several later chapters. The .22 LR is in many ways the most useful cartridge in existence. A rifle or handgun chambered for this round can be used for many purposes.

22 Winchester Rim Fire (WRF)

In 1890, Winchester introduced a pump action rifle that is quite possibly the most famous .22 pump rifle ever produced. Designated as the Model 1890 (also known as the Model 90 and some rifles are so marked), the rifle was chambered for either the .22 Short or a new rimfire cartridge known as the .22 Winchester Rim Fire (WRF) or Winchester Special. The 45-grain flat point bullet was offered in several loads some of which gave a velocity as high as 1,400 ft/ sec. The original load consisted of 7.5 grains of black powder and it had a muzzle velocity of 1,100-1,200 ft/ sec. Remington used essentially the same case loaded with a round nose bullet to produce the .22 Remington Special. The .22 WRF was popular for many years, but because it offered little advantage over the .22 LR, its popularity declined as the .22 LR became more highly developed.

The .22 WRF (right) is a shorter cartridge than the .22 WMR (left) but has almost identical case dimensions except for length.

The .22 WRF case is larger in diameter than that of the .22 LR. As a result, a bullet of 0.224-inch diameter fits inside the case mouth without having a section of smaller diameter at the base. This is also the situation with the .22 Winchester Magnum Rimfire (WMR), which has almost identical dimensions as the .22 WRF except for length. Therefore, the .22 WRF cartridges can be fired in rifles chambered for the .22 WMR, and they provide a lower-powered (if not lower priced) alternative to the magnum round. In the author's bolt action Ruger 77/22M, the CCI .22 WRF ammunition delivers excellent accuracy as will be described in Chapter 15.

Other Early Rimfire Cartridges

Although current rimfire cartridges are all .22 or .17 caliber, many of the rimfire cartridges of historical significance were of larger caliber. One of the most important rimfire developments was the .44 Henry cartridge developed by B. Tyler Henry, which has the distinction of being the chambering for the first successful lever action rifle. Imagine the effect of a few Union soldiers using rapid-firing Henry lever action rifles, which had tubular magazines that held 15 cartridges, against the Confederate soldiers who were using single shot muzzle loading rifles! Ballistics of the .44 Henry were not impressive by today's standards (a 210-grain lead bullet propelled by a charge of 28 grains of black powder to give a velocity of 1,150 ft/sec), but the importance of rapid, sustained fire in military operations is obvious. The .44 Henry cartridge was in production from 1860 to 1934. Another large caliber rimfire cartridge that was used in the Civil War was the .56 Spencer. Incidentally, the Henry lever action was produced from 1860-1866 and was no doubt a driving force that led to the development of the Winchester 73, which used the centerfire .44-40 Winchester cartridge.

It is easy to forget that rimfire cartridges were produced in larger calibers and in shorter lengths for use in revolvers and longer versions for rifles in many calibers.

Several other rimfire cartridges were developed about the same time as the .44 Henry. As is now the case with .22-caliber cartridges having different lengths, larger caliber "short" and "long" rimfire cartridges were common in the latter half of the 1800s. Examples include the .30 Short and Long; the .32 Extra Short, Short, and Long; the .38 Extra Short, Short, and Long; and the .41 Short and Long among others. Revolvers were often designed with cylinders to accept the shorter cartridges whereas the extra long types were most often used in single shot rifles. They were, of course, loaded with black powder. Although there is no need to review the development of all of these cartridges individually, it is necessary to mention several of them in order to trace the evolution of the rimfire cartridge design. It is interesting to note that of the approximately 75 rimfire cartridges that existed in the late 1800s, only about 10 remained in production after World War II.

Note how the current .22 Short and Long Rifle have parallels in the .25 Short and Long cartridges of a century ago.

Two cartridges that were developed somewhat later were the .25 Stevens Short and .25 Stevens Long (sometimes referred to as simply the .25 Stevens) that were introduced around 1900. These cartridges were produced until 1942, and they were popular in rifles such as the Stevens single shot models. Firing a 65-67-grain bullet that was driven at approximately 1,200 ft/sec by a charge of 11 grains of black powder, the .25 Stevens had a good reputation as a small game load. Compared to any of the .22-caliber rimfires, the larger diameter, heavier bullet of the .25 Stevens, which had a muzzle energy of approximately 208 ft lbs, dispatched many species more dependably. It would still be a useful cartridge, especially in a modern loading that would improve the ballistics and utilize bullets of better design.

Propellants and Primers

As the quest for better ammunition continued, it was recognized that black powder left a residue in the bore that attracted moisture and led to corrosion. Barrel life of the firearm was no where near as long as it is today. In the late 1890s, a new type of propellant was developed by making use of an entirely different type of chemistry. When cotton is nitrated with a mixture of nitric and sulfuric acids, the product is known as nitrocellulose, and it burns very rapidly when ignited. Moreover, the combustion produces very little smoke so this propellant is known as "smokeless" powder. This book is not the place for a review of propellant technology, but it should be mentioned that the burn-

ing rate of nitrocellulose can be controlled to a great extent by the particle size and additives. Therefore, it is possible to produce nitrocellulose and tailor it for use in cartridges having different sizes. Another development in propellant technology resulted in a type of powder known as double base powder. This type of propellant makes use of nitrocellulose to which has been added a small percentage of nitroglycerin. In addition to varying the particle size of the propellant, numerous additives are included to impart particular properties such as flowing ease, reduction of static electricity, flash reduction, etc. By controlling these characteristics, a large number of types of propellants have been developed with burning rates that vary enormously. Some propellants work best in small cases such as the .22 Short or .25 Auto whereas others perform best in large cases such as the .300 Winchester Magnum.

Remington ammunition has featured Kleanbore priming for many years as shown on these boxes of .22 LR cartridges from the 1950s.

Even with the use of smokeless powder, the problem of corrosion persisted. The cause was the residue that was produced from the primer, which contained a mixture that included potassium chlorate. Because of the resulting corrosion, primers containing potassium chlorate became known as corrosive primers. Some ammunition was loaded with primers containing mercury fulminate and after detonation the resulting mercury reacted with the brass case, which caused it to be weakened and thus unsuitable for reloading. In 1927, Remington introduced Kleanbore primers, which contained a type of priming mixture that was noncorrosive. In most modern ammunition, the primer contains an explosive known as lead styphnate, but recently primers have been developed that do not contain lead. The motivation behind this is to reduce the amount of lead that is present in the air when firearms are fired on indoor ranges. For use in rimfire cartridges, the priming mixture contains 35-45% lead styphnate, 25-35% barium nitrate, 18-22% ground glass, and 6-10% lead thiocyanate as well as some other minor constituents. The function of the ground glass is to make the mixture more sensitive to friction when crushed in the rim. On the negative side, the small amount of ground glass remaining in the bore increases the rate of wear so that even though soft lead bullets are used, the bore eventually shows the effects of erosion. A .22 LR barrel will not last indefinitely. One of the characteristics of lead styphnate is that its explosive character is destroyed by oil and some organic solvents such as kerosene. If oil or cleaning solvent seeps into a case, it may cause the round to misfire. This is one reason for the substantial crimp given to .22 rimfire ammunition, the other being that a heavy crimp is necessary to give the correct "pull" on the bullet that results in uniform velocities.

Some types of rimfire firearms can utilize the .22 Short, Long, or Long Rifle.

Hyper Velocity .22 Ammunition

Over the many years in which it has been produced, the .22 LR cartridge has undergone several changes. Most of these involved minor differences in velocity that resulted from the use of different powders or bullets of slightly different weight or shape. However, a radical departure from the norm occurred in 1977 when CCI introduced a round known as the Stinger®. The new round utilizes a 32-grain bullet that is driven by a heavier charge of powder that has a slower burning rate than the powder ordinarily used in .22 LR ammunition. To accommodate the larger powder charge, the case of the Stinger was made approximately one-tenth of an inch longer than the normal .22 LR case. The result was a round that produced a muzzle velocity of 1,640 ft/sec and a muzzle energy of 191 ft lbs. A flat trajectory resulted from the high bullet velocity so the effective range of the .22 rifle was increased. Owing to the high velocity hollow point bullet, the new round was explosive in its effect on small pests or unopened cans of pop. The term "hyper velocity" is generally applied to .22 LR

ammunition that produces very high velocity.

Very soon after the Stinger was introduced, Winchester began producing a type of hyper velocity round known as the Xpediter®. This load utilized a 29-grain hollow point bullet with a muzzle velocity of 1,680 ft/sec, which corresponds to an energy of 182 ft lbs. Federal followed suit by introducing the Spitfire®, which employed a 33-grain bullet with a velocity of 1,500 ft/sec and an energy of 165 ft lbs. The Winchester Xpediter was discontinued after being available for a few years, and the current Federal hyper velocity load is not designated as the Spitfire although the ballistics are unchanged from that round.

Remington entered the competitive field of hyper velocity ammunition with two offerings. The Yellow Jacket® features a 33-grain hollow point bullet at 1,500 ft/sec giving a muzzle energy of 165 ft lbs whereas the Viper® features a 36-grain truncated cone solid point bullet at 1,410 ft/sec for an energy of 159 ft lbs. One other hyper velocity round is produced by Aguila, and it drives a 30-grain bullet at an advertised velocity of 1,750 ft/sec to give 204 ft lbs of energy. However, the energy drops to only 93 ft lbs at a range of 100 yards. Another hyper velocity round is the CCI Quik-Shok® that uses a 32-grain bullet, but the bullet is designed so that it breaks into four pieces on impact. This produces a devastating effect on small varmints although penetration is generally less than with other types of ammunition.

Although the hyper velocity ammunition gives dramatic effects at short ranges, the light weight bullets lose velocity more rapidly than do the heavier bullets used in conventional .22 LR ammunition. The result is that the remaining energy of the hyper velocity ammunition is approximately equal to or lower than that of the slower rounds at a range of 100 yards or so. It is also generally true that hyper velocity ammunition does not deliver the best accuracy in most rifles. There have been many reports published to verify that conclusion, and based on the results of tests conducted during this work it is certainly true in the author's experience. Moreover, the longer cases of the Stinger and Quik-Shok pose a problem when used in rifles with so-called match-type chambers because the case engages the rifling just in front of the chamber. With match chambers, the rifling extends back to the front end of the chamber so the bullet engages the rifling as a round is chambered. The makers of some rifles having match chambers warn against using the Stinger ammunition in those rifles. Bullet diameter for the .22 Short, Long, and Long Rifle is 0.223 inch.

With all of these developments and those described in the following sections, there can be little doubt that this is an exciting time for the rimfire shooter. More details on the performance of today's rimfire cartridges will be presented in several later chapters in this book.

.22 Winchester Magnum Rimfire (WMR)

As wonderful as the .22 LR is, there are situations where more power is called for. In 1959, Winchester responded to that need by developing a cartridge that utilizes a case that is 1.05 inches in length and has a slightly larger diameter head and body than the .22 LR case (0.291 vs. 0.275 and 0.241 vs. 0.225 inch, respectively). Instead of using a bullet with a heel of smaller diameter that fits inside the case and a bullet that has the same diameter as the case, the new round used a 40-grain *jacketed* bullet of 0.224-inch diameter. This "magnum" rimfire is appropriately named the .22 Winchester Magnum Rimfire (WMR), and the advertised velocity is 1,910 ft/sec from a 24-inch barrel. With a muzzle energy of 310 ft lbs, the .22 WMR was the most powerful rimfire cartridge available until 2015. From the 20-inch barrel of author's Ruger 77/22M, the velocity at 10 feet from the muzzle is below the advertised value by about 75 ft/sec, but when this value is translated into a muzzle velocity it is just about the same as the advertised value.

Rifles in .22 WRF are no longer manufactured, but there is still a demand for the ammunition, which can also be fired in .22 WMR rifles.

Although initially available only with 40-grain hollow point and full jacket bullets, the shooter of a .22 WMR now has available numerous types of ammunition.

The main drawback to the .22 WMR has always been the cost of ammunition. Although some special target ammunition in .22 LR may cost as much as $20 or more for a box containing 50 rounds, the cost of most of the ordinary types is only $3.50-4.00 per box. As this is written, some promotional bulk pack ammunition in .22 LR can be bought for around $3.00 per box. Most of the types of ammunition in .22 WMR sell for $12.00 or more with the Remington Premier selling for around $16 per box. It is simply a fact of life that it costs around 20-30 cents per shot to fire a .22 WMR.

Being a larger and more powerful cartridge than the .22 LR, the .22 WMR could not be adapted to the actions of most firearms that were designed specifically for the smaller .22 LR cartridge. The actions had to be made slightly longer than those used on regular .22s, but very soon after the .22 WMR was introduced a considerable number of arms were available to chamber it. Winchester marketed the lever action Model 9422M, and Ruger offered single action revolvers with two cylinders, one in .22 LR and the other for the .22 WMR. Marlin, Savage, Anschutz, and others produced bolt action rifles for the .22 WMR soon after its introduction. Currently, bolt actions, lever actions, and autoloaders are available in the magnum rimfire calibers as are several handguns (see Chapters 3 and 4).

The major complaint about the .22 WMR has centered on the subject of accuracy. It is popularly believed that the .22 WMR does not give accuracy that is quite the equal of that given by the .22 LR and some newer rimfire rounds. This perception may be in error, but that topic will be addressed more fully in later chapters.

5mm Remington Magnum

In 1970, Remington unveiled a rimfire magnum cartridge that offered even better performance than the .22 WMR. However, that cartridge deviated from the usual rimfire caliber because it was a 5mm or .20 caliber (actual bullet diameter is 0.204 inch). The 5mm Remington Magnum cartridge produced 2,100 ft/sec with a 38-grain bullet that was efficient from a ballistic standpoint. As a result, the muzzle energy was 372 ft lbs, and the remaining energy also exceeded that of the .22 WMR at longer ranges. The 5mm Remington used a case that is slightly larger in diameter than that of the .22 WMR. Remington produced the Model 591 (box magazine) and Model 592 (tubular magazine) bolt actions, but these were the only rifles produced for the 5mm Remington cartridge. Thompson/Center produced barrels chambered for the 5mm Remington to be used on the single shot pistols that they market. The

Remington 591 and 592 were discontinued in 1974 with a total of approximately 50,000 rifles having been produced. Remington ammunition in the 5mm caliber has become highly collectible with prices for a full box often being in the $50-75 range or more. However, 5mm Remington ammunition produced by Centurion Ordnance has recently become available. Also, as the result of working with Aguila, it has been announced that three loads in 5mm Remington will be marketed in 2016.

Remington no longer produces ammunition in 5mm Rim Fire Magnum, but it is an excellent cartridge.

Centurion markets 5mm Rim Fire Magnum ammunition for shooters who still use that caliber.

The 5mm Remington (right) utilizes much heavier bullets than either of the two .17-calibers.

With greater energy and flatter trajectory than the .22 WMR, the 5mm Remington may well have been the best rimfire cartridge in modern times. Although the trajectory is not quite as flat as that of the .17 HMR with a 17-grain bullet, the 5mm Remington with its 38-grain bullet is a far more powerful cartridge. Part of the difficulty with the 5mm stemmed from the high pressure it produced, which may have been as high as 35,000 lb/in^2.

The high pressure caused the case to expand into the extractor notches, which necessitated some changes in the chamber, bolt face, and extractor grooves. Given the propellants available today, it is likely that the remarkable ballistics of the 5mm Remington could be produced with a somewhat lower pressure. Moreover, there are several rifles available today that could probably serve as platforms for the excellent 5mm Remington cartridge. The Ruger 77/22M, Anschutz, CZ 452 and 455, and others come to mind immediately. We can only hope that rifles and ammunition in this outstanding rimfire caliber become available once again. If not, a .20-caliber cartridge based on a necked down .22 WMR case but utilizing the superb Hornady V-Max polymer tipped bullets would be very interesting and useful. Given the fine rifles that are available in .22 WMR caliber, it should be a simple matter to produce a .20-caliber cartridge based on that case. A .20-caliber cartridge derived by expanding the neck of the new .17 Winchester Super Magnum (WSM) would be a power-house.

.17 Hornady Magnum Rimfire (HMR)

Perhaps no other new cartridge has generated so many printed words in such a short time by so many writers as the .17 HMR. Introduced in 2002, the .17 HMR was the first new rimfire cartridge since the short-lived (but perhaps not quite dead) 5mm Remington. However, the .17 HMR certainly will not suffer a similar fate! The number of rifles and handguns available in .17 HMR caliber is very large. This is natural because the .17 HMR case is simply a .22 WMR case necked down to hold a .17-caliber bullet. Therefore, a firearm designed around the .22 WMR can be made into a .17 HMR simply by changing the barrel. Even the magazines of rifles that hold .22 WMR cartridges will feed .17 HMR cartridges. Because so many firearms in .22 WMR caliber were already in production, there are now many that are also produced in .17 HMR, but the autoloaders present special problems that will be discussed later.

Nominal bullet diameter for the .17 HMR is 0.172 inch. The original load consisted of a 17-grain Hornady V-Max® polymer tipped bullet that was loaded to a velocity of 2,550 ft/sec giving an energy of 245 ft lbs. The well-shaped bullet has a ballistic coefficient of 0.125 so it retains velocity well, which results in a rather flat trajectory that makes hits on small pests possible out to 150 yards or more. Although many larger varmints have been taken with

In .17 HMR, Hornady markets loads with a 17-grain polymer tipped bullet (left) or a 20-grain hollow point (right).

the .17 HMR, the cartridge is at its best when used on species such as ground squirrels, crows, pigeons, and prairie dogs. Early reports by some writers described the use of the .17 HMR on species as large as coyotes, but many more reports have also described the failures of the tiny bullets on larger pests such as groundhogs, foxes, and coyotes. One of the most interesting discussions on the .17 HMR is that by C. Rodney James, which was published in *Gun Digest 2005*. In an article published in the February 2005 issue of *Predator Xtreme*, Ralph Lermayer has related some of his experiences on the failure of the .17 HMR as a cartridge for use on larger varmints. Eventually, loads employing 20-grain hollow point bullets having a muzzle velocity of 2,375 ft/sec were introduced to reduce the explosive character and improve penetration. This ammunition may help reduce bullet fragmentation, but the tiny .17 HMR was never really suitable for use on larger species of varmints. Long ago, the author dispatched numerous swine for meat production using a rifle shooting the .22 Short, but sporting use is a different matter. Nonetheless, the .17 HMR is a great little cartridge that gives outstanding accuracy, and we will have a lot to say about it in other chapters of this book. Incidentally, it was the development of suitable propellants that made the ballistics given by the .17 HMR possible. Had such propellants been available at the time the 5mm Remington was introduced, the .17 HMR might never have been developed.

.17 Mach 2

The .17 HMR represents a .22 WMR case necked to hold .17-caliber bullets, but consider the potential of a .22 LR case necked to hold a .17-caliber bullet. An enormous number of rimfire rifles could become .17-caliber rifles simply by changing the barrels. In order to produce a cartridge that would hold enough

powder to give a high velocity, the case used could be that of the CCI Stinger®, which is 0.700 inch long rather than 0.600 inch of the normal .22 LR. These procedures are exactly those used by Hornady and CCI to produce the .17 Mach 2, which launches a 17-grain bullet at 2,100 ft/sec (approximately twice the velocity of sound which gives rise to the name Mach 2).

However, there is a potential problem with simply changing the barrels on .22 LR semiautomatics. The .17 Mach 2 burns more powder than a .22 LR so the chamber pressure remains high for a longer period of time. This causes the bolt to be driven to the rear at higher velocity than when .22 LR cartridges are fired. To keep the bolt from being driven back with enough force to damage the action, a heavier bolt must be used or a stronger recoil spring or both. There is no problem with bolt action .22 LR rifles becoming .17 Mach 2

Hornady is currently the only company that markets .17 Mach 2 ammunition.

pieces, but in the case of autoloaders, changes other than merely switching barrels may be necessary.

Firing a 17-grain bullet with a muzzle velocity of 2,100 ft/sec, the .17 Mach 2 produces a muzzle energy of 166 ft lbs. This is less power than that produced by some high performance .22 LR rounds, so the .17 Mach 2 is a rifle for small pests. Accuracy as good as that produced by any rimfire is the strong point of the .17 Mach 2. With its flat trajectory, small pests are in danger out to around 125 yards when the shooter does his or her part. As the first edition of this book was written, a box of .17 Mach 2 ammunition sold for about $6.99 but like all other rimfire ammunition, the cost has increased considerably. This is considerably higher than the cost of good quality .22 LR ammunition although somewhat lower than the cost of .17 HMR or .22 WMR ammunition. The difference in cost of ammunition probably would not matter to a pest hunter, but it certainly would to the casual plinker.

The .17 Mach 2 appeared with great fanfare and press releases just before the first edition of this book was published. To no surprise of the author, it showed a fast start but little momentum. Currently, only CCI produces .17 Mach 2 ammunition, but it is sold under the Hornady label, and only one load is available that utilizes a 17-grain polymer-tipped bullet. Very few new rifles are currently available in .17 Mach 2 caliber and there is now little interest in the caliber.

.17 Aguila

Another rimfire cartridge introduced at about the same time as the .17 Mach 2 is known as the .17 Aguila. Although the .17 Mach 2 utilizes the longer CCI Stinger case necked to hold a 0.172-caliber bullet, the .17

The .17 Aguila never achieved much popularity, but Aguila has announced that ammunition will be produced.

Aguila employs a .22 LR case of normal length. Powder capacity of the .17 Aguila is slightly lower than that of the .17 Mach 2 so a muzzle velocity of 1,850 ft/sec is produced with a 20-grain bullet (remaining velocity at 100 yards is 1,267 ft/sec).

However, bolt action rifles and most autoloaders that fire .22 LR cartridges can be converted to .17 Aguila caliber simply by the manufacturer changing the barrels. Even though the .17 Aguila produces slightly lower velocity than the .17 Mach 2, the difference is not enough to make any practical difference in hunting use, especially since the .17 Aguila uses a 20-grain hollow point bullet. Shots should be limited to slightly shorter ranges with the .17 Aguila, but both it and the .17 Mach 2 are suitable for small game and small pests. The almost unknown .17 High Standard cartridge is apparently almost identical to the .17 Aguila. In early 2016, Aguila Ammunition has announced the production of .17 Aguila ammunition.

.17 Winchester Super Magnum (WSM)

The newest rimfire on the scene is known as the .17 Winchester Super Magnum (WSM). It was designed by employing a relatively large rimfire case that was used to drive fasteners in the construction industry. Winchester offers loads with both 20- and 25-grain polymer tipped bullets having advertised muzzle velocities of 3,000 and 2,600 ft/sec, respectively. Producing about 400 ft lbs of energy, this is a much more potent .17-caliber cartridge than any of those described previously. Winchester has also recently

announced the introduction of a .17 WSM load that utilizes a 20-grain copper bullet with a muzzle velocity of 2,850 ft/sec. This load should provide better penetration than do the more frangible bullets of normal construction. In addition to ammunition offered by Winchester, both Hornady and American Eagle are offering .17 WSM ammunition that utilizes 20-grain polymer tipped bullets that have the same muzzle velocity as the Winchester load.

The .17 WSM is the newest and most potent of the rimfire calibers.

Although several obsolete rimfire cartridges have been interesting and historically important, the choices available today make this the most exciting time in rimfire history. Hopefully this will become more apparent as you read this book. From the point of view of the author, broader production of 5mm Remington ammunition and rifles to shoot it and the introduction of either a .20- or .22-caliber cartridge based on the .17 WSM case would make things even more interesting.

The .17 calibers include (left to right) the .17 Aguila, .17 Mach 2, .17 HMR, and .17 WSM.

Two cartridges that the author (and many others) would like to see brought back are the 5mm Remington (left) and the 25 Stevens (right).

CHAPTER 2

SAFE SHOOTING

ANYTHING THAT LAUNCHES PROJECTILES has the potential to cause injury. This is not limited to slingshots, bows, airguns, or firearms. Golf balls, baseballs, and horseshoes have all caused fatalities. In baseball, batters wear helmets for a reason. Participants in other sports wear protective equipment. However, it is in the shooting sports that safety must be paramount. Firearms launch small projectiles at high velocity so they can travel great distances. In spite of this, it is entirely possible to enjoy shooting sports for many years and fire tens of thousands of shots in complete safety even though the news media may routinely consider that anything involving a firearm is a high risk activity. In this chapter, we will describe some of the aspects of safety that shooters must follow in order to participate safely in shooting sports.

Aware of the safety issues related to the storage of firearms, Sturm, Ruger & Co. includes a safety lock with most of its products.

Devices and Programs

We are at a point in time when shooting accidents are occurring at the lowest rate they have been for many years. There are several reasons for this welcome decline. First, currently produced rifles and pistols are manufactured with more safety features than ever before. Let me cite just one example. Single action revolvers are those that require cocking the hammer for each shot (which also rotates the cylinder) and this type has been popular for about 150 years. Older single action revolvers or those designed in the same way can fire accidentally if dropped or the hammer is struck a blow because in some cases the firing pin is an integral part of the hammer and it rests against a cartridge. In other models, the firing pin is held permanently in the frame, but the hammer rests against the firing pin. In either of these types of single action revolvers, the firing pin may be held away from the cartridge by a notch on the hammer (a so-called safety notch). That safety notch may not be adequate to keep the firing pin from striking the cartridge if a substantial blow to the hammer occurs. In order to carry such a revolver safely, it is necessary to keep an empty chamber in front of the firing pin. Old timers knew this and their revolvers were treated as "five shooters" rather than "six shooters."

In 1973, Sturm, Ruger, & Company redesigned its single action revolvers to produce the "new model" single action. After the new model revolver is cocked, a transfer bar moves upward to a position between the hammer and the firing pin to transmit the blow of the hammer only as the trigger is pulled to the rear.

Older single action revolvers had to have the hammer at half cock in order to rotate the cylinder.

Loading a single action is done one cartridge at a time while rotating the cylinder.

Modern single action revolvers utilize a transfer bar to transmit the blow of the hammer to the firing pin.

Therefore, only if the trigger is pulled will the hammer strike the bar and transmit the blow to the firing pin. Neither accidentally dropping a new model revolver nor a blow to the hammer will cause it to fire because when the transfer bar is down, the hammer rests against the frame and it is not in contact with the firing pin. These "new model" revolvers can be carried safely with all six chambers loaded. This is just one example of the additional safety features that are found on some newer firearms.

Although the situation described above is in reference to single action revolvers, it also existed for some of the familiar lever action rifles with their visible, manually operated hammers. Most newer lever action rifles have safeties that block the hammer from moving forward to strike the firing pin if the hammer is struck by an accidental blow. Many models of bolt action rifles also have improved safeties. Although most older bolt action rifles required the safety to be moved to the "off" position to open the bolt, many newer ones allow the bolt to be opened without having to disengage the safety. This is a great improvement because to open the action the shooter does not have to operate the bolt of a rifle that is in firing condition. Some bolt action rifles have indicators to show when the piece is cocked, but with others there is nothing visible to show whether the action is cocked or not. Today, most semiautomatic rifles and pistols have a device that holds the action open after the last shot

has been fired. An increasing number of semiautomatic pistols have some sort of indicator that shows when there is a cartridge in the chamber. For example, on the new Ruger Mark III the loaded chamber indicator is a lever that runs along the left hand side of the frame and fits flush with the frame when the chamber is empty. When a round is chambered, the lever swings out of the frame slightly and a red dot on the top edge of the lever is visible.

All modern semiautomatic pistols chambered for rimfire cartridges have safeties. Usually they are levers located on the left hand side at the rear of the frame and are operated by the thumb of the shooting hand. It is possible as a result of handling the firearm or removing it from a holster to cause this lever to be moved accidentally. Pistols of recent manufacture often have safeties that are better designed to prevent this from happening, and the possibility of litigation has caused most firearms marketed today to have triggers that require more force to discharge the piece than was the case a generation or two ago. These and other improvements in firearms have helped reduce accidents, but the most important aspect of safety is still the human mind.

Although the changes in equipment have made the shooting sports safer, so have the numerous training programs that have been conducted or sponsored by numerous organizations. The National Rifle Association (NRA) has conducted the Eddie Eagle GunSafe®

The safety on the Ruger American is a sliding bar located on the tang.

On the Ruger 77/22, the safety can be placed in three positions.

Semiautomatic rifles like this Ruger 10/22 Carbine have a push button safety located at one end of the trigger guard.

Dual safety levers that also function as decocking levers are utilized on the Ruger SR22.

This Kimber pistol utilizes a grip safety as well as the usual safety lever.

program for many years, and more than 28 million youngsters have received instruction in what to do when encountering a firearm as a result. More information on this program is available from the NRA Eddie Eagle Department at (800) 231-0752 or from the web site www.nrahq.org/safety/eddie/. According to the National Center for Health Statistics, fatal accidents from firearms in the pre-K through third grade age group has been reduced by more than two-thirds during the operation of this program.

The Boy Scouts of America includes instruction in shooting in many areas of the country. Other groups that are proactive with regard to shooting include 4-H and Future Farmers of America (FFA) groups. Many summer camps that are operated by civic and church groups for youngsters have instruction and practice in target shooting. Other companies and groups are concerned primarily with safe handling and shooting of airguns, and this activity is frequently a forerunner of shooting firearms. Daisy Outdoor Products has sponsored national BB and airgun competition for many years. Daisy also has a trailer that has been converted to a portable range that is used in various parts

of the country to introduce boys and girls to shooting activities with airguns. Crosman Corporation also sponsors programs that are directed toward training and safe shooting.

With the emphasis on safety in shooting, most states require the completion of a hunter safety course for anyone under a certain age who wishes to get a hunting license. These courses are conducted by certified instructors who make sure that the prospective hunter is familiar with proper handling and use of a firearm. Safety is a constant thing, not a sometime thing. Changes in equipment and training have led to a drastic reduction in firearm-related accidents, but further reductions are possible. Those of us involved in the shooting sports must constantly be concerned with the safety issues of our activities.

Rimfire rifles and pistols are at the same time some of the safest and most dangerous of firearms. Because of their having relatively low noise and almost no recoil, they are convenient and pleasant to use. However, the same characteristics may also cause them to be taken lightly. This should never be the case! The author has served on a coroner's jury and has seen first hand the incredible effect that can be produced by a bullet from a .22 rimfire. He has also used a rimfire to prepare large hogs and cattle for the butcher's block. A rimfire round can produce an enormous amount of damage!

A bullet from the lowly .22 LR rimfire can travel up to a mile and a bullet from the .17 HMR or .22 WMR can travel even farther. Because the velocity is relatively low, bullets from some rimfire firearms (especially the .22 Short, Long and Long Rifle) are prone to ricochet badly. Shooting at almost any object on the ground will result in that familiar but horrible whine of a bullet on its way to somewhere else. Not only that, it may be going at some merry angle compared to the direction in which it was fired. The rimfire shooter must exercise good judgment and restraint. If you are engaged in the noble and time-honored pastime of hunting squirrels with a .22, remember that you may be able to fire at game in some directions but not others. If you miss that squirrel on a limb 40 yards away, the bullet is going to come down a long way from where you are. It may also strike a branch and ricochet in some uncontrollable and unknown direction.

A bullet from a rimfire can easily penetrate a 2×4 or several inches of flesh. The author has performed almost every test imaginable, and the power produced by a cartridge that measures only one inch in length and costs as little as four or five cents is almost unbelievable. Not far from where this is being written,

A .22 LR looks tiny beside a .458 Winchester magnum cartridge. As a result of its small size, there is sometimes a tendency to take a .22-caliber firearm lightly.

a man getting into a vehicle dropped a loaded .22 handgun, which struck the floor, discharged, and sent a bullet into his body. It penetrated several organs on its upward path and the man was killed. A rimfire has the power to be lethal from many directions, not only when a bullet hits "just right." All of the safety requirements for any firearm must be exercised in the use of a rimfire. A rimfire firearm is every bit as much a firearm as is a powerful rifle that is intended for hunting elephants. In fact, the story has been told of a shooter actually killing an elephant with a .22 LR!

Safety Rules

Many accidents are avoidable. Common sense and logic would prevent many situations from arising in which someone might be injured or killed. Millions of shooters have enjoyed their sport for many years without ever being involved in an accident. In terms of the number of man-hours involved and the very low incidence of accidents, shooting sports are safer than are many other types of activities. However, when an accident involving a firearm does occur, it is deemed a newsworthy item. Even a minor injury inflicted by a firearm will get more press coverage than a broken spine that results from a skiing accident except when the injured party is someone famous. Those of us who are involved in any form of shooting sport must remember that there is a large, vocal segment of the population who does not believe that we even have the right to own and use a firearm. They believe that the Second Amendment is some sort of collective right that was intended for militias but not individuals. That is remarkable in view of the fact that the other rights specified in the Bill of Rights are *individual* rights. Historians of my acquaintance who specialized in constitutional history at the doctoral level and studied the papers of the writers of that time say that the documents made it clear that the citizens of this country would not be reduced to serfs. It was clearly their intention that law-abiding individuals would enjoy the freedom to own and use firearms lawfully.

Although this may seem so elementary that there is no need to state it, read and follow all instructions in the owner's manual that came with your firearm! The manual may contain information regarding the operation of your firearm that you may not know even if you are an experienced shooter. Some firearms have particular features or characteristics that may have changed over the production lifetime of the model so even experience with a similar model some years earlier does not necessarily mean that the latest version operates in exactly the same way. The author recently found that a problem with a certain rifle was solved by consulting the owner's manual. It was not an issue of safety, but rather the issue involved convenience in operation of the rifle. In addition to information on safety, the owner's manual will give tips on maintenance of the firearm, which can lead to long, trouble-free service. Correct procedures for loading, unloading, and handling a firearm are important, and the owner's manual will give you the information you need to perform these functions correctly.

It is incumbent upon all shooters to use all means available to make the shooting sports as safe as possible. There are several rules that serve as a basis for conduct in the shooting sports, a sort of shooting etiquette. The list takes on several forms depending on who is drawing up the list, but the rules can be distilled to embody the following areas.

1. Treat every gun as if it were loaded.

Some gun handlers become sloppy when they "know" a gun isn't loaded. However, it is the "unloaded" gun that is sometimes involved in an accident. Never assume that a firearm is unloaded when you pick it up or someone hands it to you. With many firearms, there is no way to tell at a glance whether or not there is a round in the chamber. It may also be that there is a round in the *magazine*, and working the action may place that round in the chamber unknown to the person handling the gun. If this rule were always followed, it would prevent a firearm from being handled in a careless manner. The author knows of a case where a hole was drilled through a leg of a lamp table in a living room. The shooter thought his .22 rifle was unloaded and was attempting to release the spring tension on the firing pin by "snapping" it while aiming at a section of the table leg. It turned out that there was a round in the chamber, and a bullet was placed squarely through the table leg. Although his aim was good, his logic was defective. This type of mistake can lead to disaster. If the tension on the cocking mechanism is to be released, first insert a snap cap before pulling the trigger. If the firearm is a bolt action rifle, raise the bolt handle, verify that the chamber is empty, pull back on the trigger, and *slowly* move the bolt handle to the "down" position, which allows the firing pin to move forward in a controlled manner. Treating every gun as if it were loaded has been translated by some experts to read "*all* guns are loaded." *Always assume that this is so.*

As a young lad, the author remembers being in the home of a relative and looking around in a bedroom. Lying on the floor was a small revolver that did not look much different than the toy cap pistols that were so familiar at that age. However, when the revolver was picked up, the bullets in the cartridges were clearly visible from the front of the cylinder and the cartridge heads were visible at the rear. Having been around firearms a great deal it was immediately obvious that this was a "real" gun kept by the bed rather than some toy that had been left behind. Very carefully the revolver, a Smith & Wesson 32 Hand Ejector model, was replaced where it was found. Someone who did not know better might have been involved in a tragic accident when finding a loaded revolver. Teaching youngsters about firearm safety (even those who live in homes where there are no firearms) is a worthwhile activity. Knowing and teaching about firearms is infinitely better than trying to isolate young, curious children so they will never have contact with a firearm. Sadly, it seems today that the approach taken by many individuals is to pretend that firearms are somehow evil and must be avoided.

Many years ago, the author visited a gun shop that had handguns in a glass case. A Colt 1911 attracted his attention, and he asked to look at it. The owner handed the pistol over the case, and it was held carefully. As the author casually pulled back the slide, a loaded .45 ACP cartridge was ejected! With the action open, it was obvious that there were additional cartridges in the magazine. The author *carefully* handed the pistol to the totally baffled owner. It seems as if the pistol had been placed in the case only a day or two earlier when the previous owner delivered it to the shop to consummate a trade that had been arranged earlier. Having examined the pistol at the time the trade was made, the owner

Many firearms are shipped with a "flag" in the chamber to show that no cartridge resides in the chamber. Shown here is a Smith & Wesson Model 22A.

assumed that the previous owner had unloaded the pistol before bringing it in for transfer. *Never* assume that any gun anywhere is unloaded.

2. Never allow a gun to point in an unsafe direction or point a gun at anything you would not shoot.

Firearms, especially handguns, are short enough that simply by moving an arm or by turning one's body the muzzle may be pointed in a direction in which a shot should not be fired. Realizing that the firearm being handled may be loaded (and should always be treated as if it were!), the firearm must be controlled in such a way that the muzzle is never brought to point in a line that represents an unsafe shooting direction. Handguns should be manipulated with the muzzle pointing upward, action open, and finger off the trigger until it is safe to load the piece and assume a firing position. Rifles should be kept unloaded with the actions open and the muzzle pointed upward or in another safe direction depending on the circumstances. On ranges, special racks are usually available where all rifles are held in this condition. This writer has observed instances in which someone holding a firearm was spoken to by someone else. While turning toward the speaker, the person holding the firearm allowed the muzzle to sweep through an arc that brought the muzzle in line with another person. When holding a firearm, you must always be conscious of where a bullet would go if the piece discharged at any time. It is bad enough to have a firearm discharge accidentally under *any* circumstances, but it is much better to have it fire in a safe direction (in the air or down range) should such an event occur.

It is readily apparent that this revolver is loaded. This is one advantage of the revolver over the autoloader.

3. Always wear eye and ear protection.

Although it is by no means a common occurrence, it is possible for the case to rupture when a rimfire firearm is discharged. The author has had it happen several times, and when it does hot gases as well as bits of powder and brass are ejected around the bolt face of the rifle (or out of the front or rear of the cylinder of a revolver). These items have sufficient energy to cause eye injuries. Even when the case rim does not rupture, the gap between the cylinder and barrel in a revolver can allow bits of unburned powder or lead shavings to escape. Modern rimfire ammunition is extremely good, but the author recently had four rounds of .22 LR target ammunition from the same box misfire. Moreover, two of these rounds misfired in each of two bolt action rifles. After waiting a short time with the muzzle remaining pointed at the target, the bolt was carefully opened and the round gently removed by pulling the bolt back. In such instances, it is possible for a "hang fire" round to detonate inside the open action causing all sorts of debris to be launched in all directions. If such an event happens, the shooter had better be wearing eye protection. Depending on the type of backstop being used, it is also possible that some small particles of the lead bullet may ricochet. Eyes are delicate and it is prudent to use every precaution possible to prevent eye injury. Participants in paintball sports are certainly aware of this requirement.

Most corrective eyeglasses are made with polycarbonate lenses that are impact resistant. If the shooter is wearing glasses, the majority of bits of debris will be deflected although most glasses do not provide any protection from the sides. Good shooting glasses need not be expensive. Some suppliers of firearms market shooting glasses under their own labels. For example, Remington and Smith & Wesson offer several styles that are available from many suppliers of shooting-related products such as Cabela's. Prices range from $20-40 for most of these glasses. Inexpensive wrap around safety glasses are available that are intended for shooters of airguns. Glasses such as these are generally sufficient to afford eye protection when shooting rimfire firearms. The important thing is to get a rigid, transparent layer of plastic between your eyes and any flying objects or gases. The author regularly wears prescription glasses that have plastic shields that attach to the rails. Such shields are very inexpensive and they work.

There was a time when hearing protection was not deemed necessary when firing a rimfire. True, the report is low compared to that from firearms of higher power, but it is sufficient to cause hearing loss, especially over an extended period of time. The author competed as a member of a small bore rifle team for two years with firing conducted on an indoor range. He also has little hearing in his left ear (the one toward the muzzle), which is partially attributable to a lack of hearing protectors at that time. Rimfire firearms make a loud crack that is certainly capable of causing hearing loss. We know a lot more about these things now than we did half a century ago, and hearing protectors are commonly used in occupations from airport workers to highway construction.

Although hearing protectors are available that cost $100-300, it is not necessary to spend a lot of money to get adequate protection, especially when shooting rimfire firearms. My wife and I use hearing protectors that fold to make a compact unit. Protectors of this type are available in a wide range of decibel protection values starting at low prices. The more effective protectors have higher decibel reduction ratings, and some excellent hearing protectors are also available at hardware stores. There are many other brands and styles available in the over the ear type of protector. The in the ear plug styles are also available and most are inexpensive.

4. Do not shoot at a hard surface or water.

Almost anyone who has fired a rimfire firearm in the outdoors has heard the whine of a bullet that has been deformed but not stopped. It can happen when shooting at a pine cone and the bullet hits the target or a branch and goes off into space. It can happen when a bullet fired at a pop can makes contact with the ground and whines on its way. It will almost certainly happen if the bullet is fired at a target on the surface of water. The shooter of a rimfire firearm *must* anticipate that a ricochet is likely under these conditions. As a result, most states prohibit shooting at targets on the surface of water. A bullet that is deflected during a ricochet may be capable of traveling a long distance because the velocity may not be reduced a great deal.

Safe shooting requires the participant to wear eye and hearing protectors.

Always be sure of your backstop or shoot in an area where there is nothing that can be damaged for a long distance if the bullet continues past the target.

5. Do not cross a fence or stream with a loaded gun.

Sometimes, it may not always be possible to pass an obstacle while constantly keeping the muzzle of a firearm pointing a safe direction. There is always the chance for a foot or hand to slip causing the shooter to assume some unsafe position while trying to regain control. It may also happen that the safety or hammer of the piece may contact the fence or some part of the anatomy and be moved. Any of these events can result in an unsafe situation. If it is necessary to pass some obstacle such as a fence, unload the firearm, leave the action open, and hand it to someone on the other side of the fence. If you are alone, place the empty firearm with the action open on the other side of the fence before you cross it. When crossing a stream, unload the firearm, open the action, and cross the stream safely before reloading. Having seen the foot of a hunter slip off a wet stone in the middle of a stream and the hunter go one way and his rifle another, it can not be overemphasized that it is unsafe to cross a stream with a loaded firearm.

6. Keep every firearm unloaded until you are ready to shoot.

Some of the most unsafe situations involving firearms result from improperly storing and transporting them. Firearm safety requires that an encounter of a person with a firearm begins with an *unloaded* piece. Someone else in your home or vehicle may have access to the piece in your absence. That person may not know the characteristics of your particular firearm, which could lead to accidental discharge if the piece is loaded. Some firearms have actions that cannot be opened unless the safety is in the "off" position. If the firearm is loaded, taking the safety off prior to opening the action places it in the ready mode. Therefore, it is imperative that the firearm be unloaded so that the person handling it is not manipulating a firearm that can be discharged immediately and accidentally. An exception to this can be made if the firearm is being used for self defense, but it should be stored so that only the person to whom the firearm belongs has immediate access to it.

7. Transport only unloaded, cased firearms.

In almost every situation, it is unlawful to discharge a firearm from a vehicle on a highway. In the confines of a vehicle, handling a rifle or handgun can cause the muzzle to point at someone else or at your own body parts. It is difficult to keep the muzzle from pointing in a direction that violates rule No. 2 given earlier. Even if the firearm is cased, removing a loaded firearm from a gun case can be an unsafe practice. It is possible that while transporting the piece the safety may have become disengaged. For firearms having external hammers, the hammer may have become partially or fully cocked. It is all too easy under these conditions to accidentally discharge the firearm. In the state of Wyoming there were four gun related accidents during the 2003 hunting season. Two of them involved loaded firearms in vehicles.

State laws regarding transportation of firearms vary enormously. Some states allow firearms to be transported uncased and loaded whereas in other states, firearms being transported must be unloaded *and* cased. Even within specific states there are great differences. For example, some municipalities forbid the ownership of handguns except those registered by residents. Travelers who are transporting a handgun in such areas even when it is cased and unloaded may be considered to be in possession of an illegal firearm. In some states, firearms and ammunition cannot be transported in the same case. The point is that there are literally thousands of laws on the books that relate to firearms, their transportation, and their uses. It is your responsibility to know and obey the rules that apply in your locality.

8. Keep all guns stored unloaded and away from unauthorized persons.

We are at a point in time where certain jurisdictions require that all firearms in homes be stored in locked containers or with a trigger lock of some sort in place. The idea behind this is to prevent someone who does not know safe gun handling procedures from picking up a loaded gun and accidentally firing it. Firearms vary enormously in design. The author once handed his single action revolver to a police officer who was fully qualified for duty with a semiautomatic pistol. The officer had no idea how a single action revolver worked and thought it was some type of top-break model that had to be opened at the top for loading. Of course there was no lack of concern for keeping the muzzle pointed correctly or other safe handling rules. It was simply a matter of not knowing how the mechanism of a single action revolver worked. Someone who is unfamiliar with firearms, especially children, may find it all too easy to move some button or knob and

Trigger locks are one way to keep a handgun secure. This lock requires a special key that has a most unusual shape to open it.

The Thompson Center Classic has a hole through the rear of the trigger guard through which a special lock is placed.

place the firearm in a "ready" mode. The tragedy of a child finding a loaded gun, pointing it in the wrong direction, and accidentally discharging the weapon is a scenario that can and does happen. It should not.

Numerous attempts are being made to make it more difficult for anyone other than the primary user of a firearm (especially a handgun) to operate it. Built in smart locks that use a code or a small key that must be inserted are currently being utilized or developed. By incorporating such devices, the chance of someone other than the owner firing the piece when the owner is not around is reduced. There are several rimfire handguns with built in locks. Regardless of what safety devices are developed, the most effective safety device is a careful, well-trained person who exercises appropriate caution while handling a firearm.

9. Obey all range commands instantly.

Shooters of rimfire rifles and pistols often engage in formal or informal target shooting, which may involve training sessions. This may occur at a range or in some other safe area with a suitable backstop. When firing is conducted on a range, it may be under the supervision of a range officer especially if it is a formal match that is carried out with time limitations. If this is the case, shooters are arranged at stations on the firing line with the firearms lying on a bench or table pointing toward the target area. When the target area is clear, the range officer may call, "Ready on the left? Ready on the right? Ready on the firing line! (pause) Commence firing!" At that point, the shooters are permitted to start firing the course. At the end of the time allowed, the range officer will announce, "Cease fire!" The course of fire is over at that time regardless of whether or not all competitors have fired the number of shots

normally included in that course. As firing progresses, the range officer may issue other commands. Regardless of what these commands are or whether or not they involve you, obey all such commands instantly. In basketball, when a whistle sounds the ball is almost always lobbed toward the basket, but no shot is ever to be fired on a shooting range after a command to cease is given. It is entirely possible that the range officer has seen something that none of the shooters on the line has observed. At many clubs, there may be no range officer present, but the shooters follow the same rules. A "cold line" is observed with all weapons having actions open and magazines empty until all shooters are "ready" and the appropriate commands are given to allow the line to become "hot."

Benchrest shooting, one of the popular forms of target shooting, involves firing the rifle from a heavy bench with the rifle fully supported. The object of this type of shooting is to fire the shots into the smallest group possible although in some cases, firing is for score. All shooters must keep their firearms unloaded and with the actions open until they are actually on the firing line. In rimfire benchrest competition, bolt action rifles are to have the bolts *removed* when they are not actually being set up for firing. When any person is downrange from the benches, the rifles are to be removed from the benches and all shooters are to be away from the benches. Rifles that do not have removable bolts are to have a safety device (a safety flag) protruding from the open breech when they are resting on the benches and a person is downrange.

10. Never use a firearm when mental or motor skills are impaired.

It is a crime to operate a motor vehicle while under the influence of alcohol. Some medications can cause the user to become drowsy or sluggish, which are physiological effects that are not unlike those produced by alcohol. Anyone who has received any substance that reduces mental or motor skills should never use a firearm. Crisp mental action and physical motions are required to manipulate a firearm in a safe, efficient manner.

Weapons and Image

Image is everything someone has said. If you do not believe it, watch a candidate for office as he meets with a group of business people or for a debate dressed in a black suit, white shirt, and red tie. Watch the same candidate as he meets with occupants of a nursing home or a group of farmers and note the difference in the candidate's attire. This is not a sexist observation because equivalent dress codes also exist for female candidates. Not long ago, as this is being written, a news report from the TV station in a city nearby gave the story of a homicide. As the announcer was talking, the graphic on the screen showed a handgun, the word "murder" and the outline of a body. You have probably seen such things before. However, in this instance, the victim had been stabbed to death! The desired connotation had nonetheless been conveyed to the viewers as they heard about a murder.

Let us look at one instance of how statistics and image are used in relation to reporting data regarding shooting sports. A study, published shortly before the first edition of this book was written, reported that an "estimated 21,840 injuries" resulting from non-powder guns (air rifles, paintball pistols, and BB guns) were treated in the year 2000. That estimate may or may not be accurate, but the implication is that the number is *known* because it is not given as "over 20,000", which would clearly show that it is an *estimate*. As bad as the use of the use of the word "estimated" is, there was another factor in the report that was even worse. In the lead paragraph of the report was the phrase "...undermining the notion that such weapons are harmless..." Did you ever hear a baseball announcer say, "Jones dropped his *weapon* and headed for first base" during a baseball game? Is a baseball bat a weapon? Absolutely, if it is used as a weapon. What about a golf announcer making the statement, "Jones had a good swing with the weapon." Is a golf club a weapon? Absolutely, if it is used as a weapon. If you think these are absurd examples, what about watching a TV show on cooking only to hear the chef say, "Slice the cold dessert with a warm-bladed weapon." In this book, the only time the author will use the word "weapon" is in Chapter 12 that deals with some aspects of self defense. It is true that

the same double barrel shotgun that is used when hunting quail or .22 rifle used to hunt squirrels can be used as a weapon, but it is the use that determines what is a weapon. The person who "rode shotgun" on stagecoaches had a short-barreled shotgun known as a coach gun, which was indeed a weapon.

Once, while the author was shooting on a range at a military establishment, a worker there came by and noting the .22 caliber semiautomatic pistol being used, remarked, "What a beautiful weapon." I was somewhat astonished because I regarded it as a device for punching holes in a piece of paper that was 50 feet away. That handgun was never used as a weapon. It is the contention of this author that in sporting circles the word "weapon" should generally be avoided because it conveys a negative connotation to nonshooters (who are very numerous and a growing segment of the population).

In the 10-year period 1990-2000, the total number of deaths from non-powder guns was 39 (approximately four per year), far fewer than those resulting from bicycle accidents, which have been averaging about one death every six hours or up to almost 1,500 per year! According to the Consumer Product Safety Commission (CPSC), thirty-six children die annually by drowning in five-gallon buckets! This does not include the hundreds more that drown in bathtubs, showers, toilets, etc. According to the same CPSC, children under the age of five die at a rate of approximately 150 per year as a result of playing with cigarette lighters (this does not include approximately 1,100 per year under age 15 who die in residential fires). Falls from open windows account for the deaths of approximately 18 persons under the age of 10 annually. Note the lack of media coverage of some of the other types of accidents compared to those in the shooting sports. If the intent is really to reduce accidental injuries and deaths, there are far more fruitful areas in which to work than with the shooting sports. For example, each year, almost one million children are treated for injuries involving bicycles.

During the approximately 70 years of involvement in shooting sports by the author, there has been a drastic change in firearms and the presentation of information about them. If you pick up a copy of almost any magazine devoted to guns and shooting, you will see photos of firearms that have laser sights, flashlights attached (hunting at night is illegal under almost all conditions), and a red glow at the muzzle with streaks emanating from it. Often the holder of the firearm is dressed in black and wearing a mask. Such presentation of a firearm may have a place in military or perhaps law enforcement settings. However, if a nonshooter passing the magazine rack on his way to find a copy of *Financial Fun* or *Daydreamer's Quarterly* sees several magazines with these sinister looking firearms on the cover, he or she has a mental image generated that is likely transferred to all shooting sports. Never mind that the first Gold Medal given in the 2000 Olympics was won by Nancy Johnson in women's airgun competition. As this is written in early 2016, the so-called Assault Rifle Ban that was introduced in 1994 and in force for a decade has expired. That Act was placed in force in no small measure because of the image of certain firearms. Never mind that the vast majority of such firearms were never used in criminal acts. Note that the news report described earlier used the word "weapon" as a descriptor for air rifles, paintball pistols, and BB guns. The first step in getting people on your side of an issue is to generate an image. In this case, the image of a "weapon" is being transferred to even BB guns and the paintball pistols used in a type of game or sport but not as weapons. The very likeness of an object to any type of "gun" is rejected by people who want to outlaw *all* guns.

Another word that is used frequently in many shooting publications is the word "tactical." We read about tactical pistols, tactical flashlights, tactical knives, and tactical scopes. What sort of tactics? Squirrel hunting? Shooting groups on paper targets to test accuracy? Shooting pop cans or pine cones? Tactical is the adjective form of the word "tactics," which my dictionary defines in one way as the science of maneuvering forces in combat. No wonder a nonshooter seeing a magazine that has listed the contents on the cover as articles on "tactical pistols" or "tactical knives" might think that the readers of such a magazine are (or want to be) members of some paramilitary group. There is nothing wrong with any of these "tactical" items, but they are not part of recreational or practice shooting unless the participant is training for tactics of a different sort.

Image may not be everything, but some of the gurus of the social media seem to think so. Frequently we hear of something posted on the media being removed because it shows a high school cheerleader hunting with relatives. In other cases, the post may show a teenager with the first deer. It is obvious that those owning the social media are trying to "protect" others from the evil of guns and hunting. After all, a typical tactic of the ultra "liberal" is to be tolerant of all views except on issues with which they don't

agree. All points of view are considered of equal value except those that go against the doctrine of the anti gun crowd. Some internet agencies refuse to advertise items if words like "tactical" or "sniper" are part of the text. We must be aware of these things.

We who love (a word that is not inappropriate for this author who has used rimfire rifles for 70 years) sport shooting can help give a positive image to the shooting sports. The "study" about the dangers of airguns cited above did not mention the fine work done by Daisy Outdoor Products in conducting the National BB Gun Competition because the intent was to emphasize how "dangerous" airguns are. Shooting sports in the Olympics are virtually never even mentioned in the TV coverage. We cannot expect balanced coverage of our sports in the mainstream media. A great deal of what is written in this section shows the personality, interest, and concerns of the writer. Almost all writing always does. It remains, however, that we can go a long way toward preserving the shooting sports by the image we present. In this book, the intent is going to be to present an image of shooting as a *skill*, a *sport*, and a *science* to be enjoyed safely by an enormous number of people.

Getting It Right

While spending a great deal of time in the Big Horn Mountains of Wyoming, the author and his wife became friends with one of the campground workers and his son, David. One summer, David had a friend, Josh, who came to the mountains to spend a week with him. Each afternoon, for the week of Josh's visit, it was customary to see the boys with their .22s heading out into the forest for an afternoon of adventure. It usually involved shooting a box of ammo at pine cones and pop cans that they took with them and brought back. If, as was usually the case, the boys came over to talk for a while before heading out, it was interesting to note that their rifles were unloaded, actions open, and muzzles pointing either straight up or down. They had faithfully learned the proper etiquette of handling firearms. The entire scene portrayed the very essence of our heritage and the legacy of the .22 rimfire. Watching David and Josh brought back memories from more than half a century earlier when the author and his older brother engaged in similar pursuits. There are those who wish to do away with such wonderful activities of others for their own misguided reasons. However, when, not if, this privilege is lost, America will be the poorer for it. Safe firearm handling may forestall our loss of this right assured by The Second Amendment.

CHAPTER 3

RIMFIRE RIFLES

THIS BOOK IS INTENDED to serve as a user's guide to rimfire rifles, pistols, and ammunition. Some readers are perhaps old hands in the rimfire game, but others may be newcomers. If you are a member of the former group, you may already have rimfire firearms and need this chapter only for reference. If you are a member of the latter group, this chapter will give you some insight into the factors to consider when you start evaluating the enormous number of rimfire firearms that are available in order to select equipment for your own use or perhaps for use by another member of your family.

Before you select a rimfire firearm, it is necessary to decide what you intend to do with it. It is not unreasonable for a rimfire shooter who is buying a new rifle for serious varmint hunting or competition to spend a great deal of money to attain superior performance. For these shooters, equipment at the cutting edge of capability is worth the investment. The rifles and pistols in this category are not made by the millions, as are some of the less expensive (sometimes referred to as entry level) models. By the same token, it is not necessary to spend a great deal of money if all you are going to do is to take a youngster out to hunt squirrels or shoot pop cans. Rifles that perform very well for this type of shooting do not cost a great deal of money.

In this chapter, a survey of the different types of rimfire rifles will be presented to give a general introduction to the selection of rifles available. Rifles are available with lever, pump, bolt, single shot, and semiautomatic types of actions. Within certain limits, rifles having any of these types of actions may meet the performance requirements for the intended uses. However, you are not likely to find many lever action or pump rifles that deliver tack driving accuracy, but there are exceptions. Target rifles generally have bolt actions although there are some very accurate semiautomatics. One of the first decisions to be made is that of the caliber of the rimfire rifle to be chosen. For many years, the .22 LR was about the only choice, but that is not the case today. However, rifles in all of the rimfire calibers are not available with all types of actions.

Keep in mind that a large number of variants are produced of most rimfire rifles, some of which are produced only for a year or two. They may differ in stock material, sights, blue or stainless metal, etc. It is not possible to give a complete listing that is correct and complete for any length of time as a result of these frequent changes. Therefore, to some extent the survey here is of a general nature and manufacturer's catalogs and websites should be consulted to see what is available at any point in time.

Types of Actions

In order to fire a series of shots, some means must be available for reloading. The empty case must be removed and a loaded round placed in the chamber for the next shot. Sounds elementary, doesn't it? In principle it is, but how it is done often involves some sophisticated engineering and the fabrication of intricate mechanisms. As with most forms of human endeavor, approaches to solving the problem have been many and various. Some of the earliest breech loading rifles had some sort of block that moved upward behind the cartridge to hold it in place and at the same time placed the firing pin directly between the cartridge and the hammer. The hammer could be drawn back so that the sear engaged a notch to hold it in place. When the trigger was pulled, the sear disengaged letting the spring-driven hammer go forward to strike the firing pin, which in turn struck the primer and fired the shot.

Most of the single shot rifles that incorporate a moving locking block (either falling block or rolling block) have long since disappeared from the marketplace. In the late 1800s and early 1900s, there were numerous models of such rimfire rifles that were generally of a small scale design. Replacing them were single shot bolt actions in which the bolt handle could be lifted out of its retaining notch and drawn back to open the chamber with the extractor pulling out the empty case. After a cartridge was placed in the chamber, the action was closed by pushing the bolt forward and turning the handle down into its locking notch. In some models, a cam moved the firing pin back to cock the action as the action was opened whereas in others the firing pin was held back by the sear as the action was closed. The first type is known as "cocks on opening" and the other is the "cocks on closing" type. In still other rifles, neither opening nor closing the bolt cocked the rifle. That was done after the action was closed by pulling back on a knob (the cocking piece) at the rear end of the bolt.

Because most shooters would rather load several rounds at one time and then fire them without any further handling of ammunition, the "repeating rifle" was designed. In rimfire calibers, there are two common ways in which the cartridges are held. The first type of reservoir, located in front of the trigger, is a box in which the rounds are stacked vertically. When the bolt is drawn back, a cartridge moves upward so that when the bolt is pushed forward it takes the top round out of the magazine and moves it into the chamber. A variation of this type of magazine is one in which the cartridges are held in a "box" that allows them to stack around a spindle. The rotary magazines employed by many of the popular Ruger rimfire rifles are of this type. The second type of reservoir for cartridges is a long tube that is located under the barrel or, less commonly, inside the stock. Inside the tube is a spring-loaded follower that pushes the cartridges to the rear so that as the bolt is opened, a cartridge is

To operate a bolt action, the handle must be lifted and the bolt withdrawn then pushed forward. Shown here is the famous Anschutz Model 64 action.

moved into a position that allows the bolt to carry it into the chamber as it is closed. Both of these types of magazines have been popular for many years.

Rather closely related to the bolt action with a tubular magazine is the slide or pump action. In this type of action, moving a handle located below and in front of the action backward causes the action to open and the empty case to be ejected then moving the handle forward pushes a cartridge into the chamber. Because the magazine tube lies below the barrel, the cartridge must be moved upward by a carrier as the pump handle nears its rearmost position. Pump action rifles having both external and internal hammers have been produced for many years.

A pump action like this Winchester Model 90 can be operated very quickly since only motion backward and forward is required.

Not too far removed from the pump action is the lever action in which the cartridges are also usually held in a tubular magazine. In this case, the cartridges are moved from the magazine to the chamber by operating a lever located behind the trigger. Pulling the lever down opens the action and cocks the hammer as the empty case is ejected. Pulling the lever back up pushes a cartridge into the chamber as the action is closed. The vast majority of lever action rifles produced have external hammers.

In terms of the number of units sold, the most popular type of action for rimfire rifles is that known as the semiautomatic, self-loading, or autoloading type. The bolt is held in the forward position by a strong spring known as the recoil spring. When the rifle is fired, the impulse transferred from the cartridge head to the bolt forces the bolt to the rear, which cocks the internal hammer and ejects the empty case. As the bolt is pushed forward by the recoil spring, it takes with it a cartridge from the magazine, which

Operating a lever action like this Henry requires the lever to be pulled downward then raised in order to cycle the action.

can be vertical box, rotary, or tubular type. A rifle that operates this way is often called an "automatic," but this term strictly applies to a rifle type that fires the next shot simply by holding the trigger back. With the self-loading or semiautomatic rifle, loading is automatically accomplished after each shot, but the trigger must be released and pulled for each shot.

The Ruger 10/22 autoloader requires only pulling the trigger to fire successive shots.

Each type of action has some advantages and disadvantages. The bolt action is the slowest to operate because the shooter's hand must be removed from the grip, the handle grasped, the bolt turned and pulled back, then pushed forward and closed. With the pump and lever actions, only a back and forth motion is required. With the autoloader, the trigger must be released and then pulled for the next shot. However, bolt action rifles are generally more accurate, and as a result most accurate sporting and target rifles have that type action. Some target rifles are extremely accurate autoloaders. Today, the bolt action and semiautomatic rifles are by far the most popular rimfires and there is an extensive selection of rifles

of each type. Before making a selection, handle rifles having different types of actions and evaluate them in terms of your anticipated use. You may be surprised to find how far down the list of criteria that rate of fire ranks in terms of importance. If you want a rifle that is a real tack driver, you will probably select a bolt action or one of the target autoloaders that are becoming more popular.

Calibers

Although there were once rimfire rifles available in several calibers, they are currently all either .17s or .22s. The .17 HMR, .17 Mach 2, .17 Aguila, and the .17 WSM are the choices in .17 caliber, but the .17 Mach 2 and .17 Aguila are about defunct. However, the .22 Long Rifle (LR) is by far the most popular rimfire caliber. Both .22 LR firearms and ammunition are less expensive than those in any other caliber. Of course, the choice of caliber should be made based on the use to which the firearm is to be put.

Rimfire rifles are currently available in several calibers. Shown here (left to right) are the .17 Aguila, .17 Mach 2, .17 Hornady Rimfire Magnum, .22 Long Rifle, and the .22 Winchester Magnum Rimfire. Not shown is the recently introduced .17 WSM.

Chapter 10 deals with using rimfire firearms for hunting and pest shooting. In that chapter, several factors regarding the suitability of the various rimfire calibers for specific purposes are briefly discussed. If you plan to do a lot of shooting or want to enjoy shooting for the lowest possible cost, there is no doubt that the .22 LR is the caliber of choice because of the lower cost involved. Also, the .22 LR generally gives better accuracy than the .22 Short except when the latter is fired in special target arms chambered specifically for that round. At one time, rifles chambered for the .22 Short were popular, but the choice of arms chambered specifically for the .22 Short is very limited now. Moreover, the cost of .22 Short ammunition now exceeds that of most .22 LR loads because of the difference in sales volume, and the .22 Short is not available in every corner store that sells only a few of the most popular types.

For many years, the .22 LR has been the choice of squirrel hunters when they are hunting in a location that allows a rifle to be used safely. Most rimfire rifles are capable of fine accuracy when the appropriate ammunition is used. It may take some testing with several types of ammunition to determine which types perform best in your rifle, but it pays dividends when you take a shot at a very small target that you wish to harvest cleanly. In the experience of the author, shots at small game are usually no longer than 50 yards, and the .22 LR has plenty of power to harvest squirrels at that range. Generally, head shots are made in order to minimize meat damage so the target area is not much larger than an inch in diameter. Accuracy of the rifle/ammunition combination and shooting skill are the most important factors.

Frequently, someone writing either in an advertisement or an article mentions using the .22 WMR or .17 HMR for hunting small game. Either will certainly dispatch small game species, but head shots better be made if you want much left to eat. These high velocity rounds are explosive to small targets, especially at the ranges at which squirrels and rabbits are normally taken. The primary use of these magnum calibers is in taking larger species or taking small species at long range where their higher power and flatter trajectory are advantageous. Rabbits, squirrels, and treed raccoons do not require the use of a magnum rimfire.

There is one advantage of the .22 WMR over the .17 HMR for small game hunting. Although the overall case length is shorter, an old cartridge known as the .22 Winchester Rim Fire (WRF) has almost identical head size and body taper as does the .22 WMR. Therefore, it is perfectly safe to fire .22 WRF ammunition in a rifle chambered for the .22 WMR. Because it is a specialty item having low sales volume, the cost of .22 WRF ammunition is about the same as it is for some of the lower cost (not necessarily premium) .22 WMR ammunition. The advantage of using the .22 WRF cartridges is that they feature a 45-grain bullet with a muzzle velocity of around 1,300 ft/sec so they are similar in power to a .22 LR high velocity round. This can be important when using a rifle chambered for the .22 WMR on edible game. The only factor to consider is whether the slightly shorter .22 WRF round is sufficiently accurate in your .22 WMR to justify its use. In the author's bolt action Ruger 77/22M, the CCI

.22 WRF gives outstanding accuracy. Five-shot groups average just over 0.6 inch at 50 yards so this gives the flexibility needed to use ammunition of lower power in that .22 WMR without sacrificing accuracy. However, the rifle must be sighted with the .22 WRF ammunition because the point of impact at 50 yards is 5 or 6 inches lower than where the .22 WMR hits. The .17 HMR offers no such lower-powered option in ammunition.

As will be discussed in Chapter 10, varmint hunting with rimfire rifles is an entirely different matter because recovery of edible meat is not a factor. Although one may almost certainly begin varmint hunting with a .22 LR, there are obvious advantages to the use of the .22 WMR and .17 HMR for the varmint hunter. Either will extend the range of a .22 LR by a considerable margin and will permit taking larger species. The .22 WMR is effective to about 125-150 yards whereas the flatter-shooting .17 HMR is effective to perhaps

Except for length, the dimensions of the .22 WRF and the .22 WMR are almost identical.

150-175 yards with best performance of both calibers at or close to the lower end of the ranges mentioned. As we will now discuss, this performance comes at a price when the cost of ammunition is considered. In this regard, the .22 WMR formerly had some advantage because all ammunition for the .17 HMR is of a "premium" type that costs more than most of the .22 WMR types that are not designated as premium ammunition. As this is written, the rimfire ammunition situation has been grim for a few years. Prices have risen dramatically when ammunition can be found. At present, *most* types of .17 HMR and .22 WMR are comparably priced.

Although the topic will be discussed in detail in Chapter 9, the .22 WMR is better suited to taking larger species whereas the .17 HMR is better suited to taking smaller species at longer ranges. The logical approach is probably to choose a .22 LR for plinking and small game hunting then add a .17 HMR or .22 WMR if you wish to get more involved with varmint hunting using only rimfire rifles. However, many small bore enthusiasts do serious varmint hunting with rifles chambered for the .22 LR by limiting the ranges at which shots at game are taken and choosing rifles and ammunition that are capable of giving target-grade accuracy.

If the varmints you plan to hunt are small species such as ground squirrels and crows at ranges not to exceed 125 yards or so, the .17 Mach 2 would be a suitable choice. With a muzzle velocity of approximately 2,100 ft/sec, the trajectory is quite flat out to about 125 yards making hits easy. Keep in mind that this is not a powerful round so its use should be confined to smaller species of varmints. Outstanding accuracy is reported with most rifles in this caliber so it would also function well for the squirrel hunter who is willing to pass up all but head shots. As this is written, the price of a box of .17 Mach 2 ammunition is approximately $8-10 for 50 rounds, which means that it is not much less expensive than .17 HMR. However, interest in the .17 Mach 2 has taken a plunge and very few new rifles are available in that caliber and ammunition is available only in one load and one brand.

The new .17 WSM is the most potent rimfire caliber.

When we consider the .17 WSM, we are looking at a cartridge that gives up to 3,000 ft/sec (20 grain bullet) and 400 ft lbs of energy at the muzzle. It is a far more powerful cartridge than either the .17 HMR or .22 WMR. Interestingly, the cost of .17 WSM ammunition is not much different than for the other two magnum rounds. However, since Savage introduced the original B.Mag rifle, a model having a heavy stainless steel barrel has been introduced. Ruger now offers the bolt action Model 77 in .17 WSM and Winchester offers the Model 1885 Low Wall single shot in that caliber. Although not a caliber for the small game hunter, the .17 WSM should be excellent for varmint hunting.

Selection and Cost

As with any field of endeavor, the cost of the available equipment varies enormously. Rimfire handguns will be considered in Chapter 4 so this discussion will deal with the selection and cost situation with respect to rimfire rifles and ammunition. Many years ago, firearms (and many other things) were subject to the so-called "fair trade" laws, under which the prices were set by the manufacturer. Such laws were changed long ago, but manufacturers still publish price indicators. These are simply numbers that may serve as a basis for comparison between two different models or manufacturers. Keep in mind that there is almost always a considerable difference between the manufacturer's suggested retail price (MSRP) and the actual retail selling price of any firearm. Currently, the very low end of the cost spectrum for rimfire rifles begins at a retail price of approximately $150 whereas at the upper end are models that sell for many times as much.

The number of available models of rimfire rifles is enormous. In this section, only a quick overview of some of the available models and their approximate prices can be given, and manufacturer's catalogs or web sites should be studied to see all of the options available. Another good source of information is *Gun Digest*, which contains a wealth of information in a single volume that is updated annually.

Most people usually own a firearm for a long period of time. Before deciding to buy any rifle, look at manufacturers' catalogs to try to limit your choices somewhat. Then, go to some stores and actually handle those rifles that interest you. You may find after handling a certain model that you especially like (or dislike) it. There may be some features or controls that attract (or annoy) you. The word "feel" is probably one of the most overused words, but it gives the correct connotation. The choice of a firearm is a personal matter and how a rifle looks or "feels" to you is an important consideration.

We will now try to arrive at some basic ideas related to the selection of a rimfire rifle. First, consider the caliber. A wide selection of rifles that includes bolt action, autoloaders, pumps and lever actions is available in rimfire calibers. If you are selecting a first rimfire rifle for general use, the .22 LR should be your choice. Another rifle in one of the rimfire magnum calibers can be added later if you get into varmint hunting. At that time, rifles with the whole range of action types can be considered again although you may want to select a magnum having the same type of action as the .22 LR. To simplify matters, the selection process will be approached from the standpoint of cost. Although it is unlikely that most buyers of rimfire rifles will start with a top flight, high end sporting rifle, the discussion will begin with such rifles.

Anschütz sporting rifles have long been known for their accuracy. This model fitted with a Cabela's 6-20X scope is a real tack driver.

If cost is no object and a price tag of over $1,000 to perhaps two or three times that figure is acceptable to you, a bolt action sporting rifle is probably your best choice. For many years, the outstanding rifle of this type was the legendary Winchester Model 52 Sporter, but it is no longer available. Elegant bolt action rimfire rifles are represented by models such as the Cooper Model 57M, which is priced at approximately $2,395 and Anschütz 1416 D (that has an MSRP of $1,099) or the 1416 HB (that has an MSRP of $1,199). The Anschütz 64-S Benchrest model is priced at $1,539. Anschütz sporting rifles are also built on the Model 54 Match Action with prices in the $2,100-2,300 range. Among the elegant rimfire sporters is the Sako Finnfire II, which has an MSRP of $1,440. One of the most interesting Sako rifles is the Quad Hunter, which has the flexibility of being used with four barrels (in .17 Mach 2, .17 HMR, .22 LR, and .22 WMR calibers). With all four barrels included, the price is $3,190.

All of the sporting rifles described are of superb quality and will give outstanding performance. They are known for literally "one hole" groups. For example, the Cooper Model 57M must shoot a five-shot group at 50 yards that measures 1/4 inch or less with premium match ammunition before it is shipped. Targets showing the test groups are included with these rifles when they are shipped. These are sporting rifles for the most discriminating small bore enthusiast from both performance and appearance standpoints. Some of the models mentioned are available in .22 WMR, .17 HMR, and .17 Mach 2 as well as in .22 LR.

For many years, Anschütz rimfire rifles in sporter and more specialized target configurations have been built on their famous Model 54 and 64 bolt actions. Anschütz target rifles have been consistent medal winners in international and Olympic competition. The two series of rifles are known as the 1700 and 1400/1500 series, respectively, depending on whether the action is the Model 54 or 64. Some of the target models have dominated small bore competition, and the accuracy of both sporter and target rifles is outstanding. Models are offered with standard and heavy weight barrels. Receivers have grooves 11mm in width for attaching scope mounts, but they are also drilled and tapped for mounting scope bases making it possible to use many types of scope rings. Keep in mind that except for a few of the Anschütz sporters, almost all of these high end rifles are sold without sights so a scope must be added. The price of the scope and mounts may add a considerable amount to the cost of the rifle that is in itself high.

When it comes to high performance autoloaders, the most highly regarded (and expensive) models are those produced by Volquartsen. Some of these rifles may sell for about as much as an Anschütz or Cooper bolt action. However, in terms of performance a Volquartsen is similarly capable.

In recent years, the Ruger 77/22 bolt action rifles in .22 LR, .22 WMR, and .17 HMR calibers have been popular. However, they have the MSRP of $979 with some specialty models listed at $1,069 so they are hardly inexpensive. Browning has produced an elegant bolt action rimfire sporter for many years. Known as the T-Bolt, several versions are available that differ in finish and stock material with MSRPs starting at $749.99. Browning also produces a fine lever action model, known as the BLR, which has the MSRP of $619.99.

The Ruger 77/22 will handle almost any task required of a rimfire sporter.

If you are limited to the retail price range of approximately $300-500 but still want a bolt action sporting rifle, there are numerous models from which to choose. The Ruger American series includes several rifles in .22 LR, .22 WMR, and .17 HMR calibers. They have the MSRP of $359 for the basic model in any of the three calibers. One version is available in .22 LR

The immensely popular Ruger American is now available in a version having a nicely shaped wood stock. (photo courtesy of Ruger)

with a nicely shaped wood stock having the MSRP of $459. Much more will be said about the Ruger American in Chapters 14 and 15.

Outstanding bolt action rifles are also available from Ceska Zbrojovka Uhersky Brod (CZ). The CZ 452 rifles have barrels that are threaded into the receivers, and they are widely recognized as giving outstanding accuracy. The CZ 452 is being phased out, but it is still available in certain configurations and except for the interchangeability of barrels the 452 and 455 are essentially identical. The basic CZ 455 .22 LR sporter is listed at $421 with the .17 HMR and .22 WMR versions being priced at $540. The version having the full-length stock lists for $514 in .22 LR and $540 in magnum calibers. The CZ 452/455 American features a well-shaped, checkered walnut stock, highly polished and blued metal parts, and true sporting rifle styling. Evaluations of the performance of two of these fine CZ rifles in .22 LR and .17 HMR calibers are included in Chapters 14 and 15. Other versions of the CZ 452/455 series include the Lux, Varmint, Style, Silhouette, and FS that differ in stock and barrel materials. The Varmint has a shorter barrel of heavier weight and a stock that is of a target shape. The Lux version features a longer barrel and a stock of European design, and the FS (full-stock) version has a full-length or Mannlicher style stock. Synthetic stocks are found on the Style, which has nickel finished metal and the Silhouette which has blued metal.

The European style CZ Lux is an attractive sporter. (photo courtesy of CZ USA)

This listing of options should show that Ruger and CZ bolt action rifles are available in an array of models that allow a selection to suit almost any taste. Even though these rifles are priced below the models from Anschütz, Cooper, Browning, and Sako, do not assume that they are drab in appearance. For most of us, the Ruger and CZ models represent stylish rifles that also deliver excellent performance. Of course, models are available in .22 LR, .22 WMR, and .17 HMR calibers. If you want to consider them as fine sporting rifles for shooters on a somewhat limited budget, it would not be inappropriate.

A CZ 452 represents excellent value and delivers outstanding performance in either .22 LR (top) or .17 HMR (bottom).

The CZ 452 American is a moderately priced sporter that gives outstanding performance.

All of these Ruger American and CZ 452/455 models are bolt action repeaters. The CZ has a grooved receiver and can accept the popular scope mounts that clamp in these grooves. Receivers of the Ruger American rifles are grooved for attaching scope mounts but they are also drilled and tapped to permit attaching Weaver-type rings.

Up to this point, the discussion of rifles in the medium price range has been concerned with bolt action models, but it certainly should not limited to that action type. Also in the $400-700 range are the fine Marlin 39A and Browning BL-22 lever actions all of which are excellent rifles for almost any sporting

The Marlin Model 39A has been produced for many years. It is well known as a dependable, accurate rifle. (photo courtesy of Marlin)

The Browning BL-22 is a lever action rimfire that is beautiful and reliable. (photo courtesy of Browning Arms)

purpose. The Marlin 39A (which has the distinction of being the rimfire long gun in longest production) has retail price of approximately $700. The Browning BL-22 has an MSRP of $620 depending which version is selected. As is true of other lever actions, this rifle makes use of a tubular magazine held under the barrel and typifies the superb fit and finish for which Browning firearms are famous. For several years, the Ruger 96 lever action, which has a receiver with a rounded profile with no external hammer, was produced in .22 LR and .22 WMR, but only a few were made in .17 HMR. The Ruger 96 is a fine rifle, but for some reason lever action rifles are far less popular than are autoloaders so it has been discontinued.

Numerous rimfire autoloaders are available in the $500-700 range including the Remington 552 BDL Speedmaster and some of the Browning Buck Mark models. Target type autoloaders in this price range include the Ruger 10/22T and Browning Buck Mark Target models. The Ruger 10/22T has a heavy, beautifully finished hammer-forged barrel and comes with no sights. With a blue barrel, the list price is $579 whereas the stainless steel version has a list price of $629. Retail prices are normally about $100 lower. Performance of the Ruger 10/22T is discussed in Chapter 14. For shoot-

ing that may involve low level bench rest or silhouette competition, the choice would be a toss up between the Ruger 10/22T and the Browning Buckmark Target depending on personal preference. Following the great success of the Buckmark pistol, Browning added a longer barrel and attached a stock to produce the Buckmark rifle. It is available in either sporter or target version with an MSRP of $699.99. At 7.5 pounds without sights, the Ruger 10/22T and the recently discontinued T/C Benchmark are somewhat heavy for general field use, but either would be an outstanding rifle for the hunter who likes to sit in the woods watching for squirrels. Keep in mind, there is a lot of personal preference in these *suggestions* (not necessarily to be taken as the author's *recommendations*), but they are based on experience with several of the rifles described.

One of the best known .22 LR autoloaders of all time is the Browning Semi-Auto .22 (known as the Model SA22) that is one of the most streamlined rifles ever made. It utilizes a tubular magazine that is located in the stock so there is no box magazine protruding from the bottom of the action or tube under the barrel. Also, empty cases are ejected from the bottom of the action so there are no cutout sections on the sides of the receiver. Left-handed shooters appreciate not having

Autoloader fans have available a deluxe model in the stylish Remington 552. (photo courtesy of Remington)

Built on the same action as the pistol with the same name, the Browning Buck Mark is a reliable, accurate rifle with unusual appearance. (photo courtesy of Browning Arms)

With its heavy hammer forged barrel, the Ruger 10/22T is well known for its accuracy. (photo courtesy of Ruger)

One of the most stylish autoloaders ever produced is the Browning Semi Automatic.

empty cases ejected across their faces from the right hand side of the receiver. As in the case of most other Browning firearms, the Semi-Auto .22 is available in several grades that differ in the amount of engraving and inlay work. Known as Grade I, the lowest priced SA22 has a list price of $699.99 whereas the elegant and ornate Grade VI has a list price of $1,579.

Suppose that you want to get a rimfire rifle that is capable of good performance, but your budget will not allow even a $350 retail price or you simply do not want to spend more for the rifle. In this under $350 category, there are a number of choices that will still allow you to go plinking, small game hunting, or varmint shooting successfully. Because rimfire rifles are part and parcel to inexpensive shooting, there is a broad range of rifles in this category. First, there are the numerous bolt action repeaters (having either box or tubular magazines) from makers such as Marlin, Ruger, Mossberg, and Savage. These are sturdy, dependable rifles that normally give good accuracy (around one-inch groups at 50 yards) when appropriate ammunition is used.

It is the experience of this author that these lower priced rifles frequently seem to show a greater difference in accuracy with the type of ammunition chosen than do bolt action rifles such as the Ruger 77/22, CZ 452/455 American, or target models. Testing several types of ammunition will usually allow you to find one or two types that perform very well in a specific rifle. For example in the tests (see Chapter 14), the bolt action Marlin 25N (forerunner of the Model 925 and current XT-22) gave an average group size for five

five-shot groups at 50 yards of only 0.78 inch with Wolf Match Target ammunition. The average group size was also under an inch when using CCI Green Tag and Federal Match Target ammunition. Several versions of the Savage bolt action models known as the Mark II series (or the 93 series in magnum calibers) provide excellent performance, and they are inexpensive rifles. The point is that even an inexpensive rifle may give performance equal to that of more expensive models if some testing is carried out to find the ammunition that performs best in that particular rifle.

If a bolt action is not your choice, other rifles in the under $300-350 price category include many that have other types of actions. Economically priced autoloaders that generally sell at retail for $200-250 include the Ruger 10/22 Carbine, the Remington 597, the Marlin 60, Savage 64 series (which includes 10 variants!), Henry Lever Action, and the Henry U.S. Survival rifle. Some of these models are available in several versions that differ in metal finish and stock configuration. In terms of units sold, these are the most popular rimfire rifles made. For example, the legendary Ruger 10/22 autoloader is normally available for under a price of $300 in the Carbine, Compact, and Takedown versions. All of these are competent, dependable rifles that are adequate for informal rimfire sport shooting.

One of the most successful .22 LR autoloaders of all time is the Ruger 10/22 Carbine with about 5 million having been produced since it was introduced in 1964. This model is offered in several variants, but the most popular is that with a carbine style hardwood stock and 18.5-inch barrel. It has suggested price of $309 but is

The Savage Mark II bolt action rifle is a dependable, low cost model that gives performance beyond its price. (photo courtesy of Savage

The rimfire shooter who wants good performance at a rock bottom price need look no farther than the Marlin Model 925 or XT. (photo courtesy of Marlin)

One of the most popular rimfire rifles of all time, the Ruger 10/22 Carbine is the standard by which other autoloaders are judged. Shown is the 40th Anniversary version. (photo courtesy of Ruger)

The Remington 597 offers good performance at a reasonable price. (photo courtesy of Remington)

heavily discounted to a retail price of around $250 in many stores. The 10/22 has been produced in an enormous number of versions, many of which are dealer exclusives. For example, to commemorate the 40th Anniversary of the 10/22, a special version was produced that has a large nickel silver medallion embedded in the stock. A version known as the 10/22 Rifle was formerly produced that had a 20-inch barrel with no barrel band and a stock of sporter lines. It never competed well with the standard 10/22 and was discontinued after being produced for only a few years.

It is difficult to imagine a better choice than the Ruger 10/22 Carbine autoloader if an inexpensive rifle with that type of action is desired. Moreover, once you have a 10/22, it is capable of being modified almost without limit. Such upgrades are not merely cosmetic because match grade barrels are popular options. However, in the same general price range as the Ruger 10/22 Carbine is the Remington 597. This rifle is available in several variants that feature different metal finishes and stock materials. The weight and dimensions of the Remington 597 make it a convenient rifle to carry while hunting, and the matte finish and synthetic stock render it resistant to harsh conditions. Another autoloader that has been popular for many years is the Henry U.S. Survival AR-7 Rifle. This model can be disassembled and the barrel stored in the hollow stock.

The autoloader that has been produced in greater numbers than any other is the Marlin Model 60 in its numerous versions. For approximately $200, it is possible to buy a Marlin Model 60 autoloader because one of the large "marts" regularly sells this model for around $175 in the blue metal and hardwood stock configuration. Versions having stainless steel metal parts and composite stocks are also available in the under $300 category. Almost any combination of barrel and stock from blue and hardwood to stainless steel and laminated is available in versions offered for this popular rifle. Getting one of these rifles and adding an inexpensive scope (see Chapter 5) enables a shooter to enjoy rimfire shooting with a minimum outlay of cash. One of the interesting facts about the Marlin 60 is that it has been produced for many years carrying not only Marlin's name but also the names of other retailers such as Western Auto, Coast to Coast Hardware, etc. The Marlin Model 60 is one of the true classics among American .22s. We will have a great deal more to say about the Marlin Model 60 in Chapter 14.

Also in this general price range is the Henry lever action (MSRP $360), which should be given serious consideration. The experience of the author is that the Henry lever action will give accuracy at least as good as most inexpensive autoloaders, and it is light, compact, attractive, and classic in styling (see Chapter 14). As a .22 for woods roaming and plinking that costs around $300, it is hard to beat one of the Ruger 10/22 versions, the Marlin 60, the Remington 597, or the Henry lever action. They can be used very successfully for plinking pine cones or potting squirrels.

Bolt action rimfire rifles in the magnum calibers normally sell for approximately $25-50 more than the similar model in .22 LR. For example, the lowest priced variant of a Marlin Model XT (22 LR) bolt action

The autoloading Henry U.S. Survival rifle is a takedown model, and the barrel and action can be stored in the stock. (photo courtesy of Henry Repeating Arms)

With millions produced, the Marlin Model 60 is extremely popular. Several versions are available, and performance is excellent. (photo courtesy of Marlin)

has a retail price of around $150 whereas the .22 WMR and .17 HMR versions have MSRP values of $220-250. A similar situation exists for the Savage bolt action rimfires. For example, the Mark II G has an MSRP of $242 whereas the Model 93 G in magnum calibers are listed at $285. However, both Marlin and Savage also produce bolt action rimfires that have heavy stainless steel

Lever action fans who want a rimfire need look no further than the Henry.

barrels and laminated stocks that sell for considerably more than the basic models. It should not be inferred that a relatively inexpensive Marlin or Savage bolt action gives poor performance. Some of these models perform quite well as will be described later in this book (see Chapters 14 and 15).

Although the cost of a bolt action rifle in one of the magnum calibers may be around $20-25 higher than that of a comparable .22 LR, this is not the case for autoloaders. For some autoloaders, there is a greater difference in price of the .22 LR and .22 WMR versions. The reason for this is that in the .22 LR caliber, the receiver can be made from cast aluminum. Because of the much

higher power of the magnum calibers, the receiver must be made of steel, and the bolt assembly must be more massive to handle the stresses that occur during blow back of the action. Although they are similar in appearance and model numbers, the autoloading magnum rifles and those in .22 LR are essentially different rifles. A similar situation exists for the Henry .22 WMR lever action for which the MSRP is $499.95 compared to the .22 LR version which lists at $360.

Not only is the cost of the firearm important, but also the cost of ammunition must be considered. I just finished reading an article in which the author described his use of a .17 Mach 2 on "barnyard pests, sparrows, and starlings." There is nothing wrong with such a practice, but it is massive overkill (not to mention expense) when an air rifle would work well on such species. With .17 Mach 2 ammunition selling for about $10 per box (about twice the price of .22 LR), this is not my idea of rifle for use on sparrows and starlings. Occasionally, I see someone describe a rifle chambered for the .17 HMR as a "rifle for small game and plinking." Plinking to most people means shooting pine cones, pop cans, and an occasional starling. With the ammunition selling for $12-15 per box, I do not intend to use my .17 HMR for plinking when some promotional types of .22 LR can be found for as low as $3.00 per box! It is possible to buy 500 rounds of inexpensive .22 LR for about the same price as 100 rounds of .17 HMR. However, I do not intend to use the least expensive .22 LR ammunition for prairie dog shooting (unless it performs very well in my rifle).

The Savage 93 G is an economical but capable magnum rimfire. (photo courtesy of Savage Arms)

For many years, the Marlin bolt action in .22 WMR has been a highly regarded rifle for the varmint hunter on a budget. In .17 HMR caliber, it is well known for its accuracy. (photo courtesy of Marlin)

As in the case of selecting an automobile, when it comes to selecting a firearm, personal preference plays an important role including with this author. He knows one individual who used to stoutly proclaim, "I would rather walk than ride in a Ford!" In retrospect, he should have responded with, "Get out of my car!" He knows another who insists, "Chevrolets are junk!" Well, we all have our preferences. The truth is that within the parameters of size, weight, and price most rimfire firearms are likely to prove satisfactory, and that is why many models have been produced by the millions. Even some inexpensive models have been passed down for a couple of generations and continue to function well.

This compact single-shot bolt action rifle is similar to several current models offered by Keystone Arms. They are scaled specifically for small shooters. (photo courtesy of Keystone)

Youth Rifles

Throughout the history of the .22 rimfire, it has been the caliber most often selected for the first firearm for youthful shooters. Single shot rifles of smaller proportions became known as the "boys rifles" and they were popular in the late 1800s and early 1900s. Although they were made in a variety of types, perhaps the most familiar was the falling block. This type of action has a lever located behind the trigger guard or as an extension of the trigger guard. When the lever is pulled downward, a block located behind the breech moves downward exposing the chamber into which a single cartridge is loaded. These rifles have a visible hammer with a safety notch but no other safety. One rifle of this type is the Stevens Favorite, which was one of the most popular models.

Recognizing the need for rifles appropriately scaled for boys and girls, so-called youth models are still being produced. Most are single shot bolt action models that are available with several options such as color of stock, metal finish, choice of sights, etc. CZ produces the Scout/Youth model that has a 16-inch barrel chambered for .22 LR, and it has the MSRP of $312. Keystone Sporting Arms produces a series of small single shot rifles known as the Crickett. They are available in .22 LR and .22 WMR. Barrel lengths are 16 1/8 inches and the rifles are priced from $171 depending on model. The Rascal is a small single shot

produced by Savage, and it is available with stocks in a variety of colors. Henry Repeating Arms offers a small rifle known as the Mini Bolt. It is available in .22 LR and has a 16-inch barrel. In the category of youth rifles, Mossberg offers the International Half Pint that has an MSRP of $234.

A rifle of a different type is available from Rossi. This model is a break action single shot that is available as the action with interchangeable barrels in .22 LR or .17 HMR rifle and 410 bore shotgun. A rifle/shotgun combination of this type enables a young shooter to engage in various types of activities. The enormously popular Ruger 10/22 is available as the Compact model that has a shorter stock (without barrel band) and barrel. It is furnished with sights, but the Ruger Compact 10/22 (MSRP $339) can accept the enormous array of aftermarket parts that are available for the standard 10/22. In that way, the Ruger Compact can change configurations as the skill, maturity, and

For smaller shooters, the Ruger 10/22 Compact is scaled appropriately.

interests of the shooter change.

If a bolt action repeater in a youth version is desired, Ruger produces the American in versions that have shorter barrels and stocks. The Ruger American features a removable comb/butt component that can be removed and a different component having different dimensions can be attached. Moreover, the Ruger American utilizes the reliable rotary magazine that is used in the 10/22. Ruger American rifles (MSRP $359) are available in .22 LR, .22 WMR, and .17 HMR calibers.

In addition to the models described above, there are others available from other manufacturers. For many years, there were few choices available for a true

One of the oldest and simplest designs in rimfire rifles is the Stevens Favorite. (photo courtesy of Savage Arms)

youth rifle, but as in other areas of rimfire sports, this is an exciting time and youthful shooters have not been neglected.

Selecting a Rimfire Varmint Rifle

Having dispensed with some suggestions for the selection of a rifle in .22 LR caliber, let us now suppose that you have identified varmint hunting as a developing passion and that you need to select a rimfire rifle to be used primarily for that work. Chapter 10 includes a more complete discussion of hunting guns and ammunition. Keep in mind that the varmint rifle must first and foremost be accurate. At this point, you should consider carefully the types of varmints that you will hunt most. If the emphasis is to be on ground squirrels, crows, and small varmints up to the size of prairie dogs, the author would select a rifle chambered for the .17 HMR. It shoots with a flatter trajectory than the .22 WMR, and because the ammunition is loaded with premium bullets, the average .17 HMR will probably deliver slightly better accuracy than the average .22 WMR. Because the bore in a .17 HMR barrel is so small, barrels have thicker walls than those on .22 WMR rifles, which is likely one of the factors contributing to excellent accuracy. Experience has shown that there is not a great deal of difference in accuracy between .22 WMR and .17 HMR rifles as long as ammunition of equivalent quality is used in identical rifles. There is a belief, probably with some validity, that manufacturing tolerances may be smaller for .17 HMR rifles and ammunition than with the .22 WMR.

The .17 Mach 2 is a fast shooting little rimfire and even though numerous manufacturers started producing rifles in that caliber after it was introduced, it faded rapidly. One seldom sees a rifle in that caliber and very few new .17 Mach 2 rifles are produced. It is a cartridge for which, quite frankly, there was little if any need. A good .22 LR will accomplish all that can be done with a .17 Mach 2 except at slightly longer range and do it more cheaply. At this time (early 2016) only one maker is producing .17 Mach 2 ammunition. Avoid this one unless you really must have one for experimentation.

On the other hand, if the varmints are likely to include species as large as foxes or coyotes, the .22 WMR will be a better choice than the .17 HMR. The larger, heavier bullets hit with more authority, which is needed to anchor such species. Keep in mind that because the overall sizes of the .17 HMR and .22 WMR cartridge cases are similar, the same rifle action can sometimes be used as a platform for either. Only the barrel needs to be different (except for autoloaders) and even the same magazine can be used with either cartridge. Therefore, in a specific model, the rifles are identical except for caliber. In terms of ammunition cost, the .17 HMR and .22 WMR are approximately equal.

Suggestions for specific arms in .17 HMR, and .22 WMR run parallel to those given for .22 LR rifles. If your budget can accommodate a price tag of over $1,000 (perhaps well over $1,000), the Anschütz, Cooper, Kimber, Sako, and similar sporting rifles are elegant, and they give outstanding performance. Two of the outstanding new rifles in .17 Mach 2 were produced by Anschütz, the Models 1502 and 1702, that were built on the famous 64 and 54 actions, respectively. All are elegant rifles that give a high level of performance.

In the $500-1,000 price range, the experience of this author leads to the conclusion that two of the outstanding choices are the CZ 452/455 and Ruger 77/22M or 77/17. Both rifles are capable of excellent accuracy with perhaps a very small edge to the CZ. Semiautomatic rifles in the magnum rimfire calibers that are intended primarily for varmint hunting do not excite the author. True, they often give good performance, but most are unlikely to equal the accuracy of a good bolt action and accuracy, not rate of fire, is what varmint hunting is about. Notable exceptions are the autoloaders produced by Volquartsen, which are known for their superb accuracy, but these are more expensive. If you enjoy hunting with a lever action rifle, by all means consider the Henry in .22 WMR or .17 HMR caliber. The Henry is sufficiently accurate for taking varmints as far as the calibers permit. Another, more modern lever action is the Ruger Model 96 that was produced in .22 WMR and .17 HMR calibers, but is now, sadly, discontinued.

A number of options exist for the rimfire buyer who does not want to spend over $300-350 for a pest rifle chambered for the .22 WMR or .17 HMR. Outstanding among these are the bolt action rifles from Marlin, Savage, and Ruger American, and they typically give excellent accuracy. These are available with standard or heavy weight barrels that are blued or stainless steel. Stock options include hardwood, laminates, and composites. Price is determined by the variant selected, but the lowest price combinations start at approximately $250-275. At an even lower price are some of the break action single shot rifles available from Rossi. With a good scope in place, these are sturdy, dependable rifles that can perform well as pest rifles.

The choice of rifles in .17 WSM is quite limited. Savage makes the B.Mag in two versions, one having a slender sporter barrel and the other a heavy stainless barrel. Ruger offers the Model 77 and Winchester markets the Model 1885 Low Wall single shot.

Ancillaries

After selecting a rifle, the majority of rimfire shooters will probably add other peripheral equipment to their outfits. Aftermarket barrels, stocks, triggers, and sights constitute a rather large industry, which will be covered in Chapters 5 and 13. Although many rimfire shooters will not change the barrels or stocks on their rifles, many new rifles will require the addition of sights because an increasing number of fine rimfire rifles are being sold without sights. In most cases, that will mean that a scope must be mounted on the rifle. That is especially true of the models in .22 WMR and .17 HMR calibers that are intended for use at ranges up to 150 yards, and this includes some of the moderately priced Marlin and Savage rifles. It is unreasonable for most people to expect to hit a ground squirrel or crow at 150 yards with open sights. Therefore, the majority of rimfire shooters will make choices of scopes to mount on their rifles. Scope sights and mounts are discussed more fully in Chapter 5, but some general comments will be made here.

Several types of scopes are available that are intended specifically for use on rimfire rifles. Such scopes are adjusted optically to eliminate parallax at a range of 50 yards because this is a typical range for using .22 LR rifles. Most scopes intended for use on centerfire rifles are adjusted to be free of parallax at a range of 100 yards, and thus they will work equally well on rifles chambered for .22 WMR or .17 HMR. In fact, any scope that is suitable for use on centerfire rifles will prove to be satisfactory on these magnum rimfires because they are often used at ranges comparable to those at which centerfire rifles are used. Some scopes are equipped with a focusing or "adjustable" objective (denoted as AO) so that they can be focused accurately on targets at varying distances. This is probably the best of all choices because focusing on a target corrects for parallax at the distance at which the scope is focused. Therefore, such a scope works equally well on all types of rimfire rifles.

As in the case of rifles, scopes are available in an enormous range of prices. Some of the elegant models that carry the most prestigious names sell for up to $1,000 or more. The average rimfire shooter should not be daunted by such figures because it is possible to get a very capable and satisfactory scope for a reasonable price. To some extent, the scope should match the

rifle. It is not likely that a $50 scope will be found on a Cooper Model 57M sporting rifle that sells for over $2,000, and it is not likely that a $1,000 Swarovski scope will be found on a Savage 93 G bolt action, Henry lever action, or Ruger 10/22 semiautomatic, all of which sell for under $300. There is nothing wrong with a $1,000 scope on a $300 rifle, but it probably will not be set up that way in most cases.

Because scopes that are intended to be used on centerfire rifles are satisfactory for use on .17 HMR and .22 WMR rifles, the range of available models is enormous. They are produced with fixed powers of magnification that include 2.5X, 4X, and 6X on up to target models of 24X, 32X, or higher magnification. Because of the advances in optics, zoom lenses for cameras have become much more common than are those of fixed focal length. This trend is also observed in scope sights. If you look at a catalog from a scope manufacturer, you will see that there are many more models available with variable magnification than there are of fixed power. Scopes with variable power are available in several ranges of magnification, but 2-7X, 3-9X, 3-12X, and 4-16X are the most common, although other ranges are available. Eye relief of scopes intended for use on centerfire rifles is around 3-4 inches, but rimfire rifles produce almost no recoil so that is never a problem.

Scopes made specifically for use on rimfire rifles (especially those in .22 LR caliber) are sometimes more compact and lighter in weight than are those intended for use on centerfire rifles. This is reasonable because most rimfire rifles are slimmer and lighter in weight than most centerfire models. So-called rimfire scopes are produced by many manufacturers in a wide range of prices, and to some extent the old caveat "you get what you pay for" applies to scopes. Large suppliers of outdoor equipment such as Cabela's and Scheel's market scopes with their own brand labels. Three of the scopes in the Cabela's Rimfire line are a very nice 3-9X rimfire model that has a catalog price of $79.99, a 2-7X for $69.99, and a 4X model that sells for $49.99. These are good quality scopes that are representative of lower priced models that provide good value and reliable service. When mated to a rimfire rifle of modest cost, the combination gives the shooter a rifle capable of fine performance. The author has used two of the Cabela's scopes with complete satisfaction.

Tasco markets a line of scopes that includes 4X and 3-9X rimfire models that sell for under $50. BSA offers a 4X rimfire scope for under $40 including mount and it is the model the author's brother has mounted on

Two superb rimfire scopes are the 3-9X AO Simmons 1022 T (top) and the 4X Cabela's Rimfire (bottom).

The excellent Weaver 2.5-7X rimfire scope works very well on a compact rifle like the Ruger 10/22 that is shown here with a Hogue Overmolded stock.

his Remington 597 autoloader. Simmons offers a line of scopes called the .22 Mag® models. Included are 4X, 3-9X, and 3-9X AO versions. They are priced in the $40-70 range depending on model. Bushnell markets several popularly priced scopes for rimfire rifles. The scopes mentioned are typical of the budget class of optics, but all are capable of enabling the shooter to get good performance from a rimfire rifle. Although one may prefer a better scope, the author has used a number of low priced scopes on his rimfires with complete satisfaction. If nothing better can be afforded, you would mount one on your rifle, sight in carefully with ammunition that you know to shoot accurately in your rifle, and enjoy rimfire shooting.

Moving upward in price gives the rimfire shooter many more options. Weaver offers rimfire scopes in 4X, 2.5-7X, and 3-9X AO models with the first two selling for around $150 and the last for around $250 because of its AO feature. The author has had experience with some of these scopes and they are superb. Another scope that the author has found to be well suited for use on a rimfire rifle is the Nikon Pro Staff 4X model. It is corrected for parallax at 50 yards and is generally available for a retail price of about $100. Nikon recently introduced a 3-9X rimfire scope that sells for approximately $130, and it should be a superb optic for any rimfire. Although many other scopes could be discussed, these are representative models in the mid-price range. Higher priced optics of outstanding quality are available from manufacturers such as Burris, Leupold, Sightron, Swarovski, and Zeiss. These outstanding products will meet or exceed any reasonable expectation for a scope.

Having discussed rifles and scopes does not mean that these are the only items that you will find useful in rimfire shooting. Except possibly for shooting from a bench, a sling should be considered as a necessary piece of equipment. Most rimfire rifles are sold with either swivels or studs for attaching them. Notable ex-

ceptions are the lever action rifles and a few autoloaders including the Ruger 10/22. However, it is possible to install swivels on these rifles. Front swivels that clamp around tubular magazines simplify that part of the problem for lever actions and some autoloaders. A sling not only makes carrying the rifle easier, but also it is an aid to steady aiming under field conditions. The classic military sling is a two-part affair, but an adjustable nylon strap will suffice for most uses. A rifle with a composite stock will not look out of place with a nylon strap. On a fine sporting rifle with a checkered walnut stock, an elegant leather sling would be more appropriate.

One item that is closely related to the rimfire rifle is a case to carry it in. This is often given very little attention and almost any case that will hold the rifle is placed in service, but a fine case that fits properly is a good investment. Many cases simply are not proportioned well for enclosing a rimfire rifle, which is often shorter than a rifle in a centerfire caliber. Good cases are not expensive with many of the models with nylon shells selling for around $20 or so. If you are so inclined, a heavy canvas duck case with leather trim can be obtained for around $50-100 or so. Finally, if you expect travel by air with your rimfire rifle you will need a case that meets FAA requirements. Probably more shooters take centerfire rifles on long hunting trips by means of air travel, but it is not uncommon for the rimfire enthusiast to take his or her special rifle to competitive events or on that special prairie dog shoot. The lockable hard case that meets FAA requirements may be a necessity for such shooters.

The rifle, scope, and sling constitute the basic shooting unit. Other aftermarket options will be discussed in more detail in Chapter 13 and ammunition will be discussed in Chapters 6 and 7. It is an exciting time for rimfire enthusiasts, and there has never been a time when the rimfire rifle shooter had such a wide selection of rifles and related items.

CHAPTER 4

THE RIMFIRE HANDGUNS

IN CHAPTER 3, an overview was presented of many of the rimfire rifles that are currently available. In the case of rimfire handguns, the primary uses for many shooters involve recreational shooting in the form of plinking but handguns are often used for hunting and dispatching pests. Rimfire handguns are not normally the first choice for defensive purposes although they may certainly be used in that manner. There is also a great deal of interest in formal target shooting (both paper and silhouette targets) for which specialized, high end equipment is required (see Chapter 13). These uses for rimfire handguns will be considered separately.

Basically, rimfire handguns fall into the broad classifications as "sport" and "target" models. Sport models generally have shorter barrels and may not have adjustable sights or at least may have sights that are not as sophisticated as those on target models. Rimfire handguns intended for high level competition usually have rather long barrels and the best possible sights

Popular rimfire handguns are produced in (left to right) single and double action revolvers and semiautomatic pistols. The guns shown are (left to right) the Colt Frontier Scout, the Smith & Wesson K-22, and the Smith & Wesson 422.

that are fully adjustable. Some of the most sophisticated target handguns are single shots that are designed for ultimate accuracy rather than rate of fire. Although revolvers were popular target handguns in the past, the majority of target pistols today are semiautomatics. In this chapter, a discussion of rimfire handguns is presented and some specific models are discussed, but it is not meant to be a catalog of all currently available models. For that type of coverage, consult the current edition of the *Gun Digest 2016* (see Appendix A).

Before progressing to the subject of rimfire handguns, it is appropriate to make clear certain factors related to terminology. The inclusive term "handgun" applies to any firearm that can be fired with one hand. Long ago, the term "pistol" was used to describe such a piece, and the pistols of that period had a single chamber and a single barrel that was loaded from the muzzle. As firearm technology developed, it was soon observed that one shot was quite limiting in some situations so double barreled pistols were made. At that time, they were still loaded from the muzzle. Further developments led to "pistols with revolving chambers," which we would now call a "revolver," but they are still appropriately called pistols. Still later, pistols were developed that had one barrel and one chamber that could have several cartridges held in a magazine. Although in some circles these autoloaders and the single shot types are referred to as "pistols" and those with revolving chambers are called "revolvers," the historical use of the term "pistol" was in the same sense that the term "handgun" is now used. It was a global term used to describe a piece with any type of action. It may be supposed that the old song, "Pistol Packin' Mama" did not necessarily distinguish whether she had a semiautomatic or revolver! If I remember correctly, she had a .44 caliber, which indicates that it was of the "pistol with a revolving chamber" type.

Practical Considerations

Rimfire handguns are available that range from tiny derringers and revolvers to target pistols that are a foot long and weigh three pounds. One would neither choose the former for target shooting nor the latter for concealed carry. The choice of a rimfire handgun must be made with the primary end use in mind although there will certainly be some overlap possible. The selection may represent a compromise. For example, a rimfire handgun with a barrel of medium length and good sights could easily be suitable for informal target shooting as well as hunting. A rimfire handgun with a 3-inch barrel might serve for self defense and pop can plinking. If a handgun with a 6-inch barrel and target sights is selected, it would serve well for small game hunting and formal target shooting. No one handgun is going to be the best choice for covering the entire spectrum of rimfire handgun shooting sports.

The principles involved in choosing a rimfire handgun are no different than those involved in choosing anything else. Personal preference weighs heavily in the decision as does intended use. A handgun for concealed carry should not have a long barrel and high, adjustable sights with sharp corners. A handgun for hunting squirrels or formal target shooting should not have a 3-inch barrel and fixed sights. The type of handgun should be matched to the functions it will perform. Fortunately, there is considerable overlap and one handgun can be used in a variety of ways even if some compromise is involved. For general sport use, the handgun chosen should have a barrel that is 4-6 inches long. Barrels shorter than four inches give short sight radius, which makes accurate shooting more difficult whereas a barrel longer than about six inches makes the piece too long for convenient carrying.

In recent years, the use of scopes or other optical sights on handguns has become more common. The reason is quite simple--there is only one distance at which the shooter's eye can be focused. The target and the front and rear sights are at different distances from the eye so all cannot be in sharp focus simultaneously. In a scope, the crosshair or other type of reticule appears to be at the same distance as the target. It is simple to align the reticule on the target and squeeze off the shot. Just as in the case of rifles, the level of accuracy achieved with a handgun is much greater when a scope is used (see Chapter 17). Although scopes are not part of the equipment allowed for formal target shooting, the hunter of pests and small game is under no such restrictions. A scope-sighted handgun can give outstanding accuracy that may equal that of some

rifles. A brother of the author regularly hunts squirrels with a scoped Ruger Mark II 22/45. If you plan to engage in the growing sport of handgun hunting, you may wish to give some consideration to the ease of mounting a scope on the handgun you select. In this regard, the Smith & Wesson 22A and 22S Models are excellent because they are sold with a permanently attached scope rail in place. Only the scope and rings are needed to attach a scope.

Revolver or Semiautomatic

When one is choosing a rimfire handgun for plinking and pest control, the choice must first be made between revolver and semiautomatic. Revolvers come with one of two types of actions. A single action revolver must be cocked manually for each shot, whereas a double action revolver can be fired simply by pulling the trigger. This action causes the cylinder to turn to place a fresh round under the firing pin while moving the hammer to the rear. When the trigger is pulled sufficiently far to the rear, the sear is released and the hammer falls causing the gun to fire. This action can be repeated to fire successive shots until the cylinder is empty. Any cartridge that fits correctly in the cylinder can be used. Therefore, Short, Long, Long Rifle and shot cartridges can be loaded in any cylinder that is designed to handle the .22 LR.

Single action revolvers must be loaded one chamber at a time. On most current models, there is a loading gate at the rear of the cylinder on the right hand side that swings to the side to expose a chamber. A cartridge can be inserted in a chamber, the cylinder rotated to expose the next empty chamber and

A single action revolver must be loaded one cartridge time while rotating the cylinder to expose each chamber.

another cartridge inserted. The process is repeated until all chambers have been loaded. After the cartridges have been fired, the empty cases are removed by opening the loading gate and moving an ejector rod to the rear. This forces the empty case out of the back of the chamber. Rotating the cylinder to the next chamber and moving the ejector rod backward knocks out another empty case, etc. Loading and removing empty cases are slow processes with a single action handgun.

Virtually all double action revolvers of today have a cylinder that swings out of the frame on the left hand side. A latch, located on the left hand side of the frame behind the cylinder on most models, must be moved, which unlocks the cylinder so it can be swung out of the frame. An ejector rod that is located at the front of the cylinder can be pushed backward, which forces all of the empty cases out at the same time. As a result, loading and unloading are accomplished much faster than with a single action revolver. However, for a great deal of sport shooting, rate of fire as determined by the speed of loading and unloading is of no importance.

By swinging the cylinder out the frame, all chambers in a double action revolver can loaded at one time.

Semiautomatic handguns hold cartridges in a magazine that is contained within the grip. In firing, the force generated by firing a round moves the slide to the rear against a strong recoil spring, and it also cocks the hammer (which may or may not be externally visible). The spring forces the slide forward, which allows it to engage the top cartridge in the magazine forcing it into the chamber. Therefore, the semiautomatic is actually a self-loading handgun. Incidentally, it is sometimes found that a particular semiautomatic handgun will cycle more reliably with some types of ammunition than with others. You may have no way to test this before you buy the piece, but if you find that your pistol "jams" with some particular brand or type of ammunition, by all means try a few others before you assume that the pistol is defective. The experience of this author with several pistols that have been fired with a wide range of ammunition is that most rimfire pistols are remarkably forgiving with respect to type of ammunition used. Of course, .22 LR semiautomatic pistols will not function reliably with .22 Short, Long, or shot cartridges.

Semiautomatic pistols hold the removable magazine in the grip.

In order to ready a semiautomatic for firing, the magazine must be loaded with cartridges. There is often a great deal of difference in the ease of inserting cartridges into the magazines of different semiautomatic pistols. A long spring inside the magazine places pressure on the magazine follower, and the spring tension increases as the spring is compressed by each successive cartridge. The magazines of some pistols have a small button on the side which allows pressure to be applied to compress the magazine spring that way rather than by applying force from the top by pressing on the cartridges. Some magazines have buttons on both sides of the magazines so that the follower can be pulled downward and held there as cartridges are inserted. Check the magazine of any semiautomatic pistol that you consider buying to see how easily it can be loaded.

Moving a cartridge from the magazine to the chamber requires the slide to be drawn back and released.

After a loaded magazine is inserted in the grip of the pistol, a cartridge must be moved from the magazine into the chamber. This is accomplished by pulling the slide fully to the rear and letting it go. The strong recoil spring forces the slide forward and as it moves, it takes with it the top cartridge from the magazine. Here a word of caution is needed. Some pistols allow the slide to be drawn to the rear only when the safety is in the "off" position. When the slide on such a pistol moves forward during the initial loading, the pistol is ready to fire! Other models allow all operations to be conducted with the safety in the "on" position, which is highly desirable. Generally, it is the older models that must have the safety off to operate the slide. It is an advantage to be able to open the slide with the safety on.

A great many semiautomatic handguns intended

for plinking have sights that are not fully adjustable. It may be possible to move the rear sight laterally in its retaining notch, but there may be no provision for elevation adjustment. This may not be as bad as it sounds at first. Rimfire handguns for plinking are intended for use at short range. The targets may be no more than 10-15 yards away , and at such distances small sighting errors are likely to be unnoticed. Moreover, the difference in point of impact caused by using different types of ammunition will be small enough that the average shooter will probably not notice the difference. Handguns having fixed sights are entirely practical for a lot of reasons. First, if the handgun is going to be carried in a holster, there is no possibility of changing sight settings by inserting or removing the gun from the holster. Second, fixed sights are sturdy enough that some bumps and scrapes can be endured without affecting the sight adjustment. That may not be the case with target pistols having precise, adjustable sights that are less robust. Third, at the average distance at which the handgun is used there may be no need to adjust the sights. Fourth, if you do not need adjustable sights on your pistol for its intended uses, there is no need to pay for them. High quality adjustable sights often add $50-100 to the cost.

Rimfire handguns for general use often have rear sights that are not adjustable.

Firing at a 4-inch black circle at 50 yards is an entirely different matter as is trying to take squirrels at ranges of 25-30 yards. In these cases, the hand gunner is looking for all the accuracy possible and that means adjustable sights that are set for the type of ammunition being used at the appropriate range. The same fine handgun with adjustable sights makes an appropriate piece of equipment for target shooting as well as an effective tool for hunting small game and pests.

In summary, if you plan to shoot pine cones and pop cans at short range, almost any rimfire handgun will serve well. A low-end model with a short barrel and fixed sights will work just fine. If you want a

handgun that you can use to hunt small game and pests or if you want to participate in more serious target shooting, a model having a longer barrel and adjustable sights is in order. Whether the handgun is a revolver or autoloader will be dependent on your personal preference. There is a wider choice available in the case of semiautomatics and they are more popular than revolvers today. It is the opinion of many, including this author, that the revolver is generally safer for inexperienced users. With an autoloader, the pistol is ready to fire just as quickly as the action cycles and puts a fresh round in the chamber. With a revolver, immediately after a shot the hammer is down and the chamber in line with it holds an empty case. A double action revolver can be fired again by pulling the trigger, but the long, heavy double action pull is required, which is not likely to be accomplished by slight pressure applied by an inattentive shooter. This is not so with the autoloader which requires only light finger pressure to fire again.

A few single shot handguns are available. One often sees an article dealing with "handgun" hunting in which a single shot pistol having a barrel as long as 14-16 inches is used on a piece that is chambered for a cartridge that is normally used in centerfire rifles. These "handguns" may even have a bolt action or break action that is identical to that used on some models of rifles. The stock has been cut off and reshaped to give a pistol grip, but in reality these "pistols" are short rifles. They almost always have scope sights attached. Instead of "handgun" hunting, the sport is more appropriately called "hunting with a short rifle with the stock cut off" hunting. In order to effectively use a cartridge that is normally used in rifles, the barrels are of necessity longer than those used on handguns. In the area of rimfire handguns, there are a few single shot models and in calibers such as .22 WMR and .17 HMR they are effective for hunting and pest control. As a handgun for the general uses for which rimfire handguns are appropriate, the single shot is really a minor player in a big game.

Calibers

Along with the type of action, the choice of caliber needs to be made. In rimfire rifles, identical models are available in .22 LR, .22 WMR, and .17 HMR calibers and some are also available in .17 Mach 2. This is by no means the case with handguns, and comparable models are not always available. One outstanding exception is the Ruger Single Six convertible that comes with one cylinder that chambers the .22 LR and another that chambers the .22 WMR. It is possible to offer a combination such as this even though the bullet diameter for the .22 LR is 0.223 inch, whereas that for the .22 WMR is 0.224 inch, and the small difference causes no problems. This is a single action revolver that gives the shooter the choice between two power levels (and price levels in ammunition). Another manufacturer that offers a single action revolver with two cylinders is Heritage.

Rimfire handguns have been produced in the (left to right) calibers .17 Mach 2, .22 LR, .17 HMR, and .22 WMR.

One factor to consider when discussing handgun calibers is the difference in velocity that results from the short handgun barrel compared to that of a rifle. The .22 LR develops maximum velocity while traveling approximately 16 inches in a rifle barrel. If the barrel is longer than about 18 inches, the velocity is actually slightly lower because of the bullet being slowed by friction. In a 6-inch handgun barrel, the velocity produced by a given load is somewhat lower than it is when the same load is fired in a rifle. In most cases, there is approximately 125-150 ft/sec difference between the velocity produced by a 6-inch barreled handgun and the velocity given by the same load in a rifle. Moreover, because there is a gap between the cylinder and barrel in a revolver (usually 0.002-0.008 inch), some gas escapes through this gap and is not used to push on the bullet. As a result, a revolver having a given barrel length generally gives slightly lower velocity than that produced by a semiautomatic having the same barrel length and firing the same type of ammunition. Incidentally, barrel length of a revolver does not include the cylinder in the measurement. The barrel length for a semiautomatic is the distance from the breech to the muzzle.

The fraction by which the velocity from a handgun is lower than that given by a rifle depends on several factors. First, even with the same barrel length (which does not include the length of the cylinder), a revolver will generally give a velocity that is approximately 50 ft/sec lower than that of a semiautomatic. As will be discussed in Chapter 8, most types of ammunition give about the same velocity from a 6-inch barreled revolver as from a semiautomatic having a 4.5-inch barrel. Of course, the length of the gap between the cylinder and barrel has a significant effect. A gap of 0.003 inch results in less velocity loss than does a gap of 0.007 inch.

Revolvers such as this fine Colt Frontier Scout have a gap between the barrel and cylinder that allows gas to escape. Some loss in velocity is inevitable.

A semiautomatic with a 5.5-inch barrel will give approximately 50 ft/sec higher than one with a 4.5-inch barrel (see the table of velocities presented in Chapter 8). It should be remembered that there are other factors that influence bullet velocity from semiautomatic handguns. Dimensions of the chamber and bore as well as bore smoothness have some effect on velocity. Therefore, it is possible for a particular handgun with a 4-inch barrel to give velocities that are as high or higher than those from another specimen with a 4.5 or 5-inch barrel.

As a result of their using larger charges of slower burning powders, some of the hyper velocity loads in .22 LR suffer a greater loss than do ordinary cartridges when fired in handguns. This effect is even greater in .22 WMR and .17 HMR calibers, which need longer barrels to allow the powder charges to burn efficiently. In a handgun with a 6-inch barrel, the 40-grain .22 WMR bullet that is driven to about 1,900 ft/sec in a rifle achieves only approximately 1,450-1,500 ft/sec, which generates an energy of almost 200 ft lbs. Although an energy this high does not make a .22 WMR handgun a better choice than most centerfire calibers for defensive uses, it is more effective than a .22 LR, .25 Auto, and some other low-powered calibers. Although they can not fire ammunition of any other caliber or accept another cylinder, there are several double action revolvers available in .17 HMR caliber. With cylinder swapping options that exist for some single action revolvers, a handgun in .17 HMR could use a cylinder chambered for the shorter .17 Mach 2 if one exists as an option. The 2005 Ruger catalog listed the .17 HMR/.17 Mach 2 combination for the Single Six Hunter, but the 2016 catalog lists only the .17 HMR.

Handguns intended for hunting have long barrels that produce high velocity. The Ruger Single Six Hunter shown here has a rib for attaching a scope and has interchangeable cylinders for firing .22 LR and .22 WMR cartridges. (photo courtesy of Ruger)

The Ruger Single Six Hunter has a 7.5-inch barrel. In .17 HMR caliber, the 17-grain bullets are given a muzzle velocity of approximately 2,000 ft/sec from a revolver barrel of this length. This represents a velocity that is about 600 ft/sec lower than the same load gives in a rifle. The 20-grain bullets that are driven at 2,375 ft/sec from a rifle achieve only 1,725-1,750 ft/sec from the handgun barrel. Much of the effectiveness of the .17 HMR that results from high velocity is lost when it is fired from handguns. In fact, the velocity of the .17 HMR bullets from handguns almost exactly duplicates that from the .17 Mach 2 when fired from a rifle. Although not equal to the performance of a .17 HMR rifle, the handguns offer flat trajectory when compared to any other handgun in a rimfire caliber. They are suitable for taking small game and varmints.

If you are selecting a handgun specifically for hunting small game and pests, you may wish to consider a piece chambered for one of the magnum calibers. However, because the primary use of a rimfire handgun is for pleasure and target use, the caliber that makes the most sense is the .22 LR. With a good handgun chambered for the .22 LR, you can do a lot of shooting because the cost of ammunition is so low. In some cases, the rimfire handgun is an understudy for a centerfire piece and the choice of handguns in .22 LR is very broad indeed. Because of this, it is possible in many cases to select a rimfire handgun that operates in much the same way as a centerfire model, which makes training with the rimfire have some carryover value.

Keep in mind that with a product as popular as rimfire handguns, there are very many models available from a large number of manufacturers. It is not possible in a single volume to describe all of the models available and only a brief survey of the

products will be presented in this chapter (with details of performance of some to be shown in Chapter 17). Selection of a handgun is an expression of personal preferences and there will not be an attempt to rate the guns based on the author's views.

Revolvers

The most famous single action revolver of all time is the legendary Colt Single Action Army, also known as the Peacemaker, which was introduced in 1873 and which was for a time a military sidearm. In 1957-1977, Colt produced a scaled-down model known as the Frontier Scout that was chambered for the .22 LR, but it was also marketed later with a cylinder that chambered the .22 WMR. Although these models have been discontinued, they are sometimes found as used guns. Single action revolvers of the Colt style (and Ruger single actions made prior to 1973) suffer from the condition that a blow on the hammer can cause the revolver to fire. The firing pin makes direct contact with the cartridge in alignment with it. Even though the hammer can be moved back to engage a safety notch, this was not totally effective in keeping the firearm from being discharged. Accordingly, users of this "old style" revolver normally carried them with only five cartridges in the cylinder and an empty chamber below the hammer.

Several years ago, the single action Colt Frontier Scout revolvers were quite popular. Shown here are two fine examples of this model.

By far the most commonly encountered single action rimfire revolvers at the present time are the Ruger Single Six models in various forms and the small scale revolver known as the Ruger Bearcat. All current Ruger single action revolvers are designed to be carried with all chambers loaded because the firing pin cannot be struck by the hammer until the trigger is pulled causing a transfer bar to be moved into position to transit the blow from the hammer to the firing pin.

The Ruger Bearcat is a small single action revolver that makes a good trail gun. The small grip allows shooters with small hands to fire it comfortably. (photo courtesy of Ruger)

Ruger has offered the Single Six in .17 HMR caliber for several years. For some time it was offered as the Single Six Hunter version, which has a 7.5-inch heavy barrel. The top rib of the barrel has the curved grooves milled into it so Ruger scope rings can be attached, and it is also grooved for attaching tip-off style mounts. This handgun weighs about 45 ounces, and it is clearly intended for hunting small game and pests. The 2016 Ruger catalog shows the Hunter version offered only with .22 LR and .22 WMR cylinders.

The Ruger Single Six Convertible is both rock solid and versatile.

By virtue of having two cylinders, a Ruger Single Six Convertible can fire all of these types of ammunition.

Many years ago, two of the most popular target revolvers were the double action Colt Officer's Model Match and the Smith & Wesson Masterpiece, both of which were available in .22 LR. These fine revolvers were capable of outstanding performance even in

formal competition. In addition to these models with 6-inch barrels, both Colt and Smith & Wesson produced target grade revolvers with 4-inch barrels that were intended to serve as companion pieces to the centerfire firearms carried on duty by many police officers. The Colt Diamondback was available in both .38 Special and .22 LR as was the Smith & Wesson Combat Masterpiece. These models are no longer produced. However, Smith & Wesson offers two widely differing models of double action revolvers in .22 LR. The first is the Model 617 that is a full size revolver weighing 41 ounces and having a list price of $829. This stainless steel model with a full-length barrel lug can be considered as a modern replacement for the legendary K-22 Masterpiece target revolver. The Model 317 Airweight is a small frame 8-shot revolver that is available with a three-inch or one and seven-eighths inch barrel. Weights are only 11.9 or 10.5 ounces respectively, but these small revolvers have MSRP values of $759. The Model 351PD is chambered for .22 WMR and has the MSRP of $759. The Models 43C and 351C have shrouded hammers for double action only firing as defense guns. The classic Model 48 in .22 WMR caliber is available with either a 4- or 6-inch barrel with the MSRP of $949 and $989, respectively.

Available in .22 LR, the Smith & Wesson Model 617 makes a good choice for any type of shooting. The same gun is available in .17 HMR and .22 WMR. (photo courtesy of Smith & Wesson)

Another fine double action .22 revolver is the Ruger SP 101, which is available as a 6-shot stainless steel model having adjustable sights. With a suggested price of $769, it represents the middle ground in the price range. This is a very sturdy revolver that weighs 34 ounces and has adjustable sights. It is an excellent choice for the backpacker, woods roamer, and small game hunter. Ruger has also introduced the massive GP100 in .22 LR caliber (MSRP $829).

Taurus offers an extensive line of revolvers chambered in .22 LR, .17 HMR, and .22 WMR calibers. These include the Hunter (12-inch barrel, 56.8 ounces) and Tracker (6.5-inch barrel, 45.6 ounces), which are available in all three calibers. These models have list prices of approximately $480. In addition to these

The Taurus double action revolvers are available in blue or stainless steel. They are outstanding firearms at reasonable prices. (photo courtesy of Taurus)

The Smith & Wesson Model 41 is the premier autoloader for high level target shooting. (photo courtesy of Smith & Wesson)

models built on large frames, there is also a series of rimfire revolvers that are built on medium frames that are available in wide range of finishes, barrel lengths, etc. These models have list prices in the $550 range and weights run from 25-30 ounces.

Autoloaders

Autoloading pistols have become enormously popular in recent years. The standard handguns for military and law enforcement use are almost always autoloaders. Moreover, in addition to the century old Colt 1911 style single action pistol (which must be cocked to fire the first shot), many of the most popular models are designed to be fired double action (by simply pulling the trigger for the first shot) and then they can be fired single action thereafter. Both of the types have external hammers and most have a manual safety. In recent years, a type of pistol known as the striker fired style has become very popular. Such pistols are fired by simply pulling the trigger, which causes an internal "striker" to be moved to the rear against spring pressure, and firing occurs when a certain point is reached in the trigger movement. In essence, such pistols are like a "double action only" revolver, which has no visible hammer. Striker fired pistols have become the norm in law enforcement work and they are chosen by many for personal defense. Although numerous brands are available, it was Glock who led the way in development of striker fired pistols.

When it comes to autoloaders, the rimfire shooter has an enormous range of models from which to choose. Even if some of the classic models such as the Colt Woodsman are no longer being produced, the spectrum of products available encompasses the Smith & Wesson Model 41, a high-level competition model, on one end and the diminutive Beretta Bobcat on the other. There are many models in between. The Smith

& Wesson Model 41 is available in 5.5- and 7-inch barrel lengths with weights of 41 and 42 ounces and has a list price of $1,369. The Beretta Bobcat has a 2.4-inch barrel, weighs 11.8 ounces, and has a list price of $410. There is truly a rimfire autoloader for almost any taste.

Autoloaders from a particular manufacturer can often be considered as a family of related products that share many common features. For example, popular sport pistols include the Browning Buck Mark that is available in numerous configurations from the long, heavy-barreled Silhouette competition model to a 4-inch barreled sport model that is intended as a camp, trail, or plinking model. The Buck Mark 5.5-inch barreled standard model comes with excellent sights that are fully adjustable and a trigger action that is about as good as that on almost any other mass-produced pistol. Having experience with two of these fine pistols, this author can attest to the fact that groups smaller than one-inch at 50 feet on an indoor range are the norm with factory sights when using appropriate ammunition. There is also a target version that has

The Browning Buck Mark is an outstanding handgun for sport shooting or hunting. Its performance is unsurpassed by any autoloader in its price range.

For target or silhouette shooting, the Brown Buck Mark 5.5 Target is a superb choice. It is equipped with target sights and a scope rail. (photo courtesy of Browning Arms)

a 7.25-inch fluted barrel. List prices range from $389 for the camper model to $589 for a target model. The Silhouette version comes without sights but has an accessory rail for mounting optional sights.

Labeled by Ruger as "The number one .22 pistol in the world," the Ruger Mark II (and the more recently introduced Mark III) may well be just that. The Ruger Mark II was introduced in 1982, but its forerunner was introduced in 1949, and the Ruger autoloader has been in production ever since. More than a dozen variants of this enormously popular pistol were available as the newer Mark III went into production. The Standard model comes in blue (the stainless version is a Sports South dealer exclusive) with fixed sights and has a list price of $429. Available barrel lengths include 4.75 and 6 inches. Several "target" models are available including those known as Target, Hunter, and Competition models all of which have adjustable, target-style sights. List prices range from $499 to $729 depending on the specific version. These versions with adjustable sights are furnished drilled and tapped so that a Weaver-type scope base can be attached. One target model that is available in both blue and stainless steel is produced with a 10-inch bull barrel, and it weighs approximately 51 ounces. The Ruger Mark series autoloaders have established an enviable reputation for reliability and durability in the more than half a century that they have been in production. The one-millionth pistol was produced in 1979 and total production is approximately four million.

Ruger's Mark III Standard model is one of the most durable and dependable rimfire autoloaders made. It is also a beautiful piece. (photo courtesy of Ruger)

After production of over three million Mark II pistols, the first Ruger Mark III pistols became available in 2004. Major changes include safety features such as a loaded chamber indicator, a magazine disconnect, and a key lock system. The stainless steel Mark III 678 Hunter model features a 6 7/8-inch fluted barrel. The receiver is drilled and tapped for attaching a scope rail that comes with the pistol. Another version of the Mark III is known as the Model 512, which has a blue finish and a 5.5-inch heavy

barrel (list price $499). Another successful autoloader from Ruger is the version known as the 22/45. This model features a polymer grip frame that has the size and angle that duplicate the feel of the famous Colt 1911. The Model 22/45 (list price of $305 for the basic model) has also been upgraded to incorporate features of the Mark III. The final 1,000 of the Mark II pistols were shipped in November 2004 carrying the "One of One Thousand" logo on top of the receiver.

Ruger Mark III pistols are drilled and tapped for attaching a scope rail, and they continue the tradition of Ruger durability.

A unique rimfire pistol is the Charger produced by Ruger. It is based on the Ruger 10/22 carbine with a shorter barrel and the stock cut off behind the pistol grip. Along with the takedown version of the 10/22, Ruger produces a takedown version of the Charger pistol.

Within the last few years, Ruger has introduced another rimfire pistol that has become quite popular. Known as the SR22, the little pistol has a visible hammer and is thus of the double action/single action type. It is the opinion of the author that this is the safest form of autoloading pistol. The pistol is provided with dual safety levers, which also function as decocking levers. Barrel length of the standard model is 3.5 inches, but Ruger announced a 4.5-inch version in early 2016. The Ruger SR22 features a polymer frame and an aluminum slide. The fixed barrel is made of

Ruger produces the Charger that utilizes many of the features of the famous 10/22 Carbine. (photo courtesy of Ruger)

stainless steel. In order to permit the user to alter the grip, each SR22 is furnished with two polymer sleeves that fit over the grip frame itself. Thus, it is a simple matter to provide the shooter with a choice of two grip sizes. Although the SR22 is a compact pistol that weighs only 18 ounces, it is fitted with excellent sights. Not only are white dots employed to increase visibility, the rear sight is fully adjustable for windage and elevation. With an MSRP of $439-479 and selling prices that are typically about $100 less, the SR22 is an excellent choice for general use. We will have a great deal to say about this pistol in Chapter 17.

The Ruger SR22 is a compact and versatile pistol.

Kimber markets an autoloader that is a clone of the Colt 1911, and it is available in .22 LR caliber. The slide is made of aluminum in the .22 LR pistols so the weight is only 23 ounces. In the .17 HMR pistols that were offered briefly, a steel slide was used so the weight in that caliber is approximately 31 ounces. As was discovered by other firearm manufactures, it was soon realized that a pistol firing a 17-grain bullet was of limited usefulness, regardless of the velocity. Consequently, the Kimber Rimfire Target and a lot of other firearms in that caliber were not in production long. One of the really interesting features of the Kimber 1911 style pistols in .45 Auto caliber is that they can be converted to .22 LR by installing a Rimfire Target Conversion Kit. This unit consists of an aluminum slide, stainless steel barrel, guide rod and spring that replace the slide assembly of the centerfire pistols. The units are available in either black or stainless finish and can be installed very quickly. The result is a .22 LR pistol that has exactly the same grip as the .45 Auto and which has controls that function in exactly the same way on both pistols. Excellent adjustable sights are standard on the Rimfire Target Conversion Kit and, as expected, it performs flawlessly and will be described in Chapter 17.

By means of the Kimber Rimfire Conversion Unit, this Custom II has been converted into a .22 LR pistol.

One of the famous centerfire pistols is the CZ Model 75. CZ markets the CZ 75 Kadet Adapter II that converts the centerfire pistol to .22 LR. Other conversion kits are produced for some of the most popular centerfire models.

In addition to the Model 41 target model, for many years Smith & Wesson produced an extensive line of .22 LR pistols in the 22A and 22S series. As this is written in early 2016, the 22A and 22S pistols have been discontinued with the introduction of a model known as the 22SW Victory, but new pistols in the older series are still available from some dealers. The pistols were produced with various finishes with barrel lengths of 4, 5.5, and 7 inches, and the barrels can be easily interchanged. The 22A models have alloy frames and weigh around 30 ounces. The 22S models were made with stainless steel barrels and frames, which make them weigh over 40 ounces. All of the 22A and 22S versions were provided with scope rails that accept Weaver-type bases so a wide variety of optional sighting equipment can be mounted, and the accuracy displayed by these fine pistols makes them suitable for hunting. With the wide selection of options in finish, grips, and other options available, almost any taste can be satisfied by one of the Smith & Wesson pistols.

The Smith & Wesson 22A is available with several choices of barrel lengths and grips. The pistol shown has a 5.5-inch barrel and plastic grips with rubber inserts.

Beretta markets an extensive series of pistols known as the Model U22 Neos. Barrel lengths of 4.5 or 6 inches are available in several finishes and the list price is $325 for most versions. Beretta also produces the Model 87 Target that is a high quality piece that has a suggested price of approximately $900. Another Beretta model that is more conventional in its appearance is the Cheetah or Model 87, which has been available with a choice of 3.8- or 4.4-inch barrels. The Cheetah can be fired in the double action mode for the first shot.

Sigarms markets an interesting rimfire pistol known as the Model P226 Classic. It is patterned after the famous P226 and with a 4.5-inch barrel weighs 23.7 ounces. With an MSRP of $636, it is not an economy model, but it can accept Sig's X-CHANGE Kit™ to convert the pistol to fire 9mm, 40 S&W, or 357 Sig cartridges. As with other pistols that can be converted to fire other calibers of ammunition, the kit consists of a complete slide assembly and a magazine.

High Standard has produced rimfire autoloaders for many years. After being out of production for some time, current models include the Victor, Trophy, Olympic, Citation and Supermatic. These are pistols that have established an enviable reputation.

One of the interesting and useful members of the lineup of .22 autoloaders is the Walther P22. This pistol is designed with the look and feel of the famous Walther P99 centerfire pistol that is widely used in law enforcement and military work. With a polymer frame, the basic P22, which has a 3.4-inch barrel, weighs only about 18 ounces. The target model, which has a 5-inch barrel and adjustable sights, weighs approximately 20 ounces. Both models have many unique features one of which is a replaceable back strap that can be interchanged to alter the grip size.

The P22 also comes with a built in lock that requires a specially designed key to place the pistol in a firing configuration. Dual safety levers are mounted on the top of the receiver at the rear, but they do not function as decocking levers. Moreover, barrels of different length are interchangeable to convert a sport model into the target version.

The Bersa Thunder, which bears a strong resemblance to the Walther PPK, is available in .22 LR caliber. It is a double action/single action pistol that features a 3.5-inch barrel and a safety that also functions as a decocking lever. Available in several versions, the Bersa Thunder sells for approximately $300.

There are also several compact pistols available in .22 LR that are intended for carry or defense. These include the tiny Beretta Bobcat with a 2.4-inch barrel and a weight of only about 11.5 ounces. The Bobcat has a list price of approximately $410. Taurus produces a small double action only (DAO) model known as the PT22. It has a 2.75-inch barrel, weighs only 12.3 ounces, and has a list price of slightly over $270.

Frequently, one reads on the chat room of some internet forum how the writer just loves a particular handgun. In the next post, another participant tells how his specimen of the same model jams frequently and is a piece of junk. It may be that the first writer owns a particularly good sample whereas the other got one made on Friday as they used to say. Part of the difference may lie in the types of ammunition being used in the two pistols. Certain types of pistols function much better with some types of ammunition than with others. For example, some older pistols were designed to handle standard velocity loads by making use of a rather soft recoil spring. Modern high velocity loads should not be used extensively in such models. Still other pistols seem to function best with high velocity loads. Ammunition such as CCI Stinger

The Walther P22 is a compact, lightweight sport pistol with easily interchanged barrels. This Target model has a 5-inch barrel with a muzzle weight. (photo courtesy of Keith House)

The Bersa Thunder .22 mimics the famous Walther PPK. (photo courtesy of Bersa)

and Quik-Shok is produced with a case length that is approximately 0.1 inch longer than the standard .22 LR case. It should come as no surprise that such ammunition might not feed reliably in certain semi-automatic pistols.

If a rimfire pistol fails to function flawlessly, there are four things to check in seeking a remedy for the situation. First, make sure that the action is clean and properly (but not overly!) lubricated. During firing, autoloaders have unburned powder deposited in the action and that can result in enough gunk so that the bolt does not cycle smoothly. Second, check the loading ramp that leads into the chamber. It should be smooth and correctly shaped. Third, check the lips on the magazine. If a magazine is dropped on a hard surface, it is possible for the lips to become bent. Because this is the component from which the cartridges are fed into the chamber, the bent magazine may not allow the pistol to function correctly. Fourth, try different ammunition. Some slight variation in dimensions between types of ammunition is inevitable, and different types of lubricant may make a difference in feeding. If these simple factors do not solve the problem, have the pistol checked by a competent pistolsmith.

Thoughts on Selection

Gone are the superb Colt Match Target Woodsman and some of the High Standard pistols of many years ago. They are now highly prized as collectors' pieces. Even with the disappearance of these fine firearms, the rimfire hand gunner has a wealth of choices that includes both autoloaders and revolvers. What follows should not necessarily be taken as strongly as if they were recommendations. The author is merely making some summary comments based on first-hand experience.

For sporting purposes, it would be hard to fault the Ruger Single Six, especially with the extra cylinder in .22 WMR caliber. Such a handgun is suited to

With its heavy barrel and target sights, the Ruger Mark III Target is an accurate and reliable handgun.

plinking, small game and pest shooting, and woods roaming. The Ruger single actions are famous for their durability. In .17 HMR caliber (or .17 Mach 2 with the optional cylinder), a Single Six is a good choice for small varmints at long handgun ranges (although you will probably need a scope for taking varmints under such conditions), but it does not really fit the role of a plinking handgun, and it is far less versatile than the .22 LR/.22 WMR version. The Ruger Single Six Hunter has a built in rib that accepts Ruger rings for ease in scope mounting. The large frame Smith & Wesson double action revolvers such as the Model 617 are superb handguns that can readily accept scope mounts. The Taurus revolvers represent excellent values as well. A handgun from any of these famous makers should make a superb choice for all around use.

The autoloader fan will find a wide selection of models in a broad spectrum of price ranges from which to make a selection. Before selecting any rimfire autoloading handgun, you should examine several models to determine how the size, weight, and handling characteristics compare. If an autoloader is your cup of tea, it is hard to imagine a more reliable, dependable rimfire handgun than the Ruger Mark III Standard model. As a plinking pistol for the outdoorsman, the Standard model is more than adequate, but one of the variants with adjustable sights would be a better choice if the pistol is to be used as a training piece for formal target shooting or for small game or pest shooting. Another excellent choice for general use would be one of the several versions of the Browning

Ruger's Single Six has been a popular rimfire handgun for half a century. The three-screw model shown here was purchased in 1958.

Buck Mark. In the experience of the author, they are extremely accurate and reliable, and the Buck Mark Standard weighs only 32-33 ounces. Buck Mark pistols are provided with excellent adjustable sights, and they are known to have good trigger action.

The recently discontinued Smith & Wesson 22S and 22A were produced with either stainless steel or alloy frames with barrel lengths ranging from 4 to 7 inches so a sport, target, or hunting configuration can easily be achieved. The recently introduced SW22 Victory is an attractive pistol having a stainless steel finish. The MSRP is $409-459 depending on sights and finish.

The Beretta autoloaders of the Neos U22 series (MSRP $325) have a futuristic style. Several versions are available that have different features, and they are autoloaders that can have a scope attached for producing the ultimate in accuracy for hunting and pest shooting. For plinking and sport shooting, the Walther P22 or Ruger SR22 would make a fine choice. With their light weight and small grip size, they would be superb choices for women and younger shooters who may have small hands. Moreover, the grip size can be modified on these models by changing the replaceable back strap insert, and it is a simple process to interchange barrels on the Walther.

Although there is probably not a great difference in inherent accuracy between most of the models mentioned, there may be a considerable difference in trigger action and sights. These characteristics may allow you to shoot some handguns more accurately than others. As in the case of rifles and perhaps to an even greater extent, the choice of a handgun is a personal matter, and subjective factors play a large role in the enjoyment derived from using the piece. For example, one of the handgun designs that is extremely popular with many shooters is one that does not excite the author to any great extent. If you were to handle such a pistol, you might find your emotions so stimulated that it would be your top choice. It is this type of preference that makes both single action revolvers and semiautomatics immensely popular. There are many fine rimfire handguns available from which to make a good selection.

Ancillaries

The person who is getting equipped to enjoy the sport of rimfire handgun shooting will probably want items in addition to the handgun. Although it is possible to enjoy such shooting with only a handgun and some ammunition, other items will be added to the shooter's kit if the sport becomes addictive. Most semiautomatic pistols are sold with one or two magazines included. If only one magazine is furnished, you probably should add another either to have as a spare in case something happens to one or just as a convenience. It is much easier to have two loaded magazines handy so that when one is empty it can be removed and the other inserted to continue shooting.

Probably the most frequent purchase by the hand gunner is a holster. Traditional material for constructing holsters is leather, but in recent years various synthetic materials have become widely used. There is little question in the minds of many purists that the leather holster is more attractive. However, it also requires more maintenance and the residual chemicals from the tanning process can lead to corrosion if the handgun is left in the leather for a long period of time. A friend once showed the author a fine old Swedish military pistol that he had left in its original holster for a long time. The bluing had been removed over large areas of the pistol by the chemicals in the leather thereby decreasing the value of the pistol considerably. The owner thought that because the holster came with the pistol they should be stored together with the pistol inside. Leather also tends to become brittle with age unless treated with an appropriate solution to replace lost natural oils. It should be remembered that leather is also a material that is used to polish metals. If a leather holster fits loosely

The Smith & Wesson SW22 Victory is the replacement for the earlier 22A and 22S. (photo courtesy of Smith & Wesson)

A fine leather holster like this one produced by Browning for the Buck Mark series is durable and attractive.

enough that the gun slides around in it, the bluing is going to be worn off in short order at the contact points. Make sure that a leather holster is made for your specific handgun. It has become more popular to produce a compromise holster that fits a certain general handgun type such as "large frame auto, 3.5-5-inch barrel." Do not settle for this type of holster without trying it with a handgun of the same model and barrel length as yours. If it fits well, it will be satisfactory. If not, keep looking or buy another type. One drawback to the leather holsters made for specific firearms is that they are expensive. It is not uncommon to find models that cost $75-100 or in some cases even more.

For many years, the author owned only a few leather holsters. As the cost of fine leather holsters escalated, nylon holsters became more popular. These are generally produced in several sizes each of which fits several handguns of similar dimensions. Although this can present a problem with a leather holster, it is acceptable if the holster is made of nylon. In fact, the author has one pistol for which no leather holster could be found in the price range acceptable. The result was that a nylon holster produced by Gun Mate was selected and it worked so well that another of the same type was obtained for another hard to fit handgun. In addition to Gun Mate, there are several producers of fabric holsters some of which are Bianchi, Blackhawk, and Uncle Mike's. Nylon holsters require very little maintenance, they do not tend to rub off bluing, and they are inexpensive. Some of the very good models sell for $25 or less with some being available for $12-15.

Don't forget that you will have to transport your handgun both in a vehicle as well as in the field. Almost all states have requirements for transporting firearms in vehicles that require the piece to be in a closed case. Today, many handguns are shipped from the manufacturer in a foam padded plastic case or in a case that is molded to hold the gun securely. These containers are adequate for transporting the handgun and most have a hole where a lock can be attached to keep the gun secured. A hard case made of aluminum or other material is an inexpensive addition to the shooters kit. Padded fabric cases having zipper closures are available in sizes to fit any pistol.

In recent years, the development of handgun grips has made it possible for the shooter to change the grip of his or her pistol. In some cases, the grips may be desirable to enable the shooter to handle the piece better but in other cases the effect may be primarily cosmetic. There are special grips made of wood, staghorn, composites, rubber, or laminated materials. They may have finger grooves that permit a better grasp of the grip or they may be made with a non-slip surface. Grips made of hard rubber give an especially good feel, they are not slick, and they give a more pleasant feel in cold weather. Grips of this type are made by several manufacturers, but the grips from Hogue are very highly regarded. Pachmayr, Altamont, and Eagle Grips are also producers of extensive lines of grips.

There was a time when the purchaser of a handgun had a choice of a "target" model with adjustable sights or a "sport" model with fixed sights. In many cases, the guns were identical except for barrel length and sights. If there is one aftermarket area that has expanded exponentially, it surely must be handgun sights, the majority of which are produced with increased visibility as the main feature. It is true that many handguns are equipped with fixed sights that make it impossible or difficult (which can usually be interpreted as expensive) to make a change in sighting equipment. However, there

Nylon holsters are available for almost any handgun. They are inexpensive and entirely adequate for most purposes.

are optional sights for many handguns that have white dots on either side of the notch in the rear sight blade and on the back surface of the front sight. These dots make it easier to align the sights in dim light. Other sights have dots that glow in the dark to make it possible to see them in very dim light. In some cases, the rear sight has the square notch outlined with a white line and the front sight has a white or red insert that makes the sights more visible. In the recent past, the fiber optic inserts have become quite popular. The front sight has an insert that lies along the top of the post whereas the rear sight has a fiber optic element embedded on either side of the notch. Such sights are visible in low light, but in some cases the top of the front sight does not have a square shape. For most handgun shooting, the square topped post front sight and adjustable rear sight with a square notch make a combination that is hard to beat.

Optical sights for handguns have become immensely popular in recent years. These include scope, red dot, and laser sights. Although laser sights are useful for shooting at night or possibly in law enforcement and military applications, lasers can be dangerous. The author has watched youngsters playing with a laser pointer. One was pointing the beam directly in the face of the other! The warnings on lasers are there for a reason. It might be appropriate to point out that laser surgery on the eye has become an important technique. The danger of lasers being used carelessly is real and significant. Laser sights will not be discussed further in this chapter.

If you are in the same age group as the author, it is easy to remember a time when a scope on a handgun was regarded as a novelty. That is not the case any more. Hunting for both small and large game with handguns has become much more common. Enhanced handgun performance has also been a factor because it is practical to shoot at targets at longer ranges, which makes improved aiming devices more important. Mounting scopes on handguns is so common that some models are sold with scope rails in place. Others are available with integral ribs along the tops of the barrels where scope bases can be attached. For an enormous number of other models, aftermarket mounts are available. Most of the major scope manufacturers produce scopes specifically for use on handguns. The point is that a scope can be mounted on almost any handgun except the very small pocket pistols and some single action revolvers.

Although early handgun scopes were of very low magnification, the models currently available include

Red dot sights like this model from Simmons have become very popular for use on handguns. They offer some of the advantages of a scope but are faster to use.

fixed powers that may be as high as 8X, and scopes having variable magnification are quite popular. One of the scopes with which the author has had most experience is the superb Weaver 1.5-4X variable. Eye relief of scopes for use on handguns is normally 12-16 inches so that the piece can be held at arm's length and fired in the normal way for a handgun. There is no question that a scope on a handgun enables the shooter to make shots routinely that would have been impossible or accidental under other circumstances.

The so-called red dot sight has been produced for many years in one form or another. This sight has a red dot projected onto a lens that the shooter then looks through to place the red dot on the target. The red dot is produced by battery power, and the intensity (brightness) of the dot can be varied widely by means of a rheostat. The location of the red dot in relation to the point of impact can be adjusted by means of adjustment knobs just as in the case of a scope. Because of the way in which the optical system is designed, there is no problem of parallax so the shooter merely places the red dot on the target and squeezes off the shot. Red dot sights are available with dots that cover a specific area on the target at a specific distance. Those with 3 MOA and 4 MOA are probably the most popular. Sights of this type can also be used on shotguns, muzzle loaders, and rifles. In the mind of the author, the main disadvantage to the red dot sight is that it produces a large blob on top of an otherwise trim handgun. This is no problem for the hunter using a handgun, but it makes it impossible to carry the piece in a holster. Nevertheless, the red dot sight is very popular, and there is a great difference between the red dot sights available today and those early models of a generation ago.

In this chapter we have presented an overview of the field of rimfire handguns. Obviously, not all models have been discussed. In Chapter 17 more detailed descriptions of some of the models will be presented.

CHAPTER 5

SIGHTS AND SIGHTING

IN ORDER TO HIT A TARGET WITH A RIFLE, some sort of aim is required unless the target is very close. Hitting a pop can at 15 yards with a shotgun requires no more than pointing the gun at the can and firing. Hitting the can at that distance with a rifle bullet, although not difficult, requires a more accurate aim by making use of some sort of sighting equipment. Hitting a pop can at 100 yards requires even more accurate aiming. A pop can at 300 yards is a small target and hitting it requires very accurate aiming. Hitting a one-inch circle at 300 yards would require an extremely accurate aim and would be possible only when the rifle is equipped with appropriate sights (even if the rifle were sufficiently accurate). The object of sighting equipment is to align the bore so the bullet will hit the point of aim on the target. To a considerable extent, the level of accuracy desired will dictate the sighting equipment required. In this chapter, the types of sights most appropriate to rimfire firearms will be discussed.

Open Sights

Aiming a rifle is accomplished by means of sights. Rifle sights have been made in a bewildering array of types over the centuries. In fact, acquiring old sighting equipment has become a passion for many collectors. Sights fall into two general categories, metallic and optical types. Metallic sights include the so-called open sight and the aperture or peep sight. Open sights often consist of a bead or post near the muzzle and a blade with a notch in it mounted near the rear end of the barrel. Aligning the post or bead front sight with the notch in the rear sight allows the barrel to be pointed at the target correctly. As will be discussed, there are numerous variations in open sights some of which are much better than others.

Aligning the sights on the target requires the shooter to establish simultaneously the relationship

Handguns like this Colt Frontier Scout have sights that consist of a blade front and a notch in the frame for a rear sight. They are durable but not adjustable.

between three objects, the rear sight, the front sight, and the target. This relationship is known as the sight picture, and it must be the same for each shot if consistency is to be achieved. Suppose the rear sight has a square notch and the front sight consists of a post with a square top. Correct sighting requires that the post be placed in the notch so that the tops of both are in horizontal alignment. The front post must be centered in the notch in the rear sight with a small sliver of space on either side of the post. Next, the relationship between the top of the post and the target must be established. When the target is a black circle (the "bull") on a piece of paper, one procedure is to have the sights adjusted so that the top of the post is positioned at the bottom edge of the bull. This is known as a "six o'clock hold." The problem with this arrangement is that if bulls having different sizes are fired at, the sights must be adjusted to compensate for the size difference otherwise the distance from the top of the post to the center of the bull is different and shots will strike either high or low relative to the center of the bull. The situation is even more difficult when the target may be a squirrel at 40 yards for one shot and a starling at

(a)   (b)   (c)

Three modes of aligning handgun sights on a target are illustrated. In (a), there is a six o'clock hold on a small bull; in (b), a six o'clock hold on a larger bull; and in (c), the sights are aligned on the center of the bull.

25 yards for the next. It can be rather difficult to assess what is a six o'clock hold on a pest. For this type of shooting, it is better to have the sights adjusted so that the point of impact coincides with the top of the post. Then, you can simply align the rear and front sights as described above and place the top of the post where you want the point of impact to be.

Although the situation described deals with a rear sight with a square notch and a post front sight, the situation is similar when the rear sight has a "U" notch and the front sight is a bead. The sights should be adjusted so that the bead rests in the "U" and the top of the bead is used as the specific point to determine the alignment on the target. Most often found on rifles for plinking and hunting, the bead front sight is more difficult to place exactly on a paper target because of its rounded top. It is the experience of this author that the top edge of a circular bead becomes rather indistinct in dim light and tends to reflect light in direct sunlight. These conditions can lead to sighting errors, and they explain why a rifle sighted in correctly for one person may not prove to be correctly sighted in for another.

Almost all open sights have some provision for adjustment. On many rimfire rifles, the rear sight element can be moved up or down by sliding an elevator blade that is nothing more than a ramp that has a series of notches or steps. The elevator moves forward or backward in a slot cut in the rear sight. Notches cut in the sight elevator ramp hold the rear sight at a particular height. To raise the point of impact on the

A front sight consisting of a ramp with a bead on a post is a common type of sight.

target, the rear sight is raised (elevated), which causes the muzzle to be raised in order to align the front sight in the rear sight notch. In almost all cases, changing elevation by one "notch" movement gives *some* change, but it may not be very precise from notch to notch. If the rifle is shooting *high*, the rear sight must be *lowered* to make the point of impact coincide with the point of aim. Note that *the rear sight must be moved in the direction in which the point of impact needs to be moved on the target* in order to sight in the rifle.

The rear sights on many rimfire rifles are adjustable for elevation by sliding a ramp with a series of notches for setting the height.

This rear sight is adjusted for elevation by loosening two screws and moving the sight blade. Windage is adjusted by moving the sight laterally.

On many rimfire rifles (especially inexpensive ones), the rear sight is attached to the barrel by means of a dovetailed groove cut laterally into the barrel. Lateral (horizontal) sight adjustment is known as the windage adjustment. The only way to move the sight laterally to adjust the point of impact is by sliding the entire sight. This requires tapping on the side of the sight base to move it in the groove. This needs to be done carefully in order to avoid marring the surface of the sight base and the barrel. For this purpose, the Lyman gunsmith's hammer is a useful tool. This small hammer has three interchangeable striking surfaces and a brass punch that is stored in the handle. The brass punch can be placed against the edge of the sight base and tapping it moves the rear sight laterally. A small amount of discoloration may occur as brass from the punch rubs off on the steel sight base, but it is usually easy to remove by rubbing briskly with an oily rag. If you do not have a special hammer for sight movement, you can get by with any small hammer and a small piece of brass rod having a diameter of about 1/8 or 3/16-inch. Brass rods of this type are available at most hardware stores. Many handguns have sights that are similar to those utilized on rifles and are adjusted in the same way.

The Lyman gunsmith's hammer is a useful tool for many purposes, including moving rear sights in their retaining notches.

Another brief comment will be made here on the subject of tools although the subject will be discussed in greater detail in Chapter 11. A serious shooter knows that mounting scopes or peep sights and some firearm disassembly and adjustment are an integral part of the shooting activity. Keeping things tight is required even if other changes to the equipment are not being made. Most firearms have parts attached by screws. One thing that detracts from the appearance of a firearm is screws that have been badly deformed by using improper screwdrivers. If you are serious about your firearms and keeping them in proper working order and looking good, invest in a set of gunsmith's screwdrivers. They are not expensive, and they provide a way of having the right tool for the job. In some cases, the bits are removable and store in the handle. Two of the most common kits are those available from Hoppe's and Pachmayr. These sets contain bits having blade, Phillips, and hex fittings. The Pachmayr set also has torx bits.

Peep Sights

As in the case of an open rear sight, an aperture or peep sight (sometimes referred to as a receiver sight) also makes use of a front sight consisting of a bead or blade. However, the rear sight is mounted on the receiver near the eye and has a small hole or aperture through which the shooter looks at the front sight and its relationship to the target. Because the human eye looks through a hole at the brightest point, the *center* of the aperture is naturally selected for looking at the front sight and where it is placed on the target. The shooter looks *through* the aperture rather than *at* it. With such a combination, it is possible to align the sights in relation to the target much more accurately than can be done with open sights. In fact, some types of competitive target shooting require the use of metallic sights, and when this is the case, it is a high quality aperture sight that is chosen. These sights have adjustment screws for moving the aperture laterally and vertically so precise and reproducible sight adjustment is possible. Today, because of the availability of telescopic sights, aperture sights are much less popular now than they were in the past except for formal target shooting. They were once very popular on hunting rifles. Some of the peep sights for use on hunting rifles could be adjusted then the settings locked in by means of locking screws. Some even allowed the slide to be removed and replaced without changing the point of impact. Generally, target type peep sights have large knobs that are easy to grasp and turn so that they can be adjusted quickly without tools. Some of the most sophisticated aperture sights that are intended for high level competition are elegant instruments that sell for $300-400. Fine accuracy is possible when using an aperture sight if the shooter has good vision.

Peep sights are available in numerous configurations for the various shooting sports. Small models are available that clamp in the grooves that are present on the receivers of most rimfire rifles. Other models attach by means of screws to the side of the receiver. In times past, many rimfire rifles came drilled and tapped for receiver sights as well as with grooved receivers for attaching scope mounts. An example of that type of rifle is the Winchester 69A, which is shown in the photo. Other than target rifles, few models are

One type of peep sight from Williams mounts on the dovetail grooves normally used for mounting a scope. A higher front sight is frequently needed when using this type of sight.

Peep sights like the Lyman model shown here on a Winchester Model 69A Target rifle are widely used in target shooting.

now marketed with provision for attaching peep sights to the receivers by screws.

Generally, the receiver sight is somewhat higher than an open rear sight. Therefore, the front sight must also be higher than the usual bead sight found on most rimfire rifles. Peep sights are normally used in combination with a front sight on a ramp or with a special target type front sight. Some of the target front sights have interchangeable inserts so that the shooter sees either a post or an aperture depending on which insert is selected.

The sight picture when using a peep sight is an important consideration. With the human eye automatically locating the center of the aperture, the top of the front sight and its placement on the target are the primary concerns. Generally, the eye is placed so that the top of the front sight is located in the center of the aperture. Then, the rifle is aimed with the top of the post placed on the target in one of two ways. In the first, the rifle is held so that the round target bull rests on top of the post with a tiny sliver of light between the post and the bull. The reason the post is not placed exactly on the bull is that with the post and bull both being black it is not easy to see just how far the post is riding up on the bull. Therefore, it is preferable for

there to be a very thin sliver of light separating the top of the post and the bull.

In the second procedure, the sights are adjusted so that the point of impact coincides with the location of the top of the post on the target. In that way the post is placed on the center of a round bull. If targets of different sizes are fired at, the shooter will know that the bullets will strike where the top of the post rests on the target. This procedure should be followed for any aperture sight that is to be used in hunting situations because of different sizes and shapes of targets that may be located different distances from the shooter.

In competitive shooting, the target-style peep sight is usually used in conjunction with a high front sight that has a hood. Many such front sights have a series of inserts in the form of circular blades that can be changed to suit the situation. A set of these insert blades usually consists of several apertures of different diameter and one or more posts of varying widths. When viewed through the aperture of the receiver sight, the aperture in the front insert makes another ring that then surrounds the bull on the target. The result is a series of concentric rings that can be aligned with very little error to obtain high accuracy.

A

B

C

Figure A shows the sight picture for a 6 o'clock hold using a peep sight. Figure B shows a 6 o'clock hold on a larger bull. If the rifle is sighted as in Figure A, the shots will be below the center of the larger bull. Figure C shows the sight picture when the rifle is sighted to hit at the center of the bull. Shots will be centered regardless of the size of the bull.

Hooded front sights with interchangeable inserts are extremely popular with target shooters.

Ammunition testing is best accomplished by making use of a scope of high magnification like the 6-24X Tasco being used here by the author's wife, Kathy.

Scopes

Telescopic sights (usually referred to as "scopes") are not a recent development. They were used by snipers as long ago as the Civil War. For many years, scopes were fraught with several problems. They were relatively expensive, relatively fragile, and subject to problems such as fogging (condensation of moisture inside the scope under cool, humid conditions). These problems have largely been solved and scopes are so common today that many rifles are sold with no iron sights in anticipation that a scope will always be mounted on the rifle. Even a relatively inexpensive scope can be rugged, fog proof, and have accurate adjustments.

Inside a scope is some sort of reticule that can be aligned on a target to give the aiming point. Reticules consist of crosshairs, dots, circles, or some combination of these. The scope is constructed so that the target and the reticule appear in the same optical plane. The shooter merely aligns the reticule on the target and squeezes the trigger. A scope is the simplest, and for most people, the most accurate type of sight available.

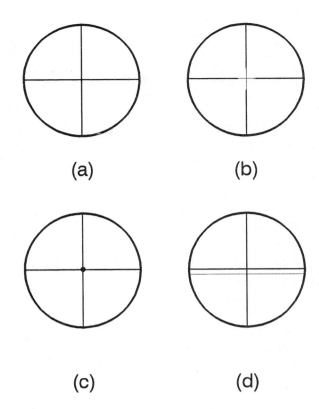

Types of reticules include (a) crosshair; (b) duplex; (c) crosshair with dot; and (d) rangefinder.

The fact that a scope magnifies the target enables the shooter to see it more clearly. Therein lies one of the great advantages of this type of sight. With a circular aperture and a front sight and target of regular shape, it is possible to obtain an accurate and repeatable sight picture with a peep sight. However, such an arrangement does not allow the shooter to see better. When the target has an irregular shape (as in hunting), the ability to see the target larger and clearer is an enormous advantage.

A phenomenon that comes into play when looking through a scope is known as parallax. Parallax is the apparent movement of an object when the point of observation changes. It can be illustrated by the following procedure. With one arm extended, point your finger at an object and look at your finger and the object with one eye closed. Holding your arm stationary, look at the object with the other eye. Note how the object appears to have moved. What actually moved was the point of observation. When you look through a scope that has the reticule positioned on a target, the reticule may appear to move on the target as you move your eye from side to side. If so, the scope has parallax error when the target is at that distance.

Many people have trouble estimating distances with any degree of accuracy. They cannot tell whether an object is 50 or 90 feet away. There is a very elementary way that makes use of parallax to estimate the distance that separates you from an object. With your arm extended, point your finger at the object while looking at it with one eye closed. Close that eye and open the other. From the size of the object, estimate approximately how much it appears to move as you look at it first with one eye open and then the other. The object is approximately 10 times this distance from you. This procedure sounds crude (and it is), but you may be surprised how well you can estimate distance in this way after a little practice. There are numerous references distances that can be used. For example, most adults are approximately 5-6 feet tall. If you are estimating the distance to some object with a person in your field of view, you can estimate the apparent movement of the object in relation to the height of the person. Suppose a paper target of normal size is located at some unknown distance from your shooting position. Try the procedure described above remembering that the target is probably about 1 foot in width. If it appears to move approximately a distance that is 10 times the size of the target (10 feet) when you observe it using each eye, it is probably about 100 feet away.

Most scopes that are intended for use on centerfire rifles are adjusted to have no parallax at a distance of 100 yards. A scope that is intended for use on a rimfire rifle is normally free of parallax at 50-60 yards. Some scopes that are designed for use on muzzle loaders or shotguns are parallax free at 75 yards. Unless the eye is positioned rather far from the axis of the scope, the parallax results in a very small error at normal rimfire ranges (25-100 yards). In his youth, the author saw some very fine marksmanship demonstrated with a rimfire rifle that had a Weaver K4 scope mounted even though that scope was intended for use on centerfire rifles and was free of parallax at 100 yards.

One type of scope has a front lens (objective) mounted so it can be rotated to focus the scope on targets at different distances. Scopes with an adjustable objective are designated by "AO" following the other description. For example, a scope designated as 2-7 X 32 AO is a variable scope with a magnification range of 2-7 power and an adjustable objective of 32 mm diameter. Scopes of this type are advantageous for the rimfire shooter who may use the rifle on targets from 25-75 yards for the .22 LR or out to 150 yards if the rifle is a .17 HMR, .17 WSM, or .22 WMR because parallax can be eliminated at the range for which the scope

One of the superb optics for rimfire rifles is the Simmons 3-9X AO rimfire scope shown here mounted on a Ruger 10/22T.

The 6-20X Cabela's Outfitter scope features an adjustable objective.

is focused. However, such scopes tend to be rather expensive, but there are exceptions.

In the early days of scope use, the crosshair (fine wires) was by far the most common type of reticule. As time went on, it became clear that in dim light the fine wires were difficult to see, especially in a wooded area. Designers then produced scopes with reticules that consisted of a horizontal wire but instead of a vertical wire a tapered post was used. The idea behind this design was that the heavy post could be seen in dim light and if the rifle were sighted in so that the point of impact was at the top of the post, shots at game would be possible. Another type of reticule consists of a crosshair with a dot at the point of intersection. This is still a popular reticule with the size of the dot being selected appropriately depending on scope magnification and the anticipated targets. For example, high powered scopes for use on varmints or targets have a very small dot. Scopes intended for use on large game are generally lower in magnification and have reticules with larger dots.

Scopes have also been produced that have a standard crosshair but an additional horizontal wire separated from the intersection by some specific amount that corresponds to a known distance at a given range. For example, the distance between the horizontal wires might represent six inches at a distance of 100 yards (which is equivalent to 12 inches at 200 yards, 18 inches at 300 yards, etc.). The idea behind this type of reticule is that it is possible to use the distance between the horizontal wires to estimate range. Suppose that a groundhog sitting vertically just fills the distance between the horizontal wires. If we assume that the groundhog has a height of 12 inches, then the range must be approximately 200 yards. The successful use of this procedure requires the shooter to know the approximate size of the target being shot. Moreover, some such scopes have lines that are separated by distances to correspond to the trajectory of specific calibers.

As mentioned earlier, the fine crosshair reticule of some scopes can be difficult to see in wooded areas in dim light. Because of this, another approach to reticule design is the crosshair that has considerable thickness except near the intersection where the wires are thin. That way the outer portions of the reticule are easily seen and point the way to the fine crosshair, which permits an accurate aiming point. Sometimes known as duplex or dual-X reticules, they offer some of the better features of the standard crosshair while offering greater visibility. Almost all of the scopes that are intended for use on rimfire rifles (so-called rimfire scopes) have this type of reticule.

There are several other types of reticules some of which may be produced by only one manufacturer so they may not be readily available on numerous types and brands of scopes. Almost all of the scopes owned by the author have either the duplex or fine crosshair type of reticule. The Weaver V-16 Classic that was obtained specifically for testing purposes was ordered with the fine crosshair reticule because it permits the most accurate aim. Other scopes that are intended primarily for target shooting are offered with the fine crosshair reticules. For general use on rimfire rifles, the author could get along with no other type of reticule. It is the reticule that is found in some of the older scopes such as the Weaver K4, K6, and K10 models that were made in El Paso, TX many years ago. These older models are not only collectible, but also are satisfactory scopes for use on rimfire rifles.

Several other scopes in the author's collection would have fine crosshair reticules if it were possible exchange them easily. A Leupold Vari-X II 2.5-7X scope in the collection has a reticule that is very close to being the perfect reticule for the author. The reticule consists of a crosshair, but the wires are tapered so that where they cross the wires are very fine even though they get thicker toward the edges of the field of view. This

This fine Weaver 2.5-7X rimfire scope has adjustment knobs that require a coin to turn. Each click moves the point of impact 0.25 inch at 100 yards.

reticule is easy to see in dim light, but the fine wires at the intersection permit a very accurate aim. Although several types of reticules have been described, there are numerous others that have been produced. It is rather like tread design on tires–almost endless in variety and each one better than all the rest. Even after using many scopes having a variety of types of reticules, the author prefers the tapered crosshair type.

Another type of option exists with scopes made today. Although scopes were originally made with steel tubes that were polished and blued, it is now possible to buy scopes in other finishes. Almost all scopes have tubes that are made of "aircraft grade" aluminum, but aluminum cannot be blued by the processes used to blue steel. Instead, available finishes on scopes include both gloss and matte black, nickel, and even camo. Therefore, it is possible to equip a rifle with a scope so that the finishes of the rifle and scope match. To my mind, rifles made of stainless steel look very good when the scope has the nickel finish. However, a camo finish on an optical device seems a little extreme to my conservative taste.

Adjustment of a scope for windage and elevation is made by turning knobs located on the scope turret. Divisions are referred to as "clicks" and one click moves the point of impact a specific amount on the target. Of course, it is actually the point of aim that is being moved so that it coincides with the point where the barrel is sending the bullet. On most scopes, one click amounts to 0.25 inch at 100 yards so it takes four clicks to move the point of impact one inch. Other scopes have clicks that are equivalent to 0.5 inch at 100 yards and some of the scopes intended mainly for target shooting have 1/8-inch clicks. These are usually the models that have high magnification. When selecting a scope for general use including plinking and small game or pest hunting, the magnitude of the adjustment produced by one click is relatively unimportant. Most shooting with a rimfire .22 LR is conducted well inside of 100 yards, and at 50 yards one click moves the point of aim only one-half as much as it does at 100 yards. Thus, a scope that has 0.5-inch clicks at 100 yards changes the point of impact by only 0.25 inch at 50 yards. If a rimfire rifle will produce one-inch groups at 50 yards, the group size itself measures four clicks even if the scope has 0.5-inch click adjustments. Only with extremely accurate target rifles and scopes of relatively high magnification does the amount of change produced by one click become important. The vast majority of scopes used on rimfire rifles have 0.25-inch clicks at 100 yards so it is actually not a problem to adjust the scope so that the point of impact and point of aim coincide to within the accuracy limit of the rifle.

Some scopes are constructed with adjustments that are measured in terms of minutes of angle (MOA) rather than in inches. A minute of angle is one-sixtieth of a degree of angle. On a target at 100 yards, the distance represented by one MOA at the firing point amounts to 1.047 inches. Therefore, the difference between 1 MOA and 1 inch is so slight that it is insignificant in most instances. One click amounts to 0.262 inches in one case and 0.250 in the other. A very accurate rifle might produce groups measuring one inch at 100 yards. Moving the average point of impact (not that of any specific shot) exactly one inch or 1.047 inches will not cause any discernable difference. At 50 yards, it is even less important because one click represents 0.125 inch if four clicks equal one inch at 100 yards or 0.131 inch if four clicks represent one MOA. The difference is a mere 0.006 inch.

Of more importance than the magnitude of the correction produced by one click is the accuracy and reproducibility of the adjustments. In other words, does a change of four clicks produce a change of

Adjustments on the Cabela's 6-24X AO are of the target type, which can easily be turned by hand after the covers are removed. Each click represents 1/8 inch at 100 yards.

exactly one inch in point of impact? To test this, start with the rifle sighted in at 50 yards and fire a group of three or five shots. Next adjust the scope so that the point of impact is changed by some specific amount and shoot another group to see if the point of impact moves the expected distance from the first group.

One procedure for checking the accuracy of scope adjustments is known as shooting the square. In order to demonstrate this procedure, a Ruger 10/22T with a Weaver 2.5-7X rimfire scope in place was used to fire a three-shot group at 50 yards. Next, the elevation was adjusted by turning the knob 24 clicks to raise the point of impact. Because the scope has 0.25-inch clicks, that change should move the point of impact six inches at 100 yards or three inches at 50 yards. Another three-shot group was fired. The scope was then adjusted 24 clicks to move the point of impact three inches to the right and another three-shot group was fired. After adjusting the scope 24 clicks to shoot lower, another three-shot group was fired. Finally, adjustment was made for 24 clicks to the left, which would bring the point of impact back to the original position and three more shots were fired. The photo shows the results obtained. It is apparent that the point of impact at 50 yards was changed almost exactly three inches by each of the 24-click adjustments. The final three shots merged nicely with the first three shots to give a six-shot group. This exercise demonstrated that the Weaver scope has adjustments that perform exactly as they should.

When scopes were first coming into common use, the magnification was almost always fixed, and 2.5, 4, and 6 were the most common magnifications. Scopes having these magnifications are still available as are scopes having 8, 10, 16, 24, and 32X power. Scopes of high magnification are generally labeled as "target" or "varmint" scopes. However, scopes having variable power are extremely popular now and new scopes of fixed magnification are rather rare. Scopes with numerous ranges of magnification are available. Some of the most common ranges are 2.5-7X, 3-9X, 4-12X, 4-16X, 6-24X, etc. On most scopes, the magnification is changed by rotating a ring located just in front of the eyepiece. Unless one has an extremely accurate rifle and is interested in extremely accurate bullet placement, most shooters will be well-served by a rimfire rifle fitted with a 2.5-7X or 3-9X scope. It has been observed by many shooters that the scope is almost always set on the highest power available and left there.

There is always a question as to whether changing the power of a scope might produce some change in

This photo illustrates "shooting the square" with a Weaver 2.5-7X rimfire scope in which 3-shot groups were fired at 50 yards as the scope was adjusted 24 clicks up, right, down, and left while aiming at the black dot. Note that the first three shots and the last three give a group of less than one inch after all adjustments have been made.

Although these BSA scopes are intended for use on air rifles, they work very well on rimfire rifles. Shown are (top to bottom) the 3-12X, 2-7X, and 4X models all of which have adjustable objectives.

the point of impact because the optical characteristics may be slightly different at different magnification. In order to test this, one can simply fire a group at 50 yards with the scope set on each magnification. The author tested a Weaver 2.5-7X rimfire scope in this way. Using an accurate Ruger 10/22T and SK Jagd Standard Plus ammunition, one shot was fired with the scope set on 3, 4, 5, 6, and 7 power to produce the group shown in the photo. The group is simply a ragged hole that measures approximately 0.36 inches with no indication that the point of impact changes as the magnification is changed. This is the type of performance that characterizes a scope of good quality.

This 0.4-inch group was fired at 50 yards with a Ruger 10/22T that was fitted with a Weaver 2-7X rimfire scope. One shot was fired at each power setting from 2X to 7X with no shift in the point of impact.

Most of the discussion presented has been directed toward the rifle shooter, but it need not be so. Handgun shooters have not been ignored by the makers of scopes and mounts. Except for some of the small, short-barreled models, most of the popular handguns are amenable to mounting a scope. The major disadvantage of having a scope on a handgun is that it is no longer compact and convenient to carry. A special holster is needed to hold a scoped handgun, but this is not particularly troublesome to a hunter who is stalking or still-hunting in a woods. Some rimfire handguns are capable of outstanding accuracy, which can be achieved only when a scope is employed. Most of the manufacturers mentioned in connection with rimfire scopes for rifles also have available models for use on handguns. In the case of handgun scopes, there is generally no distinction between those intended for use on centerfire or rimfire handguns because both types of handguns are generally used at similar ranges. There are many fine handgun scopes available from makers such as Simmons, Weaver, Leupold, Bushnell, and others.

Because rimfire rifles produce almost no recoil, the majority of scope mounts have enough strength to hold a scope in place. Three scope-mounting systems are commonly used on rimfire rifles. First, the top of the receiver may have grooves for attaching scope mounts that clamp in the grooves. On rifles made in the U.S. or made elsewhere for the U.S. market, the grooves are 3/8-inch (0.375 inch) apart but in other countries the groove separation is often 11mm (0.433 inch). Many clamp-on scope mounts have enough latitude in movement of the clamps that they will work on rifles having grooves of either width. However, some mounts that are intended for use on rifles having the narrower grooves are held open farther by wider

For accurate shooting, it is hard to beat the combination of the Smith & Wesson 22A topped with a Weaver 1-4X handgun scope.

The Weaver Quad Lock comes in low, medium, and high versions. Four independent straps hold the scope to the bases of the rings.

One of the most famous scope mounts for use on rimfire rifles is the Weaver Tip-Off mount that clamps in the grooves along the receiver.

The Leupold Rifleman mount shown here is sturdy and simple. Each part of the mount contains only two screws.

grooves so that when they are tightened there is a great deal of force on the movable side plate of the clamps. When the locking screw is tightened sufficiently, that part of the mount can be bent because most of the inexpensive mounts made for use on rimfire rifles are made of aluminum. This can draw one end of the scope laterally out of alignment with the bore to such a degree that it may be impossible to sight in the scope. There are many sturdy clamp-on mounts available. One mount that has been marketed for many years is the Weaver Tip-Off mount. Made of steel, this is a proven, durable mount. Leupold produces the Rifleman mount that is made of aluminum, but it does not have a thin side section that can be bent during tightening. Another durable mount is made by Burris. It has a curved, movable side plate, but it is very sturdy. All of these mounts have been used by the author with complete satisfaction.

Because some scopes have large diameter objectives, it is necessary to select a mount that holds the scope high enough to clear the barrel. One mount that will accomplish this is a mount available from Beeman that is intended for use on spring piston air rifles that produce heavy recoil. Although made of aluminum alloy, this massive mount is extremely sturdy and has enough latitude in adjustment to work well on rifles having either 3/8-inch or 11mm grooves. This is the mount chosen by the author when mounting a BSA 3-12 X 44 AO airgun scope on a rimfire rifle. It also provides enough height to allow most scopes to clear the open rear sight.

Although most rimfire rifles are produced with grooved receivers, some are produced with the receivers drilled and tapped to accept separate scope bases to which rings are attached. One type of scope base has been produced by Weaver for many years and such bases are generally known as "Weaver-style" bases. The bases are made to properly fit only on specific rifles

because of the differences in the shapes of the receivers. These bases are used in conjunction with rings available from Weaver and numerous other companies. The Savage B.Mag and 93 G and the Thompson/Center Classic are designed to utilize Weaver style bases. The Ruger American rimfires have receivers that are both grooved and drilled and tapped for attaching scope bases. Some Anschutz rifles have also been produced with grooved receivers that are also drilled and tapped to accept Weaver style bases. This provides maximum versatility in scope mounting systems.

Ruger bolt action rimfire rifles of the Model 77 series have a unique proprietary scope mounting

The massive Beeman mount is extremely sturdy. It provides enough height for large scope objectives to clear the barrel.

Ruger scope mounts clamp in notches on raised sections of the receivers. The tab in the base of each ring fits in a groove to prevent movement of the scope forward or backward.

Mounting a scope on a pump rifle like this Winchester Model 90 is difficult because the top of the action moves and empty cases are ejected upward.

system. The receiver has milled notches and the Ruger scope rings have matching tabs that clamp in those notches. In addition, transverse slots in the top of the receiver accept small tabs that protrude from the bottom of the scope rings so that there is no possibility of the scope shifting forward or backward. Ruger rings are available in three heights (low, medium, and high) in both blue and stainless steel. Although Ruger supplies rings of its own making with its rifles, several other manufacturers also produce rings to fit Ruger rifles. Those used by the author with complete satisfaction include the models from Leupold and Warne.

Although grooved receivers are almost universal, a few rimfire rifles have no such provision for mounting a scope. For example, some pump action rifles have an open top action from which the breech block rises as the slide is operated. Such rifles eject empty cases upward and there is no way to attach a scope mount to the top of the action. However, the Henry pump

rimfire rifle has a closed top receiver that is grooved to accept scope mounts. Because it ejects empty cases out of the side of the receiver, the Henry pump rifle can easily have a scope attached even though the rifle has an external hammer.

Red Dot and Laser Sights

In recent years, a type of optical sight known as a red dot sight has become available and popular. Essentially, a red dot (red is used because it is quickly visible against almost any background) sight projects a battery powered red dot onto a lens. The sight is constructed so that when the shooter looks through the sight the dot can be placed on the target in much the same way as is the reticule of a scope. Moreover, when used correctly there is no parallax involved so sighting becomes as simple as moving the firearm so that the dot aligns with the target. In order to be useful in different lighting conditions, a rheostat is built in so that the brightness of the dot can be varied by turning a dial. Adjustments similar to those on scopes are provided so that the firearm can be sighted in just as when a scope is used, but they provide no magnification. Of course, if the battery dies, the red dot sight is cannot be used.

A red dot sight is usually mounted on a firearm in much the same way as a scope. One model that is available from Simmons is designed specifically for use on firearms having grooved receivers, and it

Weaver-type bases attach to the receiver and the rings clamp to the bases.

comes with an integral mount that clamps directly in the grooves. However, in most cases, it is necessary to have a base or bases to which the red dot sight can be attached. Because the Weaver-style base is so common, some red dot sights come with a rail along the bottom that can be attached to the base.

The basic idea behind the use of a red dot sight is that the bright dot can be located quickly on the target and there are only two things to align, the dot and the target. Obviously, the dot covers part of the target. For many of the more common sights, the coverage of the dot is three minutes of angle (3 MOA), but for others it may be 4 or 6 MOA. Dots of these sizes cover 1.5, 2, and 3 inches on a target at a distance of 50 yards. As a result, the red dot sight is not going to be used when firing at a target 50 yards away to get the smallest group. The red dot is a popular sight for International Practical Shooting Confederation (IPSC) events, which involve speed and accuracy in handgun firing.

The word LASER is the acronym that comes from Light Amplification by Stimulated Emission of Radiation. In recent years, small lasers have been developed that project a small beam of light that is usually red or green in color. It was inevitable that someone would originate the idea that if the laser were attached to a firearm and adjusted so that the beam and the bullet path coincide, the laser beam could be used in sighting. Moreover, the beam can be seen in the dark so the sight would be effective for shooting in the dark. This has obvious advantages for law enforcement and military tactics and possibly for self defense. A large fraction of the handguns produced, including many rimfire models, have an integral rail below the barrel specifically for mounting laser sights or compact flashlights.

From the point of view of the author, there is little justification for shooting a rimfire firearm in the dark. Recreational and sport shooting are not normally done in the dark. Target competition is conducted in daylight or on lighted ranges. However, the primary reason for leaving laser sights to another forum deals with safety issues. Lasers are inherently dangerous and come with warning labels attached. When shined into an eye,

Brightness of the red dot is controlled by a rheostat that has eleven brightness settings.

The Simmons red dot can be adjusted for windage and elevation by means of adjustment screws that are similar to those used on scopes.

Red dot sights are popular especially for use on handguns. This Simmons model is inexpensive but effective.

This Smith & Wesson 22A has a Sightron 4R33 red dot sight attached, which makes accurate shooting possible.

This small laser sight is attached to the rail on a Ruger SR22.

there is no sensation of pain although irreparable damage is being done. Furthermore, the damage may be done very quickly. Laser pointers are very common and inexpensive. Having seen the complete ignorance demonstrated by children allowed to play with laser pointers, it seems incredible that we would want to mount a laser on a rimfire firearm of the type often used by young shooters. Laser sights have their place, but they must be used carefully.

LaserMax CP-1022 Laser

Laser sights have become much more popular in recent years, especially on handguns. Some are so small that they are incorporated into the grip panels in such a way that there is no protruding lump either on or below the barrel. Models are also available that replace the guide rods in semiautomatic handguns. Ever looking to expand options available on rimfire rifles, Ruger has partnered with LaserMax® to produce a laser sight known as the CP-1022 specifically for the immensely popular 10/22. One version of the Ruger 10/22 comes equipped with the CP-1022, but it can also be mounted on the standard Carbine and Take-down versions that have a barrel band. As a result, this sight will be described in rather more detail.

The LaserMax CP-1022 sight has the laser mounted in a barrel band assembly that replaces the original. As a result, the sight does not change the overall configuration of the rifle. The laser is turned on or off by means of a switch that is activated by moving a bar laterally. The housing of the CP-1022 is made of black polymer so it complements the composite stocks well. Power for the laser is supplied by a 1/3N lithium battery.

As in the case of other red laser sights, the wavelength is 635 nm. Literature supplied with the Laser-Max CP-1022 indicates that the beam is visible up to 100 yards and that may be possible in low ambient light. However, this sight will be most effective at considerably shorter ranges. The instructions also indicate that the laser is set for a distance of 25 yards. After mounting the sight, a target was placed at 25 yards and the first five-shot group was very close to the center of the bull.

LaserMax produces a laser sight that replaces the barrel band on the Ruger 10/22 Carbine.

When the LaserMax sight was installed, this nice five-shot group was obtained at 25 yards.

If sight adjustment is necessary, that can easily be accomplished with the CP-1022. A small hole on the bottom of the sight contains a screw that can be turned with a small Allen wrench that is supplied with the sight. Elevation changes are made by turning this screw. Windage is adjusted in a similar way by turning a small screw located on the right hand side of the sight. After the laser sight is adjusted carefully, it can be used to adjust either open sights or a scope by making the points of aim coincide. The LaserMax CP-1022 is available on certain Ruger 10/22 models or as a separate item. This interesting sight has the MSRP of $129.95 but can usually be found at retail for about $80-85.

Majestic Arms "Instant Optics"

It is not uncommon for shooters to want to achieve greater accuracy with a firearm. Scopes have long been commonly used on rifles, but scopes and red dot sights are also suitable for use on handguns. For some shooters, it may seem that attaching a mounting system and optical device and sighting it in is a complex process. In some cases it can be. However, almost all rifles and several handguns are marketed with some provision for attaching a scope or red dot sight. The receiver may already be drilled and tapped to attach scope bases or the handgun may have a rail for mounting auxiliary sights. Ruger Mark III autoloading pistols are drilled and tapped to attach the scope base provided with the pistols. Smith & Wesson pistols in the 22A series have a rail that runs full length of the receiver and barrel. Scope bases are readily available for attaching to the Browning Buck Mark making it easy to mount a scope.

It would seem to be a simple process to remove the filler screws from the receiver of a Ruger pistol and fasten a base to which rings can be attached. Then the optical device with rings attached could be fastened to the base. Let us suppose that a red dot sight is to be mounted on a Ruger Mark III rimfire. The steps described will result in the sight being mounted on the gun. However, as a result in variations in scope rails, rings, gun parts, and where the adjustments of the sight may be set, there is no telling where the bullets will hit the target when the first shots are fired.

It would be convenient if the equipment and process of mounting the sight were such that the sighting in was essentially complete when the sight is mounted. Dino Longueira of Majestic Arms (Staten Island, NY) has solved that problem for the owner of a Ruger Mark III pistol. By utilizing a carefully machined Ruger receiver, Picatinny scope rail, Weaver Grand Slam® quick-detachable rings and a Bushnell Trophy red dot sight, Majestic Arms offers a complete package (dubbed by the author as "instant optics") that is previously adjusted so that simply attaching it to the pistol results in the first shots hitting close to the point of aim on a target placed 25 yards away. Only minor adjustment will be needed to finish the sighting in process.

Majestic Arms Instant Optics packages with the Bushnell Trophy red dot sight include units for both the Ruger 10/22 rifle (shown) and Mark III pistol.

Testing of the Majestic Arms optics packages showed that they performed extremely well.

The Majestic Arms red dot handgun package was mounted on the author's Ruger Mark III Target model that has a heavy 5.5-inch barrel. After placing a target at 25 yards, a five-shot group was fired from a bench with the pistol supported on a rest. The result was a small group that was clustered close to the center of the target. The Majestic Arms package performed exactly as it was designed and advertised to do.

In addition to the "instant optics" package for the Ruger Mark III, Majestic Arms offers a scope and mounting hardware for the Ruger 10/22. In this case, the package consists of a scope rail, a Weaver Grand Slam® Quick Detachable rings, and a 4-12 X 40 AO Bushnell Banner scope or a Bushnell Trophy red dot sight. Preliminary sighting in has already been done so that when the scope or red dot is mounted the shots will hit close to the point of aim. Both of the Majestic Arms instant optics rifle packages were tested on the author's customized Ruger 10/22 at 25 yards while shooting from a bench. Firing five shots with each resulted in small groups that were clustered very close to the point of aim.

When tested on both a handgun and rifle the Majestic Arms "instant optics" packages performed extremely well and exactly as described. Originally offered for the Ruger Mark III and 10/22, packages are being developed for other popular firearms. If a shooter wishes to avoid some of the hassle of mounting an optical sight and sighting it in, the Majestic Arms sight systems provide relief. To read more about the equipment and products offered, visit www.majesticarms.com.

Never before has the rimfire shooter had so many options for equipping a rifle or handgun with sights. There are sights available for any type of shooting and virtually any type of firearm.

CHAPTER 6

RIMFIRE AMMUNITION IN NON-MAGNUM CALIBERS

MODERN MANUFACTURING TECHNOLOGY is the basis for the high quality rimfire ammunition available today. The basic materials of cartridge construction consist of lead, brass, nitrocellulose propellant, and lead styphnate in the primer, and this has been the situation for many years. However, the array of rimfire ammunition available today includes products that were not dreamed of only a few years ago. Having shot .22 rimfires for approximately 70 years, the author is amazed at the variety of ammunition that is currently produced. In this chapter, we will attempt to give an overview of the ammunition offerings from many companies, both domestic and foreign. How well the author remember when as a young lad a rimfire shooter bought the yellow box labeled Winchester, the green box labeled Remington, or the blue box labeled Federal. CCI did not begin to produce rimfire ammunition until 1963, but now produces an extensive line of products some of which are among the most innovative in the field. Although some of the foreign producers of ammunition were in business many years ago, their products were seldom seen. The situation now is quite different from what it was in the days when the author was but a lad.

The Sporting Arms and Ammunition Manufacturers Institute (known as SAAMI) provides standardization of ammunition so that specifications are nominally uniform from one manufacturer to another. Test procedures are also standardized according to SAAMI specifications so that all ammunition makers are testing the same characteristics by the same techniques (barrel lengths, dimensions, etc.). Firearms are tested with overloads (proof loads), and SAAMI specifies those procedures as well as the standard dimensions for chambers and bores. If the specification for a .22 LR with a high velocity load is a velocity of 1,255 ft/

Ammunition in .22 LR is produced all over the world.

sec, that velocity or one very close to it will generally be specified for loads from other manufacturers. Sometimes there are minor variations because the hollow point bullet produced by one company weighs 37 grains whereas that from another firm weighs 36 or 38 grains. One finds that the performance data from most ammunition manufacturers are rather uniform. Of course, bullet designs, bullet lubricants, etc. vary from one company to another.

Rimfire ammunition is produced all over the world. There are literally hundreds of types loaded by dozens of loading companies both foreign and domestic. In this chapter, several specific types of ammunition will be described, but this is in no way a complete catalog of the offerings worldwide. Generally, if a particular load is produced by one manufacturer, a different company will offer a similar product. In some ways, the products described in this chapter reflect wide availability rather than an attempt at being globally inclusive. In most cases, the types of ammunition described are those with which the author has had first hand experience. Some of the ideas discussed in this chapter will be revisited in later chapters because

A Summary of Non-Magnum Rimfire Ammunition Types*

CARTRIDGE	BULLET TYPE	WT. GR.	VEL, FT/SEC MUZ./100 YD	E, FT LB MUZ./100 YD	NOTES
.17 Aguila	JHP	20	1,850/1,353	152/81	A, PMC
.17 Mach 2	JPT	17	2,100/1,510	166/88	H, CCI, E
.22 Short CB	SRN	29	710/581	32/27	CCI
.22 Short	SRN	29	830/679	44/30	CCI TGT.
.22 Short	SRN	29	1,095/903	77/52	A, CCI, R
.22 Short	HP	27	1,105/879	73/46	CCI
.22 Long CB	SRN	29	710/581	32/22	CCI
.22 Long	SRN	29	1,215/922	95/55	CCI
.22 Long	SRN	20	375/183	6/--	A Colibri
.22 Long	SRN	20	500/---	11/---	A S. Colibri
.22 Long Rifle	HP	38	1,000/854	84/62	PMC Mod.
.22 Long Rifle	HP	38	1,050/901	93/69	R, E Sub.S.
.22 Long Rifle	SRN	40	1,050/---	98/---	Wolf MT
.22 Long Rifle	SRN	40	1,033/---	95/---	Wolf Match
.22 Long Rifle	SRN	40	1,080/930	105/75	Most Mfrs.
.22 Long Rifle	SRN	40	1,150/976	117/85	W T22
.22 Long Rifle	HP	38	1,280/1,020	140/90	Most Mfrs.
.22 Long Rifle	SRN	40	1,255/1,020	140/93	Most Mfrs.
.22 Long Rifle	SRN	40	1,312/1,100	154/107	E
.22 Long Rifle	HP	37.5	1,312/1,100	143/100	E
.22 Long Rifle	HP	40	1,280/1,001	146/89	W P.P.
.22 Long Rifle	STC	36	1,410/1,056	159/89	R Viper
.22 Long Rifle	HPTC	33	1,500/1,075	165/85	R Yel.Jkt.
.22 Long Rifle	HP	32	1,640/1,124	191/90	CCI Stgr.
.22 Long Rifle	HP	40	1,435/1,112	183/110	CCI Vctr.
.22 Long Rifle	SFP	40	1,235/1,015	135/91	CCI SGB
.22 Long Rifle	HP	30	1,750/1,191	204/95	A
.22 Long Rifle	SRN	30	1,750/1,191	204/95	A
.22 Long Rifle	SRN	48	1,040/904	115/90	L Scoremax
.22 Long Rifle	SRN	60	950/802	120/86	A SSS

*In some cases such as that of the 40-grain round nose .22 LR, the high velocity load is listed as 1,235, 1,250, 1,255, or 1,260 depending on the manufacturer. These are not considered as constituting different loadings. Velocities for the standard velocity .22 LR are given as 1,050, 1,070, 1,080, or 1,085 depending on the manufacturer.

Abbreviations: SRN=solid round nose; SFP=solid flat point; HP=hollow point; STC=solid truncated cone; HPTC=hollow point truncated cone; JPT=jacketed polymer tip; JHP=jacketed hollow point; JSP=jacketed soft point; FMJ=full metal jacket; TGT=target.

Notes: Most Mfr. indicates that this load or one very similar to it is offered by most manufacturers. A=Aguila; CCI=CCI; E=Eley; F=Federal; H=Hornady; L=Lapua R=Remington; W=Winchester; PMC=PMC; Vctr.=Velocitor; Stgr.=Stinger; SGB=small game bullet; P.P.=power point; Mod=Moderator; MT=Match Target; Sub. S.= Subsonic, SSS=Sniper SubSonic.

rimfire ammunition is a central theme in a book such as this. It should be mentioned that there has been a shortage of rimfire ammunition for some time so describing what is *manufactured* is not the same as what is *available*.

Selection

In the history of rimfire ammunition presented in Chapter 1, a brief discussion of several of the currently popular calibers was given. In this section, we will give an overview of what the various ammunition manufacturers are producing in those calibers. Before we progress to a discussion of specific calibers, there should be an overview presented of the types of rimfire ammunition currently being shown in catalogs. An attempt has been made to reduce this information to a single table although the offerings of many manufacturers, especially foreign ones, were not studied. The summary of the types of rimfire ammunition available is presented in the accompanying table. Actual velocity data from testing and factors affecting velocity will be discussed in Chapter 8.

For many years, the author did exactly what a large number of rimfire shooters do. He went to a couple of local stores in small towns and surveyed the ammunition available on the shelves. Eventually, after studying the ammunition catalogs from several companies, it became apparent that there were many options that had never been previously considered. For example, there are some ammunition makers that produce a complete line of products whereas others may produce only two or three types. On the national scene, the best-known producers are CCI, Federal, Winchester, and Remington. On the other hand, large importers of foreign made rimfire ammunition include Wolf, PMC, and Aguila among others. When added to offerings from the famous international makers such as Lapua, RWS, Eley, CIL (Canada) and Baikal, it becomes apparent just how enormous the number of rimfire products has become. Most sporting goods stores will carry several types of rimfire ammunition, but you can be sure that many other types of cartridges are available.

The table contains an enormous amount of information, especially when one considers that there are actually a very large number of target loads manufactured around the world all of which utilize a 40-grain solid bullet with a muzzle velocity of around 1,080 ft/sec and are thus represented by a single row in the table. In some cases, the entry is for a single load. For example, the Lapua Scoremax (which has now been discontinued) is unique in that it employs a 48-grain solid lead bullet. Similarly, the Aguila Sniper Subsonic (SSS) is loaded with a 60-grain solid bullet. With the table containing a summary of the relevant data for ammunition in non-magnum rimfire calibers, we will now progress to a discussion of each cartridge. As it turns out, the order of discussing the cartridges is in the order of their historical development as it progresses through the series from the .22 Short, Long, and Long Rifle calibers.

Projectiles

When the author became a rimfire shooter, one had a choice of ammunition with solid round nose bullets or hollow points. There were two velocity levels, standard velocity and high velocity, but hollow pointed bullets were usually available only in high velocity rounds. If there were other options, the author knew nothing about them for many years. Today, those early types of projectiles are still available, but so are many others. Standard velocity ammunition is often used for target shooting. The author participated as a member of a very successful Air Force ROTC rifle team, and the equipment used consisted of Winchester Model 52D target rifles and Federal standard velocity ammunition. The loading companies have optimized the velocity of that load so that the bullets travel at velocities that are lower than the velocity of sound. As a projectile (or airplane) goes through the sound barrier, there are shock waves that build up on the nose. This causes some instability in the bullet's flight, which can reduce accuracy. Consequently,

The Lapua Scoremax has a 48-grain bullet while the Aguila SSS utilizes a 60-grain projectile in a short case.

Remington target loads represent a joint offering with Eley.

is available from PMC including Scoremaster and Match Rifle loads, which have 40-grain round nose solid bullets. Both of these gave good accuracy in the rifles tested, as did the Wolf Match Target. Unlike the Wolf centerfire ammunition that is made in Russia, the Wolf Match Target rimfire ammunition is made in Germany. A great deal more will be said about this load in Chapter 14. In addition to the products listed, outstanding ammunition is produced by RWS, Eley, Aguila, Lapua, and others. The problem is one of availability because you simply can not walk into your local "mart" and find most of these brands. For almost all of the types just mentioned, the muzzle velocity is approximately 1,080-1,150 ft/sec.

types of .22 LR ammunition intended for target use are loaded to subsonic velocities. Minor variations may be present in the profiles of projectiles from different manufacturers. In some cases, the highest quality target ammunition offered by a company is really nothing more than lots of the standard velocity load that are particularly uniform. Just as the old Federal load showed the author long ago, some of the most accurate types of ammunition tested in this work were the standard velocity, solid bullet loads. A check of the results displayed in Chapter 14 will confirm this conclusion. In most of the rifles tested, the CCI Standard Velocity ammunition was very accurate with the Winchester T22 being very close in performance in some rifles. These loads should always be tried if you are searching for ammunition that gives high accuracy at a lower cost than the special ammunition used in high level competition.

Also among the types of standard velocity ammunition with the 40-grain solid point bullet that should be tried when searching for highest accuracy are CCI Green Tag and Federal Gold Medal Target (Federal product number 711B). After being discontinued for a time, Federal Ultra Match is once again available at retail for around $20-25 per box. The Federal 711B load is a standard velocity round, but it is essentially a target load that sells for a retail price of approximately $4.00 per box. This ammunition also exhibited outstanding accuracy in some of the rifles tested. Target ammunition is also available from Remington in the load known simply as Remington Target (Product Number 6122). In a liaison with the renowned Eley company in England, Remington markets three grades of target ammunition. These are the Target Rifle, Club Xtra, and Match EPS in the order of increasing quality (and price). This is really excellent ammunition for the target shooter. A wide variety of rimfire ammunition

Although the emphasis in this discussion has been with regard to accuracy, the standard velocity .22 LR should also be considered as a hunting load. The rationale is simply that such ammunition gives good accuracy (often superb accuracy) so it is easier to put the bullet in the desired location on the target. Strange as it may seem, bullets from standard velocity .22 LR loads are not affected as much by wind as are the high velocity ones. In the author's old Winchester 190 semiautomatic, the best accuracy obtained when several types of ammunition were tested was with the CCI Standard Velocity. The average group size using this load in both a Ruger 10/22 and a 10/22T was well under an inch. With this type of accuracy, it is easy to perform sniping on pests and small game. Penetration by the relatively slow moving solid bullets is outstanding.

The CCI SGB cartridges offer the small game hunter a flat pointed projectile for greater impact.

High velocity ammunition is also produced with 40-grain solid bullets. In fact, this may be the most popular type, and prices cover a broad spectrum. Federal Champion (which was formerly known as Lightning) can sometimes be found for approximately $3.00 per box. In the same price range are the Winchester bulk loads known as 222, 333, and 555 (indicating the number of rounds in the container), as well as bulk packs from CCI, Federal, and Remington. These "price leader" loads may perform well in some

Although the velocity of the 60-grain bullet from the Aguila SSS load is low, it is a useful cartridge.

rifles, and they certainly should be tested to find out. If one or more of them give good accuracy in your rifle or handgun, by all means use them. The author particularly likes to shoot such ammunition in a handgun because gilt-edge accuracy is not particularly important given his ability with a handgun.

Moving up in price, one finds the Federal, Winchester, Remington, CCI, PMC, and other brands loaded with the 40-grain bullets. Some brands have bullets that are copper plated rather than uncoated, lubricated lead. As with any other type of ammunition, the major concern is accuracy in your particular firearm. One should never hesitate to choose any of these loads when sniping varmints or hunting small game as long as it has been determined in advance that they are accurate in the rifle being used. There is no substitute for the confidence that comes from firing consistently small groups with your rifle and ammunition.

Solid bullets are not always of the round nose variety. CCI produces a load known as the SGB® (Small Game Bullet) that contains a 40-grain flat point lead bullet. On impact, the flat point bullet produces a greater shock effect than that resulting from a round nose bullet. The result is produced without the destructive effect and with greater penetration than given by a hollow point bullet. Moreover, this load has shown excellent accuracy in several rifles. Being a specialty load, the price is somewhat higher.

Aguila produces a load known as the SSS (SubSonic Sniper) that utilizes a 60-grain solid point bullet. To produce a round having the SAAMI overall length for a .22 LR, the long bullet requires a shorter case than that normally used in .22 LR cartridges. Consequently, the SSS load may not function reliably in some rifle actions. Nominal muzzle velocity is only 950 ft/sec, but the heavy bullet gives excellent penetration. Some writers have reported that accuracy of this load may not be acceptable in all firearms. This is not surprising because with a rifling twist of one turn in 16 inches the slow moving, heavy bullet may not be adequately

stabilized, which could affect accuracy.

During the testing of a large quantity of ammunition comprising a considerable number of types, one load that the author had never used before became a favorite. The European firm, Lapua, produces some of the finest rimfire ammunition available. One type that was formerly produced is known as Lapua Scoremax, and it was loaded with a 48-grain solid bullet. This load was intended for target use, specifically silhouette shooting in which a heavy blow is needed to knock over the metal animal. Not only is a heavy blow needed, the ammunition must deliver target-grade accuracy. In keeping with its special nature, Scoremax was not cheap. The author has several boxes in reserve for special circumstances.

Hyper velocity loads for the .22 LR have become popular. Shown here (left to right) are the CCI Stinger, Winchester Expediter, Federal Spitfire, Winchester Super-Max, Winchester Superspeed, Remington Yellow Jacket, and Remington Viper. Some of these are no longer available.

As was described briefly in Chapter 1, the hyper velocity loads in .22 LR have become very popular. All make use of lighter bullets propelled by larger charges of slower burning powders to achieve velocities of approximately 1,500-1,650 ft/sec. With hollow point bullets at high velocity, the hyper velocity loads produce dramatic effects at short ranges. However, the point of impact of the bullets from hyper velocity loads is frequently quite different from that of heaver, slower bullets from ordinary rounds. Do not buy a box of hyper velocity ammunition and go hunting without sighting in your rifle with that ammunition. Accuracy has never been a strong point with hyper velocity loads, so do some accuracy

The CCI Stinger on the left has a case that is longer than that of the standard .22 LR.

testing with this type of ammunition before you depend on it to bring home your next meal.

Another innovative bullet design from CCI is known as the Quik-Shok®. Loaded in a longer case like that used for the Stinger, the Quik-Shok bullet weighs 32 grains and has a muzzle velocity of 1,640 ft/sec. However, the bullet is designed to break into four pieces on impact to maximize the devastation on pests. As in the case of the lightweight bullets used in other hyper velocity loads, the bullet used in the Quik-Shok loses its velocity rapidly.

The .22 Short

Being the original .22 rimfire, the .22 Short has the distinction of having been in continuous production longer than any other cartridge (disregarding BB and CB caps which contain no powder). That span is approximately one and one-half centuries! However, the .22 Short is less popular now that it was in former times. About the only firearms produced specifically for the .22 Short today are some specialty target pistols and a couple of models of tiny autoloading handguns. Many years ago, Winchester produced the Model 1890 pump rifle and the Model 74 autoloader that were chambered for the .22 Short only. Browning produced the sleek Model SA22 autoloader in .22 Short. In some cases, these rifles were known as "gallery specials" because of their use in shooting galleries. The author can well remember how the county fair always had a shooting gallery, and how he once won a small lamp for knocking over some number of consecutive targets. As the world has become more civilized, such activities are no longer tolerated.

The use of the .22 Short in chambers designed for the .22 LR is often discouraged by someone on the grounds that the shorter cartridge will lead to corrosion that will make chambering the longer cartridge difficult. All the author can offer on this

Although the .22 Short (left) is not as popular as the .22 Long Rifle, it is a useful cartridge.

point is that if it were to happen it would take a lot of firing of the .22 Short to cause a problem. All that is required is to brush the residue out of the chamber with a nylon brush wet with a powder solvent. Having said that, it must be conceded that .22 Shorts fired in a .22 LR chamber do not normally give highest accuracy. The bullet from the shorter cartridge must jump some distance before it gets to the rifling, which usually is detrimental to accuracy. Although this is one factor, there is another that is likely to be equally important. The stubby little 29-grain bullet used in the .22 Short requires less spin to stabilize it in flight than does the longer 40-grain bullet used in a .22 LR. The rate of twist used in .22 LR barrels is one turn in 16 inches whereas the optimum twist for the .22 Short bullet is about one turn in 21 inches. Therefore, the short bullet is over stabilized in barrels with the faster twist. Firearms designed specifically for the .22 Short normally have the slower twist that is optimum for the cartridge.

Current offerings in the .22 Short are not nearly as extensive as are those for the .22 LR. Winchester, Remington, and CCI produce .22 Short ammunition with a 29-grain solid point bullet that has a nominal muzzle velocity of 1,095 ft/sec and an energy of 77 ft lbs. Aguila, Eley, and RWS also produce .22 Short ammunition including some that is intended for target shooting. Although this power level certainly looks puny, keep in mind that this is almost exactly the remaining energy given by a bullet from the .17 HMR at a range of 200 yards, and some people seem to think that it is a good load for coyotes at that range! When of all the species taken by the author with an old Winchester 90 pump using .22 Shorts are remembered, there is never tendency to take this round lightly. If an air rifle firing a .177-caliber pellet weighing 7.9 grains at 1,000 ft/sec can be used to hunt pests and small game, think about the possibilities when using a .22 Short that has a larger diameter bullet weighing almost four times as much traveling at the same velocity.

The .22 Long

The .22 Long makes use of the same 29-grain bullet as is used in the .22 Short at approximately the same velocity so is suited to the same uses as the Short. As of this writing, CCI seems to be the only U.S. producer of the .22 Long and that load has a 29-grain solid bullet at an advertised muzzle velocity of 1,215 ft/sec and a muzzle energy of 95 ft lbs. Although most stores that sell rimfire ammunition do not carry the Long, there is little reason to try to find it because it is not a

The Aguila Colibri and Super Colibri cartridges make use of 20-grain bullets that are propelled only by the priming.

The .22 Long (middle) offers little power advantage over the .22 Short and generally does not give the accuracy of the .22 LR.

better cartridge than the .22 Short and does not even approach the .22 LR. One advantage, a minor one, is that the case length of the Long is identical to that of the Long Rifle so there is no likelihood that a ring can be produced in the chamber as a result of firing a cartridge having a shorter case.

Aguila produces two rounds, the Colibri and Super Colibri, that make use of the Long/Long Rifle case containing 20-grain bullets that are propelled by the priming mixture (they are "*sans poudre*"). These are low velocity loads that are intended for exterminating small vermin or shooting indoors in a suitable place with a suitable backstop. The Colibri and Super Colibri have essentially the same power as some airguns. The boxes of the lower powered Colibri cartridges carry the warning that they are not for use in *rifles* because having such low power there is a chance that the bullet would become lodged in the barrel.

The .22 Long Rifle

If there is a universal cartridge, it surely must be the .22 Long Rifle. Loaded throughout the world, the .22 LR is used for recreation, sport shooting, and hunting. It is also the basis for several shooting sports that are designed specifically for the use of rimfire firearms. Originally produced with a 40-grain lead bullet propelled by a charge of five grains of black powder, the .22 LR has undergone enormous changes over the lifetime of the cartridge, which is well over a century. The .22 LR has reached an almost unbelievable state of technical development, and the number of ammunition types is quite large. This discussion is rather an expansion of that presented earlier under the heading of projectiles.

Probably the most commonly encountered type of .22 LR ammunition (in terms of number of stores that carry it and the number of rounds expended annually) is the high velocity load that utilizes a 40-grain solid bullet at a nominal velocity of 1,225-1,275 ft/sec depending on the manufacturer. Current offerings include the

Bullets in .22 LR caliber usually have the shape of either a round nose or a truncated cone.

economical Federal Champion, Remington Thunderbolt, CCI Blaser, and Winchester Wildcat varieties that are the promotional price leaders at right around $3.00 per box. However, the regular varieties of this loading that sell for about $4.00 per box are also available from numerous manufacturers. The hollow point high velocity load has a bullet that weights 36-38 grains and a muzzle velocity of approximately 1,275 ft/sec. These loads have been the mainstay of the small game hunter, pest shooter, and plinker for many years.

Another of the ubiquitous .22 LR loads is the 40-grain solid bullet loaded to so-called standard velocity, which is around 1,050-1,100 ft/sec depending on the manufacturer. Prominent among this type of load are the Federal Gold Medal Target (Load No. 711B), Remington Target, CCI Standard Velocity, Wolf Match Target, and numerous others. Some of these types carry the designation as "target" loads even though they may not sell for a premium price as do

Ammunition like the Federal Ultra Match and Lapua Midas loads are intended for use in competitive shooting.

the cartridges intended for high level target shooting. The T22 from Winchester is essentially a standard velocity type although with a velocity of 1,150 ft/sec it is actually more of an intermediate between the high and standard velocity rounds. Some rifles give accuracy with standard velocity ammunition that rivals that given with the highest quality target ammunition, which is intended for competitive shooting. This will be clear from the test results presented in Chapter 14. The accuracy of standard velocity ammunition comes as no surprise to the author after using it for competitive shooting in a Winchester 52D.

At the upper end of the ammunition spectrum there are several types of ammunition that are intended for target competition at the highest levels. These include Federal Ultra Match, Eley Tenex, Lapua Midas, Winchester Supreme, and similar loads from other manufacturers. A price of $20-30 per box is not unusual for ammunition of this degree of excellence. In many instances, the velocity matches that of the standard velocity load, which makes it possible to practice with a lower cost round then to switch to the high level target loads for use in competition. Although the intended use of the high priced target ammunition is for competitive shooting, many hunters using rimfire rifles choose to use this type of ammunition because of its outstanding accuracy. Careful, accurate bullet placement is more important than the additional 100-150 ft/sec velocity given by high velocity loads. Having seen how some of rifles perform with the standard velocity and target cartridges, the author has begun to consider target loads for small game hunting.

The handgun shooter has not been forgotten. Several ammunition manufacturers such as RWS, CCI, and Eley produce .22 LR ammunition specifically for pistol competition. In fact, Eley produces a complete line of pistol ammunition.

There are a few types of .22 LR ammunition that

deserve special mention. The author and many other rimfire shooters lament the fact that Lapua Scoremax has been discontinued. Why have they been so impressed with Lapua Scoremax? First and foremost, in a bolt action Ruger 77/22 with an old Weaver K-10 scope attached, the average size for five 5-shot groups at 50 yards was only 0.60-inch and the smallest was only 0.46-inch! With that level of accuracy, the target will be hit if the author does his part. Second, the heavy 48-grain bullet gives real smash and penetration on game. From the 22-inch barrel of my Ruger 77/22, the average velocity at eight feet from the muzzle is 1,042 ft/sec, which corresponds to an energy of 117 ft lbs. Keep in mind that this is a bullet that is 20% heavier than the usual weight for solid .22 LR bullets, and as a result it is not as prone to deflection by wind nor does it lose its velocity as rapidly as do 40-grain bullets. Lapua Scormax is a superb load.

Hyper velocity ammunition has become quite popular in recent years. Following the introduction of the CCI Stinger in 1977, other types of cartridges appeared that made use of bullets weighing 29-35 grains pushed by larger charges of slower burning powder. With velocities in the 1,500-1,700 range, the trajectory is less curved, and the lightweight bullets give explosive results on small game and varmints at short range. One negative factor related to hyper velocity ammunition is that accuracy is not always as good as with some of the more pedestrian loads. Of the hyper velocity rounds, the Remington Yellow Jacket is a favorite of the author for several reasons. First, the Yellow Jacket does not utilize a case that is longer than the conventional .22 LR. The longer cases used in some hyper velocity loads can engage the rifling in match-type chambers. Second, they seem to give better accuracy in

Shot cartridges have been popular for many years. The CCI load uses a plastic shot capsule while the Winchester and Remington varieties employ the crimped case.

some of my rifles than do other hyper velocity loads. Third, the 33-grain bullet has enough mass to impart a significant blow and the large hollow cavity assures expansion. Even with the desirable features of hyper velocity loads, the fact remains that the lightweight bullets lose velocity rapidly so their advantage is lost if the range is longer than about 75 yards.

Although not listed in the table, .22 LR cartridges loaded with No. 12 shot are available for dispatching small vermin and birds at short (no, make that very short) range. Fired from a rifled barrel, the shot spreads quickly so that an effective pattern is not maintained beyond the range of a dozen or so feet. The CCI shot cartridges have the shot load contained in a plastic case that is loaded in the same manner as a bullet. Shot cartridges from other manufacturers have the shot load held a long case that is crimped at the top. Except for revolvers in which the shot cartridges work very well, shot cartridges must be used in a single shot mode, and they may not eject reliably from autoloaders.

The .17 Mach 2

Necking down an existing case to hold a bullet of smaller diameter has long been an honorable pastime for cartridge designers. The .243 Winchester case is that of the .308 Winchester necked to hold a bullet of 0.243-inch diameter and a .25-06 Remington utilizes a .30-06 Springfield case necked to hold a 0.257-inch bullet. If necking the .22 WMR case to hold a 0.172-inch diameter bullet is successful, why not neck a .22 LR to hold a bullet of that diameter? While we are at it, let us use the case of the CCI Stinger because it is slightly longer than that of the .22 LR and then a slightly greater powder charge can be used. The result produced by Hornady is the cartridge known as the .17 Mach 2 so named because it gives a velocity that is close to twice the velocity of sound. This cartridge was also given a flying start because most firearms chambered for the .22 LR (and that is an enormous number!) can be made into .17 Mach 2 pieces simply by changing the barrel. There is a problem with certain autoloaders because the .17 Mach 2 uses a larger charge of slower burning powder than the .22 LR, which results in the pressure staying high for a longer period of time. This causes the bolt to be driven back at a velocity that may exceed the design limit of the rifle and could damage the firearm.

As of this writing in early 2016, the only .17 Mach 2 load available is with a 17-grain Hornady V-Max® polymer tipped bullet that gives a muzzle velocity

The .17 Mach 2 cartridge makes use of a case having the same length as the CCI Stinger .22 LR round.

of 2,100 ft/sec, which corresponds to an energy of 166 ft lbs. The ammunition is available only with the Hornady brand although loads carrying CCI and Eley labels were formerly available. With a velocity of 2,100 ft/sec, the trajectory is sufficiently flat to make hits on small targets possible at ranges up to 125 yards or so at which range the velocity is 1,756 ft/sec and the energy 75 ft lb. Accuracy is reported to be superb for this cartridge, which should allow it to be an excellent choice for small pests. The .17 Mach 2 started fast, but its popularity has decreased almost as quickly and only Hornady ammunition is now available.

The .17 Aguila

If necking a CCI Stinger case to hold a 0.172-inch bullet produced a useful cartridge, why not neck the standard length .22 LR case in the same way? That is precisely the origin of the cartridge that is known as the .17 Aguila. The load consists of a 20-grain hollow point bullet that produces a nominal muzzle velocity of 1,850 ft/sec. This makes the .17 Aguila only slightly less powerful than the .17 Mach 2, and it is suitable for the same purposes.

One advantage of the .17 Aguila is that as a result of the powder charge being smaller than that used in the longer-cased .17 Mach 2, the pressure does not remain as high for as long a period so the back thrust on the bolt is lower. Accordingly, it is possible to add a barrel chambered for the .17 Aguila to most autoloader

The .17 Aguila load is based on the .22 LR case of standard length necked to hold a .17-caliber bullet.

actions that work for the .22 LR. This is of no consequence for bolt action rifles or revolvers in which the longer .17 Mach 2 works satisfactorily. Whether the .17 Aguila will achieve and maintain much popularity remains to be seen. It is interesting to note that in early 2016 Aguila has announced that it will produce .17 Aguila ammunition.

Matching the Ammunition to the Target

No one wishing to hunt bear with a .30-06 Springfield would go to a sporting goods store and say, "I want a box of .30-06 ammunition." If you did, you might be sold a box of 125-grain soft points (in former times it could have been 110-grain bullets) that are better suited to varmint hunting. The bear hunter would likely select one of the .30-06 loads with 165-180 grain bullets, perhaps of premium construction. The rimfire shooter should also give some serious atten-

tion to the anticipated use of his or her firearm before utilizing ammunition that is unsuitable.

If there is one aspect of rimfire ammunition availability that has changed over the years it is in having the ability to select a type of ammunition for specific purposes. This will be discussed in more detail in Chapter 10, but the general principles will be discussed here. It must be said at the outset, regardless of the type of ammunition and projectile, the primary requirement is being able to place that projectile in a location where it can achieve its potential effect. Accuracy is paramount in rimfire shooting. After all, that is what rifle shooting in the sporting sense is all about. It is why most of us try to select an accurate rifle and add sighting equipment to enable us to achieve that high degree of accuracy. So before you look at ballistics tables from ammunition manufacturers and decide that you want to use the XYZ Pest Popper on your next prairie dog shoot, by all means get a couple of boxes and do some testing. You may find that a four-inch group at 50 yards precludes your doing good work with your rifle even if the Pest Popper has a devastating blow.

Target shooters who shoot paper targets for score (silhouette shooting is a somewhat different matter) want the most accurate ammunition available. Power is not required and may even be detrimental in shooting paper targets. Trappers who may have to dispatch animals often use the least destructive load available. For such use, the lowly .22 Short works very well in either the solid or hollow point form because pelt damage is to be kept to a minimum level. Varmint hunters want (and need) the most destructive rimfire load to prevent wounded animals from escaping. Fortunately there are rimfire cartridges that handle all of these chores.

Browning has now introduced a new line of ammunition that includes a .22 LR load that features a 40-grain hollow point bullet with a muzzle velocity of 1,435 ft/sec.

CHAPTER 7

MAGNUM RIMFIRE AMMUNITION

IN CHAPTER 6 an overview of the characteristics and availability of rimfire ammunition in calibers based on the .22 LR case (either standard length or the longer version utilized with the CCI Stinger) was presented. In this chapter, attention will be given to the various types of rimfire ammunition that are not based on the .22 LR case, and strictly speaking that begins with the .22 Winchester Rim Fire (WRF) that was introduced in 1890. The next major development was the .22 Winchester Magnum Rimfire (WMR) that was introduced in 1959. In more recent times, cartridges such as the 5mm Remington Magnum (1969), .17 Hornady Magnum Rimfire (HMR, 2002), and .17 Winchester Super Magnum (WSM, 2015) have been introduced.

In this chapter, the general types of ammunition in these calibers will be discussed and the accompanying table presents the characteristics of the loads. Included in the table is the 5mm Remington Magnum, which is listed for comparison even though it has not been produced by Remington for almost 30 years (current production is from Aguila). The author (among many others) certainly wishes it were still available and that new rifles were being produced in that excellent caliber. A casual glance at the data for that round shows that it gives impressive performance, but that subject will be explored in more detail elsewhere.

In the sections that follow, the magnum rimfire calibers will be discussed and the characteristics of most of the loads will be discussed.

The .22 Winchester Rim Fire (WRF)

The .22 WRF was all but dead for many years. Rifles in that caliber were no longer being produced, and many shooters of the original Winchester Model 1890 pump action rifles had moved on to other models or had passed from the arena of shooting sports. Finally,

The current lineup of ammunition for rimfire magnums includes (left to right) .22 WRF, .22 WMR, 5mm Remington Magnum, .17 HMR, and .17 WSM.

A Summary of Magnum Rimfire Ammunition Types

CARTRIDGE	BULLET TYPE	WT., GR.	VEL, FT/SEC MUZ./100 YD	E, FT LB MUZ./100 YD	NOTES
.17 HMR	NTX	15.5	2,525/1,829	236/119	H
.17 HMR	JHP	17	2,550/1,757	245/116	CCI
.17 HMR	JPT	17	2,550/1,901	245/136	H, CCI, W
.17 HMR, A17	JPT	17	2,650/2,050	264/159	CCI
.17 HMR	JHP	20	2,375/1,776	250/140	H, W, CCI
.17 HMR	FMJ	20	2,375/1,776	250/140	CCI
.17 HMR	JHP	20	2,375/1,754	250/137	CCI
.17 WSM	JPT	20	3,000/2,504	400/279	W, F, H
.17 WSM	JPT	25	2,600/2,230	375/276	W
.17 WSM	COPPER	20	2,875/2,237	384/294	W
5mm Rem. Mag.	JHP	38	2,100/1,606	372/217	R (obsolete)
5mm Rem. Mag.	JHP	40	2,300/1,905	383/235	A
.22 WRF	SFP	45	1,300/1,023	169/105	W
.22 WRF	JHP	45	1,300/1,056	169/112	CCI
.22 WMR	JPT	30	2,200/1,571	322/164	CCI , H, W
.22 WMR	JHP	30	2,200/1,375	322/126	CCI, F
.22 WMR	JPT	33	2,000/1,495	293/164	R Premier
.22 WMR	JHP	34	2,120/1,437	339/156	W Vmt HV
.22 WMR	JHP	40	1,910/1,326	324/156	W, R, P, F, A
.22 WMR	FMJ	40	1,875/1,366	312/166	CCI
.22 WMR	FMJ	40	1,910/1,326	324/156	W, R, P, F
.22 WMR	JHP	50	1,530/1,197	260/159	F
.22 WMR	JSP	40	1,875/1,385	312/170	CCI
.22 WMR	Gold Dot	40	1,050/898	99/72	CCI, 2" bbl.
.22 WMR	FTX	45	1,000/868	100/75	H, 1 7/8" bbl.
.22 WMR	FTX	45	1,700/1,222	289/149	H, 24" bbl.
.22 WMR	JHP,PDX1	40	1,295/---	144/---	W, handgun

Abbreviations: SFP = solid flat point; HP = hollow point; JPT = jacketed polymer tip; JHP=jacketed hollow point; JSP = jacketed soft point; FMJ = full metal jacket.

Notes: A = Aguila; F = Federal; H = Hornady; P = PMC; R = Remington; W = Winchester.

Although it is over a century old, the .22 WRF (right) is still available and can be fired in rifles chambered for the .22 WMR.

The CCI load available for the .22 WRF utilizes a 45-grain hollow point bullet.

Winchester's cartridges in .22 WRF feature a 45-grain flat point bullet.

as is so often the case, it was discovered that a small residual demand for the cartridges persisted. Winchester responded with a manufacturing run of .22 WRF in 1986. Perhaps the users of .22 WMR firearms discovered that the .22 WRF cartridges performed respectably in their guns because the demand was such that Winchester is again showing the .22 WRF ammunition in its regular catalog of ammunition. In the seemingly never-ending expansion of their rimfire line, CCI also markets the .22 WRF loads. The specified diameter of the rim and case near the base is only approximately 0.004 inch larger for the WRF than for the WMR. Such a small difference allows the shorter WRF case to chamber easily in WMR rifles. Bullet diameter for the WMR is 0.224 inch whereas that of the WRF is nominally 0.226 inch. However, because it does not have a tough jacket, the larger diameter bullet of the WRF swages to 0.224 inch readily and it still gives accuracy that is acceptable for shooting small game and pests at moderate ranges.

The CCI load in .22 WRF consists of a 45-grain jacketed hollow point bullet at a nominal velocity of 1,300 ft/sec, which produces 169 ft lbs of energy. At 50 yards, the velocity is 1,147 ft/sec and the energy is 132 ft lbs, and at 100 yards the values are 1,056 ft/sec and 112 ft lbs. A high velocity .22 LR has a muzzle energy of about 135 ft lbs and a remaining energy at 100 yards of 91 ft lbs. Consequently, the .22 WRF is slightly more powerful than the .22 LR, but not enough to make much difference in practical terms. However, the fact that .22 WMR rifles can fire .22 WRF ammunition is a bonus.

Winchester's .22 WRF load consists of a 45-grain flat nosed plated bullet that has a muzzle velocity of 1,300 ft/sec, which gives an energy of 169 ft lbs. However, the bullet has a different shape than that used in the CCI version of the cartridge so the remaining velocity at 100 yards is 1,023 ft/sec and the energy at that distance is 105 ft lbs. With a bullet that is 5 grains heavier than most .22 LR solids, the .22 WRF

is slightly better as a game load than is the .22 LR. Some rifles that are chambered for the .22 WRF will not quite equal the accuracy shown by .22 LR firearms especially because there are so many more options in ammunition for the .22 LR shooter to choose from.

The availability of .22 WRF ammunition enables shooters with vintage rifles to continue to use these arms. Quite by surprise the author found that .22 WRF ammunition gives accuracy that is quite good in his Ruger 77/22M. Therefore, a lower powered load is now available, but the rifle must be sighted in for that load. There is no real cost savings because a box of the specialty .22 WRF sells for approximately the same price as a box of the more powerful .22 WMR.

Shooters who like the .22 WMR have available a wide range of ammunition from which to choose.

The .22 Winchester Magnum Rimfire (WMR)

As we move upward in the ammunition hierarchy, we come to the .22 WMR. This round was introduced in 1959 to provide the varmint and small game hunter with a round that extends the range and effectiveness of the .22 LR. With a 40-grain jacketed bullet that has a higher velocity at 100 yards than a similar weight bullet from the muzzle of a .22 LR, the .22 WMR is a much more powerful round. Muzzle energy of most .22 WMR loads is over twice that of a .22 LR high velocity load. This is important for the varmint hunter, but it may well be massive overkill for the small game hunter who would like to have something left to cook. One possible exception, where legal, is the use of the

.22 WMR on wild turkeys. Rabbits, squirrels, and opossums up trees are simply not that hard to kill, and a standard velocity .22 LR solid round or a hollow point will do the job very well when placed accurately. After all, hunting small game and pests with air rifles is becoming more common, and the vast majority of them do not have even the energy of a .22 Short! What is important is bullet placement.

As a varmint cartridge, the .22 WMR is in a different league from the .22 LR. Varmints as large as fox or coyote are fair game for the .22 WMR as long as the range is reasonable (100 yards or so) and an accurate rifle is used. The .22 WMR is an excellent choice for groundhogs or marmots when the range is under about 125 yards. The original load for the .22 WMR as introduced by Winchester was a 40-grain jacketed hollow point bullet loaded to almost 2,000 ft/sec. The current velocity is advertised as 1,910 ft/sec. Because of the explosive nature of the hollow point bullet, a 40-grain bullet with a full metal jacket was offered. For many years, those constituted the choices of ammunition in .22 WMR produced by Winchester and CCI. Unlike the Winchester load, which uses a jacketed bullet, some manufacturers load .22 WMR ammunition with plated bullets. In most instances, these work just about as well as the jacketed bullets but may give less penetration. In recent years Hornady announced a .22 WMR load that utilizes a 25-grain bullet known as the NTX®, but the load is listed as suspended on the Hornady website.

As with other rimfire calibers, the choice of ammunition in .22 WMR has grown dramatically in recent years. Soon after the hyper velocity loads in .22

Bullets loaded in .22 WMR ammunition include a wide range of bullet styles.

The Winchester 30-grain Varmint HV load is fast and accurate in most rifles.

A 50-grain hollow point bullet is employed in the .22 WMR Federal Classic load.

One of the outstanding .22 WMR loads is the Remington Premier that utilizes a 33-grain polymer tipped bullet.

Speer has introduced a .22 WMR defense round that features the 40-grain Gold Dot bullet.

LR were introduced, the .22 WMR was to experience the same evolution. Bullets as light as 30 grains were loaded to velocities in the 2,200 ft/sec range. Most of these bullets had gaping hollow points so that they would blow up small varmints. However, they also lost velocity rapidly so that at a range of 100 yards, the remaining energy was only 120-130 ft lbs out of the 320 ft lbs produced at the muzzle. If the range extends to 125 yards or more, the trajectory is not much flatter than that of the 40-grain load, which starts out slower but retains velocity better. As stated elsewhere in this book, there is no free lunch.

In recent years, Winchester has opted for a lighter bullet at higher velocity, but chose to use a 34-grain hollow point loaded to 2,120 ft/sec in the Supreme ammunition line. Because this bullet retains velocity better than the 30-grain loads, it gives a remaining energy at 100 yards that is virtually identical to that of the 40-grain load. However, the Winchester Supreme load employed a bullet that has a large cavity so it is not noted for deep penetration. The current 34-grain

offering from Winchester is labeled as the Varmint HETM load and it is listed as giving a velocity of 2,120 ft/sec. Winchester also offers the Varmint HVTM load that utilizes a 30-grain bullet at 2,250 ft/sec. Remington has taken a different approach by marketing the Premier .22 WMR load that utilizes a 33-grain Hornady V-Max® polymer-tipped bullet. The nominal velocity is specified as 2,000 ft/sec, but my chronograph indicated a velocity that was slightly higher. Moreover, this load gives good accuracy in my Ruger 77/22M, and it does not produce quite the explosive effect of the lightweight hollow pointed bullets.

Going the other way in trying to improve the effectiveness of the .22 WMR cartridge for use in some situations, Federal produces a load, called the Game-Shok®, that utilizes a 50-grain hollow point bullet loaded to a nominal velocity of 1,530 ft/sec and my chronograph indicated almost exactly that velocity at eight feet from the muzzle of a 22-inch barrel. However, the 50-grain bullet holds its velocity well so the remaining energy at 100 yards (approximately 158

The .22 WMR Gamepoint load from CCI features a soft point bullet.

One of the new .22 WMR loads is the Critical Defense from Hornady that utilizes a 45-grain polymer tipped bullet.

ft lbs) exceeds that of most loads having a bullet of 40 grains or less. True, the trajectory is more curved, but it is certainly flat enough for shooting varmints at 100 yards. If larger species such as fox or coyote are your targets, try the 50-grain Federal load in your rifle. A .22 WMR load featuring the 50-grain Gold Dot® bullet was offered by CCI for a few years, but it has recently been discontinued. Some may still be found. Federal also produces the .22 WMR load known as V-Shok® that gives a 30-grain Speer TNT® bullet a muzzle velocity of 2,200 ft/sec and energy of 322 ft lbs. At a range of 100 yards, the velocity and energy are 1,419 fps and 134 ft lbs, respectively.

Some critics of the .22 WMR have commented on the accuracy of this caliber. Having experimented with this caliber in several rifles over the years, my belief is that the problem is not with the caliber but rather with the cartridges. In some cases, plated

Shot cartridges in .22 WMR are very effective at short range.

bullets are asked to perform at near centerfire rifle velocities whereas in others, the bullets are jacketed but they are by no means premium bullets. The result is that some combinations may not quite produce the accuracy expected. More discussion of this topic will be presented in later chapters. Some tests have given results reported by other authors indicating that in identical high quality rifles using premium ammunition there is nothing lacking in accuracy produced by the .22 WMR cartridge.

Another .22 WMR load that is useful is the shot cartridge produced by CCI. The plastic capsule holds 1/8-ounce of No. 12 shot, and it will certainly take out a rodent or snake at short range. This load is particularly convenient to use in a revolver.

From the foregoing discussion, it can be seen that there is a wide range of ammunition for use in the .22 WMR. For a lower powered alternative, even the .22 WRF can be used. In spite of the offerings, none of the manufacturers produces what this author would like to have. That would be a .22 WMR load that makes use of a 40-grain premium spitzer bullet with a polymer tip. The ballistic coefficient of such a bullet would be approximately 0.15-0.18, which is much higher than any bullet now offered in .22 WMR ammunition. It is also much higher than any bullet that is offered (or probably will be offered) in .17 HMR because the author has been informed that experimental loads utilizing 25-grain bullets cannot produce velocities sufficiently high to give an explosive effect. Therefore, .17 HMR loads with bullets having great enough weight to give a ballistic coefficient much over 0.125 are unlikely.

Aguila produces this excellent 40-grain soft point load in .22 WMR.

Ammunition shortages led to several companies introducing new types of ammunition and this is the 40-grain JHP load from Armscor.

Fiocchi has become a major supplier of ammunition and offers this jacketed soft point load.

Even if the muzzle velocity of the hypothetical .22 WMR load were only 1,850 ft/sec, the down range performance would far exceed that of any .22 WMR or .17 HMR load now available. Of the 303 ft lbs of energy it would produce at the muzzle, calculations indicate that 197 ft lbs would remain at 100 yards and 159 ft lbs would remain at 150 yards in contrast to the 139 and 102 ft lbs given by the .17 HMR at these ranges. Will such a .22 WMR load be produced? Probably not, but if it is the author wants a generous supply and will also volunteer to conduct field testing for the manufacturer who produces it.

The .17 Hornady Magnum Rimfire (HMR)

The .17 Hornady Magnum Rimfire (abbreviated as HMR and sometimes given the nickname "hummer") is one the most written about cartridges of all time. In fact, it may even hold the title! We are,

it seems, caught up in the velocity craze again, this time in the area of rimfire cartridges. The word "again" is used because such a craze existed many years ago when Roy Weatherby introduced the line of center fire cartridges that constitute the Weatherby magnums. With large belted cases and free bored chambers, the velocities produced by the Weatherby magnums are high. As with any other area of human endeavor, there are newer series of cartridges that eclipse the Weatherby magnums in velocity.

In the .17 HMR, a new standard for velocity produced by a rimfire cartridge was established. The case for the .17 HMR cartridge was formed by necking a .22 WMR case to hold a bullet of 0.172-inch diameter. A 17-grain polymer tipped bullet was driven to a velocity of 2,550 ft/sec. The trajectory of that bullet is considerably less curved than that of any fired from a .22 WMR cartridge.

The .17 HMR has been enormously successful. New ammunition offerings have appeared rapidly.

The .17 HMR is based on the .22 WMR case necked to hold .17 caliber bullets.

Both polymer tipped and hollow point bullets are loaded in .17 HMR caliber ammunition.

Small bullets at high velocity expand violently or disintegrate on impact so reports of the effects of the .17 HMR began to detail dramatic kills on everything from sparrows to coyotes. However, some writers also began to report that even on groundhogs the bullets sometimes blew up without penetrating sufficiently to drop the animal on the spot so they made it back to their holes. An increasing number of such reports began to appear and they somehow offset the reports of dramatic one-shot kills on coyotes at over 200 yards. The designers decided that a heavier bullet of different construction would be appropriate so a load featuring a 20-grain hollow point bullet having a velocity of 2,375 ft/sec was produced. Such a load is offered as the CCI Game Point® and the Hornady XTP®. These loads join the 17-grain polymer tipped loads from Hornady, Federal, CCI, and Remington as well as the 17-grain hollow point load from CCI.

With the sharp pointed bullet at high velocity, the trajectory of the .17 HMR has relatively little curvature for a rimfire so hits at long ranges are possible. Moreover, the bullets used in .17 HMR ammunition are of the premium "varmint bullet" type so accuracy of most .17 HMR rifles is outstanding, which also contributes to scoring hits at long ranges. The bullets are tiny and explosive so they are suitable for smaller varmint species. Hornady also offers the NTX® load that utilizes a 15.5-grain bullet having a muzzle velocity listed as 2,525 ft/sec. The bullet does not have a lead core and it is sharply pointed so it has a remaining velocity of 1,828 ft/sec and energy of 119 ft lbs at a range of 100 yards.

In terms of firearms, the .17 HMR was given a flying start because most firearms, except autoloaders, that could function with a .22 WMR could be altered to .17 caliber by means of a different barrel. Case and rim diameter and rim thickness is the same for both calibers. The number of firearms chambered for the .17 HMR is very large. The problems with autoloaders chambered with .17 HMR has been solved by several manufacturers (see Chapter 15), and a new load designated as the A17

Concurrently with the introduction of the Savage A17 Rifle chambered for the .17 HMR cartridge, CCI introduced the A17 load that features a 17-grain bullet having a muzzle velocity of 2,650 ft/sec.

has been developed by CCI. It gives a 17-grain polymer tip bullet a muzzle velocity of 2,650 feet per second.

Comments on the .22 WMR and .17 HMR

Ammunition in .22 WMR caliber is currently *cataloged* by manufacturers in the largest variety of loads since its introduction. *Availability* of such ammunition is another issue. As this is written in early 2016, the recent situation with regard to rimfire ammunition is the worst it has been since WW II. Shelves are starting to have stacks of at least some type of .22 LR. Even when .22 LR ammunition was seldom available, it was relatively easy to find .17 HMR ammunition. However, .22 WMR ammunition has been almost impossible to find for some time and that situation continues. It would seem to suggest something about the relative popularity of .17 HMR and .22 WMR firearms, which is not surprising because .22 WMR firearms have been produced for a much longer period of time. Although the .17 HMR quickly achieved great popularity, perhaps not everyone let dust settle on .22 WMR rifles just to get a new .17 HMR.

Although the author has a great attachment to almost all rimfire calibers, especially the ubiquitous .22 LR, it is only fair to state that the .22 WMR stands at least tied for the top spot with him. When the .17 HMR appeared in 2002, it received glowing praise and manufacturers cranked out guns in that caliber very quickly. Some even predicted that it would lead to the demise of the .22 WMR. The .17 HMR is a good and useful cartridge, and it is still popular. However, the .22 WMR can do some things that the .17 HMR simply cannot do.

The effectiveness of the .17 HMR is largely a function of the velocity of the tiny 17- and 20-grain bullets so it has never been a popular caliber for handguns. There is simply too much difference between the velocity produced by a rifle and handgun in that caliber. Certainly this also applies to the .22 WMR, but the larger .22 caliber bullets are still effective at handgun velocities.

In fact, some .22 WMR handguns are employed for defense. This trend is recognized by ammunition manufacturers who have introduced loads that are advertised and marketed as "defense" loads. Among them are the Speer Gold Dot®, Hornady Critical Defense®, and Winchester PDX1®. All are designed to give bullet expansion at the low velocity produced in handguns having short barrels. None of the Winchester PDX1 load has been available for testing by the author, but the Hornady Critical Defense and Speer Gold Dot loads have been tested in both a handgun and a rifle. Of course any of the .22 WMR loads with jacketed soft point or hollow point bullets could be utilized for defense, but based on experience they do not give much expansion when fired from a short barreled handgun.

The .22 WMR is a cartridge that is useful in more situations than just vaporizing small varmints. To be versatile, a cartridge needs to have a balance between bullet weight, diameter, and velocity. It is the opinion of the author that the .22 WMR is superior in that regard to the .17 HMR, which delivers high velocity, but with bullets that are lacking in diameter and weight to be effective on a wide range of targets.

My perceptions of the .17 HMR and .22 WMR are summed up quite well by noted author Layne Simpson in a superb article on rimfire rifles and cartridges that appeared in the September 2014 issue of Shooting Times (p. 54-62). Simpson said "If I could have only one, I would choose the .22 WMR without hesitation. … Both are great little cartridges, but the soft spot in this rifleman's heart will always be the .22 WMR."

The .17 Winchester Super Magnum (WSM)

If a little does good, a lot will do better is the old cliché. Decreasing bullet diameter from 0.224 to 0.172 and necking the .22 WMR case to hold the small

The .17 WSM from Winchester is the newest and most potent rimfire cartridge.

Fans of the .17 WSM now have a 20-grain load available from American Eagle.

Hornady has entered the .17 WSM ammunition market with a load that utilizes a 20-grain V-Max bullet.

bullets resulted in the .17 HMR. Shooters of small varmints appreciated the flatter trajectory and excellent accuracy given by most .17 HMR rifles. But all was not happy among varmint shooters when the .17 HMR was found to be lacking in power for quickly dispatching larger species such as fox, coyote, and even large groundhogs unless they were hit in exactly the right spot. Moreover, it was found that the very light 17- and 20-grain bullets drifted badly when shooting in windy conditions. In order to rectify some of these issues and to reestablish preeminence in rimfire calibers, Winchester introduced the .17 Winchester Super Magnum (WSM) at the Shooting, Hunting, Outdoor Trade (SHOT) Show in 2013.

Like the 5mm Remington, the .17 WSM is not based on the case of a previously utilized cartridge. Rather, it is based on a considerably larger case that was used to project fasteners in the construction industry. The case is both longer and larger in diameter than that utilized by the .17 HMR. Additionally, the .17 WSM is loaded with two types of bullets that weigh 20 grains (the heaviest offered in the .17 HMR) and another weighing 25 grains. The latter load is marketed as being intended for use on species as large as coyotes.

Remington 5mm cartridges are seldom seen and command high prices as a result of being collectible.

Shooters who use the 5mm Rimfire Magnum have a source of ammunition from Centurion.

Just announced by Winchester in early 2016 is a .17 WSM load that features a 20-grain solid copper bullet for which the muzzle velocity is listed at 2,875 ft/sec.

There is no doubt that the .17 WSM takes varmint hunting with a rimfire rifle to a different level, but there those who still describe less than stellar performance of the round on coyotes. Some even insist that the only .17-caliber rifles that should be used on coyotes are the centerfire calibers such as the .17 Remington. Not having taken a coyote with a .17 WSM, the author is not going to make an issue of the sport, but will categorically state that he would have no hesitation to use his Savage B.Mag in .17 WSM caliber with the 25-grain bullets for such use. However, no shot would be taken at a coyote that is farther than about 100 yards. Used with good judgment and restraint, the .17 WSM should be an adequate caliber for coyotes.

The 5mm Remington Magnum

Introduced in 1969, the 5mm Remington utilized a case that is slightly larger in diameter than that used in either the .22 WMR or .17 HMR. The initial 5mm Remington load featured a 38-grain hollow point bullet with a muzzle velocity of 2,100 ft/sec giving a muzzle energy of 372 ft lbs. The bullet diameter was 0.2045 inch. Originally, Remington marketed two bolt action rifles to fire the cartridge. The Model 591 utilized a box magazine whereas the 592 had a tubular magazine. The rifles were discontinued in the early 1970s and the only other rifles chambered for 5mm Remington caliber were the Thompson-Center single shots having a barrel in that caliber.

The 5mm Remington is a potent rimfire cartridge. As a result of the bullet weight and diameter, retained velocity and energy at 100 yards were higher than for either the .22 WMR or the .17 HMR. Reports from users indicated that the round performed well on even larger varmints such as fox or coyote. Although the Remington rifles were reported to be accurate and the ammunition performance excellent, the 5mm Remington was not successful in the market place and Remington ceased ammunition production in 1980.

But it seems that all is not lost. Ammunition in 5mm Remington is once again available under the Centurion brand. It now appears that Aguila Ammunition and Centurion Ordnance have established a collaboration to produce three or four loads in the 5mm Remington caliber. On the Aguila website, loads featuring 30-, 40-, and 45-grain bullets are listed as "coming in 2016," but actual ballistic data are not definitive at the time of this writing. It is to be hoped that the ammunition will indeed become available for those shooters who already have rifles in 5mm Remington caliber. However, it is also to be hoped that some manufacturers will produces rifles in that caliber. The 5mm Remington generated a pressure of about 33,000 psi, which is significantly higher than that of either the .22 WMR or .17 HMR and about equal to that produced by the .17 WSM. As a result, any new rifle in 5mm Remington caliber would have to employ a strong action, probably with a more robust lockup mechanism than just the root of the bolt handle. Both the Ruger 77 and Savage B.Mag utilize dual locking lugs and the actions could be adapted to handle potent calibers. Perhaps there are other candidates, but the author hopes to see new rifles to fire 5mm Remington ammunition and new loads from other manufacturers in the near future. However, a .20 or .22 caliber cartridge based on the .17 WSM case would be a welcome addition to the magnum rimfire lineup.

CHAPTER 8

INTERNAL BALLISTICS FOR BEGINNERS

BALLISTICS IS THE BRANCH OF SCIENCE that deals with problems related to launching and motion of projectiles. *Internal* ballistics concerns the forces acting on the projectile and its motion during the firing process. *External* ballistics is the branch of science that deals with the motion of the projectile after it leaves the firing device. The more a shooter knows about ballistics, the better he or she will understand the performance of the chosen firearms and ammunition and how to use them effectively. In this chapter, the basic principles of internal ballistics will be presented, and Chapter 9 will deal with external ballistics along with some discussion of the performance characteristics of current rimfire ammunition.

The science of internal ballistics involves the transformation of energy from one form into another. When the primer explodes, the powder is ignited and the chemical energy stored in the powder is converted into the kinetic energy of the bullet and heat that is transferred to the bullet and firearm. As a result of the powder being transformed into gaseous products and the expansion of the gas, the bullet increases in velocity as it is forced down the bore. Consequently, the physical principles involving force, work, and energy form the basis of internal ballistics.

Ignition

Shooters who use centerfire firearms have several variables that are under their control, especially if they load their own ammunition. The type of primer, type and amount of propellant, and the type of bullet and its seating depth are all variables over which the reloader has some control. These are the most important factors in determining the internal ballistics related to firing a shot. Other than selecting the

type of ammunition to be fired, the rimfire shooter has little control over the internal ballistics of the firearm. However, an understanding of the basic principles of internal ballistics is helpful when interpreting what is happening as a shot is fired. The discussion presented here makes use of some elementary ideas from physics, but it should be adequately clear for most purposes. Therefore, in this section we will explore what happens between the time the firing pin strikes the cartridge and the bullet exits from the muzzle.

As a firearm is discharged, the first thing that happens is that the sear releases the firing pin (or hammer) as a result of pressure applied to the trigger. From the time the sear is released to the time the firing pin strikes the cartridge is known as the lock time. It is desirable to have a short lock time so there will be as little movement of the firearm as possible while this part of the firing sequence is taking place. Generally, the bolt action rifles that are designed for target shooting have very short lock times that measure only a couple of milliseconds. Firing pin design, length of firing pin travel, and tension of the spring that moves the firing pin determine the lock time of a particular firearm. Generally, firearms with exposed hammers that must swing upward and forward as they are released have longer lock times. The lock time is a characteristic of the action of a particular firearm and in most cases there is little that

Note the dimpled cartridge head previously used by Federal in the .22 LR Ultra Match rimfire round. Ignition occurs as the firing pin strikes the rim of the case and spreads forward.

can be done to alter it except by a trained gunsmith. On the other hand, for some rifles, modifications can be made by installing certain aftermarket parts. This will be discussed briefly in Chapter 13.

A rimfire cartridge rests in the chamber with the rim against the rear end of the barrel. Rifles designed to deliver the highest level of accuracy have chambers that have slightly smaller dimensions than those of ordinary rifles. This serves to hold the cartridge in more precise alignment with the bore and assures more uniform ignition. As the bolt is closed (regardless of whether the bolt is operated manually or automatically), there must be some clearance between the bolt face and the breech, which is sufficient to accommodate the rim of the cartridge. This distance is known as the headspace. For the .22 LR rimfire cartridge, the headspace is normally in the range of 0.043-0.046 inch. Accordingly, headspace is checked by means of two gauges, a so-called "go" or minimum gauge, which the bolt should close on fully, and a "no go" or maximum gauge on which the bolt should not close. For the .22 LR, the former measures 0.043 inch whereas the latter measures 0.046 inch. In rimfire rifles, the bolt face has a recess that provides this clearance.

The rim thickness of most rimfire ammunition is in the range 0.037-0.042 inch and averages around 0.040 inch. If the headspace is less than about 0.040 inch, there will be some compression of the cartridge rim as the bolt closes. In autoloaders, this might keep the bolt from closing fully whereas in bolt action rifles the force generated as the bolt is turned may be sufficient to compress the cartridge head *slightly*. If the headspace is excessive, the case can rupture because it is not supported properly.

On the other hand, if the headspace is greater than about 0.048 inch, the cartridge can move forward when impacted by the firing pin, which may give erratic ignition. Consequently, it is desirable to have the headspace be within the range of approximately 0.043-0.046 inch. Tests have been conducted in special rifles in which the headspace can be varied by positioning the barrel in the breech and locking it in place. It was found that the best accuracy resulted when the headspace was approximately 0.044 inch. When the headspace was about 0.004 larger than this value, the shots resulted in groups that were elongated vertically, which probably resulted from ignition that was not uniform. Neither the minimum nor maximum necessarily represents the most desirable condition although there is no convenient way to adjust headspace in most rimfire rifles. However, the amount by which

the firing pin extends past the bolt face during firing is also important because if the headspace is slightly large but the firing pin extends a few thousandths more than normal from the bolt face these factors can compensate to give the same degree of crushing of the cartridge rim. The bolt face on a rimfire rifle is recessed or counter bored approximately 0.040-0.045 inch and the firing pin protrusion is usually slightly less than that amount so the firing pin does not rest against the edge of the chamber or strike it when the firearm is dry fired without a cartridge in place. These aspects of firearm function concern target shooters who are trying to obtain the maximum accuracy from super accurate rifles, and designers of firearms must consider these factors.

Many rimfire shooters who try to obtain the highest possible accuracy measure the thickness of the rims of their ammunition. In this way, ammunition can be segregated into groups of cartridges that will give more uniform indentation by the firing pin. Other shooters question whether this is effective, but instead weigh unfired rounds and group them in that way to try to obtain maximum uniformity in ammunition. Any means that may result in the highest shot to shot uniformity has probably been tried!

Shooters who install aftermarket barrels on their rifles (see Chapter 13) should at least be aware of the ramifications of headspace and the fact that headspace may be different when a different type of barrel is installed. Some barrel manufacturers such as Green Mountain Rifle Barrel Company produce shims that are actually thin washers having a thickness of 0.002 inch that can be placed around the shank of a barrel before it is attached to the action, and in this way the headspace can be adjusted. Of course, this procedure can only increase headspace to correct for instances in which it would otherwise be too small.

Rim Thickness

As part of the study of .22 LR ammunition, the decision was made to determine the rim thickness for several types of ammunition. Special commercial rim thickness gauges are available for the serious experimenter, but they are not absolutely necessary. A .22 LR cartridge will slip snugly into the neck of a fired cartridge such as the .222 Remington or .223 Remington. In this instance, the author had available fired .222 Remington cases because of owning a rifle in that caliber. An empty case was inserted in a case trimmer in order to assure that the case mouth was uniform and perpendicular to the axis of the case.

A dial caliper can be used to measure rim thickness by using a .222 Remington case to hold the .22 LR cartridges.

Rim thickness was determined by measuring the length of an empty .222 Remington case, then setting the dial to read zero.

Measuring the length of the .222 Remington case with a .22 LR cartridge inserted in the neck allowed the thickness of the rim to be measured directly. For this cartridge, the rim thickness is 0.042 inch.

After the case was prepared, its length was measured with an accurate caliper and found to be 1.691 inches. With the empty .222 Remington case between the jaws of the caliper, the caliper was set to read zero. Then, with a .22 LR round inserted in the neck, the jaws were closed against the base of the .22 LR cartridge and the head of the .222 Remington case. In that way, the thickness of the rim of the cartridge could be read directly. By this simple procedure, a rim thickness gauge was available that made it possible to read the thickness quickly to three decimal places.

Two dozen types of .22 LR ammunition were selected from the large number of types on hand and measurements of the rim thickness of a random sample of 20 cartridges were performed. For all of the cartridges, the rim thickness was never above 0.042 inch or below 0.037 inch. The results obtained are summarized in the accompanying table. In the table, the entry below each rim thickness gives the number of cartridges in the sample out of the 20 that gave that measurement. For example, with the CCI Velocitor, six cartridges had a rim thickness of 0.040 inch whereas 14 had a thickness of 0.041 inch.

Although it is not possible to correlate rim thickness with the accuracy displayed by a certain type of ammunition, the data show some interesting facts. First, some types of ammunition have rims that are very uniform in thickness. For example, the rims of the 20 Federal Ultra Match cartridges all measured 0.042 inch. For some of the other ammunition types (CCI Green Tag and SGB for example), 19 out of the sample of 20 rounds had the same thickness (0.041 or 0.042 inch). In other cases (Remington Club Xtra and Winchester T22), the majority of the rounds had the same thickness and the remainder were very close to that measurement. Second, the data shown in the table reveal that certain types of ammunition have

rims that tend to fall toward the maximum thickness. For example, the rims of all cartridges of the CCI ammunition types are in the range 0.040-0.042 inch. Rim thickness for other types of ammunition tends to be toward the minimum end of the range. All 20 of the cartridges in the samples of Winchester T22, Remington/Eley Club Xtra, Eley Silhouex, and Remington Cyclone have rims that fall within a range of 0.037-0.039 inch. Cartridges of some other types of ammunition show a range of rim thickness that fall toward the middle of the 0.037-0.042 inch range.

Whether these differences in rim thickness will manifest themselves in the accuracy given in a particular rifle has yet to be demonstrated conclusively. Tests were performed using a CZ 452 that gives outstanding accuracy. With Remington Thunderbolt that had not been sorted, the group size was 1.76 inches for five five-shot groups at 50 yards. Cartridges were then sorted according to rim thicknesses of 0.038, 0.039, 0.040, 0.041, and 0.042 inches. For the sorted cartridges, the average group sizes were 0.84, 0.83, 0.67, 0.68, and 1.04 inches, respectively. Far better accuracy was achieved when the cartridges tested had the same rim thickness.

Undoubtedly, specific rifles will perform better with ammunition for which the rims tend toward larger thickness whereas others probably give better accuracy with cartridges having thinner rims. Keep in mind that the headspace in the rifle and how far the firing pin protrudes from the bolt face are also important factors. Uniformity in rim thickness may be more important than whether the rims tend toward minimum or maximum thickness. One thing is certain and that is in the rifles tested, Remington Target ammunition did not give the best accuracy and it also has a large dispersion in rim thickness. Federal Gold Medal Target, CCI Green Tag, and CCI Standard Velocity all have little dispersion in rim thickness and

Rim Thickness for 24 Types of .22 LR Ammunition

Entries Indicate the Number of Cartridges Having That Thickness Out of a Sample of 20 Cartridges of Each Type.

AMMUNITION TYPE	RIM THICKNESS, INCHES					
	0.037	0.038	0.039	0.040	0.041	0.042
CCI Blazer	0	0	0	0	13	7
CCI Green Tag	0	0	0	1	19	0
CCI Mini Mag	0	0	0	3	17	0
CCI SGB	0	0	0	0	1	19
CCI Standard Velocity	0	0	0	14	6	0
CCI Velocitor	0	0	0	6	14	0
Eley Silhouex	4	9	7	0	0	0
Federal Champion	0	0	2	8	10	0
Federal Gold Medal Target	0	0	0	2	18	0
Federal Ultra Match	0	0	0	0	0	20
Lapua Scoremax	0	0	0	17	3	0
Lapua Super Club	0	0	0	9	11	0
PMC Scoremaster	0	0	0	12	7	1
Remington Cyclone	3	8	9	0	0	0
Remington Golden Bullet	0	1	7	9	3	0
Remington Match Xtra Plus	0	0	11	9	0	0
Remington Thunderbolt	0	4	9	7	0	0
Remington Target	4	5	8	3	0	0
Remington/Eley Club Xtra	0	16	4	0	0	0
RWS Target Rifle	0	0	4	15	1	0
Winchester Power Point	5	10	4	1	0	0
Winchester Supreme	0	0	0	3	17	0
Winchester T22	5	15	0	0	0	0
Wolf Match Target	0	10	7	3	0	0

all gave excellent accuracy in most of the rifles tested (see Chapters 14 and 16).

Rim thickness is only one factor to consider, but if your rifle doesn't shoot particularly well with the type of ammunition you are using, the data shown in the table indicate that not all ammunition is identical. Other types may perform much better in a particular rifle so some testing should be carried out if accuracy is a goal. A great deal of additional data is needed before definitive conclusions can be drawn about the relationship between rim thickness and accuracy. Moreover, in no way is a conclusion justified that one type of ammunition is any "better" another. Such a fact can be determined only with respect to a particular firearm by experimentation.

Many competitors believe that better accuracy is achieved if cartridges are sorted by rim thickness and then fired with others having similar rim thickness. Doubtless, there would be some effect but whether is large enough to be observed without firing a very large number of groups is unknown. As mentioned earlier, some competitors believe that cartridge weight is more important than rim thickness and sort their cartridges that way.

In order to assess the rim thickness of 17 Mach 2 ammunition, the rims of 20 cartridges of each of the two types that were available at the time the first edition of this book was written were measured. As a result of both the Hornady and CCI ammunition being loaded by CCI (currently available in only the Hornady brand), it came as no surprise that the rims appear identical. What was a surprise was that for each load all 20 cartridges measured 0.042 inch. Uniformity of

For a 20-cartridge sample of .17 Mach 2, every cartridge had a rim thickness of 0.042 inch.

this level is normally observed only with the highest quality target ammunition as is the case for Federal Ultra Match and CCI Green Tag. Reports on the 17 Mach 2 indicate that the round is exceptionally accurate and such uniform rim thickness is probably one reason.

Cartridge Weights

As mentioned earlier, the uniformity of cartridges with respect to weight is sometimes considered to be a factor in determining the accuracy of ammunition. One must remember that a cartridge consists of the case, bullet, powder, and primer although the bullet and case comprise most of the weight. When several cartridges are weighed and found to have rather wide variation, differences may be due to variations in any of the components. In a way, the deviation in the weight of a cartridge from the average weight is meaningless unless a large number of cartridges are considered. However, in another way the uniformity of cartridge weights is meaningful. Uniform cartridge weights indicate that all components are assembled into uniform units.

Consider two cartridges that have identical weights. This could indicate that the weights of the components in each cartridge are identical. However, identical cartridge weights would result if the case of one cartridge is 0.0050 grams heavier than that of the other but the bullet is 0.0050 grams lighter than that of the other. In other words, weight variations could compensate to yield identical cartridge weights. Although this conceivably could occur for any two cartridges, it would be very unlikely to occur in a sample of 20 cartridges so that differences in weights of the components exactly compensate. In a much more realistic situation, weighing 20 cartridges will show that some cartridges are made from lighter cases and lighter bullets whereas others will have the opposite situation. Variations in cartridge weights

will give an indication of the overall uniformity of the cartridges.

The fact that cartridges have uniform weights does not necessarily assure that they will also be highly accurate and give small groups. However, there is value in knowing the overall uniformity of ammunition as long as the data are not used to try to *predict* accuracy. Wide variations in cartridge weights for a given type of ammunition indicate less control in the manufacturing process or less rigid standards for uniformity.

To determine how several types of .22 LR varied in terms of weight distribution, 14 types were selected and 20 cartridges of each type were weighed on a laboratory balance (which weighs in grams not grains). The cartridges weighed were the first 20 out of the box with no selecting being done. The weights for the 20 cartridges of each type were tabulated and the highest and lowest weights were recorded. For the 20 cartridges of each type, the average weight was calculated and the standard deviation of the weights was determined. Although it is tempting to ascribe weight differences to the lubricant, such difference between individual rounds is small. One of the "greasy" target rounds was carefully wiped off and reweighed only to find that 0.0004 gram of lubricant was removed. The differences in weight between cartridges in the samples are far too large for differences in lubrication to have much effect. The accompanying table shows the results obtained.

The data shown in the table reveal some interesting facts. First, the range of weights obtained for the 20 cartridges and the standard deviation for Federal Ultra Match show it to be unbelievably uniform and have the lowest standard deviation. This is not unexpected given that this ammunition is intended for competitive shooting at the highest levels and sells for about $20-30 per box of 50 rounds. Although this ammunition was discon-

A sensitive balance can detect small differences in cartridge weights.

tinued for a time, Federal has reintroduced it in slightly altered form and it has recently been seen on dealer's shelves for $20-25 per box.

Several types of ammunition, such as CCI Green Tag and Velocitor, Federal Gold Medal Target, Lapua Super Club, and Winchester Power Point, have low standard deviations in weight. Perhaps not coincidentally, all of these types are noted for accuracy even though they are not all "target" types. However, the standard deviation for the Wolf Match Target is larger than that of most other types, but that ammunition is known to produce excellent accuracy in most rifles. In this case, examination of the data showed that three of the 20 cartridges of that type had weights that deviated significantly from the others. When the standard deviation was calculated for the other 17 cartridges in the sample, the value was 0.0141 instead of 0.0183. Wolf rimfire ammunition is produced in Germany by SK-Jagd and the results presented in Chapter 14 show that it gave some of the smallest groups obtained in the tests. Finally, for the cartridges weighed the largest standard deviation found was for the hyper velocity Remington Yellow Jacket, which may be one of the reasons this and most other hyper velocity loads do not normally give accuracy equal to that of other types of ammunition. Keep in mind that hyper velocity ammunition is intended for other purposes than highest accuracy so the situation is not as bad as it may at first seem. However, the weight uniformity of CCI Velocitors and Winchester Power Points is outstanding, which may also be why these hunting loads gave excellent accuracy with most of the rifles used in the tests.

Is there something about weight uniformity of .22 LR ammunition that is indicative of its accuracy potential?

Some competitors believe that there is but others do not. At this point, given the accuracy data shown in Chapter 14 and the data presented here, rim thickness would be measured and cartridges segregated by weight if the highest degree of accuracy were sought. In some events, a difference in bullet placement of 0.01 inch might mean the difference between winning and finishing high. To have every advantage possible in such instances, the author would both segregate ammunition both by rim thickness and cartridge weight.

For the vast majority of rimfire users who are engaged in plinking, hunting, and pest shooting, the rifles used are likely not accurate enough to tell the difference between cartridges of the same type that have slightly different weights. As long as a type of ammunition is selected that gives sufficient accuracy in a particular rifle, the effect produced by variation in cartridge weight is not likely to be detected by a shooter of average ability using ordinary equipment.

Tables that summarize many measurements do not always convey a complete picture of the data analysis. For example, it is helpful to see a graphical comparison of the data for a sample of 20 cartridges of a given type that shows how the weights of the individual cartridges compare to the average weight. To illustrate weight variations for a specific type of ammunition,

Results of Weighing 20 Cartridges of Each Type

CARTRIDGES	WEIGHT, GRAMS[a]			
	Highest	Lowest	Average	Std. Dev.[b]
CCI Green Tag	3.2986	3.2734	3.2895	0.0074
CCI Standard Velocity	3.3077	3.2500	3.2811	0.0217
CCI Velocitor	3.3397	3.3275	3.3336	0.0040
Federal Gold Medal Target	3.2691	3.2508	3.2577	0.0059
Federal Ultra Match	3.3564	3.3483	3.3521	0.0018
Lapua Super Club	3.3676	3.3290	3.3470	0.0091
PMC Scoremaster	3.3486	3.3149	3.3261	0.0117
Remington/Eley Club Xtra	3.3285	3.2950	3.3089	0.0124
Remington Target	3.3732	3.2988	3.3299	0.0223
Remington Thunderbolt	3.3938	3.3308	3.3623	0.0167
Remington Yellow Jacket	2.9258	2.8358	2.8751	0.0246
Winchester Power Point	3.3692	3.3459	3.3581	0.0074
Winchester T22	3.3361	3.2990	3.3140	0.0134
Wolf Match Target	3.3536	3.3103	3.3304	0.0183

[a] To convert to weight in grains, multiply by 15.432.
[b] Std. Dev. is the standard deviation, a statistical measure of variance.

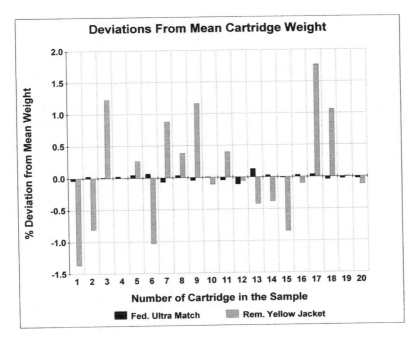

Deviations From Mean Cartridge Weight

This bar graph illustrates the difference in deviation of cartridge weight between high velocity ammunition and a high-grade target load.

the *deviation from the average* was determined for each cartridge in the 20-cartridge sample. Then, for each cartridge, the percent deviation from the average weight was calculated because it is not correct to compare the actual deviations for types of cartridges that have different average weights. That is why the percent deviation (a relative measure) was determined rather than using the actual values for the deviations. After the percent deviations were obtained, a graph was made showing the percent deviation for each cartridge in the 20-cartridge sample. The accompanying figure shows the results of this type of analysis for the ammunition that gave the smallest (Federal Ultra Match) and the largest (Remington Yellow Jacket) standard deviations. Note the difference in the lengths of the bars corresponding to these cartridges. The solid bars represent percent deviations for Federal Ultra Match cartridges and the shaded bars represent Remington Yellow Jackets. Short bars mean that the weights of the individual cartridges do not deviate much from the average weight.

Having shown the graph for the most and least uniform cartridges of those weighed, it is appropriate to show a comparison of two cartridges that are more typical in respect to weight uniformity. For this comparison, a graph was prepared showing percent deviation of the weights of 20 cartridges from the mean for Winchester T22 and Remington Club Xtra. These types are more typical than are Federal Ultra Match or Remington Yellow Jacket, and the graph shows this clearly. In preparing the graph, the same scale was used

so that the characteristics of these types of ammunition can be compared to those shown in the previous graph. Note that the weight variations are greater than for Federal Ultra Match but much smaller than for Remington Yellow Jackets. Note also that there is not much difference in the lengths of the bars (weight variations) for Remington Club Xtra and those for Winchester T22. This is expected because these are both types of ammunition that are used in intermediate level target competition. The standard deviations for the two types of cartridges are almost identical, which is reflected in bars of similar lengths in the graphs.

The graphs show how the weights of the 20 cartridges in each sample are distributed around the average weight with some being higher than the average and some lower. There is no reason to perform this type of detailed analysis for all 14 types of ammunition, but such a graph shows clearly how differences between the standard deviations of several types of cartridges are determined by the variation in weights for the individual cartridges. The longer the bars, the larger the standard deviation.

Some serious experimenters have weighed cartridges and after grouping them by weight fired them in highly accurate target rifles. With the highest quality ammunition (such as Federal Ultra Match), grouping by weight made almost no difference. With inexpensive ammunition where the weights were less uniform, grouping cartridges by weight gave smaller groups when cartridges of similar weight were used. These results are exactly as one would expect. When you look at the weight distribution diagram for Federal Ultra Match, it is clear that segregation of cartridges by weight will not help much because uniformity is already assured. With ammunition having large variations in cartridge weight, it is possible to get a sample of cartridges that is more uniform if they are grouped by weighing. Competitors who already use ammunition of the highest quality are probably wasting time by weighing cartridges. Someone who is trying to achieve the highest accuracy possible while using a type of cartridge with somewhat larger weight

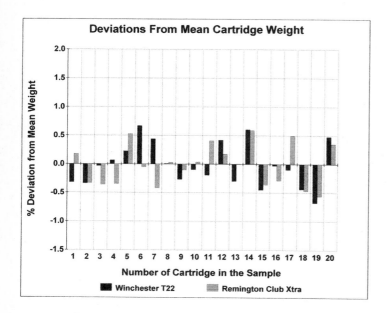

Deviations From Mean Cartridge Weight

Number of Cartridge in the Sample

■ Winchester T22   ▨ Remington Club Xtra

This bar graph shows that two common target loads have similar weight distributions.

variations could probably do better if the cartridges were segregated by weight.

Comparing the deviations in weight for the two types of cartridges chosen is not meant to imply that one is "better" than the others because they are designed to serve different purposes. However, the data shown in the table reveal that there can be significant differences in cartridge uniformity when several types of ammunition are studied. If a particular type of ammunition performs satisfactorily in your rifle and does what you expect of it, by all means use it. If you are searching for the ultimate in accuracy, explore all the avenues available, and these include considering not only rim thickness but also cartridge weights. Segregating ammunition with a narrow range of values of these characteristics may result in some improvement in accuracy.

Another factor that is known to affect the grouping ability of rimfire cartridges is the concentricity. This factor relates to whether the axis of the bullet is aligned with the axis of the case. In other words, if the cartridge does not have good concentricity, the bullet will be tipped sideways when the cartridge rests in the chamber. Theoretical studies have been conducted to determine how the grouping ability of the ammunition will be related to the extent to which the axis of the bullet and case are not in alignment. A special gauge is used to measure the concentricity of the case and bullet. This is an advanced topic that will concern few rimfire shooters. Certainly those who buy

ordinary rimfire ammunition and use it for sporting purposes will never have occasion to question this characteristic of their ammunition. However, for those individuals who are concerned with competition at the highest levels, an understanding of the problem is important. For those readers in this category, the excellent article by Frank Tirrell in *Small Caliber News*, Vol. 7, No. 2, Fall 2004, pp. 40-42 will be of great value.

Firing Pin Impact

In rimfire cartridges, the primer is contained in the rim of the case. The firing pin crushes the folded rim causing the primer to explode, which in turn ignites the powder. Smokeless powder burns generating gaseous products that expand rapidly against the base of the bullet. This force applied to the base of the bullet moves it down the barrel with increasing velocity. As the bullet engages the rifling, it is engraved by the lands, which causes the bullet to spin. Part of the energy produced by the burning powder is used in deforming the bullet, heating the bullet and barrel, and overcoming friction between the bullet and the barrel. Although the bullet has kinetic energy because of its motion, it also has a smaller amount of energy as a result of its rotation.

There is another aspect of the impact of the firing pin on the cartridge rim that has a bearing on exactly how firing occurs. That factor is the shape of the firing pin and the corresponding shape of the dent that it makes on the cartridge base. If the firing pin hits too far toward the outside of the cartridge or hits inside the rim toward the center of the cartridge, ignition is not as efficient as when the firing pin strikes the cartridge in the optimum manner. When you examine empty cases from cartridges that have been fired in different rimfire rifles, it is clear that there is a considerable difference in how the firing pin strikes the rim. Some firing pins have a wedge-shaped tip whereas others have rectangular or round tips. Moreover, a rather heavy but reproducible force on the firing pin is necessary to produce uniform shot to shot ignition. When the rifle is held in a horizontal position, the powder rests on the bottom of the case but the firing pin on most rimfire rifles strikes the top edge of the cartridge base. Some of the highest quality target rifles have actions designed to deliver the firing pin blow to the bottom edge of the cartridge base so that the priming mixture is in better contact with the powder. Although all of these factors must be considered by engineers when designing a firearm, particularly one designed for the highest level of competition, they are

These empty cases show great variation in firing pin dents. The case on the right is a Federal Ultra Match cartridge that has a dimpled case head to control ignition.

usually beyond the control of the shooter. The vast majority of rimfire shooters will never have occasion to alter these aspects of internal ballistics, but it is important to understand the basic principles.

Pressure

After ignition has occurred, the powder begins to burn rapidly and generate gaseous products, which exert pressure on the base of the bullet. Owing to the small case volume, rimfire cartridges utilize powder that is fast burning compared to the powder used in larger centerfire cartridges. The burning powder gives a rapid increase in pressure, and when the pressure inside the case is sufficiently high, the bullet is forced out of the case. Depending on the design of the firearm, the bullet may already be touching the rifling before firing as is the case in rifles with so-called match chambers. In most ordinary rimfire rifles, there is some small distance between the chamber and where the rifling begins so the bullet must move that distance before it engages the rifling. This distance is known as the free bore of the rifle. When the bullet starts its motion in contact with the rifling, there is greater resistance to the initial movement of the bullet so the pressure rises rapidly. When the rifle has some extent of free bore, the maximum pressure is reached after the bullet is already in motion. The result is that higher velocity can be achieved with a pressure that is still below the design limits of the firearm. This is not much of a factor with rimfire firearms, but free boring is commonly used in magnum centerfire rifles so that the highest velocity can be achieved within prescribed pressure limits. Perhaps the best known application of the principles related to free bore has been with the Weatherby magnum rifles and cartridges. Generally, better accuracy is achieved when the bullet starts out in contact with the rifling or very nearly so. Most rimfire match rifles and more expensive sporters are designed that way.

As more of the powder burns, the pressure increases and the bullet is accelerated as it moves along the bore. In a .22 LR cartridge, the small charge of fast burning powder is consumed rather quickly and after that, the bullet velocity may actually decrease as the bullet moves farther along in the barrel. Many tests have been conducted in which the same .22 LR rifle was fired with barrels of varying length (usually by successively shortening the same barrel), and the results of these tests show that the maximum velocity is produced in barrels that are approximately 16-18 inches in length. In longer barrels, the velocity decreases after the bullet has traveled farther than that distance down the bore. However, the difference between the velocity produced in a 16-inch barrel and one of 20 inches is only a few feet per second, and the difference is not the same for different types of ammunition. Because of the larger charges of slower burning powder used in the .22 WMR and .17 HMR ammunition, the velocity continues to increase as a bullet moves through a barrel longer than 16 inches. Accordingly, most rifles in .17 HMR caliber have barrels that are 22 inches in length whereas those in .22 WMR average around 20 inches. In the very small .17 caliber bore, the volume of the bore is small so the confined gas continues to exert pressure on the bullet, and the extra two inches of barrel length results in some increase in velocity.

The question often arises as to whether an auto-loader gives lower velocity than a rifle with a closed breech when the same ammunition is used in both and the barrel lengths are identical. Does the motion of the bolt in the autoloader rob the bullet of some of its velocity? Tests have shown that velocities produced by the bolt action rifle are usually slightly higher than those produced by the autoloader. However, it is not the motion of the bolt being blown back in the autoloader that is responsible. The bullet has exited the barrel before the bolt has been moved backward a significant amount. The main factor responsible is the difference in chambers of the rifles. In order to accept a variety of types of ammunition and feed them rapidly and reliably as the bolt slams forward, autoloaders often have chambers that tend toward the maximum dimensions. Bolt action rifles have the cartridges fed by hand and locked in place as the bolt is turned manually. Consequently, bolt action rifles can have tighter chambers than autoloaders and also have the rifling extend back to the front end of the chamber (known as a match-type chamber). The smaller chamber dimensions and the rifling holding the bullet in the cartridge case until the pressure has risen causes the pressure generated in a bolt action to be slightly higher and that is probably responsible for any difference in velocities given by the two types of actions. Only a few autoloaders are built with match type chambers and they are usually target rifles such as the Ruger 10/22T and the Thompson/Center Benchmark. However, the T/C Classic sporter (which is no longer produced) also has a match type chamber.

It is an interesting fact that the majority of types of smokeless propellants have about the same chemical composition and energy content. However, there may be an enormous difference in the burning rates of powders, which controls the rate at which the chemical energy is released. The burning rates of nitrocellulose propellants are determined by particle size, shape of the particles, additives, etc. Because shooters of rimfire ammunition do not reload ammunition (although it has been done), selection of the propellant is not a factor as it is when shooters reload centerfire ammunition. The total energy content of the powder charge is released during the event of firing the cartridge. Much of that energy is lost as heat to the surroundings (the barrel, case, and bullet) and some is carried away as kinetic energy of the moving gases.

The expanding gas generates a force on the base of the bullet that is determined by the pressure (measured in pounds per square inch) and the area of the base of the bullet (measured in square inches). However, unlike the pressure inside a tire, the pressure generated by the expanding gas is not constant. It increases rapidly up to a maximum then decreases as the bullet continues to move. For a .22 LR high speed cartridge, the maximum pressure may reach a value as high as approximately 25,000 pounds per square inch (written as 25,000 psi or 25,000 lb/in^2). The maximum pressure generated by .22 WMR and .17 HMR cartridges is not much different, but higher pressure is maintained longer than in the .22 LR because of the larger charges of slower burning powder used in these rounds. This does not mean that the force acting on the base of the bullet is 25,000 pounds because the area of the base is only a fraction of a square inch. For example, the base of the bullet is circular, which means that the area is given by the formula $A = \pi r^2$.

For a bullet that is 0.224 inch in diameter, the radius is 0.112 inch so the area is

$$A = \pi r^2 = 3.14 \times (0.112 \text{ inch})^2 = 0.0394 \text{ in}^2$$

Therefore, the maximum force (F) on the base of the bullet is given as the pressure (P) multiplied by the area on which the pressure is exerted.

$$F = P \times A = 25,000 \text{ lb/in}^2 \times 0.0394 \text{ in}^2 = 985 \text{ lb}$$

Although 985 lb may be the maximum force on the base of the bullet, the average force is much lower because the maximum pressure is not maintained throughout the entire length of the barrel. Moreover, the net force is lower because part of the force is required to overcome friction, cause the rifling to engrave the bullet, and to increase the rotational velocity of the bullet. If a net force of 985 lb operated on a bullet over a distance of two feet, the work done on the bullet (and hence the kinetic energy it would acquire) would be given as the product of the force multiplied by the distance over which that force operates.

$$\text{Work} = \text{energy} = E = \text{force} \times \text{distance}$$
$$= 2 \text{ feet} \times 985 \text{ pounds} = 1,970 \text{ ft lbs}$$

Because the energy of a high velocity .22 LR bullet is only about 140 ft lbs, the net force on the base is much lower than 985 lb. In fact, 985 lb is the maximum force that would exist only at the instant when the pressure is at its *maximum* value of 25,000 lb/in^2. Throughout most of the time the bullet is in the barrel the pressure is much lower than that value.

When a cartridge is fired, the pressure varies in a predictable way. It increases beginning with the explosion of the primer followed by ignition of the powder, which generates a mixture of expanding gases. When the pressure is high enough to overcome the resistance to bullet travel caused by the crimping and friction between the bullet and the inside of the case neck, the bullet starts to move. Continued burning of the propellant causes the pressure to increase as more gas forms. As more of the propellant charge is consumed, the rate at which gas is generated decreases and the pressure no longer increases. As the bullet moves farther down the barrel, the volume inside the bore that is available for the gas to occupy gets larger and the gases are also cooled. Both of these factors cause the pressure to decrease below the maximum value. If a graph is made showing the pressure as it varies with distance of bullet travel, a curve is obtained, which shows the pressure rising to some maximum value then decreasing thereafter.

The accompanying graph shows this relationship between pressure and the distance the bullet has traveled down the bore. Note that the pressure may reach a peak value of 25,000 lb/in², but it is much lower during most of the bullet travel. Therefore, the average pressure is well below the peak pressure. We will now show in a simple way how these forces are related to bullet energy.

We can see the importance of these factors by noting that the kinetic energy of the bullet from a high speed .22 LR as it leaves the muzzle is approximately 140 ft lbs. Kinetic energy (E) and work (W) have the same units, foot pounds (abbreviated as ft lb), which expresses the amount of work done by a force measured in pounds operating through a distance measured in feet. The multiplication of distance in feet times a force measured in pounds is how we get the unit ft lb. For example, if the barrel were two feet in length, a constant net force of 70 pounds operating over this distance would involve 140 ft lbs of work or energy, which is equal to the energy of the bullet as it leaves the muzzle.

E = W = Force × Distance = 2 feet × 70 pounds = 140 foot pounds = 140 ft lbs

Although the maximum force operating on the base of the bullet may be as much as 985 lb, the average force is only a fraction of that value and the average *net* force is lower still. No matter how much total work is done on the bullet by the expanding gases, we know that the net work is only 140 ft lbs because that is how much energy the bullet has when it exits from the muzzle.

One of the simple rules from geometry concerns the area of a rectangle, which is given as the product of its length and width. This can be written in equation form as

Area = Length × Width = L × W

The equation that gives energy or work shown earlier has exactly the same form except that it involves force and distance. Therefore, we can represent the work done as the product of a force and a distance with the product being shown as the area of a rectangle. The accompanying figure shows this representation. However, this simple analogy works *only* when the force has a *constant* value. In the case of a projectile being forced down the bore, the force is not constant.

It has been shown earlier that the force on the base of the bullet is given by the pressure multiplied by the area of the base of the bullet. Because the area of the

base of the bullet does not change, it is the pressure that is changing as the bullet travels down the bore. As a result, we could make a graph showing the force on the base of the bullet as a function of distance the bullet has traveled. The result would be a curve that has the same general shape as the pressure-distance curve described earlier. Work (or energy) is the product of the net force applied and the distance over which it is applied (the length of the barrel). As shown above, there is no difficulty in performing this multiplication when the force does not change, but in the case of the bullet moving down the barrel, the force is changing. The problem then becomes one known as *work done by a variable force*. Obtaining the *net* work done on the bullet by the expanding gases (the energy of the bullet) is not as simple as multiplying a force times a distance to give an area.

By appropriate mathematical means, it is possible to determine the area under the force-distance curve even though the force has a different magnitude at each distance. In principle, we could take the area under the curve and slice it into small segments (say slices representing one inch of bullet travel) because within those *small* intervals the force is *approximately* constant. In other words, the slight curvature in the graph is ignored and it is treated as if it were a straight line across the top of the slice. The result would be a large number of slices having geometric shapes known as trapezoids for which the areas can be calculated simply. Adding the areas of all of the slices (area segments) would give the total area under the curve. Note that within each slice the product of the average force times the width of the slice (one inch in the example

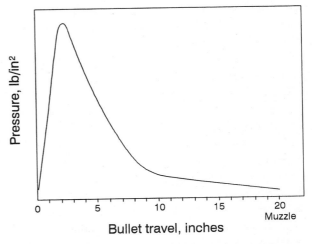

Shown in this graph is the qualitative relationship between the pressure and the distance the bullet has traveled in a 20-inch barrel.

here) gives the amount of work represented by that slice. Therefore, the *sum* of the areas of all the slices would give the *total* area under the curve. That area represents the total net work done on the bullet, which is the same as its kinetic energy. Thus, it is possible to calculate the energy of the bullet *if* the pressure is known at several distances along the bore between the chamber and the muzzle.

An interesting phenomenon is observed when two powders having different burning rates are compared. Consider powders A and B with powder A having the faster burning rate. Let us assume that the same weight of each powder is loaded in cartridges and then the cartridges are fired. The cartridge loaded with Powder A will produce a higher pressure in a shorter time so the pressure curve will rise to a high value then drop quickly. In fact, it is possible that this peak pressure may be high enough to rupture the cartridge case. When the cartridge containing Powder B is fired, the pressure will rise more slowly, and reach a maximum that is lower. As a result of the powder burning longer, the pressure will remain higher for a longer period of time than in case of the cartridge loaded with Powder A. In addition, with the peak pressure being lower, it is usually possible to use an even larger charge of Powder B, which will in turn maintain a higher pressure longer. In other words, the area under the pressure-distance curve will be larger and the resulting bullet velocity will be higher. The accompanying figure shows the relationship between these two situations. This principle is precisely the reason that larger charges of slower burning powders are used to produce high velocities without giving a pressure that is higher than the peak pressure the firearm and case are designed to withstand. Of course, in order to burn the larger charge of slower burning powder efficiently it helps to have a longer barrel.

It has already been explained that the velocity of the bullet of a .22 LR reaches its maximum velocity after traveling approximately 16 inches in the barrel. If we make a graph showing bullet velocity as a function of bullet travel, the curve will reach a plateau at approximately 16 inches and velocity will remain constant or decrease slightly as the bullet travels farther in the bore. In other words, the net force operating on the bullet reaches zero because the force on the base is small (the gas has already expanded and cooled) and it is necessary to overcome friction between the bullet and the barrel. The pressure inside the firearm at the instant the bullet leaves the muzzle will be very low. The accompanying graph shows this relationship.

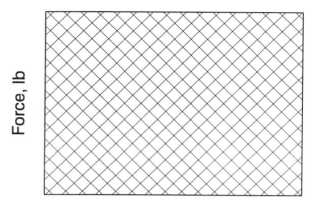

Distance, feet

The work done by a constant force is given by the product of the force times the distance through which it is applied, $W = F \times D$. This can be expressed as the area of a rectangle for which the area is the product of the length times the width. In this case, the length is the distance and the width is the applied force.

This author once had a Mossberg Model 146 bolt action .22 LR rifle that had a 26-inch barrel. How well he remembers being told to be especially careful because that big rifle would be dangerous at a greater range than the small single shot he had used earlier. In truth, the bullet velocity was probably somewhat lower than the short-barreled single shot gave, but no one had a chronograph in those days of innocence and ignorance in rimfire shooting. It was one of those cases where the rifle looked big and the basic statement sounded good so it was probably true. There are numerous such beliefs that get perpetuated, but many rimfire shooters now know better.

The basic principles of propulsion are fairly straightforward, but there is little that can be done by the shooter to alter the situation. In recent years, bullets for use in centerfire rifles have become available that are coated with molybdenum disulfide to reduce friction as they move down the bore. As a result, higher velocities (but usually less than 10% higher) can be achieved. The reloader of centerfire ammunition has another variable that can be brought into play. By utilizing a slower burning propellant, a higher average pressure is maintained because the powder burns longer but slower without exceeding the maximum pressure (which is the pressure that represents the limit for a load in a particular firearm). In other words, upon firing the pressure still increases to some maximum value, but the slower burning powder maintains a higher pressure for a longer period of time. This results in a greater average net force on the base of bullet, which results in higher velocity. Although the shooter using rimfire ammunition has no such option, the engineers designing the cartridges do. It is exactly this principle that enables the .17 HMR to achieve its high velocity because a slow burning powder (at least for a rimfire cartridge) is used.

Rimfire Rifle Velocities

As part of the work carried out in this project, the velocities were measured for several rifle and cartridge combinations. No attempt was made to fire all of the available types of ammunition in every rifle. The idea was to obtain velocities for many types of ammunition in at least one rifle. In most cases, at least 10 rounds (but in some cases as many as 25-30 rounds) were fired, and the velocities were measured using a Competition Electronics ProChrono Chronograph placed 10 feet from the muzzle. A velocity obtained in this way is known as an instrumental velocity, and it will differ somewhat from the value of the muzzle velocity published by the manufacturer for this particular load. There is some loss in velocity even in the first 10 feet of the bullet's path. The muzzle velocity would normally be approximately 20-25 ft/sec higher than it is at 10 feet. Also, velocity data published by manufacturers are obtained under controlled conditions with barrels measuring 24 inches in length for most cartridges. A particular lot of ammunition may give a velocity that is higher or lower than that specified as being nominal for that particular load. As a result, it is quite common for instrumental velocities to be somewhat different from published values. In the table, the average velocity is

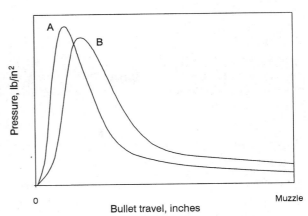

The relationship between pressure and distance of bullet travel for powders A (faster burning rate) and B (slower burning rate). Pressure remains higher for a longer time with powder B, which means that more work is done on the bullet giving it higher velocity. Powder A would produce a higher velocity in a short handgun barrel.

given followed by the standard deviation (a statistical measure showing uniformity). These values are shown in the form velocity ± standard deviation.

Although there is no need to try to explain every entry in the table, it is possible to make several observations regarding the data. Consider the case of the Federal Gold Medal Target load, which has an advertised velocity of 1,080 ft/sec. The velocity of this load was measured in five different rifles as 1,110, 1,064, 1,051, 1,096, and 1,096 ft/sec with standard deviations ranging from 26 to 41 ft/sec. Clearly, the velocity produced by this load is almost exactly that specified by the manufacturer (and statistically it can be considered to be the

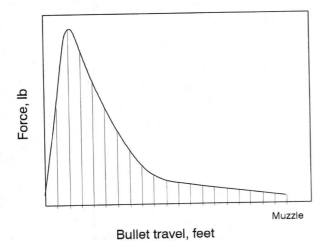

The area under the force curve gives the net work done on the bullet (bullet energy). The area can be considered as a series of slices, the area of which can be determined. Adding the areas of the slices gives the total net energy of the bullet.

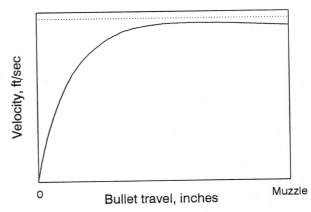

Relationship between velocity and distance the bullet has traveled down a barrel is shown. For the .22 LR, the maximum velocity is reached in about 16 inches of travel.

Instrumental Velocity at 10 Feet for .22 LR Ammunition

CARTRIDGE	VELOCITY, FT/SEC IN VARIOUS RIFLES				
	RUGER 77/22	MARLIN 25N	RUGER 10/22T	RUGER 10/22	HENRY
CCI Green Tag	---	1,048 ± 35	---	1,047 ± 32	---
CCI Mini Mag	---	1,179 ± 43	1,176 ± 61	---	---
CCI Std. Vel.	---	956 ± 36	962 ± 35	964 ± 39	---
CCI SGB	1,292 ± 52	---	---	1,207 ± 50	---
CCI Velocitor	---	1,301 ± 51	1,316 ± 56	---	---
Fed. G.M. Tgt.	1,110 ± 26	1,064 ± 41	1,051 ± 40	1,096 ± 31	1,096 ± 38
Fed. HVHP	---	1,304 ± 67	---	---	1,251 ± 54
Fed. Lightning	---	1,194 ± 48	---	---	---
Fed. U. M.	1,107 ± 45	---	---	---	---
Lapua Scoremax	1,048 ± 31	---	---	---	---
Lapua Sup.Club	1,046 ± 37	---	---	---	---
Rem. Club Xtra	---	1,049 ± 36	1,024 ± 35	---	---
Rem. Game Load	---	1,119 ± 55	---	---	---
Rem. Golden	---	1,144 ± 49	1,209 ± 43	1,111 ± 70	1,161 ± 51
Rem. Tgt.	1,153 ± 32	---	1,084 ± 35	---	---
Rem. Viper	---	1,243 ± 66	---	---	---
Rem. Yel. Jkt.	---	1,362 ± 34	---	---	---
Standard Plus	---	---	991 ± 41	1,009 ± 26	---
Win. T22	1,116 ± 37	---	1,112 ± 37	---	---
Win. PP	---	1,142 ± 50	1,174 ± 52	---	1,229 ± 42
Win. SX	---	1,150 ± 46	---	1,145 ± 66	1,119 ± 43
Win. Wildcat	---	1,168 ± 52	---	---	---
Wolf M. T.	---	1,059 ± 33	---	---	---

Abbreviations: Std. Vel. = Standard Velocity; Fed. = Federal; G.M. Tgt. = Gold Medal Target; HVHP = High Velocity Hollow Point; U.M. = Ultra Match; Sup. = Super; Rem. = Remington; Tgt. = Target; Yel. Jkt. = Yellow Jacket; PP = Power Point; SX = Super-X; Win. = Winchester; M.T. = Match Target.

same given the magnitude of the standard deviations). The CCI SGB load has an advertised velocity of 1,235 ft/sec, and the velocity was determined as 1,292 and 1,207 in two different rifles. In these cases, the standard deviations were 52 and 50 ft/sec, respectively. Winchester advertises the T22 as having a muzzle velocity of 1,150 ft/sec. The velocity at 10 feet from the muzzle was found to be 1,116 from a Ruger 77/22 and 1,112 ft/sec from a Ruger 10/22T with a standard deviation of 37 ft/sec in each case. This is in almost exact agreement with the published value. Lapua Scoremax has an advertised velocity of 1,040 ft/sec for its 48-grain bullet, and the measured velocity is 1,046 ft/sec. Numerous other examples of this type of correlation are shown by the data in the table. However, there are some instances in which the instrumental velocity is somewhat lower than the published velocity. Keep in mind that there are lot to lot variations in ammunition so the lot tested may not be among those giving high velocity, and this is normal. Also, some of the testing was conducted at rather low temperature, which tends to cause velocity to be slightly lower. Finally, it is the performance in your rifle that counts, not whether the measured velocity is close to that advertised for any load.

The .17 HMR is a high velocity cartridge, and this is one of the reasons for its dramatic performance. Several types of .17 HMR were fired through CZ 452 and Ruger 77/22 bolt action rifles to determine the velocity of 17 and 20-grain bullets. The accompanying table shows the results of these measurements when

Instrumental Velocity at 10 Feet for .17 HMR Ammunition

CARTRIDGE	CZ 452 VELOCITY, FT/SEC	RUGER 77/17 VELOCITY, FT/SEC
CCI TNT (17 gr)	2,612 ± 28	2,637 ± 28
CCI Game Point (20 gr)	2,384 ± 27	2,404 ± 40
Federal V-Shok (17 gr)	2,612 ± 26	---
Hornady V-Max (17 gr)	2,594 ± 29	2,577 ± 44
Hornady V-Max (20 gr)	---	2,440 ± 29
Remington Premier (17 gr)	2,614 ± 23	---

the chronograph was placed 10 feet from the muzzle. Because each .17 HMR load is essentially identical except for packaging, velocities of each type of load with the same bullet weight should be identical.

Velocities of .17 HMR loads specified by the manufacturer are 2,550 and 2,375 ft/sec for the 17- and 20-grain bullets, respectively. The data shown in the table indicate that the advertised velocities are met in all of the loads tested. To well within the standard deviations, velocities of all of the loads with 17-grain bullets are identical as are those of the 20-grain loads. Another observation that can be made is that the velocities are quite uniform. Keep in mind that for a velocity of 2,500 ft/sec a standard deviation of 25 ft/sec represents only 1% of the actual velocity. A standard deviation of 1% in fact represents a high level of uniformity. The two rifles gave average velocities that were well within the standard deviation so it is not possible to assign any significance to a few feet per second higher velocity for one rifle or the other. Clearly, the .17 HMR is a high velocity cartridge that yields dramatic effects on targets and uniform velocities.

Bullet Velocities from Handguns

With fast burning powders such as those used in .22 LR ammunition, the bullet is accelerated rapidly. As a result, most .22 LR cartridges will produce velocities in the short barrels of handguns that are as much as 90% of those produced when the same cartridges are fired in rifles. The percentage is somewhat lower when cartridges such as the CCI Stinger or Velocitor are considered. Because the gap between the cylinder and barrel allows some gas to escape, revolvers generally give slightly lower velocity than autoloaders that have the same barrel length. In order to show some of these effects, tests were conducted in which several types of ammunition were fired in different handguns. Five-shot strings were fired with the velocity measured at 8 feet from the muzzle. The accompanying table shows the average velocities obtained.

Average Bullet Velocities from Several Handguns

CARTRIDGE	S&W 2206 4.5"	Brwng. B.M.[a] 5.5"	High Std. HB[b] 6.75"	Colt F.S.[c] 4.75"	Colt Bunt.[d] 10"	S&W K-22 6"
Federal HV HP	1,061	1,129	1,114	1,034	1,020	1,076
Remington Golden	944	992	1,029	873	886	915
Winchester Power Pt	984	1,026	1,030	913	875	910
PMC Sidewinder	977	1,025	988	864	904	911
Federal Lightning	997	1,065	1,037	928	926	991
Winchester Wildcat	955	997	1,002	860	862	899
Remington Target	853	928	940	868	859	900
Remington Yellow Jacket	1,134	1,201	------	1,101	1,137	1,117
Remington Viper	1,044	1,099	------	996	1,027	1,067
Winchester Super-X HP	1,023	1,027	1,077	964	903	961

[a] Browning Buck Mark; [b] High Standard HB; [c] Colt Frontier Scout; [d] Colt Frontier Scout Buntline

Autoloaders like this Browning Buck Mark usually give higher velocities than revolvers of similar barrel length.

A chronograph is an indispensable tool for the serious rimfire shooter. The author uses a Competition Electronics ProChrono model.

The data shown in the table reveal some interesting trends. First, the velocities produced by the autoloaders are generally higher than those produced by the revolvers. In some cases, even the 4½-inch barrel of the S&W 2206 resulted in higher velocities than those produced by the 6-inch barreled S&W K-22 revolver. In order for the cylinder of a revolver to rotate freely, there must be some clearance between the front face of the cylinder and the rear end of the barrel. Upon firing, some gas escapes from the gap so that the force on the base of the bullet decreases more rapidly. Therefore, acceleration of the bullet is slightly lower and the bullet is retarded by friction.

Second, the 5.5-inch barrel of the Browning Buck Mark produced velocities that averaged approximately 50 ft/sec higher than those produced by the 4.5-inch barreled S&W 2206. This difference is typical of what can be expected for a one-inch difference in barrel length when the type of handgun is the same. Third, the 4.75-inch barreled Colt Frontier Scout gave veloc-

A longer barrel does not necessarily mean higher velocities. This 10-inch barreled Colt Frontier Scout gave lower velocities than did another that had a 4 3/4-inch barrel.

ities that are approximately equal to those from the 10-inch barreled version. In a long barreled revolver, gas escaping between the cylinder and barrel can reduce the pressure to the point where the force on the base of the bullet is not maintained at a sufficient level to result in increased velocity. This does not happen when a closed breech in an autoloader is involved. Moreover, the Frontier Scout having the 10-inch barrel has a rather large cylinder to barrel gap.

Finally, the bullet velocities are considerably lower than the same types of ammunition give in rifles. For example, Remington Yellow Jackets had an average velocity of 1,444 ft/sec from a CZ 452 rifle having a barrel length of 20.5 inches, but only 1,201 ft/sec (a difference of 16.8%) from the 5.5-inch barrel of the Browning Buck Mark. Federal High Velocity hollow points averaged 1,315 ft/sec from the author's 20-inch barreled Winchester 190 but only 1,129 ft/sec (a difference of 14.1%) from the 5.5-inch barreled Browning Buck Mark. Winchester Super-X hollow points averaged 1,160 and 1,173 ft/sec from two rifles but only slightly over 1,000 ft/sec from the two autoloader pistols. All of these data illustrate the principles described above.

When bullet velocities are measured from handguns, velocities for the .22 WMR and .17 HMR are much lower than they are from rifles (sometimes only 65-75% as high). The reason is that the magnum loads make use of larger charges of slower burning powders that are not burned as efficiently in short barrels. There is no free lunch.

Although it is important to understand the principles of internal ballistics, rimfire shooters can do little to change some of the parameters. The principles set forth in this chapter provide some insight to what happens during the firing process. The next chapter will describe some of the principles of the flight of a bullet.

CHAPTER 9

EXTERNAL BALLISTICS FOR BEGINNERS

IF THERE IS ONE ASPECT OF SHOOTING that is poorly understood by many shooters, it is external ballistics. Some of the questions appearing in magazines and on internet sites reveal that the person asking the question has no understanding of the bullet's flight and the factors that affect it. Because there are several variables involved, treating the flight of a bullet as a mathematical problem is a formidable task that requires knowledge of advanced mathematics. Fortunately, for effective use of rimfires this is not necessary, and it is possible to develop a good working knowledge of ballistics without resorting to the use of a lot of mathematics.

Forces on Projectiles

In an elementary view of external ballistics, there are only two forces acting on the bullet after it leaves the muzzle. At an advanced level, other forces must be considered, but they are unimportant when describing the path of a bullet over a moderate range. We leave that part of the discussion to the artillery experts and the 1000-yard competitors (who do not shoot rimfire rifles). The path of a projectile is known as its trajectory, and in this section we will consider the trajectories of bullets fired from rimfire cartridges.

The first force to be dealt with is air resistance on the bullet. Air is a mixture of gases (oxygen and nitro-

All rimfire shooters need to be concerned with ballistics of their ammunition. Shown are (left to right) the .17 Aguila, .17 Mach 2, .17 HMR, .22 LR, .22 WRF, and .22 WMR.

gen constitute about 99% of the atmosphere), which retards an object passing through it. The bullet must push molecules of the gases aside as it passes through the air. At high elevation, the atmosphere is "thinner" (there are fewer molecules in a given volume and air density is lower) so air resistance on the bullet is not as great as it is at low elevation. Atmospheric pressure depends on the number of molecules in a given volume. At a given elevation, the atmospheric pressure varies slightly over time depending on the weather conditions. For example, one day the pressure may be 29.92 inches of mercury and the next it may be 29.81 inches. The slight difference in air resistance on a projectile at these atmospheric pressures would not produce a noticeable effect on the trajectory of a bullet except perhaps at extreme ranges. It would take an incredibly accurate rifle to show such a slight difference in trajectory that results from such a small change in atmospheric pressure. However, this would not be true of artillery shells fired at an elevation of 1,000 ft above sea level at a target on the side of a mountain 5 miles away at an elevation of 5,000 ft. Such difficulties need not concern the sport shooter who uses a rimfire rifle.

Air resistance is not the same for all projectiles, even those of the same caliber. Moreover, air resistance for a given projectile is not the same at all velocities. The faster a projectile moves, the greater the number of gas molecules it encounters in a given period of time so air resistance is generally greater. This will be discussed more fully later.

The ability of a bullet to retain its velocity as it passes through air is designated by a number known as the ballistic coefficient. The higher the ballistic coefficient, the more effectively the bullet retains its velocity. Several factors contribute to the ballistic coefficient of a bullet, but the most obvious is the shape. It is easy to see why this is so. A blunt bullet passing through air forces gas molecules out of its path at greater angles, which means that the momentum of the bullet is imparted more rapidly to the gas molecules being displaced. Therefore, the bullet loses its momentum (and hence its velocity) in passing through air. A pointed bullet also forces gas molecules out of its path, but it can pass through the air while creating less disturbance. The molecules of gases are not forced outward at angles to the path of the bullet that are as great as when a blunt bullet is involved. Therefore, a sharp pointed bullet loses its momentum (and hence its velocity) less rapidly than does a blunt bullet of the same weight and diameter.

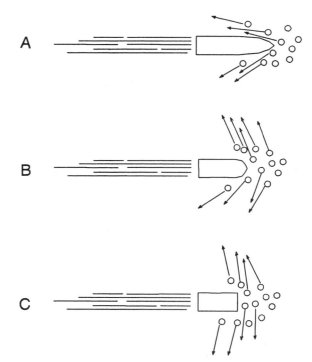

A projectile moving through the air forces molecules out of its path. A sharp pointed bullet (A) can pass through air more easily because the molecules are forced outward at smaller angles to the path. A blunt bullet (B) forces the molecules outward at larger angles, which means that they absorb more of the momentum of the bullet than in (A). A very blunt bullet (C) forces air molecules outward at very large angles, which results in even greater loss of momentum. Because of this effect, the ballistic coefficient of (A) is high, (B) has an intermediate ballistic coefficient, and (C) has a low ballistic coefficient.

These bullets have greatly differing ballistic coefficients as a result of differences in weights and shapes of their points.

A complicating feature that need not concern us here is that the ballistic coefficient is not the same even for a specific bullet if the velocity is different. In other words, the ballistic coefficient for a given bullet is not strictly a constant in all velocity ranges. Treating this effect leads into some of the interesting and deep topics in the science of ballistics, but they will not be explored in this book. Some of the references listed in Appendix A should be consulted for a complete study of this topic.

There is a simple way to calculate the ballistic coefficient for a bullet if the loss of velocity is known as the bullet travels between two points. Therefore, what we need to know is the velocity of the bullet at two points in its trajectory (for example at the muzzle and at 100 yards). Ballistics software currently available from numerous sources (such as suppliers of bullets for reloading centerfire ammunition) enables the user to input the velocity data so that the ballistic coefficient is calculated by the computer. To provide the data for the discussion presented here, this has been done for many of the available types of rimfire ammunition by taking the velocity data from the tables supplied by the manufacturer. Some surprising facts emerged from the calculations.

The calculated value for the ballistic coefficient of the various polymer tipped 17-grain bullets in .17 caliber turns out to be 0.125, which is determined by the muzzle velocity being 2,550 ft/sec and the velocity at 100 yards being 1,900 ft/sec (a loss of 650 ft/sec or 25.5%). This is exactly the ballistic coefficient published in various ballistics tables from manufacturers. However, some authors have stated that the sharply pointed .17 caliber bullets have a higher ballistic coefficient than those for bullets used in the .22 WMR. If

The ballistic coefficient of the 17-grain polymer tipped bullets used in .17 HMR cartridges is 0.125.

we take the velocity data from CCI tables, the 40-grain bullet from a .22 WMR has a muzzle velocity of 1,875 ft/sec and a remaining velocity at 100 yards of 1,375 ft/sec. Using these data in a computer program to calculate the ballistic coefficient gives a value of 0.130, which is slightly higher than that for the 17-grain bullets used in the .17 HMR. The velocity data from the Remington tables for the 33-grain V-Max bullet used in their Premium .22 WMR ammunition shows a muzzle velocity of 2,000 ft/sec and a velocity at 100 yards of 1,495 ft/sec. From these velocities a ballistic coefficient of 0.137 is determined. Even though the bullets used in most .22 WMR ammunition are not sharply pointed, their greater weight keeps them from losing velocity as rapidly as do the light weight .17 caliber bullets. When

The bullets in the .22 WMR cartridges in this lineup will have different ballistic coefficients.

the 50-grain .22 WMR load from Federal is used as a basis for calculating the ballistic coefficient, a value of 0.158 results. That heavy bullet really holds its velocity well, which is indicated by the fact that the remaining energy at 100 yards is 156 ft lbs compared to a value of 130 ft lbs for the high velocity 30-grain hollow point load in .22 WMR. The difference in energy is significant, especially when hunting larger varmints.

Another surprise arises when ballistic coefficients are calculated for bullets used in the .22 LR ammunition. For example, the CCI ballistics tables for the Velocitor load give a muzzle velocity of 1,435 ft/sec and a velocity of 1,112 ft/sec at 100 yards. These values yield a ballistic coefficient of 0.141 for the 40-grain hollow point bullet. When velocity data for the Federal Gold Medal Target load is used in the calculation, a ballistic coefficient of 0.167 results. When velocities for a considerable number of types of .22 LR ammunition are analyzed, it is found that the 40-grain solid bullets have ballistic coefficients of approximately 0.140-

0.160. The 29-grain bullet used in the .22 Short has a ballistic coefficient of only 0.104. For the 32-grain bullet used in the hyper velocity CCI Stinger, the ballistic coefficient is only 0.100 and a value of 0.106 is found for the 33-grain hollow point used in Remington Yellow Jacket ammunition. Therefore, the lightweight bullets used in hyper velocity loads lose velocity more rapidly than do the heavier bullets. These facts translate to significantly different energies for the heavy bullets and those used in the hyper velocity rounds, especially at longer ranges where a varmint may cross paths with the bullet.

Trajectory

Bullets traveling in air follow a curved path, but the line of sight from the shooter's eye to the target is a straight line. When a bullet travels down a straight rifle barrel, it is launched in the direction that the barrel is pointing. In order to take best advantage of the sights, the line of sight and the line of the bore do not exactly coincide. They are slightly closer together at the muzzle than they are at the breech. Therefore, if the line of sight to the target is perfectly horizontal, the bore being tipped slightly upward (in relation to the line of sight) causes the bullet to be launched in an upward direction that projects it above the horizontal line of sight at some distance. The bullet rises to meet the line of sight at some distance, travels above the line of sight, then crosses and falls below the line of sight at some longer distance. Therefore, the line of sight and the bullet path coincide at two distances. The longer of these distances is usually taken as the sight in distance. The deviation of the bullet path from the line of sight at one-half the range for which the rifle is sighted in is known as the midrange trajectory. Because the path of a bullet moving through air is not exactly parabolic, the midrange trajectory is not exactly the same as the maximum deviation from the line of sight. The highest point on the trajectory usually occurs at a distance that is approximately 60% of the range for which the piece is sighted in. In other words, when a .22 LR is sighted to hit the point of aim at 70 yards, the highest point on the trajectory is at approximately 40 yards instead of at the midpoint of the path (35 yards).

Most of the popular ballistics programs calculate the bullet drop, which is the distance the bullet would fall below the line of the bore at some distance when fired horizontally. This property is determined by the time of flight, and the simple laws of physics enable one to calculate how far an object would fall during

The ballistic coefficients of the light bullets used in hyper velocity .22 LR ammunition are only about 0.100-0.105, so such bullets lose velocity rapidly.

Even though the bullets in these .22 LR cartridges have different shapes, their ballistic coefficients do not differ by much.

that length of time. This is almost a useless property because shooters do not fire rifles perfectly horizontally while ignoring the sights on the rifle. The whole idea of sighting in at some distance is to optimize the trajectory. This is accomplished by adjusting the sights so that the path of the bullet rises above the line of sight and then meets it at the sight in distance. The overall drop of the bullet is immaterial except for the fact that the trajectory (which is useful) is also related to the time of flight. Comparing two bullets that have drops of 4 inches and 8 inches at some range does not mean that the one with the 4-inch drop can be sighted in at a range that is twice the other. It is also meaningless to say that the bullet that gives a drop of 4 inches shoots "twice as flat" as the other. Neither shoots "flat!"

Suppose you want to sight in a rifle so that the bullet path never deviates from the line of sight by more than a certain amount (perhaps one inch for a rimfire rifle that is used to shoot small targets). The distance at which the path of the bullet deviates from the line of sight by no more than the specified amount is known as the point blank range. This means that if the target has an overall size of two inches, the path of the bullet must not rise or fall more than one inch from the line of sight when the point of aim is the center of the target. As will be illustrated later, the point blank range for the standard velocity .22 LR is approximately 75 yards, that for the high velocity load about 85 yards, that for the .22 WMR about 125 yards, and that for the .17 HMR about 150 yards when an appropriate maximum deviation between the line of sight and point of impact is assumed.

The principles described above will be illustrated by considering several popular rimfire loads, and we will begin with the .22 LR then progress to a discussion of other cartridges. The trajectory data presented were obtained by using one of the standard computer programs.

.22 Long Rifle

As a starting point, we will consider the case of the Federal Gold Medal Target cartridge (Federal Product No. 711B), which gives a muzzle velocity of 1,080 ft/sec. If the sights are adjusted so that the bullet strikes the point of aim at 50 yards, the bullet will first cross the line of sight at approximately 18 yards and will strike approximately 0.3 inch high at 25 yards. After crossing the line of sight at 50 yards, the bullet would impact 2.44 inches low at 75 yards. All of this depends on how far the line of sight is above the bore, and that value must be specified when performing ballistic calculations. Typically, the axis of most scopes gives a line of sight that is approximately 1.5 inches above the center of the bore. If the distance between the bore and the line of sight is only 1.3 inches, all of the deviations from the line of sight would be moved upward slightly. If the sight height is 1.3 inches, the bullet would strike approximately 0.5 inch high at 25 yards when sighted in at 50 yards. The effect caused by different sight heights will be demonstrated later.

All manufacturers of ammunition provide ballistics tables for their products. However, the ranges specified usually include only 0, 50, and 100 yards when rimfire ammunition is being described. The careful rimfire shooter needs information that provides more details about trajectory at other ranges.

Calculated Trajectories for .22 LR Federal Gold Medal Target (R_0 is Sight-In Range)

RANGE, YDS.	V, FT/SEC	E, FT LB	DEVIATION FROM LINE OF SIGHT, INCHES		
			R0 = 50 YD	R0 = 60 YD	R0 = 70 YD
0	1,080	103	−1.50	−1.50	−1.50
10	1,060	100	−0.57	−0.44	−0.31
20	1,042	96	+0.06	+0.30	+0.58
30	1,025	93	+0.37	+0.73	+1.14
40	1,009	90	+0.35	+0.83	+1.38
50	994	88	0.00	+0.59	+1.27
60	980	85	−0.70	0.00	+0.82
70	967	83	−1.74	−0.95	0.00
80	954	81	−3.16	−2.28	−1.19
90	942	79	−4.94	−3.97	−2.75
100	931	77	−7.10	−6.05	−4.69

Knowing the ballistic coefficient for a bullet and its initial velocity allows the trajectory to be calculated by making use of the ballistics programs that are available from several suppliers of reloading information. The accompanying table shows the results of such calculations for the .22 LR Federal Gold Medal Target ammunition for which the ballistic coefficient of the bullet is taken to be 0.140 and the muzzle velocity is 1,080 ft/sec. These values are characteristic of standard velocity .22 LR ammunition from other manufacturers. In this example, three different sight in ranges, 50, 60, 70 yards, have been assumed in the calculations to illustrate the effect on trajectory.

The data shown in the table reveal why the common practice of sighting in a .22 LR with standard velocity ammunition at 50 yards may not be the best plan. Clearly, in this case the bullet rises to a maximum height that is much less than an inch above the line of sight. The point of impact is 0.37 inch high at 30 yards when the rifle is sighted in at a range of 50 yards. When sighting in a .22 LR for small game hunting or pest shooting, it is appropriate to sight in at 50 yards because a hunter would want to be able to hold directly on a very small target and shots at distances greater than 50 yards are uncommon. However, for shooting larger targets (such as ground squirrels sitting vertically) with a .22 LR, it makes sense to sight in with target ammunition at around 60-65 yards to give a longer point blank range. When sighted in this way, the bullet will strike about three-quarters of an inch high at 30 yards and about 0.83 inch high at 40 yards. Unless you are shooting at a very small target with a

very accurate rifle, these deviations from the line of sight will not cause misses and the bullet will strike only about an inch low at 70 yards, which is about the longest range practical for trying to shoot pests with standard velocity ammunition in a .22 LR. Of course, you could sight in at a range of 100 yards for small bore competition, but the bullet will strike approximately 3.6 inches high at 50 and 60 yards.

The powerhouse of the .22 LR cartridges is the CCI Velocitor, which gives a 40-grain hollow point bullet a muzzle velocity advertised to be 1,435 ft/sec with a corresponding muzzle energy of over 180 ft lbs. Even at a range of 100 yards the remaining energy is 110 ft lbs, which is about the same as a standard velocity round produces at the muzzle. When using this ammunition on pests and game, the rifle should be sighted in to take advantage of its flatter trajectory and power. The results of ballistics calculations that are shown in the table provide the basis for deciding the most advantageous way to sight in a rifle when using CCI Velocitors. The ballistic coefficient of this bullet is 0.141.

For most varmint shooting, a deviation of one inch from the line of sight will not cause misses. The data show that it is practical to sight in a rifle shooting CCI Velocitors at a range of 75 yards, which will give a point blank range of about 85 yards. This is about the maximum practical range for the .22 LR as a varmint rifle.

Keep in mind that game is not shot at the muzzle and that at a range of 50-100 yards the energy may be quite different from that at the muzzle. For example, a high velocity .22 LR produces about 140 ft lbs at the muzzle, but after the bullet travels 50 yards that has

Calculated Trajectories for .22 LR CCI Velocitor (R_0 is the Sight-In Range)

RANGE, YDS	V, FT/SEC	E, FT LB	DEVIATION FROM LINE OF SIGHT, INCHES		
			R0 = 60 YD	R0 = 70 YD	R0 = 80 YD
0	1,435	183	−1.50	−1.50	−1.50
10	1,396	173	−0.77	−0.70	−0.61
20	1,358	164	−0.22	−0.07	+0.09
30	1,321	155	+0.15	+0.36	+0.61
40	1,287	147	+0.31	+0.60	+0.93
50	1,253	140	+0.27	+0.63	+1.05
60	1,222	133	0.00	+0.43	+0.93
70	1,192	126	−0.50	0.00	+0.59
80	1,164	120	−1.25	−0.67	0.00
90	1,138	115	−2.25	−1.60	−0.85
100	1,114	110	−3.52	−2.80	−1.96

decreased to about 110 ft lbs. A standard velocity .22 LR produces about 105 ft lbs at the muzzle but the remaining energy at 50 yards is about 90 ft lbs. Note that the high velocity round has lost 35 ft lbs while traveling 50 yards, but the standard velocity round has lost only 20 ft lbs in the same interval. Remaining energies at 100 yards are even closer together. A hyper velocity .22 LR that uses a light weight bullet that has a low ballistic coefficient may produce 160 ft lbs at the muzzle but give a remaining energy of only 90 ft lbs out at 100 yards where the target is. Because it produces a high energy although using a bullet of normal weight, the CCI Velocitor retains its energy advantage even at extended ranges.

These .22 WMR cartridges are loaded with (left to right) 30-grain hollow point, 33-grain polymer tipped, and 50-grain hollow point bullets. The corresponding ballistic coefficients differ significantly, and the 33-grain and 50-grain bullets hold their velocity well.

.22 Winchester Magnum Rimfire

The .22 WMR is a powerful cartridge that is widely used as a varmint load, but it is almost never considered as a target round. For use on varmints, we need to determine the most efficient range for which the rifle should be sighted in. Because there are several bullet weights available in ammunition for the .22 WMR, we need to decide which load is to be used, and for purposes of illustration, the Winchester 40-grain jacketed hollow point will be considered. That load has a muzzle velocity advertised as 1,910 ft/sec with the remaining velocity of 1,330 ft/sec at 100 yards. These velocities correspond to a ballistic coefficient of 0.116 for this bullet. Our procedure is to use this ballistic coefficient and calculate the trajectories that would result when the rifle is sighted in at various distances. The accompanying table shows the results obtained from the calculations when the rifle is sighted in for 75, 100, and 125 yards.

From the table, we see that sighting a .22 WMR rifle in at a distance of 75 yards does not take full advantage of its capabilities. When so sighted, there is maximum deviation of only 0.29 inch from the line of sight at ranges between the muzzle and 75 yards. Such a slight deviation means that the point of impact is almost on the line of sight in this interval, but the bullet would strike 1.30 inches low at 100 yards and 3.79 inches low at 125 yards. Sighting the rifle in at 100 yards gives a deviation from the line of sight of almost exactly one inch at 50 and 75 yards, and the bullet strikes only 2.16 inches below the line of sight at 125 yards. The difference of one inch is small enough that it should not cause misses on small targets at shorter ranges, and the point of impact being only 2.16 inches low at 125 yards would enable hits to be made with regularity on varmints of most sizes. Sighted to hit a point of aim at 100 yards makes a .22 WMR suitable for use as a 125-yard varmint rifle if the accuracy is sufficient. At that distance, the remaining energy is almost exactly equal to that of most .22 LR loads at the muzzle.

Calculated Trajectories for .22 WMR with 40-Grain Bullet (R_0 is the Sight-In Range)

RANGE, YDS.	V, FT/SEC	E, FT LB	DEVIATION FROM LINE OF SIGHT, INCHES		
			R_0 = 75 Yd	R_0 = 100 Yd	R_0 = 125 Yd
0	1,910	323	−1.50	−1.50	−1.50
25	1,755	274	−0.25	+0.07	+0.51
50	1,610	230	+0.29	+0.94	+1.81
75	1,475	193	0.00	+0.98	+2.27
100	1,353	163	−1.30	0.00	+1.73
125	1,245	138	−3.79	−2.16	0.00
150	1,155	118	−7.68	−5.73	−3.14
175	1,082	104	−13.20	−10.92	−7.90
200	1,025	93	−20.57	−17.97	−14.51

It might be thought that sighting in a .22 WMR at 125 yards would be even better. However, the table shows that in order to do that, the bullet would strike 2.27 inches high at 75 yards. Such a deviation would make it necessary to "hold under" at ranges of 50-75 yards when shooting at small varmints or even when placing a bullet exactly where you want it on a coyote's head after calling it in to that range.

The CCI Gamepoint has a bullet that with only a small lead tip exposed and as a result it retains velocity slightly better than the bullets used in most other .22 WMR loads.

One of the types of .22 WMR ammunition that has performed well in my rifle is the Remington Premier® that fires a 33-grain Hornady V-Max® bullet at a published velocity of 2,000 ft/sec. The polymer tipped V-Max bullet has a ballistic coefficient of 0.137, which is somewhat higher than that of the 40-grain bullets with more rounded profiles. Incidentally, the measured muzzle velocity from my rifle is somewhat higher than 2,000 ft/sec, but the advertised value was used in the calculations. The accompanying table shows the results of the computer calculations for the Remington Premier load.

The results shown in the table indicate that the 33-grain V-Max bullet has a trajectory that has less curvature than that of the 40-grain bullet. With the Remington Premier load, a .22 WMR can be sighted in at 125 yards with the bullet rising no more than about 1.8 inches above the line of sight and striking about 2.5 inches low at 150 yards. If a deviation of no more than 1.4 inches can be tolerated, the rifle can be sighted in at 115 yards, which will give a point of impact that is 0.74 inches low at 125 yards and 3.34 inches low at 150 yards. The Remington Premier load makes the .22 WMR an effective varmint cartridge out to about 140-150 yards, but keep in mind that bullet energy at that distance is only 125-130 ft lbs, which is about the same as the muzzle energy of a .22 LR high velocity load.

For larger varmints such as foxes and coyotes, the 50-grain hollow point .22 WMR load from Federal is hard to beat when the range is 100 yards or less. The heavy bullet has a ballistic coefficient of 0.160 so it holds its velocity better than the lighter bullets. However, because the velocity is low with such a heavy bullet,

Calculated Trajectories for .22 WMR 33-Grain Remington Premier®
(R_0 is the Sight-In Range)

RANGE, YDS.	V, FT/SEC	E, FT LB	DEVIATION FROM LINE OF SIGHT, INCHES	
			R0 = 100 YD	R0 = 125 YD
0	2,000	293	−1.50	−1.50
25	1,868	256	−0.10	+0.25
50	1,742	222	+0.69	+1.38
75	1,622	193	+0.76	+1.79
100	1,509	167	0.00	+1.38
125	1,404	145	−1.72	0.00
150	1,309	126	−4.54	−2.48
175	1,224	110	−8.63	−6.22
200	1,151	97	−14.18	−11.42

A 33-grain polymer tipped bullet is used in the Remington Premier .22 WMR load.

the sight in distance should be only 100 yards or less. Performing the trajectory calculations for this load with a sight in distance of 100 yards shows that the bullet would strike 1.31 inches high at 50 yards, 1.41 inches high at 60 yards, 1.33 inches high at 70 yards, hit the point of aim at 100 yards, and strike 1.91 inches low at 120 yards. However, the muzzle energy for this load is approximately 260 ft lbs, but the remaining energy at 100 yards is 159 ft lbs and at 120 yards it is approximately 145 ft lbs. Within its useful range, this is a powerful .22 WMR load, and it is effective on the larger species of varmints. Before deciding that this is the load you want to use on such targets, shoot some groups to determine its accuracy in your rifle. Although it is not the most accurate ammunition in my .22 WMR, it is sufficiently accurate for use out to 100 yards or so, and it has the highest remaining energy.

.17 Hornady Magnum Rimfire

Having considered the trajectories of the .22 LR and .22 WMR, we turn now to a discussion of the .17 HMR. Because of its high velocity, the trajectory of the .17 HMR is quite flat for a rimfire cartridge. Therefore, it is possible to sight in a rifle in this caliber for a rather long range. The calculations for loads utilizing a 17-grain bullet having a ballistic coefficient of 0.125 give the trajectories listed in the table for three different sight in distances.

The calculated trajectories show that a 100-yard sight in distance does not take full advantage of the trajectory of the .17 HMR cartridge. Between the muzzle and 100 yards there is no more than a 0.33-inch difference between the line of sight and the bullet path. This difference is so small that there is little likelihood of missing even a small target, but with that sighting, the bullet will strike 2.55 inches low at 150 yards and 5.02 inches low at 175 yards. However, if the rifle is sighted in at 125 yards, the bullet will strike no more than 0.89 inch high at any distance between the muzzle and 125 yards and be only 1.43 inches low at 150 yards and 3.73 inches low at 175 yards. If the rifle is sighted in at 150 yards, the bullet will strike 1.70 inches high at 100 yards and that is a larger deviation than one should have for a rifle that is intended for use on small varmints. Therefore, the best compromise is to sight in a rifle chambered for the .17 HMR to hit about three-quarters of an inch high at 100 yards so it will hit the point of aim at 125 yards. If the targets you are shooting will allow you to tolerate a deviation of +1.0 inch, your .17 HMR can be sighted in at approximately 130 yards, which will give a point of impact that is 1.0 inch high at 80 yards. Such a sighting will result in a point of impact that is only 3.5 inches low at 175 yards.

Calculated Trajectories for .17 HMR with a 17-Grain Bullet (R_0 is the Sight-In Range)

RANGE, YDS.	V, FT/SEC	E, FT LB	DEVIATION FROM LINE OF SIGHT, INCHES		
			R_0 = 100 YD	R_0 = 125 YD	R_0 = 150 YD
0	2,550	245	−1.50	−1.50	−1.50
25	2,378	213	−0.48	−0.30	−0.06
50	2,212	185	+0.15	+0.52	+1.00
75	2,053	159	+0.33	+0.89	+1.61
100	1,901	136	0.00	+0.74	+1.70
125	1,756	116	−0.93	0.00	+1.20
150	1,620	99	−2.55	−1.43	0.00
175	1,494	84	−5.02	−3.73	−2.05
200	1,378	72	−8.74	−6.99	−5.07

However, note that the remaining energy is only about 100 ft lbs at 150 yards and only 84 ft lbs at 175 yards, a fact that should lead you to consider the .17 HMR as a varmint cartridge that is suitable for use at ranges of 150 yards or less. The .17 HMR is at its best when used on small varmints where flat trajectory is a great asset.

Ammunition in .17 HMR caliber is loaded by CCI and marketed by both Hornady and CCI that utilizes a 20-grain hollow point bullet that has a muzzle velocity of 2,375 ft/sec. The ballistic coefficient of this hollow point bullet is 0.125, which happens to be the same as that for the 17-grain polymer tipped bullet. When this load is sighted to hit the point of aim at 100 yards, the bullet would strike 0.28 inch high at 50 yards, 0.43 inch high at 75 yards, 1.12 inches low at 125 yards, 3.05 inches low at 150 yards, 5.94 inches low at 175 yards, and approximately 10 inches low at 200 yards. Because of the small deviations from the line of sight at intermediate ranges, a rifle firing this load can also be sighted in at 125 yards.

When sighted in at a range of 125 yards, the point of impact is 0.73 inch high at 50 yards, 1.11 inch high at 75 yards, 0.90 inch high at 100 yards, and 1.70 inches low at 150 yards, 4.36 inches low at 175 yards, and 8.18 inches low at 200 yards. When sighted this way, the bullet is only slightly more than one inch high anywhere along the path to 125 yards and less than two inches low at 150 yards. Therefore, the .17 HMR is an effective cartridge for use on small varmints at ranges up to approximately 150 yards, but at that range the remaining energy is only 102 ft lbs, which is only slightly higher than .22 LR loads produce at 100 yards and lower than the energy given by the CCI Velocitor .22 LR at 100 yards. Although some shooters may stretch the .17 HMR to 200 yards, the remaining energy at that range is almost exactly the same as that given by the .22 Short at the muzzle! That energy is sufficient to dispatch pests but only with precisely placed shots, which is well nigh impossible at 200 yards with bullets that are as susceptible to the influence of wind as are those fired from a .17 HMR (or any other rimfire). There is no free lunch.

.17 Mach 2 and .17 Aguila

Having considered the external ballistics of bullets fired from .22 LR, .22 WMR, and .17 HMR cartridges, let us turn our attention to the .17 Mach 2, which is sometimes designated as the .17 HM2 or .17 M2. This cartridge uses a 17-grain polymer tipped bullet that is identical to that used in the .17 HMR but with a muzzle velocity of approximately 2,100 ft/sec. A velocity of 2,100 ft/sec is exactly the velocity of the same bullet

fired from the .17 HMR after it has traveled approximately 66 yards. Therefore, the velocity and energy of a bullet fired from a .17 Mach 2 over a range 0 to 134 yards will be identical to those characteristics of a bullet fired from a .17 HMR in the interval from 66 to 200 yards. Using a sight in distance of 100 yards and a sight height of 1.5 inches, the trajectory for the .17 Mach 2 was calculated yielding the results shown in the following table.

With a muzzle velocity that approximates that of a .22 WMR firing the Remington Premier load with

Calculated Trajectory for .17 Mach 2 with 17-Grain Bullet (Sight in Range = 100 yd)

RANGE, YDS.	V, FT/SEC	E, FT LB	INCHES
0	2,100	166	−1.50
25	1,946	143	−0.16
50	1,799	122	+0.60
75	1,660	104	+0.71
100	1,530	88	0.00
125	1,411	75	−1.64
150	1,304	64	−4.31
175	1,211	55	−8.19
200	1,134	49	−13.52

33-grain V-Max bullets, the trajectory of the 17-grain bullets from the .17 Mach 2 is similar to that of the 33-grain bullet fired from a .22 WMR. Reports on the accuracy of rifles firing the .17 Mach 2 indicate that the cartridge is exceptionally accurate. Accordingly, with its trajectory, it should be possible to make hits on small species out to around 125 yards, but at that distance the energy is about the same as that given by the .17 HMR at 200 yards, which is rather anemic (about 75 ft lbs). However, this chapter is concerned with ballistics, and the tiny .17 Mach 2 is an interesting development from that standpoint. Doubtless, there will be those who will shoot animals that should not normally be shot with such a caliber and get one shot kills because a projectile having an energy at 125 yards that is equivalent to that of a .22 Short at the muzzle will kill a lot of things when placed in a lethal zone. Realistically, the .17 Mach 2 has a flatter trajectory than the CCI Velocitor .22 LR, but it has less energy at all ranges. It remains, however, that the .17 Mach 2 is a very interesting cartridge that provides outstanding accuracy and flat trajectory from rifles most of which are identical to those chambered

These cartridges are (left to right) the .17 Aguila, .17 Mach 2, .17 HMR, and .17 WSM. With their high velocity, they give trajectory flat enough to make hits possible at relatively long ranges.

for the .22 LR. Since the publication of the first edition of this book, many rifles were offered in .17 Mach 2 and just as quickly almost all have been discontinued. Few new rifles in that caliber are currently available.

While the .17 Mach 2 was being developed, the .17 Aguila was introduced. This cartridge is based on a standard length .22 LR case necked to hold a 20-grain .17 caliber bullet. Because powder capacity is slightly less than that of the .17 Mach 2, the velocity is lower and the .17 Aguila utilizes a 20-grain bullet at an advertised velocity of 1,850 ft/sc. Although not having specific information on the bullet, the ballistic coefficient was estimated to be 0.125 in order to calculate the trajec-

tory. Even though they may not be exact, the results of the calculations are sufficiently accurate to show the path of the bullet reasonably well. The accompanying table shows the data generated.

In the .17 Aguila we have a cartridge that can literally be substituted for the .22 LR in an enormous number of firearms simply by changing barrels, which is not quite the case for the .17 Mach 2. In recent years, the .17 Aguila failed to achieve much popularity and firearms in that caliber are seldom seen. In terms of ballistic performance, the .17 Mach 2 has a slight edge over the .17 Aguila owing to its larger capacity case. However, there is very little practical difference, and

Calculated Trajectory for .17 Aguila with 20-Grain Bullet (Sight-In Range = 100 yd)

DEVIATION FROM LINE OF SIGHT RANGE, YDS.	V, FT/SEC	E, FT LB	INCHES
0	1,850	151	−1.50
25	1,713	130	+0.12
50	1,584	111	+1.00
75	1,463	95	+1.01
100	1,352	81	0.00
125	1,255	70	−2.20
150	1,171	61	−5.77
175	1,101	54	−10.94
200	1,045	49	−17.88

the 20-grain bullets used in the .17 Aguila should give reliable performance on small game and pests. In terms of trajectory, the .17 Aguila shoots flat enough to make hits possible to a range of almost 125 yards in accurate rifles. The accuracy of the .17 Aguila was reported to be quite good and it should be on a par with the .17 Mach 2 in this regard. Although they are interesting developments, the author does not expect a majority of shooters to give up shooting the .22 LR for either the .17 Mach 2 or the .17 Aguila. They are both short on power except for very small animals. In early 2016, only one .17 Mach 2 load remains in production although Aguila has announced that .17 Aguila will be soon introduced.

.17 Winchester Super Magnum

In the .17 Winchester Super Magnum (WSM) we have a cartridge that is indeed a potent rimfire. Win-chester loads feature 20- and 25-grain polymer tipped bullets that have muzzle velocities of 3,000 and 2,600 ft/sec, respectively. In Winchester ballistics tables, the bullets are described as having ballistic coefficients of 0.185 and 0.230, respectively, and the muzzle energies are 400 and 375 ft lbs. The .17 WSM is the most potent rimfire, but it is still a rimfire and it cannot equal the performance of a centerfire varmint caliber such as the .223 Remington. The accompanying table shows performance characteristics of the two .17 WSM loads when the sight in range is 150 yards. This range was selected because for both loads the bullet deviates only approximately one inch or less from the line of sight at any intermediate distance.

The data show that the .17 WSM is clearly in a different class than any of the other .17 caliber rimfires. Even at a range of 200 yards, the energy is

Calculated Trajectories for .17 WSM Loads When Sighted In at 150 and 200 Yards

RANGE, YDS.	20 GRAIN LOAD				25 GRAIN LOAD			
	V, F/S	E, FT LB	DEV, IN*		V, F/S	E, FT LB	DEV, IN*	
0	3,000	400	−1.50	−1.50	2,600	375	−1.50	−1.50
25	2,875	367	−0.51	−0.20	2,508	349	−0.29	+0.10
50	2,754	337	+0.22	+0.84	2,418	325	+0.58	+1.35
75	2,636	309	+0.66	+1.58	2,330	301	+1.07	+2.24
100	2,522	282	+0.89	+2.02	2,244	279	+1.16	+2.71
125	2,409	258	+0.59	+2.12	2,159	259	+0.81	+2.75
150	2,300	235	0.00	+1.85	2,076	239	0.00	+2.33
175	2,194	214	−1.01	+1.15	1,996	221	−1.32	+1.40
200	2,091	194	−2.46	0.00	1,916	204	−3.11	+0.00
225	1,990	176	−4.42	−1.64	1,839	188	−5.55	−2.05
250	1,891	159	−6.85	−3.77	1,764	173	−8.68	−4.78

*The left hand deviation column is for 150 yard sight in range and that on the right is for 200 yard sight in.

approximately 200 ft lbs and the bullet is only about 2.46 or 3.11 inches low for the 20- and 25-grain loads, respectively. If one wishes to sight in at a slightly longer range, the bullet will rise to a greater height than the line of sight and will also fall below the line of sight at ranges of 225 or 250 yards. Even with such sight adjustment, the .17 WSM is at its best inside of 250 yards at which point the remaining energy is well below 200 ft lbs.

The data in the table show the trajectories of the 20- and 25-grain loads when the rifle is sighted in at 150 and 200 yards. When sighted in at 200 yards, both bullet paths deviate from the line of sight at 100 and 125 yards by over two inches, which might be a little too much when shooting at small varmints. For the author, considering the trajectory and the remaining energy, the most practical range to sight in a .17 WSM rifle is 150 yards.

Ballistics Tables

All ammunition makers supply ballistics tables for their ammunition. These tables show the velocity of the bullet at the muzzle and at various ranges. For the .22 LR, the ranges are usually 0, 50, and 100 yards, but may include 25 and 75 yards. For the .17 HMR, the ranges are usually for distances to 200 yards. Also given in ballistic tables is the bullet energy at each of the ranges. It is a simple matter to make use of this information for the particular ammunition being used. However, ballistics tables also include information about bullet trajectory. Such information is usually presented in terms of the difference between the point of impact and the line of sight. Negative values mean that the bullet strikes below the line of sight whereas positive values mean that the bullet strikes above the line of sight. Of course, there is some distance for which the rifle is sighted in that the point of aim and the bullet path coincide. The data in the table might be represented as follows for the .22 LR high velocity bullet where the line of sight is assumed to be 1.5 inches above the bore.

Range, yd.	0	25	50	75	100
Height, in.	−1.5	+0.05	0.0	−1.82	−5.8

In hunting situations involving the .22 LR, a deviation of the bullet path from the line of sight should not be more than about 1-1.5 inches. From the data shown above, it can be seen that when the sight in range is 50 yards, the bullet would strike only 0.05 inches above the line of sight at 25 yards. A better plan

is to sight in a .22 LR at 65 yards, which puts the bullet about 0.66 inches high at 50 yards and only about 0.83 inches low at 75 yards. So sighted, a .22 LR has a point blank range of about 80 yards. If the rifle is to be used hunting squirrels, it is better to have no more than a one-inch deviation because the lethal zone may be about one inch in size. In that case, it is better to sight in at about 65-70 yards so that the bullet is no more than an inch above or below the line of sight to a range of 75 yards. Of course the trajectory for a standard velocity round is slightly more curved, and the optimum sight in range would be approximately 60 yards.

Although these two bullets have the same diameter and weight, the one on the right has a higher ballistic coefficient.

It is clear that under most circumstances the .22 LR is about a 75-yard cartridge because of its curved trajectory. High velocity ammunition such as the CCI Velocitor will increase the range to 85-90 yards. Keep in mind that at a range of 75 yards, the average .22 would probably produce groups of about 1.5 inches so the accuracy becomes a factor also. A shooter who is very good at estimating range and using a rifle that is capable of producing groups of 1.5 inches at 100 yards can make hits at that distance on game that has a fairly large lethal zone. However, the remaining energy is less than 100 ft lbs at that range so the bullet must be placed accurately. If the accuracy is sufficient, using the CCI Velocitor round helps some because it gives a remaining energy of about 110 ft lbs. Also, with a muzzle velocity of approximately 1,400 ft/sec, a rifle firing Velocitor ammunition can be sighted in at 75

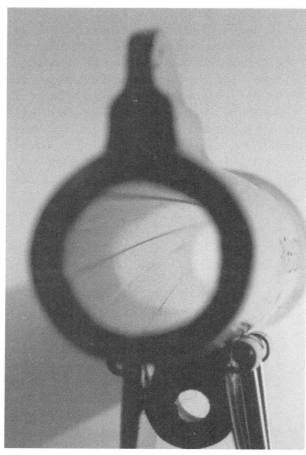

Rifling in a barrel imparts spin to a bullet passing through the bore, and that gives the bullet stability in flight.

yards and the bullet strike only 0.27 inch high at 25 yards, 0.86 inch high at 50 yards, and 2.31 inches low at 100 yards. Therefore, in an accurate rifle, CCI Velocitor ammunition gives an effective range of almost 100 yards. Trying to shoot varmints at distances greater than that involves a lot of luck because even a gentle breeze will move the point of impact a considerable distance. A 10 mph cross wind moves the .17 HMR bullet 3.5 inches at 100 yards, 8.5 inches at 150 yards, and 16 inches at 200 yards. Any bullet fired from a rimfire rifle is affected more by wind than are the heavier bullets fired from most centerfire rifles because the latter have higher ballistic coefficients.

Effect of Sight Height

When ballistics calculations are performed using one of the many computer programs available, the user must specify the height of the line of sight above the bore. Although most scopes have tubes that are one inch in diameter, scope mounts differ in height. Scopes are mounted on the receivers of rifles, but the receiver and the barrel do not have the same diameter. All of these factors contribute to the quantity known as the sight height and in this section we wish to analyze its effect on the calculated trajectory. In order to assess the effect of the sight height, calculations were performed assuming that the sight height is 1.00, 1.25, and 1.50 inches above the bore. The results for the standard velocity .22 LR load are shown in the accompanying table.

The data show the effects of the height of the line of sight above the bore. In each case the rifle is

Effect of Sight Height (SH) on Trajectory. .22 LR Federal Gold Medal Target, B.C. 0.140, Sight In Range 60 Yards

RANGE, YD	VELOCITY, FT/SEC	ENERGY, FT LB	BULLET PATH FOR DIFFERENT SIGHT HEIGHT		
			SH = 1.00 in.	SH = 1.25 in.	SH = 1.50 in.
0	1,080	103	−1.00	−1.25	−1.50
10	1,060	100	−0.03	−0.24	−0.44
20	1,042	96	+0.64	+0.47	+0.30
30	1,025	93	+0.98	+0.86	+0.73
40	1,009	90	+1.00	+0.92	+0.83
50	994	88	+0.67	+0.63	+0.59
60	980	85	0.00	0.00	0.00
70	967	83	−1.04	−0.99	−0.95
80	954	81	−2.44	−2.36	−2.28
90	942	79	−4.22	−4.10	−3.97
100	931	77	−6.38	−6.22	−6.05

Scope mounts for use on rimfire rifles come in different heights so that scopes having front bells of different diameter can be accommodated. On the left is the Weaver Tip-Off© mount while that on the right is a Beeman mount.

sighted in at 60 yards. Note that the highest point on the trajectory is 1.00 inch high (at 40 yards) when the sight height is 1.00 inch above the line of sight, but the maximum height of the bullet path is only 0.92 inch above the line of sight if the sight height is 1.25 inches. When the sight height is 1.50 inches, the maximum deviation of the bullet path is 0.83 inch. Likewise, at a range of 80 yards, the point of impact is –2.44, –2.36, or –2.28 when the sight height is 1.00, 1.25, or 1.50 inch, respectively. The higher the line of sight above the bore, the flatter the trajectory appears to be. Of course, the trajectory is exactly the same, but the point of impact deviates slightly from the line of sight because the line of sight is in a different position relative to the bore in the three cases. Note that at 40 yards the difference amounts to only 0.17-inch difference when the sight height varies from 1.00 to 1.50 inches. At 80 yards, the difference is only 0.16 inch when the sight

height varies similarly. For all practical purposes, you will never need to worry whether the center of the scope on your .22 rifle is 1.16 or 1.43 inches above the bore. There is little likelihood that you will ever notice these small differences in the point of impact unless you have a very accurate rifle.

Because the velocity is higher, the trajectory of the .22 WMR is less curved than that of the .22 LR. Therefore, the effect caused by differences in sight height will not be the same as in the case of the .22 LR. To illustrate this, trajectories were calculated assuming that the line of sight is 1.00, 1.25, and 1.50 inches above the bore. The data are shown in the table.

The data in the table show that at a range of 50 yards the difference between the point of impact and the line of sight changes by 0.25 inch as the sight height varies from 1.00 to 1.50 inches. With a rifle that gives one-half inch groups at that range, it is doubtful that a difference of only 0.25 inch would be noted on the basis of one shot. If 10-shot groups were fired with scopes having center heights above the bore of 1.00 and 1.50 inches, the average point of impact might show the effect of sight height. If the rifle were capable of firing a 1/4-inch group at 50 yards, the difference in trajectory would be evident, especially if several shots were fired with two different scopes that differed by one-half inch in height.

Having shown how the point of impact varies with height of the line of sight above the bore for the .22 LR and .22 WMR, we will now show the effect on the trajectory of the .17 HMR. As was done for the .22 LR and .22 WMR, it was assumed that the sight height is 1.00, 1.25, or 1.50 inches above the bore. When the calculations are carried out assuming a sight in range

Effect of Sight Height on Trajectory of the .22 WMR, 40-Grain H. P., B.C. = 0.116

RANGE, YD	VELOCITY, FT/SEC	ENERGY, FT LB	BULLET PATH FOR DIFFERENT SIGHT HEIGHT		
			SH = 1.00 in.	SH = 1.25 in.	SH = 1.50 in.
0	1,910	323	−1.00	−1.25	−1.50
25	1,759	275	+0.44	+0.25	+0.06
50	1,617	232	+1.18	+1.05	+0.93
75	1,485	196	+1.09	+1.02	+0.96
100	1,365	165	0.00	0.00	0.00
125	1,258	141	−2.25	−2.19	−2.13
150	1,168	121	−5.88	−5.75	−5.63
175	1,094	106	−11.10	−10.91	−10.72
200	1,036	95	−18.13	−17.88	−17.63

Effect of Sight Height on the Trajectory of the .17 HMR, 17 Grain Polymer Tip Bullet, B.C. = 0.125

RANGE, YD	VELOCITY, FT/SEC	ENERGY, FT LB	BULLET PATH FOR DIFFERENT SIGHT HEIGHT		
			SH = 1.00 in.	SH = 1.25 in.	SH = 1.50 in.
0	2,550	245	−1.00	−1.25	−1.50
25	2,384	214	+0.09	−0.11	−0.31
50	2,226	187	+0.80	+0.65	+0.50
75	2,070	162	+1.06	+0.96	+0.86
100	1,922	139	+0.83	+0.78	+0.73
125	1,781	120	0.00	0.00	0.00
150	1,648	102	−1.51	−1.46	−1.41
175	1,523	88	−3.82	−3.72	−3.62
200	1,407	75	−7.07	−6.92	−6.77

of 125 yards, the data shown in the following table were obtained.

The data in the table show that when the .17 HMR is sighted in at 125 yards, the point of impact is 1.06 inch high at 75 yards when the sight height is 1.00 inch, but it is 0.86 inch high at that distance when the sight height is 1.50 inches. Again, the trajectory appears to be flatter when the sight height is greater. However, it is unlikely that a difference in point of impact of 0.20 inch at 75 yards will ever be noticed. Moreover, even at 200 yards the difference in point of impact is only 0.30 inch, which will clearly be outside the accuracy limits. If you fire enough shots, you might find that the average point of impact is slightly different, but on any individual shot the difference will never be seen. In spite of this, it is still useful to understand the principles involved and how they affect the trajectory.

The number of myths regarding the science of ballistics is surprising. It is all too frequent that someone is overheard making claims regarding a .22 rifle sighted in at 50 yards that still hits right on the point of aim at 100 yards. If the point of aim at 100 yards is hit with a .22 that is sighted in at 50 yards, it is accidental because the bullet should have hit about 7 inches low if the ammunition was of the standard velocity type. A bullet from the high velocity .22 should hit about 5 inches low under these conditions. One also hears about some shooter having a .17 HMR sighted in at 100 yards who holds "dead on" a crow at 175 yards and makes a kill. So sighted, the .17 HMR hits about 5 inches low at 175 yards so the crow was having a bad day.

Wind Deflection

When a moving projectile is subjected to a force, some change in its path is produced. The attraction of gravity causes the path of a bullet fired horizontally to be bent toward the earth. Wind blowing across the path of a projectile causes it to be moved laterally on its way to the target. How much the path is bent depends on the wind velocity and the characteristics of the bullet.

If you have ever driven along a highway following a motorcycle you may have observed one of the curious effects produced by a crosswind. The force of the wind on the cyclist causes the cycle to tip into the wind rather than away from it. The same phenomenon happens with a bullet that is subjected to a crosswind. The nose tends to tip into the wind just as an arrow does during its flight. The process can be viewed in another way by remembering that the area of the bullet is larger toward the base than at the point so the force of the wind is greater in that region of the bullet. Tipping the bullet causes the drag produced by passage through air to be altered, which results in a curved path for the bullet in a cross wind. This problem is a complex one because there is also an elevation or depression in the path of the bullet, which will not be discussed in this elementary treatment. As it turns out, a wind blowing from the right (3 o'clock) causes the bullet to move to the left (9 o'clock) and upward slightly whereas a wind from the left (9 o'clock) causes the bullet to move to the right (3 o'clock) and down. Although the effect is slight, wind directly opposing the direction of the bullet motion will move the bullet downward whereas wind in the direction of the bullet path will cause a slight upward movement of the bullet. The reader interested in greater detail of these problems should see the article

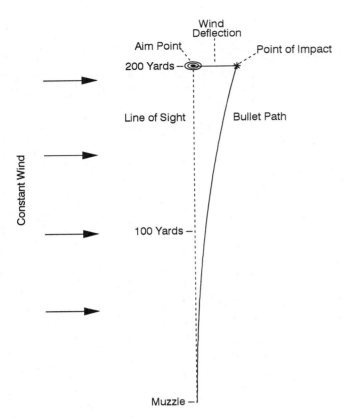

Wind Deflection

Aim Point

Point of Impact

200 Yards

Line of Sight

Bullet Path

100 Yards

Constant Wind

Muzzle

This figure shows the effect of a constant wind blowing from 9 o'clock. Note that the deflection at 200 yards is more than twice that at 100 yards.

by Frank Tirrell published in *Small Caliber News,* Vol. 7, No. 1, Spring 2004, pp. 14-20.

Interestingly, it is the extent to which air resistance slows the bullet on its path that determines how much deflection will be produced. If a bullet were to maintain the same velocity after leaving the muzzle, there would be no decrease in velocity as a result of air resistance. In other words, we are considering the bullet to be traveling in a vacuum. If the distance to the target is known, it is a simple matter to calculate the time of flight in a vacuum, T_v. The value of T_v would be the distance (range) divided by the velocity, V. For example, if the range is 100 yards (300 feet) and the bullet has a velocity of 1000 ft/sec, the time of flight, T_v, would be

$$T_v = \frac{\text{Range (ft)}}{\text{Velocity (ft/sec)}} = \frac{300 \text{ ft}}{1,000 \text{ ft/sec}} = 0.300 \text{ sec}$$

When fired in air, the bullet experiences a loss in velocity on its way to the target as a result of air resistance. The extent of that loss in velocity is related

to the ballistic coefficient of the bullet. Bullets having high ballistic coefficients lose a smaller fraction of their velocity in traveling a given distance than do those having low ballistic coefficients.

The loss in velocity of a bullet as it passes through air is related to the difference between its time of flight in a vacuum and the actual time of flight through the atmosphere. If we call the time of flight in air Ta, the wind deflection is related to the quantity $(T_a - T_v)$. The wind deflection, D, can be expressed by the relationship

$$D = 12 \text{ W } (T_a - T_v)$$

In this equation, W is the wind velocity in feet per second and 12 is a conversion factor to convert the deflection in feet to the value in inches. Wind velocity is usually expressed in miles per hour, but as a result of wanting to calculate deflection in either feet or inches we need the wind velocity in those units. It is an easy matter to convert from miles per hour to feet/sec because one mile per hour is equivalent to 1.467 ft/sec.

If we consider a .22 LR standard velocity load firing a 40-grain bullet at 1,080 ft/sec, the time of flight in a vacuum (T_v) to a target 100 yards (300 feet) away would be

$$T_v = \frac{300 \text{ ft}}{1,080 \text{ ft/sec}} = 0.278 \text{ sec}$$

Because the bullet loses velocity due to air resistance, the actual time of flight (T_a) is 0.301 sec. Suppose we want to see how much deflection a 5 mph wind coming directly across the path of the bullet would cause. This would be known as a wind from 9 o'clock (or 3 o'clock). By making use of the conversion factor given above, we find that a 5 mph wind is equivalent to 7.335 ft/sec. Therefore, the wind deflection in this case would be

$$D = 12 \text{ W } (T_a - T_v) = 12 \times 7.335 \ (0.301 - 0.278) = 2.02 \text{ inches}$$

This result shows that a standard velocity .22 LR bullet will be deflected slightly over two inches at 100 yards by a 5 mph cross wind. If the wind were 10 mph, the deflection would be exactly twice as great because the wind velocity, W, is used as a multiplier in the equation.

The question naturally arises as to what would be the deflection if the wind is blowing at an angle to the path of the bullet instead of directly across it. In such a case, the extent to which the bullet will be deflected depends

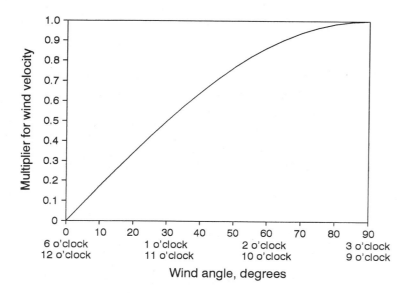

Winds from 3 and 9 o'clock
have full effect on the bullet.
Winds from other angles have
effects given by the multiplier
on the vertical axis.

on the angle. If the wind is directly in line with the path of the bullet, the deflection is zero, whereas if the angle is 90° (a cross wind) the deflection is a maximum. If the wind is blowing at an angle to the bullet path, there are two components to the total wind velocity. There is a component of the velocity that is in the direction of the bullet path and a component that is perpendicular to the path. It is the component of the wind velocity that is across the bullet path that determines the amount of deflection. This can be worked out mathematically as a function of angle, but it is not necessary because the accompanying figure shows how to adjust for the angle as it varies from 0 to 90°.

We now know how to compensate for the angle of the wind, but we still have a problem with the actual time of flight. The time of flight in a vacuum is easily obtained by simply dividing the range in feet by the velocity in ft/sec. Calculating the actual time of flight in air is a complex problem that makes use of the ballistic coefficient because that is the quantity that determines air retardation. For the introduction to ballistics presented in this book, it is not necessary to actually calculate the time of flight in air. It is one of the quantities that is contained in the output from calculations performed using the software available from several sources so we will just assume that the value is known.

Shooting Uphill and Downhill

When a bullet is fired at an angle upward or downward, the effect of gravity is not the same as it is when the bullet is fired horizontally. When the bullet travels horizontally, the effect of gravity is at right angles to the bullet path so the effect is maximum. If

the bullet path is upward, there will be a horizontal component and a vertical component to the motion. Only the component of the velocity in the horizontal direction is affected strongly by gravity. Suppose one were shooting at a crow on a rock ledge that is 50 yards distant and that ledge is 50 yards high. The length of the path of the bullet can be calculated to be 70.7 yards, but it is only the horizontal component of 50 yards that is affected by gravity. Now let us suppose that the rifle is sighted in at exactly 70 yards. Will the bullet strike exactly at the point of aim on the crow? The answer is no because the bullet experiences the effective gravity over only the horizontal distance, 50 yards, rather than the full effect of gravity over the entire distance. Therefore, the bullet will strike above the point of aim at the target. The effect would be exactly the same if the target were in the bottom of a ravine 50 yards deep and the shooter were at a point 50 yards horizontally and 50 yards vertically from the target.

Clearly, the effect depends on how steep the firing angle is. The bullet drop is related to that angle by the trigonometric function known as the cosine (which is abbreviated cos). The actual bullet drop will be that for the same horizontal distance multiplied by the cosine of the angle. For example, in the case above, the angle is 45 degrees and the cosine of that angle is 0.707. Therefore, the bullet drop would be only 0.707 of what it would if the bullet were fired horizontally over a distance of 70 yards. The results show that the bullet will strike higher relative to the point of aim than it would if the shot were at a target on the horizontal plane. It should be apparent that the extent of the error will depend on the firing angle. The accompanying table

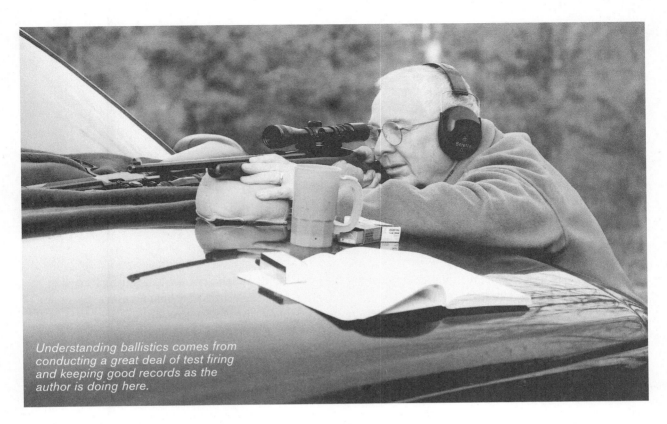

Understanding ballistics comes from conducting a great deal of test firing and keeping good records as the author is doing here.

Corrections for Bullet Drop When Firing at Angles (Up or Down) From Horizontal

ANGLE	MULTIPLY BY	ANGLE	MULTIPLY BY
0	1.000	50	0.643
10	0.985	60	0.600
20	0.940	70	0.342
30	0.866	80	0.174
40	0.766	90	0.000
45	0.707		

shows how the bullet drop for shots fired at different angles will be related to the drop when the shot is fired horizontally. The drop for shots fired at each angle is determined by multiplying the amount of drop for a horizontal shot by the multiplier indicated. From the table, it is evident that when firing at a 20-degree angle the drop is 94% of what it would be for a shot taken horizontally. Even when the angle is 30° the multiplier is 0.86 so the difference in point of impact will be only slightly above where it would be for a shot taken horizontally. In most cases, the uncertainty in point of impact that is produced by aiming error and the limitation imposed by the accuracy of the rifle will make it unnecessary to adjust the point of aim. However, on those longer shots at steep angles, it must be remembered that the bullet will strike higher than it would if the target were on the same horizontal plane as the shooter.

In this chapter, an introduction to exterior ballistics has been provided with special emphasis on each type of rimfire cartridge. Some of the concepts will be revisited in later chapters as we discuss ways to use rimfire firearms most effectively.

The approach in this chapter has been to try to develop some appreciation and understanding of external ballistics and to explain the factors that affect bullet trajectory. The presentation has only scratched the surface of this important topic, but the basic ideas presented are adequate for practical shooting situations as they apply to rimfire rifles. For a more complete treatment of the subject of ballistics, consult the references listed in Appendix A.

CHAPTER 10

RIMFIRES AS HUNTING TOOLS

ALTHOUGH THE TOOLS and techniques employed have changed, hunting is an activity that has been practiced for thousands of years. For well over a century, rimfire firearms have been the choice of many hunters of small game and pests. Today's hunter who plans to use a rimfire firearm has the widest range of equipment and ammunition ever available. This chapter presents an overview of rimfire equipment and ammunition with the hunter in mind. Although much of this chapter is written with reference to the use of rifles, the handgun hunter can apply most of the principles equally well. This is as it should be because the use of an accurate handgun for taking small game and pests is entirely appropriate although the ranges will probably be shorter in most cases than if a rifle is used. Also, some of the rimfire handguns (both revolvers and autoloaders) are sold with scope rails in place because they are intended to be hunting arms.

An experienced hunter who uses a rimfire rifle or handgun in his or her sport may simply use the tools that are already available with little thought to making changes or selecting new equipment. On the other hand, someone who is just getting started in hunting with rimfires may benefit from a discussion of some of the guns and ammunition available as an aid to making selections. In this chapter, the conclusions presented are those of the author. Because of the recent introduction of some of the products and the lack of opportunity to use them, the discussion is based on limited experience and testing in some cases. In any case, the information and opinions are intended to serve as a guide for hunters who use rimfire firearms.

What Rimfires Can Do

In discussing the use of rimfires for hunting (whether game or varmints), it is necessary to set forth some basic principles. The first of these deals with the types of species that can be harvested humanely with a rimfire firearm. A .22 WMR generates approximately 300 ft lbs of energy at the muzzle and a .22 LR approximately half as much. Even the new .17 WSM has a muzzle energy of only 375-400 ft lbs. A modern centerfire rifle such as the .30-06 Springfield or 7 mm Remington Magnum produces as much as 3,000 ft lbs of energy. It is clear that all rimfire rifles have very low power compared to centerfire pieces. Therefore, the use of rimfire firearms should be confined to taking small species except under survival or emergency conditions.

Having said that, it must be pointed out that very large species have been killed with a .22 rimfire. Such is the case of a woman in Montana who killed a grizzly with a .22 LR as it chased her horse in a corral. All manner of large game has fallen to the lowly rimfire. As a young lad, this writer dispatched a large number of hogs with one shot each using a Winchester Model 90 pump firing the .22 Short. The hogs were shot between the eyes at a distance of 10-15 feet. When the bullet is placed exactly right, a rimfire will produce

For the small game hunter, an accurate rimfire has long been the chosen tool.

Although out of production for many years, this Winchester Model 320 performs as well as any current model.

death to almost anything. However, no one is going to advocate using a .22 Short as a cartridge for hunting deer although it will certainly kill a deer.

Under hunting conditions, it may not be possible to place the bullet in exactly the right spot so the hunter must use a firearm that will anchor the target with less than ideal bullet placement. Therefore, the firearm must have more power than would be needed to dispatch the species in cases where the bullet strikes perfectly. That does not mean that you need a .338 Winchester Magnum to hunt coyotes. What it does mean is that the less powerful the rifle used, the more accurately the bullet should be placed in a lethal zone and the more important the choice of ammunition becomes. Shooting ability and sighting equipment also become factors to consider.

Terminal Effects

It doesn't take much energy to make a hole in a piece of paper. Dispatching small game and pests is another matter, and larger pests constitute yet a different situation. It is easy to get caught up in the power game and assume that the most powerful cartridge you can get in your rifle is the best choice. That is not always so. There is currently a great deal of interest in hunting with air rifles, and only a few of the most powerful models even approach the power of a .22 Short. One instance to my knowledge involved a hunter taking a fox with a .177 caliber air rifle that fires a 7.9 grain pellet at slightly over 900 ft/sec (a muzzle energy of about 14 ft lbs) by placing that pellet precisely between the eye and the ear of the fox. Contrast that airgun with the lowly .22 Short that fires a 29-grain bullet at slightly over 1,000 ft/sec (corresponding to a muzzle energy of 70 ft lbs) and you will see just what a correctly placed projectile from a .22 rimfire could do.

Does this make the .22 Short a cartridge to choose for hunting foxes and coyotes? No, but this author has dropped numerous large hogs for the block with a .22 Short placed squarely in the forehead at short range. Keep in mind that there is a great difference between what a particular load will kill and what species are suitable for hunting with the same load. Hunting involves harvesting animals in a humane way even when the bullet may not be placed exactly between the ear and the eye. Field situations may not permit that kind of shot placement.

The theme for the famous book, *Use Enough Gun*, by Robert Ruark, came about as a result of trying to take a hyena with a .220 Swift shooting a 48-grain bullet at approximately 4,000 ft/sec. After nine shots in which the frangible bullets simply did not penetrate the tough hyena, Ruark called out *"Toa bundouki m'kubwa,"* which in Swahili means "bring out the big one" or something to that effect. He then shot the animal with a .470 Nitro Express. Will a .220 Swift kill a hyena? Absolutely, especially with the excellent bullets that are available today, but penetration of a tough animal can still be a problem with light bullets at high velocity. Would a .22 LR kill a hyena? Absolutely, but the bullet would have to be placed exactly right, and a .22 LR certainly should not be used to hunt hyenas. The shooter using any rimfire should select appropriate ammunition for the type of game being harvested. Two factors that are involved in bullet performance can be considered as penetration and rate of energy transfer to the target. A discussion of these factors is presented here.

Penetration

Penetration exhibited by a specific bullet in some medium depends on several factors. The weight, type of construction, and velocity of the bullet are the most important considerations. For a bullet of a given caliber, penetration is generally greater the heavier the bullet. If the bullet does not expand significantly (the typical 40-grain solid point .22 LR bullet does not expand much in fleshy targets), the diameter of the wound channel is small. A heavier bullet will penetrate deeper because it has larger mass for the same frontal area even though the heavier bullet will have lower velocity. Tests conducted by the author using heavy .45 caliber, hard cast handgun bullets that give no expansion have shown that very deep penetration can be obtained even though the velocity was only about 800 ft/sec. In .22 LR caliber, the bullets are essentially pure lead, and most solid bullets weigh 40 grains. However, the discontinued Lapua Scoremax® load utilized a 48-grain bullet that was loaded to a velocity of 1,040 ft/sec in target grade ammunition. Excellent accuracy is exhibited by this load in rifles tested by this author. A 60-grain bullet at 950 ft/sec is used in the Aguila SubSonic Sniper load. Because of the long, heavy bullet, this load makes use of a case that is significantly shorter than that used in typical .22 LR ammunition in order to meet the restrictions on overall cartridge length. Therefore, the SubSonic Sniper load does not work through most actions of semiautomatic firearms.

It can be amazing to see just how deeply a .22 LR can penetrate. This writer has served on a coroner's jury and examined autopsy photographs showing that a .22 LR fired from a short barrel (the velocity was probably not over 900 ft/sec) penetrated almost completely through the body of an adult male. For use on small game and pests, the penetration given by solid bullets is excessive because a considerable amount of the energy of the bullet is wasted after the bullet leaves the animal. In order to reduce penetration and cause more of the energy of the projectile to be transferred to the animal, hollow pointed bullets can be used. The expanding bullets do not penetrate as deeply in animal tissue because they make a wider wound channel so the rate of energy transfer to the target is higher.

After its introduction, the .17 HMR quickly became an extremely popular round for taking small varmints for a good reason. Most of the rifles chambered for the .17 HMR produce excellent accuracy. The sharp pointed bullets traveling at high velocity give flat trajectory, which makes it easy to hit the target even at ranges of 150 yards or so. However, most negative observations regarding the .17 HMR relate to bullet performance. Within the last few days as this is being written in early 2016, another writer shared his experiences with the .17 HMR on game. A fox taken in the neck at a range of 50 yards collapsed instantly. A coyote hit in the chest at a similar distance took off for parts unknown. The tiny 17-grain bullet does not give sufficient penetration to be reliable for dispatching such large varmints unless the bullets are placed exactly right. However, the .17 HMR was never intended for use on varmints the size of a coyote except perhaps when head shots are taken at short distances. Although there are a lot of cases where the .17 HMR has worked satisfactorily, there are many instances where it has not. It is similar to Ruark's experience when using the .220 Swift on a hyena.

Ammunition in .17 HMR is available with either 17-grain polymer tipped bullets or 20-grain hollow points.

The expansion of this CCI Gold Dot bullet from a .22 WMR assures rapid energy transfer.

In an effort to reduce the instances where bullets fragment without penetrating sufficiently, CCI and Hornady introduced ammunition for the .17 HMR that utilizes 20-grain hollow pointed bullets of more sturdy construction. With the heavier bullet, the muzzle velocity is only about 2,375 ft/sec, but that is still fast enough to give a trajectory that is sufficiently flat. Generally, reports from people who have used these cartridges on game indicate that the 20-grain load performs better than those utilizing 17-grain bullets.

A 17-grain polymer tipped .17 HMR bullet at high velocity is explosive. Tests show that when the bullet is still traveling at high velocity fragmentation occurs in many types of test media. However, at ranges of 150-200 yards where the velocity is much lower, the bullets often penetrate a varmint without expanding significantly. It is an interesting but significant fact that penetration at longer range is generally deeper than for the same bullet at shorter ranges. Expansion is assured when the velocity is high but when the velocity decreases and expansion is less, penetration is greater. This behavior points out one of the difficulties in designing bullets for use on game. Reliable expansion is needed at long range, but the bullet must not fragment at short range. When small varmints are the targets, fragmentation may actually be desirable in order for the bullet to expend all of its energy on the critter and not on the landscape. It is just that when a caliber as small as the .17 HMR is considered, a coyote is not a small critter.

For larger varmints, the 50-grain Federal Classic load in .22 WMR is an excellent choice.

The new .17 WSM is a much more potent caliber than are the other .17s.

The most common form of .22 WMR ammunition is probably that with the 40-grain hollow point or full metal jacket bullet. However, ammunition is also available with hollow point bullets that weigh as little as 30 grains or as much as 50 grains. Federal produces a 50-grain load that is advertised to give a muzzle velocity of 1,530 ft/sec from a rifle, which corresponds to a muzzle energy of 260 ft lbs. This velocity is almost exactly equal to that obtained at 10 feet from the muzzle when the load was fired from the author's Ruger 77/22M. However, the heavy bullet retains its velocity well and published data show a remaining energy at 100 yards of 159 ft lbs. Because the velocity is lower, the 50-grain bullets do not expand as violently and as a result give deeper penetration. This provides better performance on larger varmints such as foxes and coyotes. CCI also produced a .22 WMR load with a 50-grain Gold Dot hollow point for a time, but that load has been discontinued.

In order to stabilize a bullet in flight, the bullet is caused to spin by the rifling in the barrel. The longer the bullet of a given caliber, the higher the rate of rotation required to stabilize the bullet in flight, but the velocity of the bullet is also a factor in determining rotational stability. Barrels for most rifles chambered for the .22 WMR are given a rate of twist of 1 turn in 16 inches. With the low velocity of the 50-grain bullets, especially from handgun barrels, stability is marginal and some firearms are not highly accurate with the 50-grain loads. In most of the .22 WMR rifles that this author has used, both of the 50-grain loads gave good accuracy.

When it comes to the .17 WSM, we arrive at a rimfire caliber that might be considered suitable for use on species as large as coyotes or small species at ranges that extend to perhaps 250 yards. The trajectory of either the 20- or 25-grain load is sufficiently flat to make hits possible to that distance, but by that point the energy will be only 150-175 ft lbs and wind deflection may be a problem. Even with the .17 WSM, which has been touted as a cartridge for use on coyotes, the author will keep shots to within 150 yards and place

the bullets in a lethal zone. The .17 WSM is a wonderful cartridge and a quantum leap up from other rimfires, but it is still a rimfire that utilizes bullets weighing only 25 grains or less.

Smash

The essential idea behind shooting animals is to dispatch them cleanly and quickly. In order to do this, part or all of the kinetic energy of the bullet must be used to displace material (tissue, bone, and fluids) in the target. In other words, there must be energy transfer to the target. Any residual energy that remains is lost by virtue of the bullet passing through the target and continuing on its way with considerable velocity. A more desirable situation is for the bullet to expend its total energy on the target. This is one of the reasons that the .17 HMR is devastating to small varmints because the tiny bullet at high velocity disrupts a lot of tissue and seldom exits from the animal. There is no need for a bullet that will penetrate 10 inches of flesh when shooting prairie dogs because after about half that much penetration, the bullet is on the other side of the prairie dog making a furrow in the ground.

Recognizing that rapid transfer of energy is desirable when taking small game and varmints with a rimfire, some means of making the bullet change shape after entry is desirable. One solution to the problem is to make a bullet with a hollow cavity in the nose. Upon impact, the walls of the front section of the bullet collapse or rivet giving the bullet a larger diameter. This in turn causes it to displace a larger amount of material, and that leads to rapid energy transfer to the target. Penetration is less than with a solid point bullet, but the impact is considerable because the bullet transfers a greater percentage of its energy to the target. Ordinary .22 LR solid bullets weigh 40 grains whereas the hollow points are in the 36-38-grain range depending on the manufacturer. As a result, the hollow pointed bullets have slightly higher velocity, but the difference is negligible.

Because heavy bullets of a given diameter penetrate better than do lighter ones, another technique to give a higher rate of energy transfer is to use lighter bullets, which also results in higher velocity. Then, to further increase the rate of energy transfer, the lighter bullet can be a hollow pointed one. This is exactly the approach taken when the CCI Stinger® and previously offered Winchester Expediter® rounds appeared in the late 1970s. Winchester currently offers the Varmint HE® load that utilizes a 37-grain bullet with a nominal velocity of 1,400 ft/sec.

The CCI Stinger uses a 32-grain hollow point bullet that reaches a muzzle velocity of about 1,640 ft/sec from a rifle and almost 1,400 ft/sec from a handgun. Remington markets two types of hyper velocity ammunition that are known as the Yellow Jacket® (33-grain hollow point bullet at 1,500 ft/sec) and Viper® (36-grain truncated cone bullet at 1,410 ft/sec). Federal produces the Game-Shok® load utilizing a 31 grain hollow pointed bullet with a muzzle velocity of 1,430 ft/sec. In 2009, Winchester announced the Hyper Speed HP™ load that utilizes a 40-grain bullet having a muzzle velocity of 1,435 ft/sec, which makes it have ballistics similar to the CCI Velocitor® load. Browning has also introduced a line of ammunition that includes a load featuring a 40-grain hollow point with a muzzle velocity of 1,435 ft/sec.

A hyper velocity load known as the Super Maximum® is available from Aguila, and it gives a 30-grain bullet an advertised muzzle velocity of 1,750 ft/sec. At the other end of the velocity spectrum, Aguila also offers the Sniper SubSonic® and Subsonic® that feature bullets of 60 and 38 grains at velocities of 950 and 1,025 ft/sec, respectively.

All of the hyper velocity loads are explosive on small species, but the lightweight bullets lose their velocity more rapidly than do the 40-grain solid or

Even at handgun velocities, the Hornady Critical Defense bullet expands well when fired into water.

36-38-grain hollow points that are used in regular high velocity .22 LR loads. As a result, their explosive energy transfer is best utilized at short range. Hyper velocity ammunition is frequently not as accurate as the high velocity or standard velocity types, but it may still be quite accurate in some rifles. This should be determined before loading up with hyper velocity ammunition and going hunting.

In order to give the lightweight bullet the highest possible velocity, CCI uses a heavier powder charge in the Stinger that is contained in a case that is slightly longer than the usual .22 LR case. In most chambers, this causes no problem, but in rifles that have match chambers the rifling extends to the mouth of the chamber. When a Stinger round is chambered in such a rifle, the case engages the rifling. Because the brass case with the bullet enclosed is not easily deformed, it requires considerable effort to chamber the round as it is forced into the rifling, and it certainly does not do good things to the rifling just in front of the chamber. The instruction manuals that come with some rifles warn against using Stingers in those rifles because they have match chambers. The hyper velocity ammunition from Winchester, Remington, Federal, and Aguila is loaded in cases that are the same length as those used for regular .22 LR ammunition.

Although the CCI Gamepoint is an excellent .22 WMR load, the bullets are too strongly constructed to expand when fired at handgun velocities.

The Aguila Super Maximum has an advertised velocity of 1,750 ft/sec.

A different approach was taken by CCI in developing their Quik-Shok® ammunition. This load has the same bullet weight and velocity as the Stinger, but the bullet breaks into four segments on impact. This produces a shallow but wide wound channel and virtually guarantees that the total energy of the projectile will be expended on the animal while doing a great deal of damage. However, the Quik-Shok also makes use of a case that is longer than the standard .22 LR case with the attendant chambering problems.

One of the most successful .22 LR high velocity loads is the CCI Velocitor®. This load uses a bullet that is hollow pointed, but it weighs 40 grains. Muzzle velocity from a rifle is specified as 1,435 ft/sec, which corresponds to a muzzle energy of 183 ft lbs. Moreover, the relatively heavy bullet (for a hollow point) retains its velocity well and at 100 yards the velocity is 1,112 ft/sec and the remaining energy is 110 ft lbs. This is a higher remaining energy at 100 yards than that of any other .22 LR load. Although the CCI Stinger has a muzzle energy of 191 ft lbs, the lightweight bullet loses its velocity rapidly and the remaining energy at 100 yards is only 90 ft lbs. If you read the stories in magazines concerning varmint hunting with a .22 LR, you will see that the Velocitor ranks high with these hunters. In the experience of this author, the Velocitor gives excellent accuracy in some rifles. Two rifles tested gave an average 5-shot group size of less than one-inch at 50 yards and a couple of others grouped in just over an inch. Although this does not rival the accuracy produced by target ammunition, it is fine accuracy for a high-powered hunting round.

Another cartridge that has produced an excellent reputation for effectiveness and accuracy is the Winchester Power Point® that produces a muzzle velocity of 1,280 ft/sec and muzzle energy of 143 ft lbs. In many rifles, the accuracy of Power Points is almost as good as that given by standard velocity ammunition. Some of the rifles tested in this work gave an average of five 5-shot groups at 50 yards that was as small as 0.85 inches whereas others gave an average slightly over one inch. This is excellent for high velocity ammunition that is intended primarily for hunting.

Shot Cartridges

The shooter using a .22 LR or .22 WMR has an optional type of ammunition that is not available to the shooter of the .17 HMR. For many years, cartridges have been available from CCI that have a plastic capsule filled with small shot instead of a bullet. Owing to the small volume available, the shot are

Shot cartridges in .22 WMR are useful for small pests.

extremely small so that a sizeable number can be contained in the capsules. In most cases, the shot are No. 12 in size (about 0.05 inch in diameter). Instead of using a plastic capsule filled with shot, the .22 LR shot cartridges produced by Winchester and Federal use an extra long case that is crimped at the mouth to hold in the shot. Only CCI produces shot cartridges in .22 WMR caliber. The weight of the shot load in .22 LR is 31 grains whereas that in .22 WMR is 52 grains, which makes it a potent short-range load. Because there is no way to determine exactly how the dozens of shot will strike, there is always the possibility of some of them bouncing around. It is imperative that safety glasses be worn when shooting rimfire shot cartridges.

Shot cartridges are intended to function as a miniature shot gun for the smallest of vermin including mice, sparrows, snakes, etc. at very short range. The rifled tube causes the capsule and its contents to spin, which causes the pattern to spread out dramatically at ranges over 15 feet or so. One problem with the shot cartridges is that they do not work reliably through the actions of many firearms so they must usually be

Shot cartridges are effective on small pests and birds at short ranges. The target on the left was shot at a distance of six feet while that on the right was shot at 12 feet. The holes have been circled to increase visibility.

used in a single shot mode. Probably the best firearm for using shot cartridges is a revolver where the empty cases need not be removed at all until the cylinder is empty. The length of the case is immaterial as long as it does not protrude from the front of the cylinder.

When shot cartridges are used, it is important to remember that the pattern becomes wide at short distance. Therefore, there is not sufficient pattern density for these loads to be effective at ranges beyond a few feet. Usually, multiple hits with the tiny pellets are required to dispatch small vermin so the range must be kept to around a dozen feet or so at most. Six feet is a distance at which the tiny shot are even more effective.

Hitting the Target

The small game and varmint hunter who uses a rimfire firearm needs accurate shot placement above all else. A fox or coyote that is brain shot with a .22 Short is going to be dead in very short order whereas one that is gut shot with a somewhat more powerful rifle such as a .22 WMR, .17 HMR, or .17 WSM will not. This is why the ability to place the bullet accurately is so important to the hunter using a rimfire firearm. Many hunters select a rifle (either target or sporting) that is capable of competition level accuracy. They then experiment with many types of ammunition to achieve almost unbelievable accuracy. For this type of hunter, it is not unreasonable to dispatch a coyote called to within 75 yards using a rimfire rifle, even one chambered for the .22 LR. To try such shots with an inaccurate (not necessarily the same as inexpensive) rifle with no scope and Super Duper ammunition of limited accuracy is unreasonable. It is not the cartridge used that makes hunting a particular species inhumane. Within the limits of accurate bullet placement, the handgun hunter approaches the sport in the same way as does the rifleman. In an effort to place bullets more accurately, an increasing number of hunters using handguns are mounting scopes on them.

A very accurate rimfire with a good scope of suitable magnification may produce five-shot groups of one-half inch or less at 50 yards. A rifle that gives only "plinking" accuracy might produce two-inch or larger groups at 50 yards. The author recently read the test results for a .22 rimfire rifle that gave 1.25-inch groups at 25 yards. The lethal zone on a squirrel may be only an inch or so in diameter so a rifle that gives only plinking accuracy is not a 50-yard squirrel rifle. Neither does the rate of fire ("firepower") have anything to do with the effectiveness of a rimfire rifle that is used as a hunting tool. Although self defense is

Before setting out to hunt, determine the capability of your rifle and ammunition as the author is doing.

a somewhat different matter, it is the first well-placed shot that counts most when hunting. In fact, a fast-firing rifle may encourage a "hose 'em down" mentality. To a disciplined hunter, the type of action employed by the firearm makes little difference because it is accurate shot placement that counts. Accuracy is paramount, but the type of action is totally irrelevant in most cases.

Having said that, it should be pointed out that generally bolt action rifles are more accurate than are those with other types of actions although there are many exceptions. Some expensive .22 bolt action rifles must produce group smaller than one-half inch at 50 yards to be deemed ready for shipment. Many autoloading, lever, and pump action rifles will deliver 1.25- to 1.5-inch groups at 50 yards with most types of ammunition. Some belonging to the author will reduce that group size to about an inch if the ammunition is chosen carefully. However, two of the most accurate rimfire rifles owned by the author are a Ruger 10/22T target model and a discontinued Thompson/Center Classic, both autoloaders. Either will give groups that average well under one-inch at 50 yards with most types of ammunition, and groups measuring slightly over one-half inch are possible when the most accurate types of ammunition are selected. Individual rifles with any type of action may deliver outstanding accuracy, but usually even a modestly priced bolt action rifle may prove to be more accurate

With a good scope, the Ruger 10/22T gives excellent accuracy although it is somewhat heavy for a walking hunt.

With the right ammunition, the CZ bolt action rifles are a very good choice for hunting small game.

than rifles having other action types that cost more. This does not mean that you should always hunt with a bolt action rimfire firearm. It means that you should determine the accuracy capability of your chosen rifle and ammunition before you hunt live targets. Unless you have exceptional eyesight, it also means that you will need a scope to determine how accurately your rifle will shoot and to place bullets accurately in hunting situations.

The handgun hunter must operate within the limits imposed by the accuracy produced by the combination of gun, ammunition, and sighting equipment. Many rimfire handguns are capable of giving groups of one inch or less at 25 yards and some very accurate models might give groups of 1.5-2 inches at 50 yards. Given this level of accuracy, most hunters using handguns should limit their shots to about that distance. If your particular equipment will do better and you can shoot well under field conditions, the range might be extended somewhat.

One of the most important factors to consider when hunting is the trajectory of the bullet. That topic was discussed in Chapter 9, but it needs to be revisited briefly here in order to make clear some limitations of rimfire cartridges. Consider a .22 LR that is going to be used with standard velocity loads or with the CCI Velocitor load. If the rifle is sighted in at 60 yards in each case, the trajectories will be as shown in the accompanying figure. Note that the bullet rises slightly less than one inch above the line of sight in either case, but the path of the Velocitor bullet is never more than about 0.3 inch above the line of sight. Either bullet will take out a squirrel at any distance out to about 70 yards at which distance the bullet from the standard velocity load will strike an inch below the point of aim. As a result, when sighted in at 50 yards and using standard velocity ammunition, the .22 LR bullet deviates no more than an inch from the line of sight out to 70 yards and should be used within that limit.

Suppose you wish to use the Velocitor and sight in so that the bullet will rise no more than one inch

As shown in this graph, the Velocitor load shoots considerably flatter than does a standard velocity load in .22 LR.

The trajectory of the CCI Velocitor is sufficiently flat to allow it to be sighted in at 80 yards.

If the small game hunter wishes to use a handgun, the Browning Buck Mark has the necessary accuracy. The Weaver 1.5-4X scope is a great asset.

The Ruger Mark III Hunter is designed to be an effective implement for use on small game and varmints. (photo courtesy Ruger)

above the line of sight. The accompanying figure shows the trajectories that would result when the rifle is sighted in at 60, 70, and 80 yards with Velocitors. Note that when the rifle is sighted in at 80 yards the point of impact is one inch high at 50 yards and almost one inch low at 90 yards. So sighted the .22 LR has an effective range of almost 90 yards with the bullet striking no more than an inch above or below the line of sight out to that range.

When using the .22 WMR with 40-grain bullets, it is helpful to know the trajectory that would result when the rifle is sighted in at different distances. The accompanying figure shows that the most practical sight in distance is about 100 yards. When so sighted, the bullet rises just one inch above the line of sight at its highest point and strikes less than two inches low at 125 yards. Hits can be made on small varmints out to that distance by holding the sights directly on the target.

Because of its high velocity, the .17 HMR firing a 17-grain bullet gives a trajectory that has less curvature than that of any rimfire except the .17 WSM. In order to see how the path of the bullet depends on the distance at which the rifle is sighted in, the accompanying figure was prepared assuming sight in distances of 100, 125, and 150 yards. When sighted in at 100 yards, the midrange trajectory is only about one-third of an inch. When sighted in at 150 yards, the midrange trajectory is about an inch and three-fourths, which is

The magnum rimfire calibers deliver much greater terminal effects than does the .22 LR.

a little too much for a rifle that is at its best when used on small varmints. When sighted in at 125 yards, the .17 HMR has a midrange trajectory slightly less than one inch, which is about right. In this case, the bullet will strike about 1.5 inches low at 150 yards. This is the most effective sighting for general shooting with the .17 HMR. Although the details will not be shown here, the .17 Mach 2 has a trajectory that is not much different from that of the .22 WMR and rifles in both calibers could be sighted in similarly. The .17 WSM shoots sufficiently flat to permit sighting in at 150-175 yards and still have the path of the bullet deviate very little from the line of sight. The shooter using a rimfire rifle will be more effective when the trajectory of the load used has become very familiar.

Caliber Considerations

The groundhog (or woodchuck) has been a noble varmint for generations. In the west, the marmot (also known as a rockchuck) fills the same role. The largest groundhog that this writer ever took was sitting vertically on the edge of his hole. The distance was about 50 yards, and the high velocity .22 LR bullet hit him in the chest squarely between the front legs. The groundhog went over backwards and appeared not even to twitch. With shots such as this or head shots, the .22 LR can be used successfully on groundhogs out to 75 yards or so if the bullet is correctly placed. Although any solid body hit from a centerfire varmint rifle will smash a groundhog or marmot, this is not the case with a .22 LR. The bullet from a rimfire, even a .17 HMR or .22 WMR, must be placed in a lethal zone on the target.

Both the .22 WMR and the .17 HMR give performance that raises the bar significantly compared to a .22 LR. At 100 yards, the remaining energy for the .22 LR is approximately 90 ft lbs. Even with the CCI Velocitor the remaining energy is only about 110 ft lbs at that range. However, with a 40-grain bullet, the .22 WMR has about 155-160 ft lbs at 100 yards and the .17 HMR has an energy of 135 ft lbs. Both of these

The CZ 455 Varmint in .17 HMR is an outstanding varmint rifle. (photo courtesy CZ USA)

magnum rimfires are legitimate 125-yard groundhog or marmot cartridges in accurate rifles.

As of this writing, there are several factory loads available for the .17 HMR with most of them utilizing a 17-grain bullet having a nominal muzzle velocity of 2,550 ft/sec. Other loads from CCI and Hornady utilize 20-grain bullets that have a muzzle velocity specified as 2,375 ft/sec giving a muzzle energy of 250 ft lbs, which is almost the same as the 245 ft lbs produced by the 17-grain rounds. A 50-grain hollow point .22 WMR load from Federal has approximately 160 ft lbs of energy remaining at 100 yards. Although the trajectory of this load is not as flat as that produced by lighter bullets in .22 WMR, it packs a punch and is perhaps the most effective .22 WMR load for use on larger varmints. A .17 HMR or .22 WMR with any of these rounds far out classes the .22 LR both in energy and flatness of trajectory.

All of this is not meant to imply that the .22 LR is not a useful pest cartridge. Many people like the challenge that arises from the use of a .22 LR instead of a true varmint cartridge of higher power. Extreme accuracy is required, and before you start out, do a great deal of testing with several types of ammunition. As will be described in Chapters 14 and 15, a particular rifle

may well give groups that are twice as large with one type of ammunition as with another. Because bullet placement is vital when using a .22 LR, the hunter needs to know the performance of the ammunition being used. The hunter using a rifle chambered for the .22 WMR or .17 HMR has a little more leeway because of the greater power of these rounds. The user of a .22 centerfire such as the .223 Remington or .22-250 Remington has even more leeway because almost any solid hit with these high velocity centerfires will put the varmint out of business instantly. Many years ago when the author used a .222 Remington on groundhogs, no groundhog made it anywhere after being hit. The combination of the .222 Remington Model 700 and Weaver K-10 scope made hits almost certain out to 200-225 yards with the bullets having enough remaining energy to demolish the varmint. On one hunt, I loaned my Mossberg Model 640 Chuckster® in .22 WMR to a friend who took three groundhogs with three shots because the bullets were placed correctly. The bullet must be placed accurately in a lethal zone for varmint busting to be humane with a rimfire.

Compared to a .223 Remington or similar calibers, the trajectory of bullets fired from rimfires is quite curved. A .223 Remington can be sighted to hit the

The .17 WSM (left) is a potent rimfire, but it does not approach the performance of a .223 Remington (right).

These .17-caliber cartridges are (left to right) .17 Aguila, .17 Mach 2, .17 HMR, and .17 WSM. All are useful within their limitations.

This graph shows the trajectory of the 17-grain load in .17 HMR when sighted in at 100, 125, and 150 yards.

point of aim at 200 yards by being only about one inch high at 100 yards and only about six inches low at 300 yards. On the other hand, a .17 HMR firing a 17-grain bullet at 2,550 ft/sec sighted to hit the point of aim at 100 yards hits 8.5 inches low at 200 yards. Moreover, at 200 yards, the remaining energy is only 72 ft lbs, about the same as the muzzle energy of a .22 Short! When sighted in at 100 yards, the .17 HMR strikes only 0.1 inch high at 50 yards. A more efficient arrangement is to sight a rifle shooting the .17 HMR to hit approximately 0.5 inch high at 50 yards (which gives a point of impact about 0.75 inch high at 100 yards), a zero at 120 yards, and a point of impact of 1.4 inches low at 150 yards. Such a sighting makes hits possible at almost 175 yards (if the rifle is sufficiently accurate and it is not windy). However, the remaining energy at 175 yards is only 88 ft lbs. In fact, at a distance of slightly over 210 yards, the remaining energy of a .22 LR high velocity is almost exactly the same as that of the tiny .17-caliber bullet from a .17 HMR! Because of its curved trajectory, it would be virtually impossible

This graph shows the trajectory of the 40-grain load in .22 WMR when sighted in at 75, 100, and 125 yards.

to hit anything at such long range with a .22 LR. Some years ago, a conversation was overheard in a sporting goods store in which the clerk told of killing a coyote at 180 yards with a .17 HMR rifle. No doubt that he did it, but such a feat is probably more in the nature of an accident than an indication of the suitability of the .17 HMR for such use.

The .22 WMR has a trajectory that is more curved than that of the .17 HMR, but the heavier bullets of the .22 WMR retain more energy. The .22 WMR can be sighted in at 100 yards with the point of impact being about one inch high at 50 yards, 2.2 inches low at 125 yards, and approximately six inches low at 150 yards. At 150 yards, the 40-grain .22 WMR bullet has 15% more remaining energy than a bullet from the .17 HMR and it also has a heavier bullet of larger diameter for greater punch. The main advantage of the .17 HMR over the .22 WMR is that the higher velocity results in a flatter trajectory, which makes hits easier at longer ranges, especially on small targets.

The rimfire magnums add almost 100 yards to the performance of a .22 LR.

It is instructive to compare the magnum rimfire cartridges of today with the almost obsolete 5mm Remington Magnum of the early 1970s. That cartridge fired a 38-grain bullet at 2,100 ft/sec giving a muzzle energy of 372 ft lbs. Because the bullet is rather heavy for a 5mm caliber (0.204" diameter), it holds its velocity well because the ballistic coefficient of the bullet is 0.145. The accompanying figure shows the remaining energy for the .17 HMR, .22 WMR, and 5mm Remington as a function of distance. The 5mm has about the same energy at 200 yards as the .17 HMR does at 100 yards or the .22 WMR does as at 125 yards. Although the trajectory has more curvature than that of the .17 HMR, it has less than that of the .22 WMR. The 5mm Remington Magnum is an excellent rimfire cartridge, and we can only hope that some manufacturer will see fit to resurrect it. With the propellants available today and a Hornady polymer tipped bullet weighing about 32-34 grains, it would be a very interesting development in rimfire ammunition.

When we consider the .17 Mach 2, we face a paradox. The muzzle velocity is 2,100 ft/sec and the ballistic coefficient of the 17-grain polymer tipped bullet is 0.125. The velocity and ballistic coefficient are very similar to those for the .22 WMR, but that is where the similarity ends. A 40-grain bullet from a .22 WMR has almost exactly twice as much energy as the little 17-grain bullet from a .17 Mach 2 at all ranges out to 200 yards! In fact, the CCI Velocitor .22 LR produces more energy at the muzzle (183 ft lbs as compared to 166 ft lbs) and at 100 yards (110 ft lbs as compared to 88 ft lbs). In the .17 Mach 2 we have a cartridge that is extremely accurate, which makes hits on small animals possible out to perhaps 125 yards, but at that range the energy is well below that of a high performance .22 LR and roughly equal to that of a standard velocity .22 LR. At best, it would seem that the .17 Mach 2 should be used on species no larger than ground squirrels, which require very little killing, or perhaps crows or prairie dogs at ranges so short that the remaining energy is at least 100 ft lbs (about 80 yards). There can be absolutely no doubt that many larger species will fall to the .17 Mach 2 and shooters will tell of killing coyotes at considerable distances with it. It will kill a coyote, but so will a powerful air rifle. That does not mean that either is actually suitable for coyote hunting. When hunting squirrels at normal ranges (under 75 yards) the .17 Mach 2 will do nothing that can not be done with an accurate .22 LR with carefully chosen ammunition. The accuracy potential of the .17 Mach 2 can not be denied, but in power the cartridge duplicates that of the .17 HMR after the bullet from the latter has traveled 65-70 yards. If a cartridge with those capabilities excites you, a rifle in .17 Mach 2 caliber might have a place in your future. The same situation exists for the slightly less powerful .17 Aguila. Given the very limited popularity of those calibers you may have trouble finding a rifle to shoot them or ammunition.

Several companies offer .22 WMR ammunition loaded with bullets as light as 30 grains. However, the lighter bullets have low ballistic coefficients and they lose velocity rapidly so that the trajectory over a distance of 125-150 yards is no flatter and retained energy is less than that of the 40- or 50-grain bullets. The lightweight hollow point bullets in .22 WMR have large cavities and they are very explosive on small targets at ranges of 100 yards or less. One exception is the Remington Premier load in .22 WMR, which utilizes a 33-grain Hornady V-Max bullet that has a polymer tip similar to those used in .17 HMR ammunition. This bullet has a ballistic coefficient that is higher than that of any of the bullets used in the .17 HMR ammunition, and it is much less explosive than the 30-grain hollow points. With a muzzle velocity specified as 2,000 ft/sec (my chronograph indicates that is the actual velocity), this pointed bullet holds its velocity well, and it is quite accurate in the author's Ruger 77/22M. The Remington Premier has become a favorite load for varmint hunting when using a .22 WMR, but the explosive 30-grain hollow point loads are not used to any great extent.

When we come to the .22 LR, the curved trajectory is an even greater problem. The .22 LR high velocity ammo fires a 40-grain bullet at a nominal velocity of 1,260 ft/sec. In order to zero this load at 100 yards, the bullet must strike approximately 2.7 inches high at 50 yards. This much deviation from the line of sight is unacceptable because it makes accurate bullet placement on small targets difficult as a result of the shooter having to "hold under" at short ranges. For the small pests suitable for taking with the .22 LR, the bullet should not deviate more than about one inch from the line of sight. Probably the best plan is to sight a .22 LR to hit about one inch high at 40 yards, be zeroed at 60-65 yards and hit about 2 inches low at 80 yards. This means that the rifleman with an accurate rifle can put a bullet in a small target at approximately 80 yards on a still day. Some shooters with high quality equipment and the ability to estimate distances accurately can stretch this a bit, but the remaining energy at 100 yards is only about 90 ft lbs. The CCI Velocitor load shoots slightly flatter and has a remaining energy of approximately 110 ft lbs at a range of 100 yards. If the accuracy in your rifle is acceptable, the Velocitor is the most effective .22 LR ammunition available for use on some of the larger species of varmints.

Some types of so-called high performance or hyper velocity .22 LR ammunition have become quite popular. One such round is the CCI Stinger that fires a 32-grain bullet at a muzzle velocity of about 1,640 ft/sec, which corresponds to an energy of approximately 190 ft lbs. This round gives explosive performance at short range, but the light bullet loses its velocity rapidly so that at 100 yards it has a remaining energy of only 90 ft lbs, about the same as that from most high velocity .22 LR ammunition. However, the owner's manuals of several rifles warn against using the Stinger in those rifles. If a rifle has a so-called match chamber, the rifling begins at the forward end of the chamber so that the bullet engages the rifling as the round is chambered. The bullet does not have to "jump" to engage the rifling, and this results in greater accuracy. Stingers use a case that is approximately 0.10 inch longer than the standard .22 LR case. When a Stinger is chambered in a rifle having a match chamber, the case engages the rifling. This condition can cause difficulties in chambering the cartridge and possible damage to the rifling just ahead of the chamber. Check the owner's manual for your rifle before firing Stingers in your rifle. The CCI load known as the Quik Shok also uses a case that is longer than the standard long rifle case.

With a 40-grain hollow point bullet and a velocity of 1,435 ft/sec, this new Browning .22 LR ammunition is a good choice for hunting.

Although CCI Stinger and Quik Shok rounds use a longer case, the CCI Velocitor round does not. This and the Winchester Hyper Speed HP™ and the Browning BPR are the real powerhouses of the .22 LR family. Both utilize use a 40-grain hollow point bullet that leaves the muzzle at a nominal velocity of 1,435 ft/sec and produces a muzzle energy of 183 ft lbs from a .22 LR case of normal length. Even at 100 yards the velocity is 1,112 ft/sec and the energy is 110 ft lbs. In addition, the Velocitor gives very good accuracy in many rifles. If you feel that you want to tackle larger varmints with a .22 LR, by all means test the Velocitor or Winchester Hyper Speed HP ammunition. However, do not overlook ammunition of lower power that may give target accuracy. Winchester Power Points utilize a 40-grain hollow point bullet and have become popular for hunting with rimfires because they give excellent accuracy in a wide variety of .22 rifles. Many hunters use highly accurate rifles and target ammunition because it is better to place a bullet having an energy of 100 ft lbs in the lethal zone than it is to place one having an energy of 150 ft lbs outside that zone.

Of the small game animals taken with a .22 LR rimfire, the squirrel is probably the toughest. Given an accurate rifle with good ammunition, squirrels are

not difficult to bag. The head offers a target of about an inch in diameter, and the upper body (heart/lung area) perhaps an inch and a half. A good marksman with good equipment should have no trouble hitting such targets at 40-50 yards. Rabbits are even easier to kill and offer larger targets. Always remember that a missed shot at a squirrel in a tree sends a bullet on a path to come back to earth a mile or so away. A shot at a rabbit always carries the possibility of a ricochet. Safety must always be paramount when shooting rimfire firearms.

Small pests such as rats, ground squirrels, starlings, crows, etc. offer a challenge to the rimfire shooter only in the areas of marksmanship and hunting skill. Power requirements are secondary. Is it sporting to try to bag larger varmints such as groundhogs, marmots, foxes or even coyotes with a rimfire? Perhaps the best answer is the old cliché, "Yes, no, or yes if… ." Yes, if the hunter has an accurate rifle/scope/ammunition combination, limits the range, and shows the discipline necessary to make an accurate shot in a lethal zone. It is not uncommon for a varmint hunter to call a coyote to within 50 yards and make a head shot with a .22 LR. Under these conditions, the .22 LR is adequate. Reading a report written by a hunter who has taken almost a dozen coyotes with his Ruger 10/22 with one shot each in this way shows that it is certainly possible. The answer to the question posed is definitely "no" if one is talking about taking a sniping shot at 100-125 yards or so. Under these conditions, the .22 WMR is just barely an adequate fox or coyote cartridge, and the bullet must still be carefully placed in the anatomy of the varmint.

The .17 HMR is extremely popular. Most .17 HMR rifles give good accuracy and the trajectory is such that it easy to score hits at rather long ranges for a rimfire. Some shooters are attempting to use the .17 HMR in ways it was not intended for. Although many larger varmints have fallen and many more will fall to bullets from .17 HMR rifles, it is not a reliable killer on such species. An acquaintance who has taken several coyotes with both .17 HMR and .22 WMR rifles has told the author that there is a considerable difference in the effectiveness of the two calibers. He says that coyotes frequently travel some distance after taking a tiny .17 HMR bullet in the chest area, but that the coyotes he has hit similarly with the .22 WMR basically dropped on the spot. Neither the .17 HMR nor the .22 WMR is a great coyote cartridge, but the more powerful .22 WMR with its heavier bullets of larger diameter is better.

To complement the performance of the Savage A17 rifle, the CCI A17 load gives 2,650 ft/sec with a polymer-tipped bullet.

A .25 caliber rimfire firing a 60-grain bullet at 1,500-1,600 ft/sec would be better still, but no such cartridge is currently available. The .25 Stevens Rim Fire cartridge, which has been out of production since 1942, gave a 65- to 67-grain lead bullet a velocity of about 1,200 ft/sec. With a modern loading using propellants available today, a velocity of perhaps 1,500 ft/sec could be produced with a 60-65-grain bullet. Such a load would be considerably more effective on larger varmints than any rimfire now available. Even the original load had a good reputation for dispatching small game without destroying much edible meat. For those of us who are interested in sports using rimfire rifles, it would be nice to have such a cartridge as a choice today.

The newest rimfire is the .17 Winchester Super Magnum (WSM). The factory loads include those having 20- or 25-grain polymer-tipped bullets that have ballistic coefficients of 0.185 and 0.230, respectively. As a result, these bullets retain their velocity at longer ranges better than do those of any other rimfire cartridge. As shown in Chapter 9, a .17 WSM can easily be sighted in to hit a point of aim at 150-200 yards and has sufficient energy to be effective on a range of varmint species at such distances. One must still verify that the rifle used is sufficiently accurate to hit small targets at such ranges and keep in mind that small bullets are susceptible to deflection by wind. It is the opinion of the author that even the .17 WSM should be used with discretion on larger varmints because of the very light bullets of small diameter. The .17 WSM case is large enough that if it were expanded to hold .20- or .22-caliber bullets the result would be a cartridge that might not match the trajectory of the .17 WSM, but would hit with greater authority on larger varmints. The .17 WSM is a fine cartridge, but that case necked down to hold .20- or .22-caliber bullets would be even better.

The trajectory of the .17 WSM is flatter than that of any other rimfire caliber.

The velocity given by the .17 WSM is still well over 2,000 ft/sec at 100 yards.

The .17 WSM has a remaining energy at 100 yards that is as great as that produced by the .17 HMR at the muzzle.

Scopes for Rimfire Hunting

Assuming that you are hunting small game and pests and need to place the shot accurately, a scope is virtually a requirement regardless of whether you are using a rifle or handgun. A scope certainly is necessary if you buy one of the many rimfire rifles that are marketed with no iron sights installed, a situation that has become common in recent years. Together, the rifle and scope essentially constitute the vehicle for launching bullets accurately to harvest game or dispatch pests. But what type of scope? What power? What type of reticule? How expensive? Fixed power or a variable? All of these questions can be perplexing to someone who is selecting the equipment for rimfire shooting sports. Some of the very inexpensive scopes that can be used on rimfire rifles have tubes that are only three-quarters of an inch in diameter. They are slightly better than no scope, but they are not the type of scope used by serious rimfire shooters who prefer to use scopes of good quality with one-inch diameter tubes.

A focusing objective allows the shooter to focus the scope at the desired distance and correct for parallax at the same time.

A factor that must be considered when using scopes at different distances is parallax. Parallax can be illustrated as follows. With your arm extended, point a finger at a distant object and look at your finger and the object with only your right eye. Hold your arm stationary and look at the object with only your left eye. Note how the object appears to have moved. What actually moved was the

A hunter on a budget can still get excellent performance. In this case, it comes from a Marlin rifle topped with a Weaver K6 scope.

point of observation. When you look through a scope that has the reticule aligned on a target, the reticule may appear to move on the target as you move your eye from side to side. If so, the scope has parallax error when the target is at that particular distance.

Scopes that are intended for use on centerfire rifles are usually adjusted to have no parallax at 100 yards. A scope that is intended for use on a rimfire rifle is normally free of parallax at 50 or, in some cases, 60 yards. Some scopes that are designed for use on muzzle loaders or shotguns are corrected for parallax at a distance of 75 yards. Unless the eye is positioned rather far from the axis of the scope, parallax results in a very small sighting error at normal rimfire ranges (25-100 yards). In my youth, I saw some very fine marksmanship produced with a rifle that had a Weaver K4 scope mounted on it even

though the scope was not free of parallax at the usual distances where .22 rimfires are used. That scope was intended for use on centerfire rifles and was free of parallax at 100 yards, but it made little difference as long as the shooter was careful to place his eye in the same position for each shot.

One type of scope has a front lens (objective) that can be rotated to focus the scope on targets at different distances. This is advantageous for the rimfire shooter who may use a .22 LR rifle on targets at 25-75 yards or out to 150 yards if the rifle is a .17 HMR, .22 WMR, or .17 WSM. However, these adjustable objective or AO scopes tend to be rather expensive, but there are exceptions. Some models will be described later.

A question that arises frequently is, "What power scope should I put on my rimfire rifle?" The most logical response is, "What do you plan to do with it? What size targets do you intend to shoot and at what ranges?" For testing the accuracy of a rifle with different types of ammunition, a scope of 10-20 power is not unreasonable. In that case, you want the sighting error to be as small as possible. For most hunting situations, there is no need for a scope having this much magnification even when shooting small varmints at the longest ranges appropriate for using rimfire rifles. A variable scope that is 2-7X or 3-9X in magnification will serve quite well for almost any hunting activity with a rimfire. Of course a 12X or 16X scope will do no harm, especially when ground squirrels at ranges up to 150 yards are the targets for your .17 HMR. The Ruger 77/22 owned by the author is frequently used with a very old Weaver K10 scope whereas the Ruger 77/22M often has an old Weaver V12 (a 3-12X variable) scope attached. Both of these scopes have adjustable objectives and were bought as used scopes for a fraction of the cost of new scopes of comparable quality.

Do not overlook the possibility of finding a good used scope that someone has taken off a rifle to make

Although modestly priced, the .22 WMR Savage 93 G is a good varmint rifle that is perfectly matched with a Leupold 2-7X scope.

space for that new high powered, lighted reticule, trajectory compensating model that was deemed to be absolutely necessary. Two excellent older steel-tube Weaver K6 scopes were found at a show where the owner had them priced at $60 each. That is a good price for a scope of that quality, but by making an offer of $100 for the pair, the author obtained two fine scopes at prices far below those of comparable new scopes. The author has also been able to buy three scopes on eBay, but be careful about buying scopes that you can not look through or check adjustments on. On some older scopes the lens elements may be becoming separated or may be loose.

Marketing specialists have convinced many hunters that there is an enormous advantage to having a high-powered scope with a large objective lens, and the larger the objective the better. Realistically, such scopes are seldom if ever needed in hunting situations. When using a centerfire rifle to shoot at a crow at 300 yards, rather high magnification is almost a necessity. However, the author successfully used a .222 Remington with a 4-power Weaver K4 scope as a varmint rifle for many years. He later moved up to a Weaver K10 scope for more accurate shot placement at longer ranges, and a large number of crows and groundhogs were taken at ranges up to 225 yards or more. Rimfire rifles are not 300-yard varmint rifles. The use of a .22 LR should be at most about a 90-100 yard proposition. The .22 WMR stretches this to 125-150 yards, and the .17 HMR is useful to perhaps 25 yards farther. The .17 WSM extends this range to perhaps 200 yards. Longer shots are possible for the highly skilled, well-equipped shooter, but the average shooter with average equipment should not attempt such feats. The risk of merely wounding the target is too high.

Scopes of variable power are popular even if most of the time they are set on one magnification and left there. Many are 2-7X or 3-9X, but 4-12X, 4-16X, or 6-24X scopes are also common. If the scope is to be used for purposes of testing accuracy where the smallest possible groups are the intent, the scope should have high magnification because a sighting error of 0.1-0.2 inch is significant in such shooting. As this is written, a fly was observed crawling on a target about 100 yards away through a 20X scope. That kind of visibility is an advantage when shooting at small, stationary targets. If the scope is to be used in hunting, lower magnification is satisfactory. It is frustrating to bring a rifle to the shoulder only to find that you must search for the animal because the field of view is so small. It is also very difficult to follow a moving target if the scope has high magnification.

This Anschutz Model 164 is fitted with a Cabela's 6-24X AO Outfitter's scope. It is superbly accurate, but would normally be used for hunting with a smaller scope.

A scope having a maximum power of 7X or 9X is a good compromise that will serve almost any purpose on a rimfire rifle used for hunting. Even a good quality fixed power 6X scope is a very capable sighting tool, and in the "hunter" class of bench rest target shooting, 6X is the maximum magnification permitted. A long time favorite scope of the author is the Weaver K6. Many years ago, he witnessed some very fine shooting done with a Winchester Model 75 Sporter and a Model 69A both of which wore 4-power Weaver K4 scopes. Except when trying to achieve the ultimate accuracy, a scope of high magnification is simply not necessary. A hunter using a .22 LR for hunting small game and pests within 75 yards or so can do fine work with a good scope of 4-6 power. Some rimfire scopes are variables in the 2-7X or 3-9X range, and they represent a good compromise. Such scopes include the Weaver 2.5-7X, the Simmons 3-9X, 3-9X AO, the Leupold 2-7X, and the 2.5-7X from Thompson/Center among others. If the range is going to stretch to 150 yards or more by using a .17 HMR or a .22 WMR, a good 3-9X is very useful. Two outstanding scopes are the Weaver 3-9X AO and Simmons 1022T AO both of which are intended for use on rimfire rifles. A new entry into the rimfire scope market is the ProStaff 3-9X model from Nikon. If you are going to shoot small varmints with a .17 WSM at ranges up to 250 yards, you want one with greater magnification. All of these scopes have adequate magnification and some also have the advantages of a focusable objective.

Four excellent scopes for use on rimfire hunting rifles are (top to bottom) the Simmons .22 Mag 4X, Simmons 1022T 3-9X AO, Cabela's 2.5-7X, and Nikon ProStaff 4X.

Scopes of good quality that are intended for use on air rifles also work well on rimfire rifles. Some such scopes are very ruggedly constructed because they are built to withstand the recoil of break action air rifles. In those air rifles, a heavy piston lurches forward at the time of firing. When it reaches the forward end of the compression cylinder, it yanks the rifle forward so the scope has to be able to withstand recoil in both directions. Of course, rimfire rifles have almost no recoil backward and none forward so an airgun scope is subjected to much less stress when used on a rimfire rifle. Most of these scopes have adjustable objectives because air rifles are used at ranges from perhaps 10-

Handgun hunters have an excellent tool available in the Ruger Single Six Hunter that can readily have a scope attached. (photo courtesy Ruger)

50 yards, and it is necessary to be able to focus sharply on targets over a five-fold variation in distance. Air rifle scopes available from BSA include 4X, 2-7X, and 3-12X models, and all have AO. My experience with several of the BSA scopes is extensive, especially the 3-12 X 44 AO, which I have also used extensively while testing .22 LR ammunition.

An extensive selection of scopes awaits the handgun hunter. Both fixed and variable power models are available. Scope mounts are produced for almost all popular rimfire handguns, especially those models that would be considered suitable for hunting. For some types of hunting, a good red dot sight might be a better choice, but keep in mind that most of these sights have dots that cover 3 or 4 MOA (about 1.5 or 2.0 inches at 50 yards). That means that the dot itself might cover much of a small critter if the range is 50-75 yards. On the other hand, the crosshair of a scope could easily be centered on such a target. In the case of using handguns for hunting small game and pests, it is much more likely that the skill of the hunter under field conditions will be the limiting factor.

Let us look at the facts from the point of view of the rifleman. To hit small species of game and pests, the bullet path should not deviate more than about an inch or an inch and a half from the line of sight. Sighted to hit one inch above the point of aim at 50 yards, the .22 LR high velocity bullet strikes the point of aim at approximately 65-70 yards and falls about 2 inches below the point of aim at 90 yards. Beyond about 80-85 yards, it is necessary to "hold over" in order for the bullet to hit within one inch of the point of aim. Unless the range is accurately known, placing the bullet correctly becomes difficult because of the curved trajectory it follows even when assuming that there is no wind deflection. This writer has taken groundhogs at rather long ranges with a .22 LR, but he also stopped trying to do so abruptly after seeing one fall over then crawl into a hole. We must be humane in our sport. There is a large segment of the population that would be quite happy to see all forms of sport hunting banned. We must not give them any additional arguments to use against us as they try to accomplish that goal. Selecting the right equipment and ammunition for the job and being serious enough to take time to develop shooting skills are basic requirements for hunting.

Field Accuracy

One of the aspects of hunting that always comes as a surprise after a long absence from the woods is just how much different things look in the woods than they do on a range. Distances are uncertain. Branches, leaves, bushes, and uneven terrain all combine to give a totally different view from that of looking at a target on a stand 50 yards away. The target is black or orange on a white background and regular in shape whereas the target being sought in the woods has an irregular shape and may blend in with the surroundings.

To prepare for shooting under hunting conditions, try practicing under hunting conditions. If you have access to an area where you can safely shoot at targets on trees or stumps, try putting up some conventional paper targets and shooting them at varying distances using the same shooting positions that you will use when trying to take a squirrel at 50 yards. You may find that the bench rest compensated for more flaws in your shooting technique than you would have believed possible. Although the earth is solid, a few feet of swaying, quivering anatomy has a way of producing an unstable shooting stand. After working on conventional targets on stumps or logs, try shooting some targets that are pictures of the animals that you intend to hunt. Targets are available with silhouettes in the form of squirrels, rabbits, and

prairie dogs that are very useful for this purpose. However, you can also find photos of animals in magazines that can be cut out and taped on heavy paper. They can be placed at appropriate distances so that the scale matches the size of the real animal. For example, if you find a squirrel picture that is approximately six inches long, when shot at 25-30 yards it would be equivalent to the real animal at perhaps 50 yards.

The idea behind this type of shooting is that an irregularly shaped animal is quite different from those black circles on a white background that most of us shoot so much more often than we do game. The idea is the same as it is for the archer who practices on animal targets rather than the red, blue, gold, and black target faces that are used in target archery. It is absolutely necessary to have a suitable, safe location before you practice rimfire shooting in this way, but such practice will pay dividends when the target is an animal seen under hunting conditions. You will also get an idea of how proficient you are under field conditions, which is sometimes quite different than on a range.

Although position shooting in competition is according to strict rules, the hunter has no such restrictions. By all means lean your hand against a tree for support when shooting from a standing position. As in target shooting, a sling can be an asset to steady aiming. Take advantage of a convenient stump or log when shooting from a seated position. Remember, the least stable shooting position is standing with

The small game hunter should try to get a steady position as the author is doing here.

no support, and shots should be taken in this way only when no other option exists. The hunter using a handgun will at the very least hold the piece with both hands, but it would be much better if some sort of rest could be used.

Hunters who wish to hunt large game will find that taking a squirrel at 50 yards with a rimfire is excellent training for taking much larger species at longer ranges. This is no less true for the hunter using a handgun who wishes to move up to hunting large game with a handgun of high power. Handgun hunting is becoming very popular and hunting small game and pests with a rimfire handgun is superb training as well as being a fascinating sport in its own right. Recognizing this, manufacturers are producing more handguns that are delivered with sight rails attached. In this category are some versions of the Browning Buck Mark, Ruger Single Six, Mark III, and 22/45, and the Smith & Wesson Models 22S, 22A, and the recently introduced SW22 Victory autoloaders. Smith & Wesson and Taurus also offer revolvers that are suitable for use in hunting. It should be no problem to select a suitable handgun for hunting small game and pests.

Although general issues related to safety were discussed in Chapter 2, it is not inappropriate to mention safety here as it relates to hunting. In a story on another topic that appeared on the front page of a newspaper as the first edition of this book was being written, a sidebar described how dangerous hunting is. In 1993, there were a total of 1,199 hunting related accidents, including 101 fatalities. For 2002, the figures were 850 and 89, respectively. Self inflicted wounds amount to 39.2% of the total whereas two-person incidents account for 60.5%. Contrasted to the number of fatalities from several other sources that were cited in Chapter 2, the number is indeed small considering how many millions of people spend such an enormous amount of time engaging in the sport. However, hunter safety courses are required in many states for a good reason. In the excitement of the chase or stalk, it is easy to forget to watch that muzzle. Gun handling etiquette should be so ingrained in each hunter that it is automatic. There are sidebar writers

A hunter using a rimfire handgun would be well served with this Kimber Rimfire Target pistol.

everywhere who are trying to make a point and generate an image.

Another safety issue is illustrated by this story. It seems as if some bird hunters had taken a break and placed their guns on the ground. Along came an excited bird dog (ever see one that wasn't excited?) and stepped on the trigger area of a shotgun. The dog's weight pushed the safety to the fire position. It also moved the trigger backward slightly and the gun fired. The action should have been open with no shell in the chamber. Anticipate an unsafe condition before it arises. One of the "laws" of human enterprise states that "anything that can go wrong will."

Hunters have been using small bore rifles for well over a century. Today, such hunters have a wide range of equipment from which to choose. Both rifle and handgun shooters can obtain firearms that will prove completely satisfactory when appropriate sighting equipment and ammunition are selected.

For many years, the Smith & Wesson Model 17 K-22 was one of the top choices for the hunter who used a rimfire handgun.

RUGER STANDARD MARK III

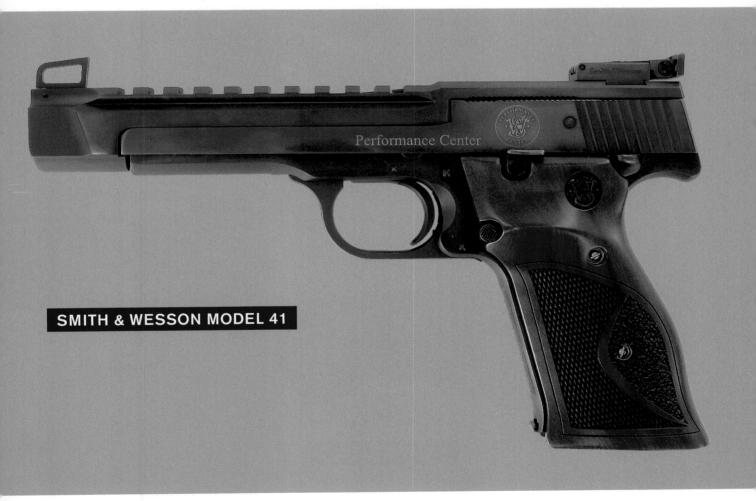

SMITH & WESSON MODEL 41

WINCHESTER 9422 TRIBUTE

RUGER 10/22 TAKEDOWN

SAVAGE RASCAL

SAVAGE B.MAG

CZ AMERICAN 455

RUGER 10/22 SPORTER

RUGER 77/22M

BROWNING 1911-22 BLACK LABEL

HENRY MILITARY SERVICE TRIBUTE

RUGER SINGLE SIX CONVERTIBLE

RUGER 10/22 CARBINE

REMINGTON 597

WALTHER P22

WINCHESTER .17 WSM

SMITH & WESSON SW22 VICTORY

SMITH & WESSON 22LR
SPRINGFIELD, MA USA

RUGER SR22

RUGER - MAYODAN, NC USA SR22P 22LR

SAVAGE 93 BSEV

KIMBER RIMFIRE TARGET

KIMBER RIMFIRE SUPER

RUGER AMERICAN 22 WMR

RUGER 22/45 LITE

SMITH & WESSON 317

HENRY U.S. SURVIVAL

BROWNING BUCK MARK RIFLE

100 FPS FASTER THAN OTHER 17 HMR LOADS!

CCI

A17

Savage Arms *The Definition of Accuracy*

➡ Optimized for the Savage Arms™ A17 rifle

VARMINT TIP
2650 FPS · 17 GRAIN

200 ROUNDS

CCI A17 AMMUNITION

RUGER AMERICAN WOOD STOCK

BROWNING SA22 GRADE VI

SAVAGE 93 FVSR LANDRY

RUGER SINGLE SIX

2.64-93763

RUGER 77/22 STANDARD

HENRY STANDARD LEVER ACTION

SMITH & WESSON 617

CUSTOM RUGER 10/22 TAKEDOWN

CHAPTER 11

RIMFIRE MAINTENANCE

MOST RIMFIRE FIREARMS are very forgiving when it comes to being neglected. They continue to perform well in spite of the debris and gunk that accumulates as a result of firing. Except for magnum calibers, rimfire ammunition does not normally use jacketed bullets, but is made using lubricated lead bullets and a noncorrosive primer so there is little erosion in the barrel. Another factor that contributes to long barrel life is the fact that the powder charges are very small so there is also very little erosion caused by hot gases

Gun care products are available any from many manufacturers.

rushing down the bore. Even with these favorable factors, rimfire rifles and handguns need and deserve some care. Most manufacturers offer models that have stainless steel barrels and actions, and they require even less maintenance. Most rimfire shooters, including this author, actually enjoy tinkering with their guns so cleaning and routine maintenance are not exactly chores to be dreaded.

Before you make any adjustment or change in your rimfire, read the owner's manual. It is very likely that if you alter your firearm you may invalidate the warranty. Do not attempt to alter such things as the trigger pull unless you are fully qualified to do so. The type of activity described in this chapter is limited to cleaning the firearm and making changes in external appearance. At work stations in factories where firearms are assembled, the assemblers have a variety of tools, jigs, and fixtures to orient parts correctly and hold them in place. The home handyman may find it impossible to get something apart or back together without these aids. My advice is don't go beyond your skills and equipment when dealing with your rimfire firearm.

While conducting the firing tests to collect the data that are shown in Chapter 14 and 15, it became apparent that some firearms seem to get messier than others, particularly the autoloaders. It was also found that as groups were fired with a CZ 452 American in .17 HMR caliber, the group size started to increase with some degree of regularity as the number of groups following cleaning increased. After four or five 5-shot groups were fired, the average group size increased by approximately 0.10-0.15 inch. Cleaning the rifle thoroughly caused the group size to be reduced. That observation is in contrast to what has been written by some authors about the small powder charges used in the .17 HMR not causing enough fouling to reduce accuracy. It may not be noted in field use, but on the range the effects were evident. There is also no question that some semiautomatic firearms function much more reliably when the action is kept clean. In this this chapter we will offer some suggestions regarding maintenance that may be of help in keeping your rimfire firearm performing reliably and accurately.

The shooter of a rimfire firearm should be observant. One simple observation that should be made is to inspect fired cases. Carefully note the appearance of the dent made by the firing pin. If the firing pin becomes damaged, the dent will probably reveal some abnormality in terms of depth or shape of the indentation. If the case head is bulged, it may mean that the firearm is developing excessive headspace and needs to be inspected or repaired by a professional. It is not likely that the average shooter will purchase headspace gauges, but if the heads of fired cases are expanded, have the headspace checked by a gunsmith. If the headspace is excessive, it could cause ruptured cases to send a spray of gases and debris into the face of the shooter, which is sufficient reason to wear eye protection when shooting any firearm.

Tools

It is not necessary for the rimfire shooter to try to do a great deal of repair or modification on a firearm. However, there will come a time when the rimfire enthusiast will need to remove some part or move a sight. One of the unsightly results of trying to loosen or tighten a screw with the wrong tool is a mangled screw head. Screwdrivers for use on screws in firearms should have the blades ground in such a way that the blade has parallel faces rather than the common tapered design. When tightening or loosening screws with slotted heads, always use the thickest driver blade that will fit in the slot. For the author, it has been found that a high quality gunsmith's screwdriver set is one of the most useful accessories. These generally have a handle to which a variety of tips

can be attached. Slotted screws were the norm many years ago, but one often encounters Phillips, Allen or hex head screws, and those with torx recesses are becoming common on firearms and scope mounts of recent manufacture. Mounting a scope efficiently also requires screwdrivers of high quality if damage to the screws is to be avoided.

Two types of gunsmith's screwdrivers that the author has found useful are those marketed by Hoppe's and Pachmayr. The Hoppe's set has a hollow handle in which the tips are stored, and the drive shaft is magnetic to hold the tips securely while working with the tool. Incidentally, the magnetic tip is also useful for locating the tiny screws that fill the holes where mounting screws are placed when attaching a scope. Working outdoors, the author has dropped the fill screws that have been found in grass or dust where there would have been no chance of finding them without a magnet. The screwdriver retrieved them. Tips include blade, Phillips, and hex points each in several sizes. It is a most convenient package. The Pachmayr screwdriver set is a complete outfit that contains the handle and a large number of tips for use with slotted (12 blade sizes are included), hex, Phillips, and torx headed screws. The whole assembly is contained in a convenient plastic case. Having the right driver for virtually any screw makes it a lot easier to do things to a firearm without causing damage to the screws. In addition to the gunsmith's screwdrivers, two sets of Allen wrenches are kept handy, one in metric sizes (in mm) and one in SAE sizes (fractions of an inch). With these tools, many firearms can be taken apart (and if you are skilled they can also be put back together).

The author once had a muzzle loading rifle that had an adjustable rear sight, but the adjustment screw was very hard to turn. In fact, one adjustment screw was ruined by assuming that the screw could be turned if enough torque were applied. After ruining the screw,

The Hoppe's screwdriver has a hollow handle that provides storage space for the bits.

This set from Pachmayr provides an assortment of tips in all popular types.

it was learned that the proper way to move a stubborn screw is to turn it a very slight amount then apply a small amount of thin oil to the threads and turn the screw back to its original position. Then back it out slightly (turning it slightly farther than the first time) then turn it back to its original position and again apply oil. This "rocking" motion cleaned out the threads and after working it back and forth instead of simply turning harder to try to move the screw, it eventually turned easily. On some firearms, it is possible that an accumulation of debris or corrosion may prevent a screw from turning with a reasonable amount of force. Try working the screw back and forth lubricating it as you go in order to avoid damaging the head of the screw. Avoid using undue force when trying to move a screw or pin. There are several solvents that can be of help when loosening parts. One of the most widely used is known as Liquid Wrench®.

Another tool that is handy to have available is the Lyman gunsmith's hammer, which is actually three hammers in one. This hammer has a choice of striking faces made of steel, brass, or Teflon that can be threaded onto the head. One of the three faces is threaded to the end of the hollow handle to form a cap. Inside the handle is stored a brass punch. When it is necessary to move a front or rear sight laterally in its retaining slot, the hammer and brass punch will allow the blows to move the sight without the brass punch marring the blue finish on the steel sight base. The hammer and punch also find other uses when working on firearms. These simple tools form the basis of the author's kit for tinkering with rimfire firearms.

One of the many useful accessories in any shooter's kit is a bore light. This battery-operated light has a curved piece of plastic rod that directs the beam outward from the end of the rod. When the rod is inserted in the bore, looking through the bore at the light makes it possible to see if the bore is clean or where there may be spots of residue that need to be removed. This is a one-size-fits-all light that is equally useful for inspecting the bores of rimfire or centerfire firearms.

Keep in mind that the person who assembled the firearm had available special tools, jigs, and fixtures to hold everything in place as the work progressed.

Lyman's gunsmith's hammer is a useful tool that provides three types of striking surfaces.

For some firearms, a special tool may be required to perform certain operations. For example, the barrel on a Winchester Model 190 .22 autoloader is held to the receiver by a threaded collar that pulls the barrel backward into the receiver. To tighten that collar, a special wrench is required that has an end shaped like a "U" but with the tips bent over. The tips fit in two matching slots in the retaining collar as the bottom of the "U" fits around the barrel. This is but one example of a special tool that is needed for removing and attaching a barrel. Even removing the extractor on some rifles requires a special tool.

In the early days of shooting rimfire firearms, the shooter had available only a very meager selection of products for maintaining the firearm. Today, the selection is truly overwhelming. The author grew up with the smell of Hoppe's No. 9 Nitro Powder Solvent on his hands, but in looking at a catalog from a company that sells shooters supplies it was found that no less than a dozen different solvents were available from that supplier alone. In fact, the number is even greater. True, some of them are specifically for removing copper fouling and whereas others are intended for removing lead. Others are intended for general use in cleaning operations. Solvents are available from most of the suppliers of shooting consumables such as Hoppe's, Outers, Birchwood Casey and many others. Keep in mind that some of these solutions contain

A bore light makes it easy to examine the bore.

organic solvents that are toxic and potentially harmful, and most are flammable. Follow all safety precautions when using these products.

Over a period that has reached almost 70 years, this author has used more Hoppe's No. 9 cleaning solvent than any other. It is still a fine choice for the rimfire shooter, but like other cleaning liquids it contains solvents that might be harmful if inhaled or absorbed through the skin. Another solvent found useful by the author is known as Shooter's Choice, which seems to be an oily solution. Hoppe's Bench Rest-9 is another solvent that does a good job with cleaning most residues out of bores. Many other gun cleaning solvents are available so by all means try a few to find one that you like to use. If you like to cut cloth into little squares, go right ahead. You will probably find that using commercially available patches is more satisfactory, and they are now readily available in the small size that is appropriate for cleaning .17-caliber firearms. You will find that it may require four or five patches in each bore cleaning session so if you shoot much get a good supply.

The primary tool used in cleaning a firearm is a good cleaning rod. For rimfire firearms today, the rod needs to be useful for both .17 and .22 calibers. Separate rods for these calibers might be useful, but a surprising number of cleaning rods and cleaning kits that contain rods are available for use with .17-caliber firearms. For cleaning .22-caliber firearms, the author always uses a rod intended specifically for that caliber. My cleaning rod is a three-section aluminum model that was obtained from Montgomery Ward about 50 years ago. Cleaning rods are made to accept accessories known as jags that screw into the end of the rod. For convenience, many cleaning rods consist of three sections that can be screwed together to make a rod of full length. Long, one-piece rods, sometimes called range rods because of where they are most often found, are available but they are not as convenient to transport as are the take-down models. Cleaning rods are most often made of aluminum or brass so that they will not scratch steel barrels. Most cleaning rods have handles that are free to rotate so that as the rod, tip, and patch follow the rifling, the handle can be grasped and moved forward and backward without it rotating. When traveling or in a pinch, a 1/8-inch dowel rod works reasonably well as a one-piece wooden rod for

Hoppe's No. 9 solvent is a classic gun care product.

A modern cleaning kit for small bores includes a rod and tips that can be used for both .17 and .22 calibers.

This three-piece cleaning rod has been in use for many years. It is made of aluminum which helps prevent damage to rifling.

use with .17-caliber rifles. Such small diameter dowels are quite flexible and easily broken unless they are handled carefully.

Techniques

Before doing anything with a firearm, make absolutely certain that the firearm is unloaded, both in the chamber and in the magazine! Wherever possible, remove the bolt and clean from the breech rather than the muzzle. Rod-end attachments include jags that have ridges or slots to hold a patch as well as brass or nylon brushes. The brushes generally have a twisted wire core into which the bristles (generally brass wires) are inserted. Although the author uses such brushes when cleaning centerfire handguns with leaded bores, he almost never uses them in cleaning a rimfire firearm. A jag pushing a patch saturated with a solvent through the barrel will thoroughly wet the bore. In order to let the solvent work, set the rifle aside with the muzzle pointing downward or else with the rifle lying flat. If the rifle is placed with the muzzle downward, place some absorbent material under the muzzle to trap excess solvent that drains from the bore. Do not set the rifle in such a way that excess solvent can drain downward into the action and stock.

After the solvent has been in the bore for perhaps 15-20 minutes, push a clean, dry patch through the bore to remove the dirty solvent and any solid residue. Push a second clean patch through the bore and examine it to see if it is clean. If the second patch indicates that the bore is still not clean, repeat the treatment with a patch saturated with solvent to wet the bore. Allow the solvent to remain in the bore for half an hour or so and repeat the process with the dry patches. Usually a couple of solvent treatments will be sufficient to soak out any residue from rimfire ammunition. In the case of .22 WMR and .17 HMR that fire jacketed bullets, it may be necessary to let the solvent work for a longer period of time to dissolve the copper-based alloy (known as gilding metal) used in the jackets. High velocity ammunition in .22 LR caliber often has copper-plated bullets, which can leave a copper residue. Sometimes, the rifle may be placed in a safe manner and left overnight to let the solvent work on the residue. In any case, it may be better to let the solvent remove the residue rather than removing it by abrasion with a brush.

Most rifles that have semiautomatic, lever, and pump actions must be cleaned from the muzzle because there is no way to open the breech to insert a rod. Special precaution must be taken not to damage the rifling at the muzzle. The rifling there is the last part of the barrel to make contact with the bullet, which must depart from the muzzle pointed straight onward rather than being tipped. If done carefully, there is little likelihood that an aluminum or brass rod will damage the steel barrel, but it can happen. One way to prevent the rod from scraping on one side of the bore is to place the tip with the patch on the muzzle then rotate the other end of the rod while applying pressure. When the tip is centered in the bore, the pressure to insert it is the least and the patch can be forced into the bore with the rod scarcely touching the barrel. Even though some authorities say never to clean a rifle from the muzzle, the author has no reservation about cleaning autoloaders that way, but he is also very careful about how the patch is inserted. Muzzle loading rifles are also cleaned from the muzzle, but it should be done carefully.

One of the proven products for firearm protection is Sheath from Birchwood Casey.

G-96 is an excellent product for cleaning and preventing rust on metal surfaces.

If the firearm is to be used in the near future, I do not coat the bore with anything. If the firearm is to be stored for a considerable time, I usually run a lightly oiled patch or a patch to which has been applied Birchwood Casey's Sheath® or G96 Complete Gun Treatment down the clean bore. Tubes containing special gun greases are available for coating the bore if the firearm is to be stored for a very long time or if it is to be stored in an environment that is severely detrimental to metals. Greases must be swabbed out of the bore before firing the gun.

When inserting a patch in the muzzle, move the rod gently to prevent damage to the crown.

With most rimfire firearms, there will be some unburned powder and other debris that finds its way into the action. For a bolt action, it is a simple matter to remove the bolt and clean it separately. It is then easy to manipulate a rag inside the receiver to wipe out debris. For autoloader, lever, and pump rifles, the bore can be cleaned as described above, but the action may have to be cleaned by simply opening it and working in the cramped space. Cotton tipped swabs (Q-Tips®) are useful for this work as is a patch moved around with a short section of dowel rod. Some rifles can be partially disassembled (field stripped) for cleaning, but others may have no simple procedures for getting the action apart. It is not possible to give general procedures to be followed because there is such a great diversity of types of actions. By all means follow the instructions in the owner's manual for your specific firearm. If you do not, it is possible that something may go "boiinng" which will require the services of a gunsmith to fix.

After the bore and action are cleaned, lubricate the parts where metal surfaces must slide while in contact with each other. On bolts, this includes the cocking

Lubricants come in many forms that are useful for specific applications.

piece where cam action cocks the rifle as the bolt is opened, trigger pivot points, extractors, etc. It is also a good idea to wipe the bolt itself with a lightly oiled rag. For the actions of autoloaders, pumps, and lever action rifles, lightly oil the moving parts. In order to lubricate some of the hard to reach parts, apply the oil with one of the syringe-type oilers or with a drop of oil on a cotton swab. If the rifle is to be used in extremely cold weather, which could cause the lubricant to stiffen to the point where cycling of the action and ignition become unreliable, use one of the special dry lubricants that are available. In any case, do not oil to excess. A very thin film is all that is required. The own-

er's manual generally gives information for lubricating a specific type of firearm.

External metal parts can be protected by applying a thin film of water repellant. Some of the most common products of this type are Birchwood Casey Sheath, G96 Complete Gun Treatment or WD-40.

The fact that many rimfire firearms are passed from generation to generation in good shooting condition testifies to the longevity of these pieces. It has been said that more firearms are ruined by improper cleaning than by neglect. Although this may be true, there is merit in using a clean, well cared for firearm. The author can still remember the sense of pride that he felt as he cleaned the little Stevens Model 15 single shot that was his first rimfire.

Restore or Refinish?

Before you decide to refinish that old firearm that you inherited from your grandfather, consider the overall situation. No doubt the piece will look better, but that is not the only factor to consider. Highly collectible firearms are usually worth more in their original condition than after they have been refinished. Collectibles have value partially because of their originality, and reworked items, while not exactly counterfeits, lose some of their heritage so to speak. In this chapter the discussion that follows involves rimfire firearms that are "users" that do not have any special value as collectibles. For "user" firearms, refinishing usually improves the appearance and thus increases the value somewhat. Of course, it also makes a difference as to who does the refinishing and the quality of the work. Refinishing usually involves buffing off the old blue from the surface and that sometimes makes markings less visible and sharp in their appearance. Too much polishing alters the legibility of the markings to the point that they may not even be legible, especially if the surface was worn and pitted to begin with. In this chapter, the discussion is directed more to keeping your "user" firearms looking good and operating properly rather than professional restoration, which is an entirely different matter. If you are in doubt as to whether an older firearm should be refinished, consult an appraiser or other expert in the field before you do something that may make the firearm look better but be worth less.

Metal Finishing

While spending a few weeks in a campground in the Big Horn National Forest in Wyoming, my wife and I became friends with David, the 15-year old son

Birchwood Casey bluing products include solutions and touch-up pens.

Touch-up pens are used like any other felt tip pen.

of the campground host. David and Josh, a friend who had come to stay with him for a week, spent a lot of time talking about and using their .22s. David showed up one day with his Ruger 10/22 that had seen considerable service to ask if a section of the barrel could be made to look better. It seems that David had held the rifle in a particular way that placed his hand around the barrel just ahead of the fore end. Sweaty hands have enough salt water present to remove bluing on steel. For a space of about six inches, the barrel on David's rifle was shiny. I assured him that although he could not make it look like new, he could make it look better and keep it from rusting.

As always, I had with me the "kit" that has a permanent home under the seat of the truck. In the kit, which is housed in a plastic shoe box, are such things as a gunsmith's hammer, a Hoppe's gunsmith's screwdriver set, adjustable wrenches, pliers, hack saw, sandpaper, steel wool, pocket knife, ruler, leather, leather punch, etc. This kit has made possible several craft projects and numerous repair jobs during camping trips. So when David wanted the barrel of his rifle to look better, out came the kit. I began by using fine steel wool to remove any layer of oxidized metal and brighten the metal. The barrel was then wiped with a paper towel that had been wet with Coleman fuel. The reason for this procedure is to remove any oils so that the bluing solution would make contact with bare metal. Commercial solvents are available for removing oils from metal surfaces, but Coleman fuel works well as does the gas line freeze preventative, Heet®.

After the metal surface was clean and oil free, I applied Birchwood Casey Perma Blue® with a piece of cloth in a back and forth motion. I then let the bluing work for several minutes, wiped the surface with a damp paper towel, and repeated the bluing process. After a few repetitions, I wiped the barrel with a wet paper towel, carefully dried it, and then wiped the surface with an oil-soaked cleaning patch. The result was not a rifle barrel that looked exactly like a new one, but it certainly looked a lot better than it did when David handed it to me.

The process that I have just described constitutes the steps that are necessary to restore the surface on blued steel. Be sure to have a bright, clean, oil-free surface and follow the directions on the bottle of the bluing solution that you are going to use. By the way, most commercial bluing solutions contain toxic selenium compounds and should be handled carefully. Follow the manufacturer's directions with regard to safety precautions. There are numerous bluing preparations available, and the ones that I have tried have worked well. Birchwood Casey offers bluing preparations in several forms that include the liquid Perma Blue® and Super Blue®. Also, a paste form of Perma Blue® is sold in tubes. If the area to be blued is small, bluing can be applied using a touch-up bluing pen that has a felt tip. Known as the Presto® Gun Blue Pen, this item is also available from Birchwood Casey. Paint pens with felt tips in flat and gloss black are also available for touch up work on black painted surfaces. Complete bluing kits are also available that include the bluing solution, steel wool, degreaser, applicators, etc. needed for the job. Other manufacturers have similar products, but I am more familiar with those described above.

Many firearms, especially rimfires, have metal parts that are not made of steel. Aluminum and its alloys are frequently used for parts that are not subjected to excessive stress or abrasion. Some parts may also be made of brass that is coated black. Birchwood Casey offers Aluminum Black® and Brass Black® to restore or touch up these parts. Older firearms and muzzle loaders often had metal parts that were given a brown finish, and a product known as Plum Brown® is

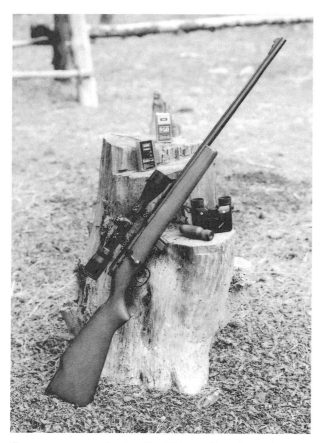

For many years, the Marlin 25 has offered good performance in a bolt action rifle of moderate price. The Marlin 25N with the modified stock is shown in Chapter 14.

This inexpensive Outers stock finishing kit contains all the items to produce an excellent finish.

available to match that type of finish. No matter what the type of finish on a metal surface is, there is a product available to restore the finish. Of course, the best practice is to avoid the loss of finish in the first place, and for blued steel alloys keeping the surface oiled or coated with G96 Complete Gun Treatment, Birchwood Casey Sheath®, or an equivalent product from another manufacturer is usually sufficient.

Wood Finishing

Many inexpensive rifles are sold with stocks that have somewhat less than exquisite shape or finish. If you are like the author, you eventually reach the point where you realize that a stock or some portion of it could be made to look better. It may need the finish restored or it may need some reshaping to give a more pleasing shape than the manufacturer was willing to produce. Let me describe both situations in terms of one such project.

Several years ago, the author bought a Marlin 25N bolt action rifle to use as a utility tool. It did not take long to realize that the stock, although it had an adequate overall shape, lacked those little touches that add elegance. The forearm was cut off square. The grip area was plain, and the finish was a muddy brown. I wanted a stock that was shaped like those on sporting rifles and a finish that gleamed. After taking the stock off, the first step involved trying to remove the finish using the usual paint and varnish removers. None of those products even touched the finish known as Mar-Shield® that Marlin applies to its hardwood stocks! That left only one alternative, abrasion, which is also known as sanding. Removing the finish on the Marlin stock took a great deal of time and effort, but I was eventually rewarded by the sight of bare wood. At that point, I was ready for reshaping the stock to produce the desired look. Before you begin to reshape a stock, examine an elegant rifle or at least look at pictures of such rifles so you will have an idea of what you are striving for.

First, the square end on the forearm was attacked with a wood rasp to give it a pleasing rounded look. Next, work began on the comb by rasping out flutes on the sides. When doing this, be sure that the flutes are directed toward the toe area of the butt and make sure that they are symmetric. Keep the top edges of the flutes sharp and make sure that the bottom sections blend in with the lower section of the stock. The stock now had a fluted comb so the next area to work was the grip. Fine sporting rifles have true pistol grips rather than the type of curved stock found on most inexpensive rifles. To produce such a grip, the author used a round wood rasp to remove wood from the area just behind the grip. The sides of the grip were shaped so that they blended in with the bottom portions of the flutes on the comb. The stock now had a pleasing overall shape and had to be prepared for finishing.

For the stock finishing project described in the text, Outers stain and filler was used followed by Birchwood Casey Tru-Oil.

To modify the factory stock on a Ruger 10/22 Carbine, the step where the barrel band fits was removed.

The stock was given a pistol grip by removing wood from the factory stock in the grip area.

Although the factory magazine for the Marlin 25N holds seven rounds, the shortened magazine holds only four.

Sand, sand, then sand some more is the appropriate admonition when finishing a stock. It is the only way to remove the scratches left by a wood rasp. During the sanding process, you can also make minor changes in the shape so that the areas where wood has been removed blend smoothly with the unmodified areas. Initial sanding was done with medium sandpaper, and followed by sanding with fine grade paper. Finally, the entire stock was sanded with extra fine paper. The stock was now wetted by rubbing with a damp cloth to raise the grain. This process causes the loose fibers known as "whiskers" to stand and after the stock is dry they can be removed by sanding with extra fine sandpaper. As a final step in preparing the wood for finishing, the stock was rubbed briskly with 0000 grade (extra fine) steel wool. By this time, the stock was slick.

Walnut has open pores that must be filled and sealed prior to applying the actual finish. This is done with a wood filler that is rubbed into the wood. Many types of wood filler are available, some of which also contain sealer, so that the wood is filled and sealed in one operation. To impart the desired color, a stain may also be applied. The stock on a Marlin 25N is made of hardwood rather than walnut so the process is slightly different. One of the classic stains for stocks on fine rifles is known as French Red. To get that look, Outers® Stain and Filler was used, which gives the reddish tone to wood. Hardwoods do not have open pores that readily accept the stain so it may be necessary to apply more than one coat of stain. Having now stained the well-shaped stock, it was time to apply the finish.

Several articles made of wood have come under my hand to be finished. This includes not only gunstocks, but also several pieces of furniture. The preparation used by the author most often is Birchwood Casey's Tru-Oil®, which gives a beautiful finish to walnut and mahogany, but it also works well on many other types of wood. Having used this product many times, it was the choice for the stock of my Marlin. My method to apply Tru-Oil® is with my fingers. I get a few drops on my hand by covering the mouth of the bottle with my hand and inverting the bottle. The oil is rubbed out to give even coverage over a small area. The process is repeated while making sure that each small area blends smoothly with others where the oil has been applied until the stock has received an even coat. Allow the

The author shortened the magazine of his Marlin 25N to fit flush with the stock. Although magazine capacity is reduced, the profile of the rifle is greatly enhanced.

initial coat to dry completely then rub the stock lightly with 0000 steel wool while being careful not to apply pressure to sharp edges such as along the bottom of the grip or along the flutes in the comb. Additional coats of Tru-Oil® can be applied in exactly the same way to give a hand rubbed, durable finish. I normally apply five or six coats of this fast-drying oil to get a finish with a high gloss. After the last coat is applied, you can decide whether you want a glossy or satin finish. To obtain a satin finish, the stock can be buffed very lightly with 0000 steel wool or by rubbing it with Birchwood Casey's Stock Sheen and Conditioner®. This product is also excellent for removing dirt and oily grime from older stocks to brighten and restore the luster to the wood.

The same finishing procedures have been carried out on the stocks of several of my air rifles and on a Ruger 10/22 Carbine, and the results have been rewarding. You may not want to remodel a stock, but it can be accomplished with only simple tools and techniques. Just work slowly and make sure that you strive for a smooth, symmetrical appearance. Many newer rifles are furnished with composite or laminated stocks, the shapes of which can not be easily altered. They are usually well-shaped because it is just as easy to mold a pleasingly shaped stock as it is an ugly one. Composite stocks on many rifles have stocks that have pressed in checkering so you will not want to make extensive changes in them. But many older rifles with wood stocks that are less than glamorous can be improved with a little work.

It should also be mentioned that after the work on the Marlin stock was completed, I grew tired of the magazine protruding from the bottom of the stock just where my hand needed to be to carry the rifle. That problem was solved by sliding the bottom plate off the retaining lips on the bottom of the magazine, removing the follower and spring, and using a hack saw to cut about 3/4-inch off the bottom of the magazine box. The spring was shortened by one full loop, and the bottom edges of the magazine box were turned outward to form lips that would hold the base in place. The shortened magazine fits almost flush with the bottom of the stock and holds four rounds instead of seven as is the case for an unmodified magazine. The work that was performed on the Marlin does not make it a work of art, but it certainly looks a lot better than the unmodified version. Moreover, instead of having just another Marlin 25N, I now have a unique rifle that I enjoy using even more than I did before. The modified Marlin 25N was the subject of a feature article, "One Man's Marlin" in the January 2005 issue of *Gun World* (Vol. 46, No. 1, pp. 16-19). Marlin must have liked the result because some of their bolt action rimfire rifles are now offered with a short magazine.

With a minimum of care and attention, it is easy to keep a rimfire firearm functioning well and looking good. Never before have there been so many fine products available to give the shooter the needed tools and materials for the task.

CHAPTER 12

CHOOSE A RIMFIRE FOR TOUGH TIMES

FIREARMS HAVE LONG BEEN an integral part of being in remote places. One of the best descriptions of this association was given by James Oliver Curwood in his 1908 adventure novel, *The Wolf Hunters* (Grosset & Dunlap, New York, 1908). Curwood wrote, "Only those who have gone far into the silence and desolation of the unblazed wilderness know just how human a good rifle becomes to its owner. It is a friend every hour of the night and day, faithful to its master's desires, keeping starvation at bay and holding death for his enemies; a guaranty of safety at his bedside at night, a sharp-fanged watch-dog by day, never treacherous and never found wanting by the one who bestows upon it the care of a comrade and friend." Curwood knew how much more effective a rifle is than a handgun, but we will consider both types of firearms. Although this was written in a work of fiction, it was written by a man who had experience in such remote places, and it is an accurate portrayal of the facts in some cases. It would be wonderful if there were more places of silence and desolation available to us today. Perhaps taking a sheep wagon to the high country for the summer is about as good as it gets. Yes, this is still done in some parts of the country.

A handgun for tough times may get a lot of use. This Ruger Single Six Convertible belongs to a cowboy in Wyoming and it has been his companion for many years.

Tough Times

Given the status of the United States and many other countries today, it is unlikely that you will ever find yourself in a survival situation. It has been stated that in the lower 48 states, there is no point that is more than 30 miles from some type of road. However that may be, there is potential value and no harm in maintaining a state of preparedness regardless of where you may be. That is certainly true in some of the more remote areas of the country where you may be many miles from the nearest phone and where those electronic marvels known as cell phones must be transported many miles to get them to a place where they can contact the rest of the world. In some situations, there is simply no substitute for self-sufficiency. This may mean in the outback, but it may also mean in times of natural disaster or as recent history teaches us, unnatural disaster. It is better to be prepared and not need to be than the other way around.

For many people (including this author) being prepared to deal with whatever arises means being armed when in remote areas. However, being armed in no way eliminates the need for skills that are useful for survival or well being in primitive areas. Knowledge of weather, plants, animals, and geography may also enable you to survive (perhaps even somewhat comfortably) until the situation changes. Whether you consider a firearm as part of your preparation for tough times is up to you. In parts of the west, cowboys still take the cattle herds and flocks of sheep to high elevation for the summer, and some of those camps are rather lonely places. The sight of a sheep herder with two or three thousand sheep on the side of a mountain is a beautiful sight that can still be seen in parts of the west. When these intrepid souls head for the high country with the sheep wagon, they know that there is no 911 to call and the cell phone doesn't

This old H&R Model 929 served its owner well on his trap line.

work anyway. If coyotes harass the flock, something must be done and not by someone else. If a rattlesnake or a large predator shows up, it may need to be dealt with. Being armed is simply part of that way of life even in the 21st century. It is not about crime statistics or even the Second Amendment as important as that is. Out there, any day may turn into a tough time so persons there must be ready.

Survival situations are not planned. Someone has said that a "survival knife" is the one you have with you when you have to survive. You do not normally choose a knife then deliberately go out to see if you can survive in a tough situation. In the same way, one does not select a firearm knowing that a survival situation is at hand. You select a firearm as part of your overall program of preparedness knowing that if such a situation does arise you have selected your equipment and prepared yourself to deal with that situation. In this chapter, we will discuss various aspects of survival situations and how a rimfire firearm is an appropriate tool. Many books have been written on the subject of survival skills, and the interested reader should consult some of these books to gain knowledge of survival skills. As you will see from these sources, firearms constitute only one aspect of survival equipment. You should be equipped to provide shelter, warmth, and perhaps food as well as protection.

Why a Rimfire?

Compared to most centerfire firearms, rimfires are low-powered. However, it is interesting to note that the .22 Short was developed initially for self defense! Why not choose something more powerful as a survival tool? Why not select a .44 Magnum handgun or a .30-06 Springfield rifle? There are instances where either of these would be a much better choice than any

rimfire firearm. In fact, if you were facing a very large animal bent on having you for a meal, nothing would seem too powerful. Like it or not, there are very few places where such animals are likely to be encountered today and in many of the places where you might find one, you are not permitted to have a firearm. It is also not likely that you will encounter half a dozen drug-crazed hooligans who are bent on doing you harm all at the same time. In such an instance, the author would want either a semiautomatic .45 or a shotgun rather than a rimfire handgun or rifle, but he would rather have a rimfire firearm than only a tiny knife. Much more likely is the fact that the mere presence of a firearm will serve as a deterrent except for the most desperate criminals. Situations where being armed is a good idea do occur even though some segments of the population would tell you to go limp and play dead. Such behavior is not part of the makeup of the writer. Of course, any possession of a firearm must be in accord with all applicable laws or you are going to be involved in a lot of paperwork. Unless you have a valid concealed carry permit for the area where you are, a firearm must be clearly visible.

The essence of having a firearm as part of your preparedness for tough times lies in the answer to what purposes you may logically expect it to serve. If you are fishing for salmon in Alaska, a rimfire firearm should not be your chosen companion. There, something on the order of a .44 Magnum or .454 Casull would be a better choice. Generally, your survival firearm will serve to obtain food, signal for help, and possibly for self protection. In these instances, a rimfire rifle or handgun may be an appropriate choice, but you may need to give some thought to protection from what? One reason why a rimfire firearm is a good choice for long term tough time situations is that it is possible to store or even carry a substantial amount of ammunition. A couple of hundred rounds of .22 rimfire ammunition can be carried more conve-

On the left are 10 rounds of .44 Magnum and on the right are 50 rounds of .22 LR. One reason for selecting a rimfire for tough times is obvious.

niently than can be a box of 25 shells for a shotgun or an equal number of rounds for a centerfire rifle. Another reason for selecting a rimfire is the cost of ammunition. Although some types of low-priced .22 LR ammunition sell for only around $3 per box of 50 rounds, the better types sell for only $4 or $5 per box. Although this may seem high, the total cost for a few boxes of the ammunition most appropriate for use in tough times is small, and this is still only a fraction of the cost of ammunition for a centerfire rifle or large caliber handgun.

A firearm selected as a part of a survival package must enable you to obtain food and possibly defend you against attack from species having two or four legs. With regard to obtaining food, a well-placed bullet from a rimfire will quickly dispatch small game such as squirrels, rabbits, raccoons, opossums, turtles, snakes, birds of many types, etc. A well-placed bullet from a rimfire will even dispatch large animals. That is not to imply that the selection of a rimfire for such uses under sporting conditions is a wise decision. It is not. However, we are not discussing sporting conditions here, but rather survival conditions. In a survival situation, it may even be prudent to be able to procure food without announcing to everything and everyone within three miles that you are there. In this case, a rimfire has a distinct advantage over a high powered rifle or a large caliber handgun. A powerful airgun would permit taking small species in an even more clandestine manner, but it would not be a good choice for defensive purposes.

It is in the area of defense that a real question arises with regard to the choice of a firearm. Many experts believe that handguns for personal defense begin with the .38 Special and go upward in power from there. Are they correct? Well, yes and no. For most situations, the author wants a firearm that is more powerful than any rimfire, but would be far better off with a rimfire from which he can fire accurately aimed bullets than he would be with a larger caliber piece that is poorly used. There is no question that a well-placed bullet from a .357 Magnum is much more effective than is an identically placed bullet from a .22 LR. When a rimfire firearm is used in a defense situation, it represents a compromise between low power and ease of use. By placing the bullets in a lethal area, a rimfire can be an effective defense round. As has been described in Chapter 4, several manufacturers produce small rimfire handguns specifically for self defense. If the adversary being defended against is large, powerful, or can shoot back, one will derive a greater sense of comfort from a

The Browning Buck Mark is a durable, reliable pistol that would serve well in tough times.

larger caliber handgun, a centerfire rifle, or a shotgun. However, a few years ago, a woman killed a grizzly that was chasing her horse by shooting it with a .22 rifle. She was also fined $1,500 for killing a protected species.

While spending some summers in mountainous national forest areas, I have often gone "out there" armed with a .22 rifle or handgun. The region has some mountain lions and black bears but no grizzly bears. Defense in the majority of instances would more likely be from a rabid skunk or rattlesnake than from a mountain lion. I do not feel particularly well armed with the rimfire, but neither do I feel defenseless. Although the author has never actually had to use the firearm to keep himself separated from some animal, he believes that there is a very good chance that he could do so if necessary. As far as two legged predators are concerned, the mere fact that I have a firearm is sufficient to indicate that I would not be easy prey. The writer once read the story of a game warden who upon starting his job realized that he would have to carry a sidearm. He tried his father's .45-caliber handgun and managed to hit the target once or twice. He switched to his Colt Woodsman .22 LR and fired his usual score in the mid-90s! His sidearm for carry while working quickly became a Colt Woodsman .22. Had he been able to use the .45 equally well, he would have been better protected with it. The truth is that the vast majority of shooters who have limited experience can shoot a rimfire firearm more accurately (and comfortably) than they can a more powerful piece although at a range of a few feet that may be a moot point. The subject of this book is rimfire firearms, so we will leave the discussion of other types of firearms to another forum.

Rifle or Handgun?

There is no doubt that a rifle can be fired with greater accuracy and effectiveness than can a handgun under most circumstances. Someone has said that a handgun is the weapon you use until you can get to your rifle. These thoughts would indicate that a rimfire rifle should be chosen for tough times, but there are other factors to consider. First, it is not easy to pick berries, operate a fly rod, or even photograph flowers with a rifle in hand or slung on a shoulder. For certain activities, it is necessary that the survival piece be immediately accessible, but occupy no hands and little space. In such cases, a handgun is a more appropriate choice. Moreover, if one is camping or staying in a cabin in a remote area, it is not always convenient to pick up a rifle as you head out to cut an armload of wood. The idea here is that in survival or emergency situations, the survival firearm must be readily accessible at all times. Walking 50 yards to a stream for water without it may be just the time you need it and find that you are 50 yards away from it. If you are in a situation where your life and well-being may depend on a survival weapon, keep it within arm's length at all times.

For camping in a fixed location for an extended period of time where some supplies can be left in a secure place, a rimfire rifle is a wonderfully effective tool. Some compact models are available that are extremely handy. For example, the Henry .22 Survival rifle has a hollow, removable stock in which the barrel and action can be stored and transported. Even some of the rifles that are not take down models are compact. One of the primary considerations is that any firearm that may determine your survival must be utterly reliable. A single shot may suffice, but when "out there" I want to be able to fire repeat shots quickly because a rimfire is none too powerful. Therefore, a repeater of some type is indicated. Bolt action rifles are generally more accurate than other types, but they also tend to be somewhat larger and heavier. For most types of hunting and self preservation, fine accuracy is not a requirement. Performance of rimfire rifles and handguns is discussed in Chapters 14, 15 and 17.

Rifle Choices

One of the autoloaders in rimfire calibers that has become the standard against which other rifles of this type are judged is the Ruger 10/22 Carbine. This short rifle utilizes a 10-shot rotary magazine that is known to be virtually jam proof. The little carbine is available in a wide range of configurations ranging from blued metal and hardwood stock to stainless steel metal and synthetic stock. The Ruger 10/22 has spawned an incredible number of after market products, and some specialty houses are devoted to selling accessories for this model only. One can obtain a match grade trigger, a wide range of types of sights, special firing pins, etc. The barrel on the

Ruger 10/22 is held in place by a novel arrangement. The bottom of the barrel has a perpendicular cut a short distance from the breech. A bar that fits in the cut is attached to the front face of the action by two large screws with Allen heads. Removing the barrel is as simple as loosening the two screws and sliding the barrel forward out of the action. For a Ruger 10/22, one can obtain about any type of after market barrel imaginable. After market accessories are dealt with in more detail elsewhere in this book, but the point being made here is that it is possible to configure a Ruger 10/22 to suit almost any taste or use. For many users, that makes the Ruger 10/22 a logical choice for a firearm to be kept at the ready when one is out there. Furthermore, this fine little carbine is sometimes found in the version with blued metal and a hardwood stock

One of the most popular rifles for tough times is the Ruger 10/22. If the owner wants to modify it, the possibilities are almost endless.

on sale for not much over $200 although the usual retail price is approximately $250-275. The version with stainless steel metal and a composite stock costs about $50 more, but with its overall length of about a yard and its weight of only five pounds, is hard to imagine a better choice for taking into the outback.

Recently Ruger has introduced the Ruger 10/22 Takedown® version. As the name implies, this 10/22 can be taken apart and gives the stock and action in one unit and the barrel and forearm in the other. Details of the operation and performance of this interesting rifle are presented in Chapter 14.

The discussion above is not meant to imply that the Ruger 10/22 is the only choice for a rimfire rifle for tough times. The Remington 597 autoloader is available with a wood or composite stock and a dull matte finish on the metal parts. This rifle also has an excellent reputation for accuracy and dependability although the available aftermarket items do not cover the spectrum of similar items available for the Ruger 10/22. Marlin also offers several variants of the Model 60 autoloader that would be entirely suitable for "out there" wear. Another rifle from Marlin is a take down model in which the barrel is attached to the receiver by means of a large knurled

The Ruger 10/22 Takedown is convenient to transport and store.

ring. This rifle, the Model 70PSS, has a synthetic stock and a stainless steel barrel, and utilizes a 7-shot magazine. Savage also markets several models of rimfire rifles that are autoloaders capable of providing dependable service at low cost. These constitute the 64 Series that offers just about any combination of stock material and finish on the metal.

A rifle chosen for tough times need not be an autoloader. Some lever and pump action rifles are available, but the range of choices is somewhat limited. Bolt action rifles abound in rimfire calibers. They range from the inexpensive models available from makers such as Marlin and Savage to the elegant sporters from Ruger, Cooper, and Anschutz. In between are models from Browning and CZ. All of these rifles are dependable and some are extremely accurate. Doubtless, not many people would opt for a rifle that costs $800-1,000 to lug around in the outback or to receive the hard knocks of camp and cabin use. Nor do they have to. Serviceable bolt action rimfire rifles are available from about $200 on up.

As mentioned earlier, bolt action rifles tend to accentuate accuracy potential and thus are larger and heavier as a group than are autoloaders. For example, a Ruger 77/22 bolt action rifle is 39.25 inches long and weighs 6.5 pounds whereas the 10/22 Carbine is only 37 inches long and weighs 5 pounds. In the comparison given, the bolt action rifle costs from two to three times as much as the autoloader. The inexpensive bolt action Marlin XT and Savage Model 64 are available with wood, laminated, or composite stocks and blued or stainless steel metal. They are capable, clip-fed rifles that are also quite durable.

A bolt action like this Ruger 77/22 is accurate and dependable.

A lever action rifle such as the Henry H001 or Marlin 39A would make an excellent little rifle to have available in remote areas. In fact, the Henry lever action is 36.5 inches long and weighs 5.25 pounds so it very convenient to carry. The author likes compact rifles. The fact that lever action rifles have no bolt handle protruding from the side of the action makes them flat and easy to carry. Regardless of the model chosen, the rifle for tough times must be fitted with a sling so that it can be carried conveniently under a variety of circumstances. Some models come with studs already in place for attach-

The Henry U. S. Survival Rifle is a lightweight autoloader that is designed for survival situations. (photo courtesy Henry Repeating Arms)

The Henry U.S. Survival Rifle is easy to assemble and disassemble, and the barrel and action store in the stock. (photo courtesy Henry Repeating Arms)

The Marlin Model 60 is a popular .22 autoloader that is reliable and accurate.

A compact lever action like this Henry is a convenient, dependable companion in remote areas.

ing sling swivels, but swivels can be attached to other rifles.

In the opinion of this writer, any rimfire rifle for tough times should have open sights. There is a trend for rimfire rifles to follow the practice that has become commonplace in recent years with centerfire rifles. When looking recently at several racks of bolt action centerfire rifles in a large sporting goods store, it was noted with interest that only a small percentage of the rifles had iron sights. Today, it is assumed that the shooter who is going to be using a fine bolt action rifle will add a scope to the piece to greatly increase its effectiveness. Although that is true in most instances, any rifle that is chosen to serve as a constant companion should have a set of open sights that do not add to the weight and bulk of the rifle. There may also be a scope mounted on the rifle, but far from a shop and range one must have a complete rifle available if something happens to the scope. Scopes are durable instruments, but it is not at all uncommon for an extra hard bump to do damage to a scope or its mount that cannot be fixed with a Swiss Army knife and duct tape.

Handgun Choices

It is possible for most people to shoot a rifle much, much more accurately than they can any handgun. Having said that, the author has sent four animal silhouettes off the rail by firing five shots at a distance of 50 yards with a revolver. It would have been just as easy to have taken small animals at a similar distance or to have placed the bullets within a small area on a larger target. The point is that if one can get within a reasonable distance from the target a handgun can be used to take small game if the shooter is willing to practice and has discipline. Keep in mind that the handgun that is going on long hikes or kept instantly available for long periods of time should not be overly large or heavy. The best choice is a handgun that is

accurate, durable, and of light to moderate weight. The fact that the handgun may be only 7-10 inches long and weigh 30-35 ounces makes it a logical choice as a piece to have available for tough times. For reasons of portability, the handgun for tough times probably will not be equipped with a scope or red dot sight.

Rimfire handguns are available in a wide range of configurations that are based on actions of the single shot, revolver, and autoloader types. For many uses, the long-barreled single shot having a bolt action is a wonderful handgun with which to plink or to shoot small game or pests in a familiar area. However, when restricted to a rimfire, most people would not choose such a piece for general use that may include defense. These specialized pieces simply are not "packin' irons." That leaves the revolvers and autoloaders from which to choose a rimfire for tough times. My personal preference is for a handgun with a barrel neither shorter than about 4 inches and nor longer than 6 inches. My current walkabout rimfire handgun is usually a Ruger SR22 having a 3.5-inch barrel, but my wife and I also have Browning Buck Mark pistols that have 5.5-inch barrels. The barrel length of the Brownings results in velocities that are approximately 75 ft/sec higher with most types of ammunition. A difference in velocity of this magnitude will not be noted in general use.

For many years, the Smith & Wesson Model 34 Kit Gun was considered to be the ultimate backpacker's .22. Made on the J-frame that Smith & Wesson uses for small revolvers, it had a 4-inch barrel and sights of target quality. This small, 6-shot revolver is also referred to as the 22/32 Kit Gun because the J-frame was considered initially as the platform for the .32 S&W cartridge. In later years, the Kit Gun was available as the stainless steel Model 63. Weighing only 19 ounces, the Models 34 and 63 are highly prized today for the

When a small, portable handgun is needed, the Ruger SR22 is a good choice.

An outstanding handgun for survival situations is the Smith & Wesson Model 34, which was known as the Kit Gun.

For many years, the Smith & Wesson Kit Gun has been a top choice for backcountry use, but it has now been replaced with the Model 317. (photo courtesy Smith & Wesson)

same reasons as they were in the past–they are small, light, accurate, and dependable. Smith & Wesson once again offers a .22 LR revolver on the J-frame. Known as the Model 317 Kit Gun™, it features a 3-inch barrel, holds nine rounds, and has a fiber optic front sight. It is a fine trail gun that has the MSRP of $759. Small frame rimfire revolvers are available from Taurus in an extensive series of models built on frames of medium size. Particularly attractive are the 4-inch barreled models that are available in blue or stainless steel in either .22 LR or .22 WMR calibers.

For military applications, the advantages of a semiautomatic pistol are obvious. Once the pistol is in play, all the shooter has to do is to pull the trigger to fire successive shots. Pressing the magazine release allows an empty magazine to drop out and a loaded one can quickly be inserted to continue the fray. However, if no additional loaded magazines are available, it takes considerable time to force rounds into the magazine one at a time and then get the loaded magazine back into the piece. Today, the vast majority of law enforcement and military agencies make use of autoloaders. Such an observation should make it clear that men and women who trust their lives to handguns know that semiautomatic pistols are reliable. I have personally fired rimfire pistols hundreds of rounds without a single jam. However, a shooter who stakes his or her life on an autoloader should not go forth with a handgun loaded with a type of ammunition that has not been tested in the piece. Different types of ammunition have bullets with slightly different shapes and dimensions, and the power level varies between standard velocity

and high velocity ammunition. As a result, a particular autoloader may not function with complete reliability with all types of ammunition. The time to find out is before you are somewhere out there and need a reliable handgun. A look at catalogs from Smith & Wesson, Colt, Kimber, Ruger, Beretta, Walther, Taurus, and others will show that autoloading handguns have become vastly more popular than revolvers.

When selecting a revolver, there are two types from which to choose. Single action revolvers must be cocked for each shot. Drawing the hammer back causes the cylinder to rotate to align a fresh cartridge with the firing pin. Pulling the trigger discharges the piece, and the hammer must be drawn back to fire another shot. Double action revolvers can be fired by pulling the trigger, which causes the cylinder to rotate and the hammer to move back simultaneously. When the trigger is pulled fully, the hammer is released and the piece fires. There are two actions involved (rotating the cylinder and moving the hammer) so the revolver is known as a double action model. Because of the long, heavy trigger pull when shooting in the double action mode, most shooters will cock the hammer manually and fire in a single action mode most of the time because the accuracy will be much better.

Double action revolvers can be fired faster by most shooters than can single action models. However, except in defensive situations, the difference in rate of fire is likely to be immaterial. If a shooter is using both hands, the hammer can be cocked quickly by using the thumb of the non-shooting hand. It is in the speed of reloading that the double action revolver has its biggest advantage. Of course, one could argue that by the time the shooter has fired six shots and the problem is still present, it may be time to try something other than reloading.

Revolvers are utterly reliable. Single action revolvers have few parts and they generally give very long life. Imagine all the cowboys, explorers, and adventurers who roamed the wild places of the earth in days gone by armed with single action revolvers. The single action revolvers of today are even more reliable because of advances in design, metallurgy, and manufacturing methods. One could realistically expect a modern single action revolver to give a lifetime of service. Of course, it is possible to abuse any firearm to the point that it gives problems prematurely. The practice of "fanning" is hard on a single action revolver. Fanning involves holding the trigger back and quickly and repetitively firing the piece by waving or fanning the shooter's hand across the hammer to pull it back and release it quickly. This places greater stress on the hand that rotates the cylinder and other internal parts.

The double action revolver that first came into use well over 100 years ago has developed into a precision, durable instrument. Although the revolver can be fired by pulling the trigger, it is possible to achieve greater accuracy by cocking the piece first and then firing. In other words, firing in the single action mode

This Taurus double action revolver is utterly dependable and capable of good accuracy. (photo courtesy Taurus)

Ruger's Bearcat is a compact, lightweight model that is a good choice for the woods roamer who likes a single action revolver.

makes it easier to achieve greater accuracy. However, if necessary a double action revolver can be placed in action quickly by simply pulling the trigger. This could be an advantage in a defensive situation, especially for a shooter who has not practiced extensively with a single action model. The feats of cowboy action shooters and gunfighters of the old days show that someone who is proficient with a single action revolver can handle most situations. Having owned and fired both single and double action revolvers for many years, the author finds little difference in the speed of the first shot because the piece is cocked as it is raised and brought to bear on the target. The revolver is cocked during recoil so that by the time the sights on either type of piece are aligned on the target, the revolver is ready to be fired again. It is when the cylinder is empty and the piece must be reloaded that the user of a single action revolver is at a severe disadvantage.

A person selecting a revolver for survival situations should handle and fire both single and double action models. In this way, the "feel" of the piece can be experienced. One area in which the double action revolver excels compared to the single action type is in speed of reloading. When the cylinder latch on a double action revolver is moved, the entire cylinder rotates out of the frame. Pushing backward on the ejector rod removes all of the empty cases at once so that fresh rounds can be inserted. Pushing the cylinder back into the frame causes the latch to lock it in place and the piece is ready to fire. A single action revolver has a loading gate on the right hand side at the rear of the cylinder. Using the thumb, this gate is swung outward exposing one chamber in the cylinder. An ejector rod is located in a fixed housing below and to the lower right hand side of the

barrel. Pushing the rod backward forces one empty case out of the cylinder. The ejector rod must be allowed to slide forward and the cylinder turned manually to bring the next chamber into alignment with the ejector rod, which is then pushed to the rear to remove another case. This procedure is repeated until all of the empty cases are ejected and then loaded rounds can be placed in the cylinder one at a time. Through practice, reloading of a single action revolver can be accomplished fairly quickly, but it is slow compared to reloading a double action revolver.

One advantage of single action revolvers such as the Ruger Single Six is that they can be obtained with two cylinders. One cylinder is chambered for the .22 LR whereas the other is chambered for the .22 Winchester Magnum Rimfire. The use of .22 WMR ammunition gives the shooter the option of having a somewhat more powerful handgun while still being able to fire the much less expensive .22 LR for most situations. One drawback to the whole idea of interchangeable cylinders is that one is not going to go walking in the wilderness with the .22 LR cylinder in place and when a situation arises where more power is desired change cylinders at that time. It could happen that while out searching for food (where the .22 LR is appropriate) one could encounter some sort of trouble where the .22 WMR would be a better choice. It is probably a simpler plan to carry the revolver with one cylinder in place while having a supply of ammunition in that caliber and not have an extra cylinder along, which would require the use of ammunition of a different caliber. The extra cylinder also takes up space and has weight, and there is considerable merit in traveling light.

Over the years, Smith & Wesson has offered some exceptional rimfire revolvers. Some have been target models that had the same dimensions and weight as those in larger calibers. Others mirrored models that were intended for law enforcement use. For example the S & W Model 15 Combat Masterpiece had a rimfire counterpart in the Model 18. The idea was that a

For extreme versatility, the Ruger Single Six Convertible is an excellent choice.

The entire range of .22-caliber ammunition can be utilized in a Ruger Single Six Convertible.

shooter could practice with greater comfort and less expense with the rimfire piece to gain proficiency with the duty weapon. Colt offered rimfire models comparable to the Officers Model Match and Diamondback centerfire revolvers. All of these fine rimfire revolvers are no longer manufactured. The trend toward autoloaders in centerfire calibers is also manifested in rimfires. There are currently many more models of autoloaders available than there are revolvers.

Autoloading pistols are available in several types and they will not be discussed in detail here (see Chapter 4). However, a personal preference will be discussed to make a point. Before the dramatic increase in striker fired autoloading pistols, the majority of centerfire pistols had a visible hammer. With some of these pistols, firing is only by double action (DAO) meaning that after each shot the hammer remains "down" until the trigger is pulled again to move the hammer backward and fire the piece. In other cases, the hammer remains cocked after each shot and pulling the trigger only releases the sear to fire the piece. The first shot can be fired double action, but additional shots are fired in the single action mode. Many autoloaders of the latter type have safeties that also function as decocking levers to lower the hammer when no additional shots are to be fired. Pressing the safety lever downward allows the hammer to fall and strike a large block that prevents it from striking the firing pin. Not only is there an external hammer whose

position is clearly visible, but also a safety lever that must be manipulated before the pistol can be fired. This is about as safe as an autoloading pistol gets.

In the case of rimfire pistols, there is no external hammer in most current models, and the safety catch is a small lever on the left hand side of the frame. It is not difficult for the safety lever to be moved as the pistol is withdrawn from a holster or pack, and the shooter is then holding a loaded pistol that requires only slight pressure on the trigger to fire. In the opinion of many shooters, pistols of this type are not as safe as are the centerfire pistols with visible hammers or either type of revolver. One exception is the Walther P22, which not only has a visible hammer, but also it can be fired double action for the first shot. This small lightweight pistol has much to recommend it, especially for shooters who like centerfire autoloaders that have external hammers. In early 2012, Ruger introduced the SR22, a small autoloader with an external hammer having a 3.5-inch barrel that can be fired in either double or single action mode. As a result, the Walther and Ruger pistols appeal to many shooters. Any firearm is only as safe as the shooter using it. A responsible shooter with good technique and safe gun handling practices will be a safe shooter with any type of handgun. Although the author regularly uses rimfire pistols of several types, he is fully cognizant of the limitations of a single mechanical safety.

There are many types of semiautomatic pistols in rimfire calibers available to the outdoorsman. One of the pistols that has stood the test of time is the Ruger Mark III that is available in a standard version for sporting use as well as several target configurations for competition. These pistols and the earlier Mark II and Standard models have been made by the millions, and they have an unsurpassed reputation for dependability and durability. Some versions are available in stainless steel, which is a desirable option for a pistol to be used under harsh conditions. The Ruger Mark III which replaced the earlier Mark II has a different type of magazine release and a loaded chamber indicator.

Another pistol that has been popular for many years is the Browning Buck Mark. As in the case of the Ruger, there are several versions available that have different barrel lengths and finishes. The Buck Mark Standard model is a highly accurate pistol that has excellent adjustable sights. The author has had considerable experience with the Ruger and Browning pistols and would unhesitatingly take to the outback with either.

Another pistol that should make an outstanding kit gun is the Walther P22, which is available with barrel

This Walther P22 has performed well for many years. (Keith House photo)

Stainless steel handguns have become the favorites for situations that involve hard use and inclement weather. The Ruger Mark II (left) and Smith & Wesson 2206 (right) would be superb choices.

A Sig Mosquito has many nice features and its operation is familiar to shooters who use a Sig centerfire.

lengths of 3.4 and 5 inches. With a polymer frame, the Walther weighs only approximately 20 ounces even with the longer barrel, which has attached a weight in the form of a fake compensator located at the muzzle. The grip is very short so persons who have large hands will probably have the little finger placed below the grip, but the pistol is extremely compact. The little Walther has dual safety levers located on either side of the receiver in the positions where decocking levers are located on many center fire pistols. With excellent white dot sights, the Walther would be a convenient choice as a rimfire pistol for tough times. With many of the features of the Walther, the Ruger SR22 is also a small, light handgun. Models are available with 3.5- or 4.5-inch barrels in all black, stainless slide and black frame, or as dealer exclusives with a black slide and colored frame. Like the Walther, the Ruger SR22 features adjustable sights that have white dot markings for ease of visibility.

Smith & Wesson, Beretta, Kimber, Taurus, and many other firms market the ubiquitous rimfire autoloaders (see Chapter 17). They are fine firearms, and the prospective buyer of a rimfire auto should examine several models to determine what feels best and

For versatility, a 1911 style .45 Auto such as the Kimber Custom II can be converted to .22 LR by installing a conversion kit.

will meet the buyer's requirements. Many shooters of rimfire autoloaders believe that the Colt Woodsman was the finest .22 auto ever made. Others feel the same way about the Smith & Wesson Model 41. However, a new S&W Model 41 or High Standard pistol or a vintage Colt Woodsman costs some serious money, and such an outlay is not necessary when selecting a handgun for tough times. There is nothing wrong with them, but they are too exquisite for rough use as kit guns. If the outdoorsman wishes to select one of these elegant models, more power (or money!) to him or her. They are fine shooters. This discussion is not meant to be a complete product review, but rather an indication that the choice of a rimfire firearm for tough times is rather large (see Chapters 4 and 17).

Caliber

Except for a few highly specialized pistols chambered for the .22 Short, there are really only three rimfire calibers available in handguns. Of these, the .22 LR is by far the most common with many more models available in that caliber. The .22 WMR has never been very popular in handguns. For a time Smith & Wesson has produced a double action revolver in that caliber, and an autoloader known as the Automag II has been available. Colt produced the single action rimfire revolver known as the Frontier Scout for many years and many of them were offered with an additional cylinder in .22 WMR. Ruger has done this for many years with the popular Single Six Convertible model.

Today, the selection of handguns chambered for the .22 WMR is only a fraction of what it is for .22 LR guns. Volquartsen markets a long barreled autoloader in .22 WMR that is intended to have a scope mounted and to be used as a varmint gun. Taurus produces an extensive line of excellent revolvers. A 4-inch barreled version is available in blue or stainless steel in either

The magnum cylinder of a Ruger Single Six Convertible can be used to fire all .22 WMR ammunition as well as .22 WRF.

When relying on a rimfire, suitable ammunition should be chosen, and the Hornady Critical Defense is one of the most effective .22 WMR rounds.

.22 LR or .22 WMR caliber. Kel-Tec offers a 30-shot .22 WMR autoloader. Actual retail price for a box of .22 WMR cartridges is around $12-15 depending on the brand and type so cost of ammunition is also a factor.

The author is going to show some of his prejudice with what follows in this paragraph, but right or wrong it is the opinion of this writer. If there is one caliber that makes little sense to me as a handgun caliber, except in single-shot guns with long barrels, it is the .17 HMR. Before you go ballistic, let me explain my thinking on the subject. At the current time, the .17 HMR ammunition lists for about $18 per box of 50 and actually retails for $14-15 per box. This prices it out of the plinking category for many shooters including me. In a handgun with 4 or 6-inch barrel suitable for convenient carrying, the velocity is much lower than the 2,500-2,600 ft/sec achieved in rifles. The performance of a tiny 17-grain bullet is dependent on its high velocity, which simply isn't produced in most handgun barrels. That is why some of the models offered in .17 HMR have barrels in the 10-12 inch range. It has been demonstrated that at fairly long ranges where the velocity has dropped to about half the muzzle velocity, bullet performance of the .17 HMR is questionable in terms of expansion even when fired from rifles. It behaves more like an ice pick than the explosive little round that it is when the bullet velocity is over 2,000 ft/sec.

The .22 WMR, which drives a 40-grain bullet at over 1,400 ft/sec and produces nearly 200 ft lbs of energy from a handgun, is a more effective cartridge. In addition, the .22 WMR ammunition is available with full metal jacketed bullets for situations where deep penetration is needed or damage to pelts must be kept to a minimum, and shot cartridges are available in .22 WMR for dispatching small pests. True, a .17 HMR handgun gives velocities high enough that a flat trajectory results, which makes it possible to hit ground squirrels at longer ranges. A scope would almost certainly be necessary to find out. I have no problem with this type of equipment for the pest hunter, but for a survival fire-

arm it seems out of place. A bullet from a .17 Mach 2 at the muzzle represents the same power level as a .17 HMR that has lost 20-25% of its velocity so the same comments apply. There are many gas stations in remote areas that sell the .22 LR, but they probably do not have .17 HMR or .17 Mach 2 ammunition on the shelves.

The author owns and uses firearms in .22 WMR and .17 HMR calibers. In rifles, both perform in a different league than the .22 LR. So much of that additional performance is lost when the rimfire magnum cartridges are used in handguns that they may not be worth the additional expense, noise, and uncertainty in availability. The .22 WMR makes some sense when used in single action revolvers that also fire .22 LR by swapping cylinders, but there is nothing to swap a .17 HMR cylinder for except another .17 caliber of lower power, the .17 Mach 2. As a stand alone handgun cartridge, it is interesting and useful as a varmint cartridge, but I do not want to pack one in the backcountry. I think that if one wants something other than the .22 LR or the .22 LR/22 WMR combination, a .38 Special or .357 Magnum makes a lot of sense. Some of the guns are no larger than most of those in rimfire calibers, ammunition can be bought relatively cheaply, effective shot cartridges are available, and with some loads a much larger degree of smash can be delivered to the target. The main drawback to centerfire handguns for extended use that it is not so easy to carry several hundred rounds of ammunition. When the cost and availability of ammunition and other factors considered, selecting the .22 LR as my handgun for tough times makes a lot of sense to this writer. However, the reasons underlying my selection may be different than for yours so you may arrive at a different conclusion.

Ammunition

When selecting equipment for tough times, consider that although you may be taking squirrels with head shots at 25 yards you may also be trying to keep something much larger away from you. Under the latter circumstances, you should load your rimfire with the most potent ammunition available as long as it gives the necessary accuracy for other chores. Personal preference may be showing here, but I do not want ammunition for tough times that makes use of a very light bullet at high velocity because penetration is very low. Such ammunition is fine for taking ground squirrels, starlings, crows, or other fragile species, but not for doing damage to the internal organs of large species.

Keep in mind that a 40-grain high velocity bullet from a handgun barrel of average length moves at around 1,000 ft/sec and generates approximately 100 ft lbs of energy at the muzzle. A high performance load such as the CCI Velocitor or Remington Yellow Jacket will probably exceed this by a small amount. If you want to shoot something a little more exotic, the Lapua Scoremax (now discontinued) makes use of a 48-grain bullet. The velocity was given as 1,040 ft/sec from a rifle and would not be more than perhaps 900 ft/sec from a handgun, but the heavy bullet would penetrate very well. In fact, at handgun velocities even the standard 40-grain solids penetrate very well. Trajectory would not be much of a factor for a survival handgun because shots would almost always be taken at short ranges. Survival situations are not those where a scoped handgun has its greatest utility, and using open sights the average shooter should limit shots to ranges under 50 yards or so. If you try shooting some groups at 50 yards with most handguns, you may find that you need to limit your shots at game to well under the 50-yard mark.

When the cost and availability of ammunition and other factors were considered, I selected the .22 LR as my handgun for tough times. If circumstances allow a rifle to be chosen, almost any high velocity ammunition that gives suitable accuracy in that rifle is satisfactory. The CCI Velocitor and Winchester Power Point are two high velocity hollow point rounds that have given outstanding accuracy in several of the author's rifles. For use in all possible situations in remote areas, a few boxes of high velocity ammunition with solid bullets would also be required. With the emphasis being on obtaining as much power as possible, it is easy to overlook the fact that standard velocity ammunition often gives better accuracy. From a handgun, the difference in velocity between standard velocity and high velocity ammunition is almost always less than 100 ft/sec. When identical barrel lengths are involved, bullet velocities from semiautomatics are usually slightly higher than those given by revolvers, part of which is due to the gap between the cylinder and the barrel. As a result, a semiautomatic firing standard velocity ammunition will give approximately the same velocity as a revolver firing high velocity ammunition. For hunting purposes,

it is recommended that you try several types of ammunition and select a type that your handgun feeds reliably through the action and shoots best.

If you are using a rifle or handgun in .22 WMR, the

As illustrated by the bullet that was recovered after firing into water, expansion the CCI Gold Dot is excellent.

40-grain jacketed hollow points will perform as well as any other type of ammunition. The author especially likes the Federal 50-grain hollow point load, but it may not give the best accuracy and the point of impact is often 2-3 inches from where the 40-grain bullets hit at a range of 50 yards. It is better to pick one load that performs well, become familiar with it, and stick with it. One additional factor for selecting 40-grain loads for the .22 WMR is that you have a choice of identical loads with hollow point or full metal jacket bullets.

The user of a .22 LR handgun also has the option of the CCI Stinger, SGB, and Quik Shok cartridges. The Stinger and Quik Shok bullets are quite fast and the latter breaks into four pieces on impact. However, both of these types of ammunition utilize cases that are longer than those in ordinary .22 LR rounds, and some autoloaders do not feed them reliably. This is not a factor when they are used in revolvers. In .22 LR caliber, the Power Point from Winchester is also a good choice. It utilizes a 40-grain hollow point bullet and gives excellent accuracy in most rimfire rifles and handguns. However, almost any of the high velocity solids will give good performance. The cost of ammunition in .22 LR is around $4-5 per box of 50 rounds, which makes it possible to practice a lot. Finally, don't overlook the fact that shot cartridges are available in .22 LR and .22 WMR calibers. These can be of use when trying to get rid of rodents or pest birds at short ranges.

The idea of surviving in some remote area while being armed with only a knife and a few matches is intriguing. No doubt there are some who can successfully do that, but just in case the author might not be among them, he wants at least a .22 LR handgun and a supply of ammunition. On the other hand, the author has never actually been faced with a tough situation of that type, but it is better to be prepared and not need to be than the other way around. It is known as preventative medicine or a strategic strike force, depending on your point of view.

CHAPTER 13

ACCESSORIES, ACCURACY, AND COMPETITION

WHEN THE AUTHOR WAS CONSIDERABLY YOUNGER, some owners of automobiles that he knew found it exciting to modify their vehicles. Such modifications were aimed at improving the performance of the machine or perhaps making it look better (a result that was dubious in many instances). Automotive supply houses offered everything from fender skirts to camshafts for most cars. Most of the acquaintances of the author simply did not have the funds available to take advantage of the opportunities to obtain such merchandise. The coin of the realm came from odd jobs such as sweeping floors at night or picking peaches in the summer. If the car ran at all, it was left as it was because keeping fuel in the tank was the primary concern. But there were many more affluent owners who bought intake manifolds so that two or three carburetors could be attached. A three-quarter race camshaft may have been installed, and dual exhausts were almost mandatory. The engine may have even been bored and stroked and had polished intake and exhaust ports. Such a vehicle was beyond the means but not the dreams of many young car owners.

Each hobby area has its own following. Today, computers have become the nemesis of many hobbyists, and the available aftermarket peripherals are endless. In days gone by, the author spent many hours perusing the catalogs and magazines that dealt with firearms. It was possible to buy stocks, sights, triggers, and other items to change the appearance and perhaps the performance of many firearms. It was with great interest that items such as Timney and Canjar triggers, Fajen stocks, and Marble's sights were studied. It did not matter that a rifle that could accept such items was not at hand. Eventually, a Mauser 98 came along and the work began with a semi-inletted Bishop stock. The military bolt handle was cut off and a Jaeger bolt handle with a neat ring of checkering

The Ruger 10/22 is the most modified rimfire in history. This 10/22 belongs to the author's son, Keith, and it has a Hogue over molded stock, a Majestic Arms barrel, and Volquartsen trigger.

around the knob replaced it. A Redfield Sourdough front sight and a Lyman 48 peep sight replaced the military sighting equipment. With the metal reblued, the result was a rather attractive sporting rifle. As is the case with other young men (or those who are young at heart), along came a single action revolver and the Mauser went in trade.

In those days long ago, most cars stayed "stock" for several reasons. Today, most rifles stay "stock" because they function satisfactorily that way. Some models have been made in the millions, so there is a substantial market and range of items to use with these rifles. The result is that there is a huge aftermarket industry in specialty parts for firearms, especially some rimfire models. Some of the items are for cosmetic changes whereas others are designed to enhance the performance of the piece. In this chapter, we will briefly explore this area of the rimfire shooting sports. Keep in mind that aftermarket products often enable the owner of a rifle or handgun in one form to change it to another. There is less reason to do this with some models because the number of options offered by the manufacturer is so large. It is possible to buy most rimfire rifles with almost any choice of stock material and metal finish initially. However, the aftermarket items are not restricted to simply choices in stock and metal finishes.

Stocks

One of the most commonly replaced items on a rimfire rifle is the stock. For certain models (particularly the Ruger 10/22), the range of optional stocks is enormous. Perusal of the catalogs and websites for suppliers such as Midway USA, Cabela's, Graf & Sons, Natchez Shooter Supply, Boyds, and many others will reveal that the selection of available stocks includes models with all sorts of configurations and compositions. The selection is so vast that only a few examples will be mentioned here. The outstanding Hogue OverMolded® stock with rubber pebbled grip surfaces is a perennial favorite for good reasons. Such stocks provide outstanding feel and controllability combined with durable construction at a price of approximately $70-75 from most sources. Other options include low cost synthetic stocks from several manufacturers. Some of the black stocks from Butler Creek sell for around $55, but they are also available with an attached bipod for about $30 more. Advanced Technology produces the Fiberforce Dragunov style stock that sells $49.99 from Midway USA. This is a skeletonized model with an open grip area in the stock. Two other stocks of the AR style are also available for $99.99, one with a folding butt section and the other with a collapsible butt section.

This Hogue OverMolded stock has a tactical configuration and is easy to handle.

The Bell & Carlson Odyssey stock can be configured to fit any shooter.

On the other end of the scale are stocks from Bell & Carlson with one model being a target-type stock that features an adjustable butt plate and comb. This composite stock sells for approximately $350. Also near the upper end of the price range are laminated and composite stocks from Volquartsen most of which sell for $300-600. Midway also offers a large number of stocks for the Ruger 10/22 in an almost endless variety of styles. Models span the range of prices from $60 to $300. Some folding stocks are available for the Ruger 10/22, but be advised that such stocks are not legal in all areas.

For many years, the only stocks available for rimfire rifles may have been those from the firearm manufacturer. That situation has changed enormously, and aftermarket stocks are now available for many makes and models of rimfire rifles. For example, Boyds Gunstock Industries offers well over a dozen laminated stocks for the very popular Marlin Model 60 semiautomatic. Sporter and thumbhole models are available starting at $129. The same is true for the older bolt action Model 25 as well as the more recent 900 and XT series, including both box and tubular magazine models. Boyds also offers an extensive line of stocks for numerous Savage rimfire rifles. Stocks for Marlin, Savage, and Remington 597 rifles are also available from Revolution Gunstocks. However, the owner of a Marlin Model 60 rimfire autoloading rifle may not find an aftermarket stock available from some stock makers. The author has been told that the cost of preparing the molding equipment for a particular stock runs up in the six figure range so the manufacturer must limit the number of models available.

When the first edition of this book was published, stocks for many Marlin rimfire rifles were available from Marlin Firearms Company. The stocks were available in several styles, but not all types are available for all rifle models. This is no longer the case and Marlin currently lists only a composite stock for a youth model bolt action rimfire. These stocks were priced competitively with those available from aftermarket sources. Midway USA lists two stocks for the Marlin 60, a plain hardwood model and another composite stock with an open butt section (Dragunov design).

Bob's Gun Shop (Royal, AR) is a source for a wide range of stocks, both new and used. Models are available to fit virtually all Marlin rifles, but stocks for Ruger, Savage, Winchester, and numerous other brands are also available. Numrich Gun Parts (Kingsport, NY) and Brownell's (Grinnell, IA) are suppliers of a wide range of gun parts. If you have an older rimfire rifle or wish to change the appearance of a new model it is not difficult to locate a stock for most models. The rimfire shooter no longer must suffer with an undesirable, unsightly stock for most rifles. This is a particularly desirable situation for the owner of an older gun that has a damaged stock or one that is in poor shape because a new stock will dress up the rifle in short order.

Shooters of rimfire handguns also have many options to help them get a grip on things. Grips are popular items to replace because the process is so easy. In many cases only a screw or two holds the panels to the frame. No doubt some shooters change the grips on handguns simply to improve the looks. For example, a pair of staghorn

Boyds Gunstocks Industries produces laminated stocks for many models of rimfire rifles including this thumbhole model for the Ruger 10/22 Takedown.

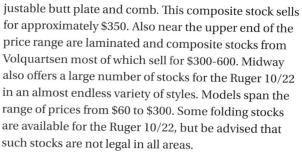

grip panels on a single action revolver makes a considerable change in its appearance. Beautiful walnut grips, for the Ruger Mark II and Mark III pistols as well as the 22/45 model, are available from Majestic Arms (Staten Island, NY). Grips for Ruger pistols are available from Hogue including those made of many types of wood or aluminum (in many colors).

Grips available for the Smith & Wesson 22A include the model shown here that has rubber inserts along the front and back straps.

In recent years, handguns leaving the factories have much better grips than those of a generation ago. Gone are most of the slick wood or plastic grips that were formerly so common. Replacing them are grips produced by aftermarket grip makers such as Hogue (Paso Robles, CA), Altamont Grips (Thomasboro, IL), (Pachmayr/Lyman, Middletown, CT) and others who supply grips for an enormous number of handguns. Most of these grips have been available as aftermarket items for many years, but in some cases the handguns are shipped from the factory with them already installed.

The primary reason that some handgun grips are made of rubber is that they give a good purchase in the hand. The grip afforded by the rubber surface is augmented by raised bumps, finger grooves, and imprinted checkering. Grips such as these are especially effective when handling a handgun in cold weather. The Smith & Wesson Models 22A and 22S are available with several options in grips. Three of the choices involve grips made of hard plastic either with or without a thumb rest. The option is also available for grips made of plastic that have rubber inserts along the front and rear surfaces. The fourth option for the S&W 22A is a large target style grip made of laminated wood. Any of these grips can be added as aftermarket options for the Model 22A and 22S pistols if the owner wishes to change grip style. My own preference is for the soft grip option with rubber inserts because it is compact but still gives an excellent feel.

Barrels

A practice that was virtually unheard of in the younger days of the author is now quite common. That practice is switching barrels on a rimfire rifle. Rifles that have barrels threaded to the action or locked in place by a transverse pin are not amenable to barrel swapping by the average shooter. Any barrel can be replaced by a competent gunsmith, but this chapter is aimed at the typical rimfire shooter. The rimfire rifles that are ordinarily considered as candidates for barrel replacement are those manufactured by Sturm, Ruger & Co. The Model 10/22 has spawned a number of aftermarket industries because the design of the rifle allows the barrel and many other parts to be replaced easily. Less popular is barrel swapping for the Ruger Models 77/22, 77/22M, and 77/17 the barrels of which until 2009 were attached to the action in a manner that is similar to that used on the 10/22. Let me say quickly that there is nothing wrong with the barrels made by Sturm, Ruger & Company for these models. There is nothing wrong with a two-barrel carburetor, but swapping the intake manifold for one that would allow a four-barrel carburetor to be used was a fairly common activity some years ago. Analogous comments could be made about camshafts and rifle barrels.

The primary motivation for changing barrels on a firearm is to enhance accuracy. In some cases, there is a change in appearance, weight, and durability, but accuracy is the most important issue. This section is not devoted entirely to the Ruger 10/22, but it will probably seem like it. In the rimfire rifle category, the ultimate in versatility with regard to aftermarket accessories is the Ruger 10/22. Modifying a Ruger 10/22 by replacing the factory parts with parts from other manufacturers (known as "tricking out" the rifle) is extremely popular. If you want to verify that, go to the eBay web site and type "Ruger 10/22" in the search blank. When the search is made, you will see a bewildering array of items that are offered for auction. Interestingly, there are always numerous factory barrels and stocks available because many people want only the rifle action to use as the starting point for building a custom 10/22. Formerly, the Ruger 10/22 in .22 WMR was fairly popular so there was a considerable array of aftermarket items for that rifle also, but the .22 WMR version has recently been discontinued. A complete survey of aftermarket parts and modifications of the Ruger 10/22 is available in the book Customize the Ruger 10/22 (2nd edition, Krause Publications, 2016) by House and House.

Much of the basis for the ease of modification of a Ruger 10/22 lies in the way in which the barrel is attached to the action. A few rimfire rifles have barrels that are threaded into the actions. These include the now discontinued Thompson/Center semiautomatic rifles and the CZ 452 bolt action models (most now replaced by the 455). The vast majority of inexpensive .22s have barrels that are fitted friction tight in the receiver then locked in place by a pin that extends through the front ring of the receiver and also passing through a groove in the barrel extension.

Barrel attachment on the Ruger 10/22 is unique. A large slot is cut across the bottom of the barrel, and a bar fits in the cut. The bar has two holes that have large Allen-headed screws that pass through them and thread into the front face of the action. Tightening these screws pulls the barrel backwards so that the barrel is drawn tightly against the action. Removing the barrel is as simple as removing two screws. However, it should be kept in mind that the receiver on a Ruger 10/22 is made of an aluminum alloy so it would be possible to strip the threads if too much torque is applied to the locking screws. Moreover, the screw holes in the rather soft receiver are subject to wear if the barrel is removed and attached frequently.

Aftermarket barrels for the Ruger 10/22 (and to a lesser degree the bolt action 77 series) span the range from around $125 to well over $300 depending on the metal and manufacturer. Some of the finest barrels are produced by Lilja Precision Rifle Barrels of Plains, Montana. Lilja produces a 21-inch stainless steel barrel for both the .22 LR and the .22 WMR versions of the Ruger 10/22. A 23-inch stainless steel barrel is produced for the Ruger 77/22 and 96 (lever action). These barrels are priced from $300-400, but they represent the epitome in replacement barrels for the Ruger semi-automatic and bolt action rimfire rifles. As is the case with many other replacement barrels, most of the Lilja barrels are cylindrical with a 0.920-inch diameter, but some tapered models are also available.

Barrels having an outstanding reputation for accuracy are produced by Green Mountain Rifle Barrel Company of Conway, New Hampshire. Configurations are available in blue and stainless steel with both smooth and fluted surfaces. Prices range from around $100 to $200 with the fluted stainless steel model being the most expensive. Also available from Green Mountain are blue and stainless steel fluted barrels for the 10/22 in .22 WMR. These have retail prices of approximately $120 and 140, respectively. However, a section of about six inches at the muzzle end has a diameter of 0.920 inch, which gives the effect of a muzzle weight. This barrel can be used with the factory stock, but it is a heavier barrel that provides greater stability for offhand shooting.

Volquartsen Custom Ltd. of Carroll, Iowa produces an extensive line of barrels for the Ruger 10/22 and the newer Ruger 10/22 Takedown. One series of barrels is of the tensioned type with a carbon sleeve surround-

Removing the barrel from a Ruger 10/22 Carbine requires loosening the two large screws as shown.

ing the barrel itself. These barrels retail for around $286. Volquartsen barrels are also available with a built in compensator at the muzzle with retail prices of approximately $270. Volquartsen produces another interesting barrel for the 10/22 that has a contour that matches that of the factory barrel throughout most of the length then widens to 0.920 inch. Volquartsen barrels have a strong following among varmint hunters and an unsurpassed reputation for accuracy. The performance of two Ruger rifles with Volquartsen barrels will be described in detail in Chapter 14.

Another Volquartsen product involves the .22 Short cartridge, which produces less back thrust on the bolt than does a .22 LR. As a result, most autoloaders chambered for the .22 LR will not cycle properly with .22 Short cartridges even if the difference in length does not cause feeding problems. Shooters of Ruger 10/22 rifles can convert them to fire .22 Short cartridges by installing an aftermarket kit from Volquartsen. The kit, priced at $259, includes a CNC-machined, hard anodized, alloy bolt, recoil rod with spring, modified magazine and a reduced hammer spring.

One of the interesting barrels for the Ruger 10/22 is produced by Majestic Arms, LTD of Staten Island, New York. This barrel, known as the Aluma-Lite, is of the dual composition type. It features an inner steel barrel produced by famed barrel maker Lothar Walther that is surrounded by an outer sleeve made of aircraft grade aluminum permanently bonded to the inner barrel. With an outside diameter of 0.920 inch and an overall length of 17 inches, the barrel weighs only 24 ounces. As a result, it is possible to obtain a barrel having the dimensions of a target barrel but having the light weight of a barrel of sporting contour. The Aluma-Lite barrel, which retails for approximately $219, has a target crown that is beveled inward to the muzzle to protect the muzzle. Accuracy data obtained with this barrel will be presented in Chapter 14.

A barrel having an aluminum sleeve is available from Tactical Solutions. Known as the X-Ring®, it weighs only 15 ounces and is available in several colors with or without a threaded muzzle. The results obtained with a Ruger 10/22 fitted with this fine barrel will be described in Chapter 14.

The Majestic Arms Aluma-Lite barrel has a steel inner barrel surrounded by aluminum. It is light in weight but very accurate.

The barrel on a Smith & Wesson 22A is unlocked by pushing inward on the latch at the front of the trigger guard.

In addition to the Ruger 10/22, another rifle that is capable of considerable alteration is the bolt action Ruger 77 rimfire in both the standard and magnum forms. Moreover, because most of the dimensions of the .17 HMR and .22 WMR cases are identical, it is convenient to convert a 77/22M to a 77/17 simply by changing barrels. Not only can that be done for the magnum version, but also a 77/22 can be converted to a .17 Mach 2 rifle by changing barrels. However, Ruger 77 series rifles manufactured after 2009 have barrels that are threaded into the receiver so barrel changing is not possible for newer rifles. Several barrel options are available, but two of them are the barrels produced by Green Mountain Rifle Barrel Company and Volquartsen. Both produce barrels in .17 HMR that can be interchanged with the factory barrels on the Ruger 77/22M. The Green Mountain barrels are available in a 20 inch fluted stainless steel model with a diameter of 0.920 inch and as a 22-inch octagonal blue sporter model. These barrels retail for about $170 and $200, respectively. Additional information on the octagonal sporter weight barrel in .17 HMR can be found in Chapter 14.

Volquartsen produces barrels in .22 WMR and .17 HMR for the Ruger 77/22M bolt action in two forms. The first is a stainless steel cylindrical barrel of 0.920-inch diameter whereas the second is a tensioned barrel enclosed in a carbon fiber sleeve. These barrels retail for about $300-350. In addition to rifle barrels, Volquartsen also produces match barrels for Ruger Mark II and Mark III pistols.

The aftermarket barrels described do not represent an inclusive list, but they are representative of those available. Generally speaking, barrels on rimfire rifles produced by Marlin, Savage, Winchester, Browning, Thompson/Center, Kimber, Anschutz, and others are not user interchangeable. However, the CZ455 is designed to allow barrels of .22 LR, .17 HMR and .22 WMR to be interchanged.

In most cases, owners of rimfire handguns have the barrel that came on the gun with no possibility for making changes other than by a gunsmith or returning the gun to the factory. There are some notable exceptions to this restriction. As this is written in early 2016, the Smith & Wesson Models 22A and 22S have only recently been discontinued but are still available from some suppliers. The pistols were produced with 4, 5.5, or 7-inch barrels. However, because of the design of the pistol, it is a simple matter to remove the barrel and its accompanying sight rail (as is done during field stripping). Barrels in all three lengths may still be available from Smith & Wesson if the owner wishes to change the barrel from one length to another. As a result, the same pistol can be fitted with a 7-inch barrel for target work or one of 4-inch length for general use.

Another barrel switching option exists for the Walther P22, which is available with barrels measuring 3.4 and 5 inches in length. The barrels are easily changed by loosening two Allen headed screws, and barrels in either length are available from the manufacturer. In fact, one available option for purchasers of new Walther P22 pistols includes barrels in both lengths as part of an optional kit.

Owners of Browning Buck Mark pistols also have the possibility of changing barrels by purchasing an additional barrel as a part available from the factory. The Buck Mark Standard pistol has a 5.5-inch barrel, but other versions have different barrel lengths. Because the barrel is attached to the frame by two large screws, it is possible to interchange barrels easily. Extra barrels are available from Browning's Parts Department at (800) 322-4626.

The Ruger Charger is in essence a 10/22 with shorter barrel and a pistol grip stock. It amenable to modification in much way as the 10/22, and trigger units and most other parts are identical.

Triggers

In addition to barrel quality, trigger action is a factor that can have a significant impact on accuracy. A long, raspy trigger pull is not conducive to reproducible let off, which in turn is not conducive to small groups. There are essentially two ways in which to improve trig-

The Ruger Charger Takedown can be heavily modified by use of aftermarket parts. (photo courtesy Ruger)

ger action. First, the entire trigger can be replaced if an aftermarket trigger is available for that particular rifle. The problem is one of availability because many rimfire rifles simply are not amenable to trigger replacement. This includes a vast number of autoloaders, pumps, and lever actions. Relatively few bolt action rimfire rifles have an aftermarket trigger option available. Part of the reason lies in the area of economics. It is unlikely that most shooters who have a $200 rimfire rifle would spend about the same amount simply to replace the trigger. Moreover, there is also the feeling of why should the trigger be replaced when barrels, stocks, and other items are going to have to be left as originals. This argument does not apply to a few rifles, such as the Ruger 10/22, because it is possible to replace everything except the receiver with aftermarket items.

Most notable in terms of trigger replacement are the Ruger 10/22 autoloader and 77 bolt action series. Outstanding among the options available for the 10/22 and 10/22 magnum are the triggers from Volquartsen known as Trigger Guard 2000 (TG2000). These are available as complete, drop-in units for about $260 for either the .22 LR or magnum version, and they represent the highest quality components for individuals seeking to produce the ultimate autoloader. Although these units include the complete trigger assembly, individual parts such as the sear, hammer, springs, and shims can also be purchased.

Jard of Sheldon, Iowa produces aftermarket triggers for both the Ruger 77/22 and 10/22 rifles. These are outstanding drop-in units that sell for approximately $180-225 depending on the model. Other trigger kits for these rifles are produced by several makers, and they are available from large suppliers. Hornet Products offers several complete trigger assemblies for the Ruger 10/22 that range in price from approximately $135 to $175. Hornet also offers a variety of other items, especially for the Ruger 10/22. Long known as a producer of fine triggers, Timney produces an outstanding unit for the Ruger 10/22 rifle. Seeing the potential of aftermarket products for the 10/22, Ruger now markets a complete trigger assembly for the 10/22. Known as the BX Trigger, it sells for around $90. Having tested all of these complete drop-in units, the author can attest to the fact that they work exceedingly well. As if these options were not enough, many firms offer gunsmith services that include trigger work. Among this list is Clark Custom Guns of Princeton, Louisiana.

In recent years, Rifle Basix has produced replacement triggers for bolt action rifles made by Marlin,

The Timney trigger assembly for the Ruger 10/22 incorporates a lever magazine release that extends back under the trigger guard.

Customizing a Ruger 10/22 often involves changing the trigger assembly, and Ruger now offers the BX trigger.

including the Model 25 (prior to 2004) and similar rifles, and Savage in addition to those for the Ruger 77 series. Marlin adopted an improved trigger mechanism known as the T-900 Fire Control System, and all of the current bolt action models make use of that trigger. The system also includes a redesigned safety. However, the author has been informed by Marlin personnel that the T-900 trigger can not be installed as an aftermarket option on earlier models such as the 25N. Moreover, Marlin does not endorse the replacement of triggers on older bolt action rifles with any aftermarket trigger. Replacement triggers for both the pre-2004 and later versions of Marlin bolt action rifles (that have the T-900 trigger) are available from Rifle Basix for $89.95. A similar model is available for Savage bolt action rifles. Both of these trigger units make use of the factory safety.

Sights

Perhaps no area involves a greater aftermarket industry than does sighting equipment. Sights are so important and of universal concern to shooters that Chapter 5 is devoted to that subject. Regardless, sights constitute such a broad area that some additional observations will be made here. Because scopes and red dot sights were covered in Chapter 5, the discussion here will concern other issues related to sights. Many fine rifles are produced and marketed with no sights mounted on the barrels. It is anticipated that these rifles will be fitted with appropriate scopes so the receivers are either drilled and tapped or grooved to accept scope mounts. It is anticipated that these rifles will never wear "open" or "iron" sights.

If the only concern were with accuracy, a scope of high magnification would be mounted on the firearm and other factors would be subjected to fine tuning. There are, however, cases in which the suitability and durability of the sighting equipment become more important than finest accuracy. Should the owner wish to do so, the factory sights can be replaced with others because aftermarket sights are available in many configurations from several producers. On most rimfire rifles, the rear sight is attached by means of the sight base fitting tightly in a dovetail groove on top of the barrel. In order to install a different sight, the original must be removed by driving it laterally out of the groove. In most cases, the width of the dovetail groove is a standard width so sights from other producers will fit satisfactorily. It is a different matter with front sights. In many cases, the sights are also attached by means of a dovetail groove, but in others the front sight is attached by one or more screws. If you wish to attach sights that attach differently, you will need the services of a gunsmith to drill and tap holes or to attach the sight base by brazing, silver soldering, or other means. Keep in mind that it is possible to attach almost any type of sight to a rifle or handgun, but it is not always as simple as tightening a screw.

Williams Gun Sight Company produces an extensive line of sights known as Firesights® and they feature fiber optic inserts. Models include front sights on ramps as well as open rear sights with fiber optic inserts on either side of the notch. One of the firms that has produced sights for generations is Lyman Products Corporation. Lyman produces not only open sights, but also peep sights and target front sights with removable inserts. Suppliers such as Midway USA, Brownell's, and Numrich have many types of sights available. Bob's Gun Shop of Royal, Arkansas offers a wide assortment of sights, many for older guns from several manufacturers. Handgun sights are available in an impressive array from manufacturers such as Millett, Trijicon, Novak, and others. These are just a few of the suppliers of aftermarket sights.

The owner of a Ruger 10/22 has the option of fitting the rifle with several types of sights that can not be mounted conveniently on other types of rimfire rifles. For example, a peep sight is produced that mounts in two of the holes on top of the receiver where the rear scope base is normally attached. A rear and front sight

Aftermarket sights are available in a wide range of styles. The white bead front and folding rear sights shown here are from Lyman.

pair known as the Zephyr Sighting System consists of a rear sight with protective ears that have an aperture mounted between them and a front sight that has a post encircled in a small circular hood. The effect is similar to that given by some types of military sights. Williams Firesights are also available specifically to fit the Ruger 10/22. Specialty firms that produce aftermarket items for the Ruger 10/22 produce other types of sights.

It is appropriate to include a caution in regard to replacement sights. Most rear sights have a rather limited range of adjustment for elevation. If the front sight is too low or too high, it will not be possible to move the rear sight enough to allow the sights to be adjusted properly. The height of the front and rear sights must be matched appropriately. Before you invest in replacement sights, make sure that the front and rear sights are compatible in terms of height.

Accuracy

Before addressing the topic of enhancing accuracy, we need to explain what accuracy is. Two terms that are often used interchangeably are *accuracy* and *precision*. When applied to the capabilities of rifles, they are often used incorrectly. A shooter who fires a small group often remarks about the "accuracy" of the rifle used. However, the ability of a rifle to place shots close together is really a measure of its *precision* (also known as reproducibility). When a quarterback places the football right on target we say that he is an *accurate* passer, which is the correct use of the word. Suppose as a practice drill three tires are set up 25 yards away from the quarterback and he is attempting to throw a football through the middle tire. If he consistently throws the ball through the tire on the left, his passing shows poor accuracy but good precision.

Suppose a particular type of bullet is advertised as weighing 40.0 grains. If 10 of the bullets have weights ranging from 43.3 to 43.5 grains with

Some handguns have sights mounted in a dovetail groove and can be replaced by other models that have correct height.

Fiber optic sights are available for a wide range of firearms.

an average of 43.4 grains, the bullet weights show good *precision* because they are all close to the same value. However, with regard to weight, the bullets show poor *accuracy* because the weight is not very close to the advertised weight of 40.0 grains. Therefore, the bullets show good precision but poor accuracy in regard to weight. It is rather like an archer who sticks six arrows in an area the size of an apple in a target at 50 yards, but with the cluster being in the lower left hand corner of the target rather than in the center. The precision is good, but the accuracy is poor.

When groups are fired at 50 yards to try to obtain the smallest possible cluster of bullet holes in the target, it

The group at the top shows good precision but poor accuracy. The bottom group shows good accuracy and good precision.

is actually precision that is being determined. In many instances, it doesn't matter whether the group is precisely in the center of the target or not because that can be corrected by adjusting the sights. However, if the cluster measures three inches across, the rifle is not capable of a high degree of precision. Although not a correct usage of the word, we speak of the accuracy of a rifle to denote that it is capable of producing small groups. That practice will be continued here, but it is important to know the difference.

There are several factors that determine the ability of a rifle to produce small groups. Some of these factors are identifiable in terms of critical dimensions and closeness of fit. Others are intangibles. The author once damaged a rear sight and called the rifle maker to obtain another. The model had been discontinued for some time but the helpful customer service representative said that there was a sight on a barrel that was not attached to a rifle. He said that all of the dimensions of the barrel were well within specification, but for some reason the barrel would not group and so it had not been used to build a complete rifle. Such is sometimes the case. A barrel that otherwise seems normal just does not shoot well.

The finish of the bore is an important consideration. Some barrels are mirror smooth and free from defects. However, the author once bought a centerfire rifle that had been produced by one of the most famous makers. Eager to test the rifle, a scope was mounted and a few sight in shots were fired. Then, the truth became

known. The rifle would not group for sour apples. After thoroughly cleaning the bore, the bore light revealed rather large machine marks that ran around the bore throughout its length. Somehow, the barrel had not been properly finished inside the bore. A call to the dealer led to a request to bring the rifle in for examination and testing in the gunsmith shop associated with the store. The gunsmith stated that the rifle needed to be returned to the manufacturer. True to the reputation of a professionally operated customer service department, it was acknowledged that the rifle had somehow slipped through with a defective barrel and a new barreled action was attached to my stock because it was a special laminated one that I wanted to keep. Otherwise, the manufacturer would have simply replaced the whole rifle. Needless to say, knowing how the customer service operation works, I have no reservation buying a rifle with that manufacturer's name on it.

Generally, you get what you pay for in terms of barrel quality and accuracy. Rifles produced by certain manufacturers are widely known for their performance. For example, Anschutz rifles have an enviable record for garnering medals in shooting competition at the highest levels. Rimfire rifles produced by Cooper Firearms of Montana must produce extremely small groups before being declared ready for shipment. Rifles from both of these prestigious makers are shipped with the test targets enclosed in the boxes with the rifles. Barrels produced by these firms are made from high quality materials with the application of rigid quality control. It should also be mentioned that the cost of such rifles is commensurately high.

Can you get a rifle that shoots accurately for a modest price? The answer is sometimes yes. The author once bought an inexpensive bolt action .22 that would place the first shot or two exactly at the point of aim. After a couple of shots, the subsequent shots would string out vertically. After installing a barrel band, the shots strung out somewhat less, but there was no obvious solution to the problem. If you examine the data shown in Chapter 14, you will see that the inexpensive Marlin 25N gave composite group averages of less than one inch with several types of ammunition. Although not indicative of the kind of accuracy given by an Anschutz or Cooper, an average of five 5-shot groups that measures less than one inch is not bad at that range. For many years, the one inch group at 50 yards has been sort of a standard for .22 rimfires. If you read the test results published in magazines for rimfire products, you will see that groups produced by "ordinary" rifles are frequently in the 1 to 1.25-inch range or larger. Groups in the 0.75 to 1-inch range indicate a rather high level of performance whereas those in the half-inch range or less are rare except for target rifles and high quality sporting rifles. Of course, the ammunition chosen always plays a major role in determining accuracy.

What degree of accuracy do you need or expect? Having worked with a sizeable number of rimfire rifles over a span of many years, the author has developed some feeling for accuracy. The rifles studied have ranged from very inexpensive single shot models to inexpensive repeaters (having bolt, lever, and semiautomatic actions) to moderately expensive sporting rifles and finally to a Winchester 52D target rifle. The author has learned not to expect one-hole groups from most rimfire rifles, but neither to expect a rifle to give a random pattern measuring six inches across at 50 yards. All of the rimfire rifles ever shot by the author fall between these extremes. For the moment, I will refrain from discussing the phenomenal Winchester 52D because it is simply the most accurate rimfire rifle I have ever fired. Period. Now, let us discuss the other types.

Most of the inexpensive repeating rifles of my experience would give groups measuring two inches or smaller at 50 yards with most types of ammunition. With a few types of ammunition, such as Remington Vipers, the groups might be as large as three inches. Generally such rifles would give groups of 1.5 inches or less with some of the ammunition that performed best in a particular rifle. Occasional groups smaller than one inch were obtained, and an average of 1.25 inches is typical. Most of the inexpensive repeating rifles fall into this category.

Some of the better performing inexpensive repeaters (such as the Ruger 10/22 Carbine, Henry Lever Action, and Marlin 25N gave groups that were smaller than 1.5 inches with almost any type of ammunition and as small as one inch with the ammunition that performed best in that model. In other words, these rifles consistently gave groups in the 1.0-1.5-inch range but with some ammunition groups of one inch or slightly less were produced.

Repeaters tested by the author that have given the best accuracy include the Ruger 77/22, CZ 452 American, Thompson/Center Classic, Ruger 10/22T, and Winchester 320. These rifles gave groups that average less than one inch with almost all types of ammunition with individual groups running one-half inch or smaller. With the most compatible types of ammunition, each of these rifles gave an average

group size that was not much larger than ½ inch. Any difference in the accuracy of the rifles listed is totally insignificant. The Remington 504 was introduced with much fanfare and flowery words, but it was produced for only a few years. Having read almost everything written about the Remington 504 bolt action sporter, it appears that the rifles described above will approximately equal the accuracy the 504 normally gives. None of these rifles will match the accuracy of a discontinued Kimber Classic, Cooper 57M, or an Anschutz 1710 nor should they be expected to. These fine sporting rifles will consistently give groups that average one-half inch or smaller at 50 yards.

One should not lose sight of the fact that for almost any use other than formal competition, a .22 rimfire rifle that will give groups of 0.75-inch or less at 50 yards is an accurate rifle. Having tested many rimfire rifles and read the results of tests for many more, it has become apparent that an inexpensive .22 LR that consistently groups in less than one inch is performing about as well as can be expected. My experience with rifles in .22 WMR caliber is much more limited in terms of the number of rifles tested. My Ruger 77/22M will consistently give groups in the 0.60-0.75 inch range with most types of ammunition. Both the author's Ruger 77/17 and his wife's CZ 452 rifles in .17 HMR will give groups averaging close to one-half inch with occasional groups of 0.3-0.4 inch.

The question arises as to whether accuracy can be improved by aftermarket items. The answer is undoubtedly yes, but only at a price. Installing a new barrel (on models where it is possible for the user to do so) will cost from $200-300 or perhaps even more. If the barrel has a different configuration than the original, a new stock may be required or the original may have to be modified to accept the aftermarket barrel. Replacement of the trigger assembly can cost from $80-250 although replacing only the sear and other parts can cost less. It is easy to invest several hundred dollars in aftermarket items in addition to the original price of the rifle. The result is likely to be a rifle that will give groups measuring one-half inch or less at 50 yards. However, the same amount of money might well have bought a new rifle that would have given one-half inch groups right out of the box. But there is something to be said for having a somewhat unique rifle that you have developed. Improvements in accuracy occur in small increments by doing a lot of little things right.

There is a tendency to fall into the pattern of thinking, "If I only had a ... (you can fill in the blank), my groups would improve." My suggestion is this: before you go too far in buying aftermarket items, try tweaking some things. First, make sure that everything is clean and tight. If you have one of the Ruger models that allows the barrel to be interchanged, make sure that the screws are tight (but not overly so for the 10/22) that hold the barrel to the action. In terms of accuracy, some of my rifles are very sensitive to the tension of the screws that hold the barreled action to the stock. Check the tightness of the screw(s) and try shooting groups with a different screw tension. My Ruger 77/17 seems to function best when the screws are tight, but not overly so. Scope mounts seem to have a way of loosening themselves so make sure that the screws are tight.

Having taken care of some of the mechanical aspects, experiment with different types of ammunition. The author's Ruger 10/22 Target gave 5-shot groups at 50 yards that averaged 0.45 inch with SK Jagd Standard Plus ammunition and groups twice that size with CCI Green Tag. Both types of ammunition are of very high quality, but the rifle works better with the Standard Plus. In my wife's CZ 452 American, the average group size was 0.54 inch with Federal Ultra Match and twice that size with Federal Gold Medal Target. Rimfire rifles give drastically different accuracy with different types of ammunition. If you experiment with many types of ammunition, it is possible that your rifle may give a level of accuracy that will meet your requirements without any modification of the rifle.

The author once knew where there was an unusual rifle in the gun rack of a sporting goods store. The previous owner had the rifle built with all of the bells and whistles imaginable. No expense was spared because the owner wanted to win a certain benchrest competition. A special barrel was mounted on a fully tricked out action with a custom trigger and all sorts of other items. The stock was precision made of metal. By the time the project was complete, the owner had spent approximately $2,500 on the rifle. After winning the particular benchrest competition, the owner decided that he had had enough of the sport and sold the rifle (at a great loss). The point is that it is possible to build a rifle that will achieve almost any desired level of accuracy, but before you do so make sure that you understand the costs involved. You may decide that the level of accuracy that will be satisfying to you can be obtained with less expense by starting with a different rifle. Regardless, the aftermarket items are available for some rifles to convert them into almost anything you desire.

Holding Steady

Steady holding of a rifle requires a weight distribution with considerable weight toward the muzzle end. The reason for this can be explained with a simple illustration. Suppose you pick up an 8-pound iron ball with one hand and let your arm hang down. Rotate the ball by simply turning your hand back and forth. Note how easy it is to twist the wrist and rotate the ball. Suppose that you have an 8-pound dumbbell in your hand and you rotate your wrist. It is more difficult to rotate the dumbbell than the 8-pound ball, but it is still easy to rotate eight pounds in this way. Finally, suppose you have an 8-pound bar that is four feet in length. Try rotating your wrist with this weight and note the difference. Rotation of the bar is much harder to start and stop because part of the weight is far from your hand, the pivot point. If you had a long rod that weighs two pounds and it had a 3-pound weight on each end, the total weight would still be eight pounds, but it would be still harder to rotate because the weights are far from the center of rotation, your hand. The four systems have the same total weight but different moments of inertia.

What does all this have to do with holding a rifle steady? A rifle that has a long, heavy barrel resists small movements better than one that has a short, slender barrel. The heavy barrel has more weight farther from the center of rotation, which is usually a point (the pivot point) somewhere between your hands. There is a reason why target rifles have barrels that measure up to 28 inches in length and nearly an inch in diameter. That much mass in the shooting mechanism (the shooter and the rifle) means that the muzzle will not waiver as much as a result of small unbalanced forces due to twitches, jerks, and muscle tension. As a member of a small bore team, the author used a Winchester Model 52D that weighed approximately 11 pounds, which was designed for steady holding and accuracy. A six-pound sporter with a slender barrel cannot be held as steady.

These principles also apply to rifles used for other shooting activities. Some rifles have such short, slender barrels that for all practical purposes most of the mass is in the action and stock and located between the shooter's hands. It is very difficult to hold such a rifle steady in the standing position because it requires so little force to cause the muzzle to dance around. Furthermore, if a scope is mounted, it is also positioned on the rifle between the shooter's hands. Such a rifle is not conducive to steady holding.

Contrast the rifle described with a lever action rifle with a 20-inch barrel of medium weight that has a full-length magazine tube below the barrel. If most people tried to hold each of the rifles steady in a standing position they would be amazed at how much difference there is in the movement of the muzzle. Short, light rifles are convenient to carry, but they are not conducive to steady holding. Target rifles are not normally short or light and for good reasons. Depending on the weight restrictions and rifle design, weights may be added to the muzzle and that also helps to reduce wobble.

To some extent, the same principles apply to handguns. Certain pistols have receivers that are heavy, but tapered barrels that are rather light in weight. Most of the weight in such a pistol rests directly above the shooter's hand, and the pistol requires very little force to cause the muzzle to move. Other pistols, especially those intended for target shooting, have longer, heavier barrels so they have a "weight forward" design. Some models even have a provision for adding muzzle weights. Muzzle motion is less pronounced with such a pistol. Formal target shooting requires a one-hand, extended arm position, which leaves the piece very mobile. In such shooting, the weight forward condition produced by a 5.5-7.5 inch heavy barrel makes it much easier to hold the pistol steady.

The Browning Buck Mark is a high quality pistol that has superb weight distribution as a result of its heavy barrel.

Some shooters may sit at a shooting bench with sandbag rests and shoot almost any rifle or pistol well. The supports offset the instability caused by an unfavorable weight distribution. However, firing from a bench rest and walking in the woods are entirely different situations. Any firearm chosen for target shooting or for hunting (where shots must often be taken from a standing position) should be evaluated with respect to its handling characteristics. It is often not a case of difference in weight of two firearms, but rather a difference in weight distribution. At various times, the author has verified how much more accurately he can fire a certain 32-ounce pistol than another that weighs 36 ounces because the former has a heavy barrel on a light action whereas the latter pistol has the opposite characteristics.

Competition

A shooter who enjoys using rimfire rifles and handguns has a variety of competitive sports in which he or she can participate. These include the formal disciplines of three-position (prone, kneeling, and standing) shooting on indoor and outdoor ranges. Competition on indoor ranges is usually conducted at 50 feet whereas in outdoor competition targets are normally shot at 50 yards or meters, and at 100 yards. A typical rifle match consists of firing from three positions (prone, kneeling, and standing) with one shot fired at each bull. Targets for use on the 50-foot range consist of 10 bulls. A "possible" score for a three-position match would be 300 points. In some matches, the sitting position is also used so 400 points are possible. Other forms of competition involve shooting only from a prone or standing position. Getting all of the points possible in a given position or the entire match is known as shooting a "possible." Competition is held on many levels, and to some extent, equipment requirements and rules depend on the level of the competition. This situation also exists for pistol competition. Competition at the highest levels requires cutting edge equipment and that is reflected in the cost. Although the specific rules for position shooting will not be given here, they can be found on the web site http://www.nrahq.org/compete/smallbore.asp, which is linked to the National Rifle Association and can be accessed through http://www.nrahq.org.

The United States Rimfire Association (USRA) sanctions a series of benchrest competitions at a variety of levels. Known as IR50/50, the course of fire consists of 25 shots for record at 50 yards or 50 meters within a time limit of 30 minutes. In order for contestants to be using similar equipment, rifles are grouped in three categories. These are known as the Sporter Class (rifle and scope must weigh 7.5 pounds or less and the scope must be 6 power or less), the 10.5-pound class, and the 13.5-pound class. The scopes used in the Sporter Class are typically high-quality 6X models produced by Burris, Leupold, Weaver, and other makers. Although some of the rifles described in Chapter 14 could be used in low level competition, at the higher levels the vast majority of the rifles are custom built. Some of the most frequently encountered actions include the Anschutz 54, Sako, Cooper, Remington (40X), or similar high quality types. Custom barrels are frequently those made by Douglas, Lilja, Hart, Walther, and Shilen. This is the ultra high precision sport in rimfire shooting. The rules are very specific and detailed, which leads to a rather long document. It can be found at http://www.ir5050.com/rules.html.

In IR50/50 contests, one shot is fired at each target with the circles representing 10, 9, etc. Inside the 10-ring is a small "X" ring, which can be used to refine the scoring. For example, a perfect score for 25 shots would be 250 with all shots touching the X ring. This is listed as 250 25X. Two competitors could have all shots touching the 10-ring for a score of 250, but the shooter having the higher number of shots touching the X-ring would be the winner. In other words, 250 14X wins over 250 13X.

In a form of benchrest shooting known as Barnyard Benchrest, the rifles used must be factory rifles that retail for no more than $500 and the ammunition used must sell for no more than $5.00 per box (as of 2016). A scope of not greater than 6 power is allowed. This sport is intended to enable shooters to compete even though they have not invested a few thousand dollars in equipment. Even with these restrictions on equipment, the grouping ability normally runs under one-half inch and sometimes well under that size. Some of the rifles described in Chapter 14 could be used in this event.

Another sport that has become more popular in recent years is the biathlon, which involves skiing over a course and stopping to shoot at targets placed at stations along the course. This is a demanding sport because the elapsed time is determined by skiing ability and how long it takes to fire at the targets. However, shooting ability is also important. Accurate placement of a bullet after the physical stress of skiing requires a great deal of skill, conditioning, and practice.

Finally, shooting at metal plates having the shapes of animals constitutes silhouette competition. As in all other shooting sports, there are restrictions on the equipment used so that shooters compete on an equal basis. The rifle must weigh not more than 10 pounds, 2 ounces including sights. There are numerous other restrictions on the rifle that include a maximum barrel length of 30 inches and specific measurements and shapes for stocks. In a category known as the Hunting Rifle division, the rifle must not weigh more than 8.5 pounds including sights. Any type of sight may be used and scopes may be of any magnification. The silhouettes are placed at different ranges, and they have different sizes, which makes for varying levels of difficulty. Matches may be conducted with ranges in yards or meters. Ranges (in either meters or yards) for the different silhouettes are as follows:

The silhouette shooter has available ammunition designed specifically for that sport.

In recent years, silhouette shooting has become a popular sport for rimfire, centerfire, and air rifles.

chicken, 40; pig, 60; turkey, 77; and ram, 100. Firing is from the standing position. Details of small bore silhouette competition can be found on the web site http://competitions.nra.org/documents/pdf/compete/RuleBooks/Sil-r/sil-r-book.pdf.

Ancillaries for competing in different rimfire sports are many and varied. In some cases, it is essential that the competitor have a special shooting jacket and glove, a mat for use in the prone position, a spotting scope, a sling for the rifle, etc. Because many of these are described in the rules for the particular type of shooting event, they will not be covered in more detail in this chapter. Rules for some types of competition include specific information on the types of ancillary equipment that is permitted. Although one may compete for fun in a variety of competitive events with modest equipment, successful competition at a high level is much more specialized in terms of the discipline itself and the necessary equipment.

As described above, there are several types of competitive shooting events that can be enjoyed by the rimfire shooter. All of these sports provide opportunities for the shooter of rimfire rifles and handguns to compete at the local, regional, and in some cases, international levels. If you have an interest in one or more of these types of shooting, find out where competition is being held and go watch the event. Note

The conversion of a .45 Auto such as this Kimber Custom II into a .22 LR is possible by installing a conversion unit that consists of a complete slide and barrel assembly.

the techniques, ammunition, and equipment being used by *successful* competitors. You will learn a great deal about the sport as well as the level of funding and dedication you will need to be successful.

CHAPTER 14

SURVEY OF SOME CURRENT RIMFIRE RIFLES

PREVIOUS CHAPTERS have dealt with safety, ballistics, hunting, and numerous other aspects of the use of rimfire rifles and handguns. Discussion of performance has been kept to a level that gives only an indication of what can be expected from certain rifles. No general assessment of the performance of several rifles has been given that could be used to show how they compare. This chapter is intended to provide concrete evidence on the performance of several current rimfire rifles, and Chapter 15 deals with some of the models chambered for magnum calibers whereas Chapter 16 is devoted to vintage rimfire rifles. Virtually all rifles and ammunition tested were bought from retail sources so the testing does not reflect any attempt to give any preference to manufacturers or suppliers. What is presented is simply the facts as they emerged during the tests.

The Study

Performance is what separates a Super Bowl contender from a last place football team. It is what determines the winner of the Winston Cup in NASCAR, and it is what gives one golfer the green jacket at the Master's tournament. Many shooters are vitally interested in the performance of various firearms. In fact, some gun and shooting magazines devote a great deal of space to presenting product review information that is at least partially based on evaluations of the performance of the firearms. A book that is concerned with rimfire firearms should present information on the performance of several models. However, because of the enormous number of models of rimfire rifles available, only a few representative models could be tested in this project. If your favorite rifle is not included, it simply because one was not available for testing. Keep in

A rimfire sporter such as the Ruger 77/22 can be used for many types of shooting.

mind that two rifles that are nominally identical may perform quite differently. As a result, another specimen might give results that are different than those presented.

Performance of rifles is primarily concerned with accuracy. Rate of fire, longevity, and looks have little to do with the performance of a rifle for most sporting purposes. It is the ability to place the bullet at the desired spot that makes a particular rifle suitable for the purpose it is employed. In this chapter, we will present the results of accuracy tests obtained with several rifles that are representative of those currently being manufactured. The operational characteristics of several models will also be described in some detail in order for this chapter to serve as a sort of abbreviated buyer's guide or user's reference.

Today, certain rifles have become (or are becoming) benchmarks against which other rifles are judged. For example, the Ruger 10/22 is the most popular autoloader currently produced, if not of all time, but the Marlin 60 is also a contender for that title. A huge after market industry has sprung up around the Ruger 10/22, and it is one of the most modified firearms in history. Upon encountering a used Winchester 190 autoloader from the 1970s, a prospective buyer might logically ask, "How does it compare to a Ruger 10/22?" Is it to be compared to a tricked out 10/22 or just the standard model in original configuration? The same comparison might be made between a Remington Nylon 66 or some other out of production autoloader. In the case of bolt action rifles, the Ruger 77/22 is one of the current standards, and the Remington 504 sort of became another for a brief time. In the case of the Remington 504, after rave reviews when it first appeared, reports of mediocre accuracy started to emerge, and it was not long before it was discontinued. In the interim, Remington has introduced the Model 547, which is a custom shop item that has a retail price of around $1,500, but the author has never seen one. At the top of the list are the elegant (a word that seems almost inadequate) rimfires from Cooper Firearms of Montana. These superb rifles have price tags of well over $2,000, but their performance is unsurpassed.

One might also ask how do some of the bolt action rifles of a generation ago compare in performance to these current models? In this chapter and in Chapter 16, we seek to answer these questions by examining the performance of current rifles and a few of those that are gone from production but not forgotten. It should also be remembered that in some cases numerous variants of the basic model are offered that may have stocks having different composition, stainless or blue steel metal, etc. As a result, the models tested should be considered as typical of the family having the same model number.

In order to test rifle accuracy, it is essential that a scope be used in order to decrease the sighting error. In the tests conducted, there was no attempt (nor was it possible) to use identical scopes on all the rifles. The scopes used represent those that might be appropriate for a particular rifle, and the magnification was sufficient to assure that sighting error would be small enough so that the accuracy potential of the rifle would be evaluated. For testing, three to five five-shot groups were fired at 50 yards with each rifle using several types of ammunition. In each case, group sizes were measured by determining the distance between the centers of the two widest holes. Test firing on this scale was carried out over an extended time period. As a result, temperature and wind conditions were not uniform nor could they be for all the tests.

RUGER AMERICAN

As fine sporting rifles have escalated in cost in recent years to the point where some list for $1,000 or more, several manufacturers have continued to produce such models, but they have also introduced other less expensive rifles. One of the most popular of the so-called "entry level" rifles is the Ruger American. It offers excellent performance in a rifle that features a polymer stock with metal bedding blocks, a free floated barrel, and Ruger's Marksman® adjustable trigger. With the MSRP of $359, the American is a lot of rifle for the money.

Building on the success of the centerfire American, Ruger introduced the rimfire version in .22 LR, .22 WMR, and .17 HMR calibers. The rimfire rifles have many of the features found on the centerfire Ruger American. The rifles feature a 22-inch hammer forged barrel that has a crown that is recessed at the muzzle. Moreover, the two Ruger American rimfires in the possession of the author have beautifully polished and blued metal parts. Ruger American rimfires utilize the rotary magazines that have always been used in the 77/22 and 10/22 rifles. However, it makes no sense to the author to tout the flush-fitting magazine and then have an ugly protruding release for it. If a flush fitting release can be adapted, my rifle will get one soon.

Compact versions are also available that have barrels measuring 18 inches in length. The stock of the American has a removable section that controls the height of the comb and the length of pull. That "L" shaped section is held in place by the rear sling swivel stud. Each rifle is shipped with two of the sections having different sizes in order to better fit shooters of different stature. On the American, the safety is a sliding bar that is located on the tang at the rear end of the action.

In addition to the general features already described, the Ruger American rimfires have numerous other nice touches. For example, the rifles are provided with open sights, as they should be. The rear

The Ruger American is a durable rifle that has excellent styling.

The Ruger American features the Marksman trigger.

Ruger American rifles are fitted with excellent open sights.

sight is an adjustable folding model having a reversible blade that has "U" and square notches on opposite sides. The front sight is a square-topped post having a green fiber optic element (which the author could get along quite well without) along the top. Together, the open sights work very well, and the folding rear sight does not interfere with scopes that have objective bells of modest size.

Although the American is fitted with open sights, the receiver is grooved for attaching clamp-on scope mounts. It is also drilled and tapped to attach two bases that can accept Weaver-type rings. As a result of these provisions, it is possible to mount a scope easily. For testing, the .22 LR Ruger American had a Weaver Classic 2-7X rimfire scope attached. Results of testing the rifle with several types of ammunition during miserable weather conditions are shown in the accompanying table.

The protruding magazine release on the Ruger American works well, but it is unsightly.

Accuracy Results for the Ruger American with Weaver 2-7X Scope

AMMUNITION	GROUP SIZE, INCHES		
	Smallest	Largest	Average
Eley Target	0.32	0.92	0.67
CCI Mini Mag	0.86	1.82	1.37
CCI Green Tag	0.31	1.46	0.98
Federal Target	0.71	1.89	1.35
Remington Game Load	1.03	1.96	1.53
Winchester Power Point	0.51	1.17	0.85
		OVERALL AV.	**1.12**

As shown by the data, the Ruger American can easily produce groups measuring smaller than one inch with many types of ammunition. In fact, with all but one of the types of ammunition the smallest groups were excellent. However, in shooting several five-shot groups, there often seemed to be an outlying shot that increased the size of some of the groups inordinately, which resulted in an average that may not be representative. For example, if only one shot in two of the groups obtained with CCI Mini Mag were disregarded, the average group size with that load would be only 0.74 inch. With a similar change, the average with Winchester Power Point would decrease to 0.53 inch instead of the average of 0.85 inch when all shots are considered. It would seem that perhaps a little tweaking of the tension of screws or testing under better conditions would show that the Ruger American is capable of consistently giving groups smaller than one inch.

In late 2015, Ruger introduced the American with a wood stock that is beautifully shaped and finished. If the specimens examined by the author are representative, this version of the Ruger American is perhaps the least expensive way to acquire a fine rimfire sporter. With the attractive stock and highly polished and blued metal, it is indeed an appealing rifle.

The Ruger American with a wood stock is an attractive, durable, and accurate rimfire. (photo courtesy Ruger)

MARLIN 25N/XT

Among the inexpensive bolt action rimfire rifles, those produced by Marlin have been some of the most successful. There are models that utilize tubular and detachable box magazines that have been produced for many years. The Marlin Model 25N was the box magazine version, but the 2015 catalog lists the current rimfire model with a box magazine as the Model XT-22 because it utilizes the new Marlin Pro-Fire™ trigger mechanism. Except for cosmetic appearance and the Pro-FireTM trigger, mechanical features of the 25N also characterize the current bolt action Model XT-22. Therefore, the performance of the 25N should be representative of the XT as well. However, a different version of the XT-22 features a tubular magazine that holds 17 rounds of .22 LR.

The older Marlin Model 25N and current XT are full-size .22s that are sturdy and dependable. They have 22-inch barrels that are pinned to the receiver, and they features Marlin's Micro-Groove rifling. The hardwood stock has a rather plain appearance although the Mar-Shield® finish is so durable that it gives a new meaning to the word! However, the wood stock on the Marlin 25N or XT can be reshaped to give a more pleasing profile and the author has done that to his (see Chapter 11). The current Model XT-22 has

These inexpensive Marlin bolt action rifles belonging to the author and his wife are dependable and accurate. The Marlin on the left with the modified stock has been described in Chapter 11.

Accuracy Results for the Marlin 25N with Bushnell Banner 3-9X Scope

	AMMUNITION	GROUP SIZE, INCHES		
		Smallest	Largest	Average
HIGH VELOCITY	CCI Mini Mag	1.00	1.60	1.31
	CCI Velocitor	0.82	1.10	0.99
	Federal High Velocity H.P.	1.02	1.65	1.34
	Federal Lightning	0.85	2.09	1.32
	Remington Game Load	0.93	1.71	1.19
	Remington Golden H.P.	1.09	1.66	1.29
	Winchester Power Point	0.89	1.39	1.17
	Winchester Super-X	1.13	1.70	1.31
	Winchester Wildcat	0.68	1.47	1.22

OVERALL AV. 1.24

	AMMUNITION	GROUP SIZE, INCHES		
		Smallest	Largest	Average
STANDARD VELOCITY	CCI Green Tag	0.56	0.98	0.77
	CCI Standard Velocity	0.69	1.53	1.07
	Federal Target (711B)	0.79	0.97	0.90
	PMC Match Rifle	0.86	1.61	1.34
	PMC Scoremaster	1.00	1.39	1.18
	Remington Target	0.89	1.41	1.14
	Winchester Supreme	0.55	1.14	0.89
	Winchester T-22	0.64	1.34	1.04
	Wolf Match Target	0.67	0.89	0.78

OVERALL AV. 1.01

pressed checkering on the grip and forearm. Although the fore end on the Model 25 is cut with a square profile, that of the XT-22 is rounded.

Sights on the Model 25N and XT consist of a square-topped post on a ramp front and a fully adjustable rear sight. Elevation adjustment is made by sliding a stepped ramp, whereas windage adjustment requires the sight to be moved laterally in the dovetail groove. With a square notch in the rear sight blade and the square-topped post, a good sight picture is afforded. The receiver is grooved so that scope mounts can be easily attached. The safety is located on the right hand side at the rear of the receiver, and the detachable magazine holds seven rounds, but it can be modified. With that capacity, the magazine is long enough that it protrudes from the bottom of the stock by an inch or so, which makes it awkward to carry the rifle while holding it at its natural balance point. These are durable, no-frills rifles, and the 25N belonging to the author has been used with satisfaction for many years.

Many shooters of rimfire rifles, including the author, do not have one of the elegant sporting rifles that cost upwards of $1,000. A Marlin XT currently sells for around $200 so the question naturally arises as to what type of performance one can expect from this basic rifle. Exhaustive tests were conducted with two Model 25s to find out. In the tests, ammunition of almost all types was utilized. The types ranged from the very expensive Federal Ultra Match (approximately $20-25 per box) to Federal Lightning (now named Champion) that was purchased for $3.00 per box. For the tests, a Bushnell Banner 3-9X scope was mounted on the rifle. The accompanying table shows a summary of the results obtained when using both standard velocity target loads as well as high velocity hunting types of ammunition.

The results shown in the table indicate that one can expect groups to average about 1 inch with standard velocity loads and around 1.25-inch with high velocity ammunition. As a check on the results, a second Marlin 25N was found to give almost identical results with a selection of the ammunition types. Is a Marlin 25N or XT-22 a worthy companion for the small game and pest shooter? From the data presented it is clear that the answer is clearly affirmative. Numerous rimfire rifles are available that will not match the performance of a Marlin 25N and XT, and many of them cost considerably more. Certainly the user of a Marlin 25N or a current XT-22 should try different types of ammunition to determine what works best in his or her rifle, but that is true of all rimfire shooters.

The Ruger 10/22 is available in several configurations. Shown are (top to bottom) the Carbine, Target, and Rifle models.

RUGER 10/22 CARBINE

Introduced in 1964, the Ruger 10/22 Carbine is one of the most frequently encountered rimfire firearms. Over 5 million of these rifles have been produced, and they are available in several versions that have different stock material, metal finish, or other characteristics. The most common version has an 18.5-inch barrel, a hardwood stock, and a barrel band that encircles the forearm and the barrel. With a length of 37 inches and a weight of about 5 pounds, the 10/22 is a compact, handy firearm. In 1997, the 10/22T was introduced and it has a heavy hammer forged barrel that measures 0.920 inch in diameter with no taper. This target version is available with blued metal and a laminated stock or with stainless steel and a synthetic stock. In 2004, a new variant of the 10/22 was introduced that was called the 10/22 Rifle because it has a 20-inch barrel and a slimmer stock without the a barrel band. However, that model has since been discontinued. The most attractive version of the 10/22 is known as the Sporter model, and it has a checkered walnut stock of good contour.

Of the numerous versions of the Ruger 10/22, the most attractive is the Sporter. (photo courtesy Ruger)

The housing for the action of the Ruger 10/22 is made of an aluminum alloy. In order to attach a scope, a scope rail is attached to the top of the receiver by four screws. Two types of rails are encountered.

The Ruger 10/22 in both Carbine and Takedown configurations can be modified extensively.

The first is a flat-topped rail that has grooves along the sides where clamp-type mounts can be attached. Beginning in 2004 a scope rail was introduced that not only has grooves along the sides, but it also has grooves across the bar, which allow rings known as the Weaver-type to be attached. The latter rail thus provides greater versatility in terms of the types of mounts that can be used.

One distinguishing characteristic of the Ruger 10/22 is the rotary magazine that holds 10 rounds of .22 LR. Because the magazine is laterally thick, the magazine well in the stock is wide, which makes the overall stock thick. The result is that the rifle is almost as thick as it is high, and that gives it a round, chunky appearance and feel when the standard stock is in place. In order to improve the handling and looks, it is possible to modify a Ruger 10/22 in many ways. Later in this chapter, the performance of modified 10/22s will be described.

Although the Ruger 10/22 has several unusual features, perhaps the most unique is the method used to attach the barrel to the receiver. The barrel has a cutout section across the bottom near the breech. A mating block fits in the slot, and it attaches to the front face of the action by two large Allen headed screws. Tightening the screws pulls the barrel extension into the action and locks it in place. Because only two screws must be removed, the barrel can readily be taken off and an aftermarket barrel produced by one of many suppliers can be installed. In fact, the design of the Ruger 10/22 is such that several parts are replaceable by someone with a modest amount of manual dexterity. Barrels chambered for the .17 Mach 2 are available for the Ruger 10/22. However, the .17 Mach 2 cartridge causes the bolt to be driven to the rear at a velocity that is higher than that produced when a .22 LR is fired in the rifle. Knowledgeable people in the industry have told the author that installing a .17 Mach 2 barrel on a 10/22 will cause the standard action to be ruined after a few hundred shots. Converting a Ruger 10/22 to .17 Mach 2 is not as simple as unbolting one barrel and replacing it with another.

A bewildering array of aftermarket parts and accessories are available for the Ruger 10/22. One can buy barrels in numerous configurations, stocks, triggers, sears, hammers, etc. that can be used to configure a 10/22 in almost any way. Several companies produce items almost exclusively for the 10/22 as aftermarket industries. The Ruger 10/22 Carbine tested was of "stock" configuration except for having a scope attached. The accompanying table shows the results of the accuracy testing with several types of ammunition.

Accuracy of the Ruger 10/22 is quite good for a short, light rifle that is intended for general use. It certainly qualifies the standard 10/22 for hunting and pest control with most types of ammunition as long as the range is around 60 yards or less. The accuracy shown by the CCI Standard Velocity and the SK Jagd Standard Plus is truly outstanding for this type of rifle. Sighted to hit a point of aim at approximately 60 yards, either of these loads would make it possible to pick off varmints out to around 75 yards. The 10/22 Carbine model gave the smallest groups with SK Jagd Standard Plus ammunition as did the 10/22T. Clearly, Ruger autoloaders like this ammunition so you should try it in your Ruger if you are looking for top accuracy.

Accuracy Results for the Ruger 10/22 Carbine with BSA 3-12X AO Scope

AMMUNITION	GROUP SIZE, INCHES		
	Smallest	Largest	Average
CCI Green Tag	0.69	1.53	1.08
CCI Standard Velocity	0.65	1.10	0.88
Federal Target (711B)	0.95	2.00	1.47
Remington Golden H.P.	0.99	1.79	1.39
SK Jagd Standard Plus	0.53	0.94	0.78
Winchester Super-X H.P.	0.68	1.88	1.31
Winchester Super-X solid	0.90	1.67	1.18
OVERALL AV.			**1.16**

The Ruger 10/22 is one of the most successful sporting firearms ever produced. It has an outstanding reputation for reliability, durability, and accuracy. In fact, the Ruger 10/22 has become a true icon among American firearms. If you do not like the appearance of the chunky little carbine, you can modify it to almost any form you desire. Although the 10/22 has a list price of $309, the usual retail price is around $250 and sometimes lower. If anyone wants a compact semiautomatic, it is safe to say that the Ruger 10/22 should be given very serious consideration.

RUGER 10/22 WITH MAJESTIC ARMS BARREL

Because a large number of shooters using Ruger 10/22 Carbines do not leave them in the stock configuration, the author decided to follow suit at least up to a point. From the large number of aftermarket options available, a Majestic Arms Aluma Lite barrel and a Hogue OverMolded Stock were chosen. The Aluma Lite barrel has a steel insert produced by Lothar Walther that is encased in a cylindrical aluminum sleeve that measures 0.920 inch in diameter. The Hogue stock that is intended for use with target barrels of that diameter fits perfectly. The combination gives a compact, lightweight rimfire. However, the old saying, "Pretty is as pretty does", seems to apply so the obvious way to find out was to start shooting.

In order to obtain small groups, one must be able to see the target clearly. Attaching a 4-16X AO Weaver Classic scope using Leupold Rifleman mounts made sure that the bull could be seen in detail. To test the modified 10/22, a few types of target ammunition were selected because the barrel is made to match standards and there is no advantage to getting good

This 0.44-inch 5-shot group was fired at 50 yards with the author's Ruger with a Majestic Arms barrel using Lapua Super Club ammunition. Four shots produced one ragged hole.

groups when excellent groups are possible. The results obtained are shown in the accompanying table.

The accuracy obtained with the Aluma Lite barrel shows what is possible when a Ruger 10/22 is modified even to a modest extent. This level of accuracy represents about the limit for the author because of vision problems. There is no question that this is an extremely accurate barrel when match ammunition is used. Can you expect accuracy be as good with hunting loads? Probably not with most types, but the Remington Game Load, a high velocity hollow point, performed extremely well. However, a hunting load will not accomplish any more than will a well-placed bullet from a target load that is traveling with slightly lower velocity but placed with greater accuracy. The Ruger/Aluma Lite/Hogue combination is capable of putting the bullet in the desired spot on the target.

The author's son, Keith, has a lightweight tack driver. His Ruger 10/22 has a Majestic Arms barrel with an aluminum shroud and a Lothar Walther steel insert. The stock is the Hogue OverMolded model.

Accuracy Results for the Ruger 10/22 with Aluma Lite Barrel and Weaver V-16 Scope

AMMUNITION	GROUP SIZE, INCHES		
	Smallest	Largest	Average
Eley Target	0.49	0.85	0.68
Lapua Super Club	0.43	0.69	0.49
Remington Game Load	0.41	0.64	0.55
Wolf Match Target	0.45	0.84	0.67
		OVERALL AV.	**0.60**

RUGER 10/22 WITH VOLQUARTSEN BARREL

In the spirit of "let's see what it can do," a Ruger 10/22 Carbine was transformed by adding a Bell & Carlson Odyssey stock, a Kidd trigger assembly, and a Volquartsen Ultralight tensioned barrel. The scope attached was the Bushnell Banner 4-12 X 40 AO scope that was part of the "instant optics" package from Majestic Arms (see Chapter 5). The results obtained are summarized in the accompanying table.

The data shown in the table make it clear that the Volquartsen Ultralite barrel is capable of outstanding accuracy. With all of the testing conducted on an outdoor range in Wyoming where conditions are usually less than ideal, it is apparent that the rifle tested is capable of half-inch groups consistently under more favorable conditions. It should be mentioned that the Volquarsen Ultralite is now permanently at home on one of the author's Ruger 10/22s. With a light stock, the result is a rifle that weighs slightly over four pounds that shoots like a target rifle. It is a superb rifle for walking varmint hunting.

The muzzle of the Volquartsen barrel has a stainless steel cap.

Groups measuring around half an inch were obtained with the Volquartsen barrel using CCI Mini Mag ammunition.

By employing a Bell & Carlson stock and a Volquartsen barrel, this Ruger 10/22 was converted into a tack driver.

Accuracy Results for a Ruger 10/22 with Volquartsen Ultralite Barrel, Bell & Carlson Odyssey Stock, and Kidd Trigger

AMMUNITION	GROUP SIZE, INCHES		
	Smallest	Largest	Average
SK Jagd High Vel, HP	0.47	0.85	0.62
SK Jagd Standard Plus	0.41	0.68	0.53
CCI Mini Mag	0.47	0.73	0.58
CCI Standard Velocity	0.48	0.74	0.57
Geco	0.61	1.15	0.83
Wolf Match Target	0.58	0.68	0.64
Remington/Eley Target	0.61	0.83	0.73
OVERALL AV.			**0.64**

The Magnum Research barrel has a cap that covers the muzzle of the actual barrel, which has a carbon fiber sleeve surrounding it.

RUGER 10/22 WITH MAGNUM RESEARCH GRAPHITE BARREL

In another effort to produce a lightweight but accurate Ruger 10/22, a Carbine was modified by substituting a Ruger BX trigger assembly for the original version. Then, the barrel was replaced with a Magnum Research Graphite Lite barrel. A Hogue Thumbhole stock was added and a Bushnell 4-12 X 40 AO scope was mounted. Testing of this rifle, which weighs less than five pounds, produced the data shown in the accompanying table.

The data shown in the table make it clear that it is no longer necessary to use a target barrel measuring 0.920 inch in diameter and weighing about three pounds to produce an accurate Ruger 10/22. For some reason, CCI Mini Mag, which usually gives outstanding accuracy, did not perform so well in this rifle. The level of accuracy with the Mini Mag is certainly adequate and some other high velocity loads performed quite well.

An overall average group size of 0.69 inch under the conditions prevailing at the range is excellent. It would be hard to imagine a more convenient rifle for hunting small game and pests than a Ruger 10/22 that weighs between four and five pounds but which has the accuracy of a target version. The Magnum Research barrel makes that possible.

This small group was obtained at 50 yards with a modified Ruger 10/22 that utilized a Magnum Research barrel.

Accuracy Results for a Ruger 10/22 with Magnum Research Barrel, Hogue Stock, and Ruger BX Trigger

AMMUNITION	GROUP SIZE, INCHES		
	Smallest	Largest	Average
SK Jagd High Vel, HP	0.49	0.58	0.53
CCI Mini Mag	0.84	1.17	1.03
CCI Standard Velocity	0.36	0.71	0.54
Wolf Match Target	0.51	0.63	0.56
Remington/ Eley Target	0.50	0.75	0.65
Remington Game Load	0.74	0.85	0.81
		OVERALL AV.	**0.69**

To give a rifle weighing less than five pounds, this Ruger 10/22 has a Macmillan stock and a Magnum Research barrel.

When tested from the bench, the Ruger 10/22 modified by adding a Tactical Solutions barrel and Hogue stock performed exceedingly well.

RUGER 10/22 WITH TACTICAL SOLUTIONS BARREL

Tactical Solutions is well known for producing both aftermarket items for the Ruger 10/22 and other rimfires as well as complete firearms. With one of the Tactical Solutions barrels being a sleeved model known as the X-Ring® and weighing only 15 ounces, it was natural to assemble a Ruger 10/22 using that barrel. This barrel has an aluminum sleeve surrounding a chrome molybdenum liner. Moreover, the X-Ring barrel is available with sleeves having several colors and with or without a threaded muzzle. For testing, a Hogue Thumbhole OverMolded stock and Kidd trigger assembly were added, and a Bushnell 4-12 X 40 AO scope was mounted. The results obtained are shown in the accompanying table.

If a shooter wishes to make a Ruger 10/22 that is both light in weight and accurate, the Tactical Solutions X-Ring barrel would be a good choice because the overall average group size was just under three-fourths of an inch. As shown by the data, groups well under an inch in average size are the norm and only two individual groups were obtained that measured over one inch. As always, the shooter should experiment to find the type of ammunition that performs best in a particular rifle.

Accuracy Results for a Ruger 10/22 with Tactical Solutions Barrel, Hogue Stock, and Kidd Trigger

AMMUNITION	GROUP SIZE, INCHES		
	Smallest	Largest	Average
SK Jagd Standard Plus	0.59	1.05	0.82
CCI Mini Mag	0.88	1.05	0.94
CCI Standard Velocity	0.46	0.89	0.74
Remington/Eley Target	0.45	0.53	0.49
Remington Game Load	0.66	0.87	0.76
Wolf Match Target	0.60	0.77	0.68
OVERALL AV.			**0.74**

RUGER 10/22 TARGET

A number of rimfire disciplines are best enjoyed when using a rifle that is a "target" model. Several manufacturers produce such rifles, and they usually employ the same action as the "standard" model but use a special heavy barrel. Ruger responded to this demand in 1996 with the 10/22T featuring a heavy hammer forged barrel that is 20 inches in length, which results in a rifle weighing 7.5 pounds. No sights are provided so this rifle is intended for use with a scope. The specimen owned by the author is the version that has a richly blued barrel and laminated stock, but another version with a stainless steel barrel and gray laminated stock is available. Operating characteristics of the 10/22T are identical to those of the 10/22 Carbine discussed earlier. Whether by design or accident is not clear, but the author's 10/22T has a better trigger pull than does the Carbine model. In fact, it is as good as can be found on almost any other autoloading rifle.

Testing of a target model 10/22 should be carried out with a scope worthy of this potential level of accuracy. In this case, the scope used was a Cabela's Outfitter 6-20X model with AO so the scope could be focused sharply and corrected for parallax at 50 yards. The accompanying table shows the results obtained.

The data given in the table show that a Ruger 10/22T is capable of fine accuracy. An average group size of 0.45 inch for five 5-shot groups was obtained with SK Jagd Standard Plus ammunition, and Lapua Super Club also performed well giving an average group size of only 0.66 inch. The Ruger 10/22 Carbine model also gave its best accuracy with the SK Jagd Standard Plus ammunition. Note that the 10/22T performed better with CCI Standard Velocity ammunition than it did with the more expensive CCI Green Tag. This was also the case with the 10/22 Carbine. Only two high velocity types of ammunition gave average group sizes greater than one inch, but even those gave some individual groups well under an inch. The 10/22T tested has not been modified in any way, but it would be interesting to see what a modified specimen would do. With the rifle weighing 7.5 pounds, adding a scope raises the weight to approximately 8.5 pounds or more. This somewhat heavy for a walking rifle, but for still hunting or calling varmints a Ruger 10/22T is a fine choice.

Accuracy Results for the Ruger 10/22 Target with Cabela's Outfitter 6-20X Scope

AMMUNITION	GROUP SIZE, INCHES		
	Smallest	Largest	Average
CCI Green Tag	0.54	1.14	0.93
CCI Standard Velocity	0.45	0.96	0.68
CCI Velocitor	0.55	1.57	1.10
Federal High Velocity H.P.	0.69	1.32	1.13
Federal Target (711B)	0.77	0.91	0.84
Lapua Super Club	0.52	0.82	0.66
Remington Club Extra	0.68	0.92	0.82
RWS Rifle Match	0.55	1.15	0.85
SK Jagd Standard Plus	0.36	0.50	0.45
Winchester Power Point	0.64	0.93	0.75
		OVERALL AV.	**0.83**

The Ruger 10/22T has a heavy hammer forged barrel, and it gives superb accuracy.

RUGER 10/22 TAKEDOWN

How do you continue to make a product that has been as successful and produced in so many variants as the Ruger 10/22 interesting to consumers? Alter it so drastically that it can be easily taken apart for transporting or backpacking. Thus in 2012 was born the Ruger 10/22 Takedown®. The Takedown features essentially the same action and controls as the Carbine but with the barrel and forearm being detachable. Both blue and stainless versions are available and they are equipped with open sights. The version tested, belonging to the author's wife, has a stainless barrel and composite stock.

Barrel attachment on the Takedown is totally different than it is on other Ruger 10/22 rifles. In a recess on the bottom of the forearm is located a release lever that when pushed forward moves a wedge that mates in a recess in the bottom of the barrel. When the rifle is cocked and the wedge is disengaged from the receiver, the barrel and forearm assembly can be rotated and pulled forward out of the action. Although adequate and sturdy, this mode of attachment of necessity must allow for some lack of rigidity. The tension of the barrel to the receiver is controlled by a large knurled ring. Open sights are mounted on the barrel so any movement of the barrel in the receiver has minimum effect on accuracy. However, when a scope is mounted on the receiver, one should not expect a Takedown 10/22 to deliver tack driving accuracy. Some sacrifice in accuracy is the result of the convenience of being able to disassemble the rifle. The 10/22 Takedown was tested

Ruger 10/22 Takedown Version With Sightron 4-12 X 40 AO Scope

AMMUNITION	GROUP SIZE, INCHES		
	Smallest	Largest	Average
CCI Blazer	1.50	3.07	2.39
CCI Mini Mag	2.18	2.41	2.31
CCI Standard Velocity	1.65	3.03	2.36
Federal Automatch	1.67	3.07	2.42
Remington Game Loads	2.20	3.67	2.73
SK Jagd Standard Plus	1.48	2.84	1.95
Winchester Power Point	1.67	2.54	2.03
		OVERALL AV.	2.31

with an elegant Sightron 4-12 X 40 AO scope attached giving the results shown in the accompanying table.

Not unexpectedly, the data shown in the table indicate that the 10/22 Takedown gives accuracy that would be acceptable for plinking at short range. The rifle is intended for recreational shooting or for packing so that some rifle will be available, possibly in remote areas. For those purposes, the 10/22 Takedown is perfectly acceptable.

For transporting or installing accessory barrels, the Ruger 10/22 Takedown can be separated into two units.

Enhancing the Ruger 10/22 Takedown by adding a Boyds stock and a Tactical Solutions barrel resulted in a beautiful rifle that performs well.

RUGER 10/22 TAKEDOWN WITH TACTICAL SOLUTIONS BARREL

As has long been the case for other versions of the Ruger 10/22, an aftermarket industry is developing for the Takedown version. Trigger assemblies that are produced by several companies can be used on either the Takedown or other versions of the 10/22. Stocks are available from Hogue and Boyds, and barrels are available from several manufacturers. In addition to testing with the factory barrel, the Takedown was tested in several combinations including a Tactical Solutions SB-X barrel, Hornet Black Max or Kidd trigger, and a Hogue OverMolded or Boyd's SS Evolution Stock. In all cases, a Sightron 4-16X AO scope was attached. The data obtained are summarized in the accompanying table.

From a comparison of the data shown in the table with that for the Takedown in factory configuration, it can be seen that considerably better accuracy is obtained with the rifle having an aftermarket trigger, barrel and stock installed. Moreover, with the Tactical Solutions barrel, the rifle weighs less than in factory configuration. The accuracy results are not stellar, but such a rifle would be suitable for use on small game or pests. The problem of barrel to action rigidity with the scope being mounted on the receiver instead of attached to the barrel still remains.

Ruger 10/22 Takedown with a Tactical Solutions SB-X Barrel

AMMUNITION	GROUP SIZE, INCHES		
	Smallest	Largest	Average
CCI Standard Velocity	0.59	1.69	1.23
Remington Game Loads	2.54	2.57	2.56
SK Jagd Standard Plus	0.78	1.83	1.30
Winchester Super X Solid	1.95	2.43	2.16
CCI Mini Mag Solid	1.03	1.08	1.05
Federal Champion	2.40	3.02	2.64
SK Jagd High Velocity HP	0.90	1.24	1.07
		OVERALL AV.	**1.71**

RUGER 10/22 TAKEDOWN WITH VOLQUARTSEN BARREL

The lack of rigidity between the barrel and the receiver in the Ruger 10/22 Takedown has been addressed in a most successful way by Volquartsen. In this case, the hardware for mounting a scope is permanently attached to the barrel. A rigid cantilever scope mount is attached to the barrel so a scope and the bore can be coaxial and remain that way. Testing a Ruger 10/22 Takedown configured with the Volquartsen barrel, Hogue OverMolded stock and Kidd trigger assembly yielded the data shown in the accompanying table.

Accuracy produced by the Ruger 10/22 Takedown with the Volquartsen barrel is excellent. Only one of the types of ammunition tested gave an average group size larger than one inch (a high velocity load) and that was very slightly larger. The composite average group size of 0.82 inch qualifies the rifle for all but the most serious target shooting. To obtain superb accuracy from a 10/22 Takedown, it appears to be necessary to have the scope mounted on the barrel. Doing so results in a rifle that is not as compact when disassembled, but the improvement in accuracy is significant.

The Ruger 10/22 Takedown is a useful and handy rifle. If it is used in situations that do not demand high accuracy, it will be found to be utterly dependable. However, with the Volquartsen barrel attached, the accuracy is so good that the rifle is permanently configured that way.

By attaching the scope mount to the Volquartsen barrel of the Ruger 10/22 Takedown, accuracy is greatly enhanced.

Ruger 10/22 Takedown with a Volquartsen Barrel, Hogue OverMolded Stock, Kidd Trigger, and Sightron 4-16X AO Scope

AMMUNITION	GROUP SIZE, INCHES		
	Smallest	Largest	Average
CCI Standard Velocity	0.29	0.86	0.57
Federal Automatch	0.58	1.08	0.82
Federal Champion	0.65	1.39	0.96
Remington/ Eley Target	0.37	0.83	0.61
Remington Game Loads	0.73	1.06	0.89
SK Jagd Standard Plus	0.47	0.90	0.65
Winchester Super X Solid	0.75	1.44	1.08
Winchester T22	0.67	1.21	0.94
		OVERALL AV.	**0.82**

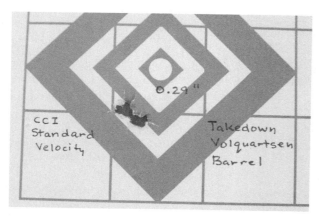

With the Volquartsen barrel attached, the Ruger Takedown gave this five-shot group at 50 yards with CCI Standard Velocity ammunition.

MARLIN 60

Arguably the most popular semiautomatic .22 rifle ever made, the Marlin Model 60 is one of the best bargains in the rimfire field. As this is written, a Marlin Model 60 is available in one of the large "marts" for approximately $175-200 in the "basic blue and hardwood" configuration. This rifle has been produced in the millions. Basically, the Model 60 is a 19-inch barreled semiautomatic with a tubular magazine that holds 14 rounds of .22 LR. For many years, the Model 60 was offered with a 22-inch barrel and a magazine that held 17 cartridges, which is the case with the rifle tested. The Marlin 70PSS features essentially the same action as the Model 60 but utilizes a box type magazine and a barrel that can be removed to make a two-piece firearm for easier transportation. The Model 795 is an economy version that features a synthetic stock and a 10 round box type magazine.

The Model 60 (and related versions) are inexpensive rifles that have several desirable features. First, the Model 60 has a hold open device that holds the bolt half way open after the last shot. Second, the rifle has a cross bolt safety of generous size located behind the trigger. Third, the receiver is grooved for easy attachment of scope mounts. Fourth, with its receiver having a rounded back, the Model 60 has sleek styling, and it has a well-shaped stock. Moreover, with an overall length of 37.5 inches and weight of 5.5 pounds, the rifle is very convenient to hold and carry. The tubular magazine gives the rifle a "weight forward" feeling, which allows for steady holding. Fifth, the Model 60 has a square-topped post front sight on a ramp and an adjustable rear sight with a square notch. This sighting equipment permits a good sight picture to be established.

One of the things about the Marlin 60 that has changed over the years is the number of options in stocks and metal finishes. The Model 60 can be obtained with blued metal and either hardwood or camo stock. Stainless steel metal parts combined with hardwood, composite, or laminated stock comprise other available options. The variant with the blued metal and hardwood stock represents the lowest price option.

The Marlin Model 60 has been a staple in the rimfire market for many years. It has been offered not only with the Marlin name but also carrying the labels of other retail chains. For many years, this was a common practice for stores such as Sears, Wards, Western

The Marlin Model 60 is a classic American autoloader. There is a reason millions of these rifles have been produced.

Auto, and hardware stores who did not produce their own firearms. Oh my! How times have changed! The Model 60 tested in this work was produced for the 60th anniversary of Coast to Coast hardware stores, and it carries an inlayed medallion to denote the occasion. It should also be remembered that the clip-fed Models 70, 795, and 7000 (target version) are essentially the Model 60 with a different means of holding cartridges.

Testing this American classic began by attaching a BSA 3-12X AO airgun scope with a Beeman mount. A few shots were fired to sight in the rifle, and it was tested for accuracy at 50 yards using six types of ammunition. It should be mentioned that these tests were conducted at Buffalo, Wyoming in December. The temperature was approximately 35 degrees F, and because of having no sandbags along, a makeshift support was used on the concrete shooting bench. Consequently, conditions were somewhat less than ideal for accurate shooting. The accompanying table shows the results obtained.

When testing rimfire rifles, one is never sure which types of ammunition will perform best, but the attempt is made to find a few kinds that give good accuracy. In the case of the Marlin 60, three of the six types of ammunition gave average group sizes of under one inch, and the Remington Game Load gave an average group size of only 0.82 inch. All six types of ammunition gave individual groups smaller than an inch. The Marlin 60 does not seem to be quite as finicky with regard to ammunition type as are some autoloaders. In fact, an aggregate group size of 1.01 inches is very good for a rifle of this type. Although the author has other .22 rimfire rifles, the Marlin 60 showed that it is the only rifle really needed for most small game hunting and plinking.

The accuracy results given by the Marlin Model 60 show that this rifle is capable of fine accuracy with certain types of ammunition. In fact, the author has no other inexpensive rimfire autoloader that will give better performance. To see if my experience with the Model 60 is typical, some time was spent reading comments posted on the internet at various sites devoted to rimfire shooting. Some of the comments were amazing. Almost every comment from a user of a Model 60 praised the accuracy of this rifle. Some of the comments by users indicated that the Model 60 is even more accurate than indicated by the results obtained in this work, which is not surprising in view of weather conditions during testing.

When you realize that a Marlin Model 60 with blue metal and wood stock sells for under $200 at some

Accuracy Results for the Marlin Model 60 Rifle with a 3-12X BSA Scope

AMMUNITION	GROUP SIZE, INCHES		
	Smallest	Largest	Average
CCI Green Tag	0.83	1.50	1.04
Federal Target (711B)	0.63	1.39	1.11
Remington Game Load	0.66	0.93	0.82
Winchester Power Point	0.97	1.56	1.25
Winchester T22	0.77	1.19	0.93
Wolf Match Target	0.62	1.07	0.92
OVERALL AV.			**1.01**

The inlaid medallion in this Marlin Model 60 commemorates the 60th anniversary of Coast to Coast stores.

stores, it is clear that it is possible to get into rimfire shooting very inexpensively. Even when a good scope is added the total cost can be less than $250, and Remington Game Load is a relatively inexpensive type of ammunition. However, as the data show, this combination is capable of producing excellent results. Keep in mind that the Marlin Model 60 is produced in several combinations of metal and stock finish so one is not restricted to a single version of this fine rifle. For many rimfire shooters, one of the versions of the Marlin Model 60 could well be all the rifle needed. The author particularly likes inexpensive firearms that give performance well beyond their cost, and the Marlin Model 60 certainly belongs in that category. This rifle is a true American icon.

REMINGTON 597

Autoloaders are the most popular type of .22 rifle so it is natural that there should be a large number of models available. In 1959, Remington broke new ground in rimfire autoloaders with the introduction of a model known as the Nylon 66. That rifle had a tubular magazine located in the buttstock that held 14 rounds. This was not a new approach to housing the magazine in a rimfire, but what was new was the fact that the stock was made of a plastic known as Zytel®. Moreover, most of the rifle was made of structural nylon that needed no lubrication and very little maintenance. Even the receiver was made of nylon but it had a thin sheet of metal surrounding it. After the Nylon 66 was discontinued in 1987, the next mass produced Remington autoloader was the Viper 522, which was produced for several years. As is so often the case in firearm development, the Viper was a transitional piece that led to the Remington 597. The Remington Model 597 is actually a family of rifles in .22 LR caliber that includes variants with different metal finishes and stock compositions. Not content with offering rifles in one caliber, magnum models have appeared that are chambered for the .22 WMR and .17 HMR although they cost much more than those in .22 LR caliber. As a result of problems caused by the pressure produced by the .17 HMR cartridge, rifles in that caliber were quickly discontinued and rifles sold were subject to recall.

The Remington 597 has several attractive features. First, it is reasonably light, but it has enough weight to hold steady. Second, the Model 597 has a metal magazine that is easier to load than are those of some other rifles. The magazine follower is bright orange in color, which makes it easy to see when the last cartridge has been removed. Third, the bolt rides on dual rails and operates very smoothly. The rifle tested had been fired fewer than 20 rounds when the testing was initiated, and the action became noticeably smoother during the firing. With a couple of shots early in the testing, ejection of the empty case was not complete because the action was stiff and the round being fired was a low powered one. After that, ejection and feeding were flawless. The stock on the Model 597 has a forearm of generous width, which allows it to rest on sandbags in a steady manner.

The Remington 597 tested belongs to the author's brother and has an inexpensive 4X BSA rimfire scope mounted. Because the rifle was already sighted in and was going to be used with that scope, it was tested that

Accuracy Results for the Remington 597 with BSA 4X Scope

AMMUNITION	GROUP SIZE, INCHES		
	Smallest	Largest	Average
CCI Standard Velocity	0.72	1.17	1.00
Federal Target (711B)	0.89	1.85	1.34
Remington/ Eley Target	0.44	1.14	0.81
Remington Golden H.P.	0.80	1.43	1.14
Winchester T-22	1.24	1.72	1.57
		OVERALL AV.	1.17

way. Therefore, the sighting error was slightly larger than in cases where a scope of higher magnification was used. In spite of that, the Remington 597 gave the excellent results shown by the data in the accompanying table.

As is true of all rimfire rifles, the Remington 597 shows preferences in ammunition. Impressive accuracy was obtained with the Remington/Eley Target with the average group size being only 0.81 inch with only a 4X scope used on the rifle. CCI Standard Velocity gave an average group size of only an inch. There is no question that the Model 597 is capable of better accuracy when fully broken in and with a scope of higher magnification attached. Under the conditions of the tests, the results are excellent with the composite group size being only 1.17 inches. Keep in mind that the Remington 597 sells for around $200 and the BSA scope used is available at one of the large "marts" for around $35 including a mount. This is an inexpensive combination that delivers performance that is entirely adequate for plinking or small game hunting. Although the range of aftermarket accessories available for the Remington 597 is not as extensive as that for the Ruger 10/22, it is a growing industry. The Remington 597 is, as it deserves to be, a very popular .22 autoloader.

HENRY LEVER ACTION

At the time when the author was growing up, it was an era in which western movies provided a significant form of wholesome entertainment. As a result, it would have been impossible to grow up not liking single action revolvers and lever action rifles. Although the author has had the former for many years, a lever action rimfire rifle eluded his clutches until comparatively recent times. Both Marlin and Winchester have produced lever action rifles in rimfire calibers for many years, but it is neither of these companies that produced the lever action rifle to be described here. No, it was the Henry Repeating Arms Company of Bayonne, NJ that produced that rifle. List price of the Henry is $360, but in one of the large "marts" it retails for around $300.

Henry lever action rifles had been admired over the years, but for some reason one had never been added to the collection. Traditional styling is evident in the Henry, but it is not just to be looked at–this rifle is for shooting. The Henry has a weight of 5.25 pounds and a steel barrel that measures 18.25 inches in length. The grooved receiver on the Henry is made of an alloy that is given a durable black finish. The Henry is fitted with a walnut stock and forearm that are made of very good wood on most of the specimens examined by the author. A tubular magazine that holds 15 rounds of .22 LR resides under the barrel. Sights on the Henry consist of a front sight that is a hooded post on a ramp and a square notch in a blade rear sight. The rear sight can be adjusted for elevation by sliding a stepped ramp under the blade. Windage is adjusted by drifting the sight laterally in the retaining notch. As is true of older lever actions, the Henry has a safety notch position for the hammer but no other safety.

To test the Henry, a Weaver 2.5-7X rimfire scope was mounted. This superb scope is compact and fits well on the little Henry. The results of the accuracy testing are shown in the accompanying table.

Although the Henry will not win any benchrest competition, the accuracy is actually quite good for this type of rifle. Many plinking rifles give 5-shot groups that measure around two inches and the Henry beats that with all of the types of ammunition tested. The accuracy with SK Jagd Standard Plus is nothing less than superb with the average group size being only 0.56 inch! With Winchester Power Points, the average group size is slightly over one inch. This suits the author fine because the Power Point is one of his favorite hunting loads, and with this ammunition

The Henry Lever Action performed very well in the tests and always fed and ejected reliably.

Accuracy Results for the Henry Lever Action with Weaver 2.5-7X Scope

AMMUNITION	GROUP SIZE, INCHES		
	Smallest	Largest	Average
CCI Standard Velocity	0.79	1.79	1.18
Federal HV H.P.	1.29	2.07	1.73
Federal Target (711B)	0.82	1.67	1.20
Remington Golden H.P.	1.38	1.78	1.56
SK Jagd Standard Plus	0.36	0.95	0.56
Winchester Power Point	0.83	1.36	1.09
Wolf Match Target	0.73	1.77	1.25
		OVERALL AV.	**1.34**

the Henry is certainly a 50-yard squirrel and pest rifle. Because of its beautiful styling and excellent handling qualities, my Henry is destined to be one of my two favorite rifles for woods roaming. It would be nice to set up shop and try to call in a predator while using the rifle that has my favorite action type.

Functioning of the Henry during the tests was impressive. There was positive and ejection of the empty case and a cartridge was fed from the magazine every time the lever was cycled. The Henry is a fine rifle, and one of the author's favorite rimfires.

RUGER 77/22

In 1983, Ruger responded to a demand for a high quality rimfire rifle with the introduction of the 77/22, a bolt action sporter in .22 LR caliber. This elegant rifle had a checkered walnut stock, a 20-inch barrel, and utilized a 10-round rotary magazine. As in the case of the Ruger 10/22 autoloader, the 77/22 bolt action is a little thick in the midsection because of the large rotary magazine, but in side view, this is one of the trimmest bolt action rifles around. At the time it was introduced, the Ruger 77/22 may well have been the most elegant rimfire sporter produced in the United States, and some would say that it still ranks high on the list.

The current Ruger catalog lists six variants of the 77/22. They consist of the combinations of blue metal with walnut stock, stainless steel with synthetic stock, and low glare stainless with laminated stock all without sights. Other models are available in .22 WMR, .17 HMR, and .17 WSM calibers (see Chapter 15).

The Ruger 77/22 tested has been a companion to the author since 1983, and it is configured as most rifles should be, complete with open sights. On the Ruger 77/22, the open sights consist of a bead on a post front sight and an excellent folding rear sight. My 77/22 was made many years ago when a walnut-stocked version could be obtained with sights.

A brief description of the mechanical features of the 77/22 will be provided. First, the action is robust, really robust. The bolt is of the two-piece type with the rear half rotating whereas the front section simply moves forward and backward in the receiver. Turning the rear section as the bolt handle is lowered into locked position causes two locking lugs to move into recesses in the receiver. The front section of the bolt has dual extractors. At the rear of the bolt on the right hand side is a rotating wing-type safety that can be placed in three positions. When the safety is in the rearmost position, both the trigger and bolt are locked. Moving the safety forward into the middle position keeps the trigger locked, but allows the bolt to be opened. In the forward position, the bolt can be opened and rifle can be fired.

One of the outstanding bolt action sporters is the Ruger 77/22 shown here with a Weaver K10 scope attached.

Until 2009, the barrel was attached to the receiver on the Ruger 77/22 in a manner similar to that used on the 10/22. A notch the bottom of the barrel has a mating block that is attached to the front of the receiver by means of two large Allen headed screws. Therefore, it is not difficult to remove and replace a barrel. However, when the factory barrel is replaced by an aftermarket barrel, it is necessary to make sure that the headspace is not excessive. Of course, the replacement barrel need not be chambered for the .22 LR, and barrel swapping to make the rifle a .17 Mach 2 was popular. As long as the headspace is satisfactory, there is no problem with a bolt action equivalent to that of excessive bolt speed that can occur when a barrel chambered for the .17 Mach 2 is installed on the 10/22 autoloader.

Beginning in 2009 (with serial number 703-58030), all variants of the Ruger 77/22, 77/17, and 77/22M have been manufactured with barrels that are threaded into the receiver. As a result, interchanging barrels (as described above) is no longer an option. However, some shooters report that accuracy produced by the current Model 77 rimfires having rigidly attached barrels is enhanced, especially with the magnum calibers.

The expected level of accuracy from a fine rimfire sporting rifle is always high so the tests with the Ruger 77/22 were undertaken with enthusiasm. In order to see the target clearly, an old 10 power Weaver K-10 AO scope was mounted on the rifle, and the author set forth to test the rifle with several types of ammunition. The results obtained are shown in the accompanying table.

The results of the tests with the Ruger 77/22 are among the most interesting obtained during this entire project, and several conclusions can be drawn. First, as with all other rimfire rifles used in these tests, the Ruger 77/22 did not like the Remington Target ammunition. This was the only type of ammunition that gave an average group size of over one inch. Second, the now discontinued Lapua Scoremax performed extremely well, giving an average group size of only 0.60 inch. That load utilizes a 48-grain bullet at a modest velocity of 1,040 ft/sec, and it is intended for hunting and silhouette applications. In this rifle, the Scoremax would be an excellent choice for accurately placed shots on predators that have been called in to moderate ranges. The author is happy that he acquired a generous supply of Scoremax when it was available.

However, outstanding accuracy was also exhibited by several other types of ammunition. One aspect of

Accuracy Results for the Ruger 77/22 with Weaver K-10 Scope

AMMUNITION	GROUP SIZE, INCHES		
	Smallest	Largest	Average
CCI Green Tag	0.65	0.85	0.72
CCI SGB	0.66	1.00	0.95
CCI Velocitor	0.71	0.99	0.84
Federal Target (711B)	0.55	1.03	0.80
Federal Ultra Match	0.53	0.99	0.77
Lapua Scoremax	0.46	0.82	0.60
Lapua Super Club	0.68	1.27	0.90
Remington Target	0.69	2.04	1.31
Winchester T-22	0.49	1.04	0.75
Winchester Supreme	0.56	1.01	0.86
		OVERALL AV.	**0.85**

accuracy found pleasing is that CCI Velocitors gave excellent accuracy with the average group size being only 0.84 inch. With the Velocitor giving a remaining energy of 110 ft lbs at 100 yards, the author is particularly interested in knowing that the accuracy is sufficient to take advantage of this powerful load. Finally, an aggregate group size of only 0.85 inch is outstanding. Having read everything published on the Remington 504 that was introduced with a lot of praise and then discontinued, it seems that the Ruger 77/22 will give at least equal accuracy.

If it were necessary to start deleting rimfire rifles from the safe, the Ruger 77/22 would probably be the last to go. It is supremely reliable, its accuracy is predictable, and its appearance is classic. It is an outstanding rimfire that is a superb choice for hunting and pest control. Yes, the author loves shooting this rifle having the obsolete Weaver K10 scope mounted with its fine crosshair reticule. When the crosshairs are placed where they should be and the trigger is squeezed while holding the rifle steady, one can be assured that the bullet will go where it should. What more can one ask from a rifle?

The CZ 452 is characterized by elegance and accuracy.

CZ 452 AMERICAN (22 LR)

Czeska Zbrojovka, abbreviated as CZ, produces a variety of firearms in their plant that they proclaim to be the largest small arms factory in the world. Among the rimfire rifles produced by this manufacturer is the outstanding Model 452 American, a classic bolt action sporting rifle that is available in .22 LR, .17 HMR, and .22 WMR calibers. This rifle has a well-shaped, checkered walnut stock and highly polished and blued metal parts, but is sold without sights. The receiver is grooved for attaching scope mounts. As this is written in early 2016 the CZ 452 is in the process of being replaced by the Model 455, but some versions are still offered so both the 452 and 455 will be described.

The same bolt action is used as the starting point for several other rifles that include the heavy barreled CZ 452 Varmint, a Mannlicher stocked CZ 452 FS, the longer barreled European-style stocked CZ 452 Lux, and the CZ 452 Silhouette, which has a synthetic stock. There are also other versions that are known as the Training Rifle and the Scout, which is a smaller scale youth rifle. The CZ 452 is available in a configuration for almost any taste in a bolt action rimfire rifle. The finish on the metal parts of most of the CZ rifles that the author has examined is quite good. Bolts are very well machined and highly polished. The trigger guard and floor plate assembly is highly polished, and the magazine fits almost flush with the bottom of the stock on rifles in .22 LR caliber. Because of the larger cartridges in .22 WMR and .17 HMR calibers, the magazines of rifles in these calibers protrude from the bottom of the rifle by almost an inch. Magazine capacity is five rounds in all three calibers.

Accuracy of the CZ 452 rifles in enhanced by the fact that the barrel is threaded into the forged steel receiver. Barrels are hammer forged and are lapped. Although some rimfire rifles may feel somewhat cheap and flimsy, the CZ 452 is anything but that. These sturdy, robust rifles are constructed of high quality

The CZ 452 American has a two-position wing type safety.

materials in the traditional way. The safety on the CZ 452 is of the wing type, and it is located at the rear of the bolt. Unlike the Ruger 77 series, the CZ has a two position safety that blocks the firing pin not just the trigger. The trigger is adjustable for weight of pull. Operation of the CZ 452 is positive and precise. MSRP prices for the CZ 452 vary slightly with caliber and features, but are generally in the $450-500 range.

Having examined the rifle in detail, it was with considerable anticipation that accuracy testing was begun. The results obtained are summarized in the accompanying table. Although a scope of high magnification was used, it has a rather thick crosshair reticule so the high magnification is not as much of an advantage as it might be.

During the testing of the CZ 452, the farther we progressed into accuracy testing the more interesting the results became. The CZ tested belongs to the author's wife, and she did all of the firing. Testing is fun, and as a result a total of 21 different types of .22 LR ammunition were tested because she was enjoying her new rifle so much. She also liked getting smaller groups than I was getting with most of my rifles!

The data show that the CZ 452 produces superb accuracy with most types of ammunition. Four types of target ammunition produced groups that averaged less than 0.60 inch. So many groups were measured that were simply ragged holes that it was almost monotonous. Such outstanding accuracy was not limited to target ammunition. Remington Game Loads produced an average group size of only 0.66 inch and Winchester Power Points gave an average of only 0.83 inch. The aggregate average group size of 0.80 inch was as good as that produced by any other stock .22 LR tested in the study. However, it must be kept in mind that the Ruger 77/22 was tested with a 10X scope whereas the CZ 452 had a 24X scope in place. Now, just wait until we get identical scopes on both rifles!

Although lacking the aftermarket modifications possible with the older Ruger 77/22, the CZ 452 is fully its equal in accuracy. There may be no more capable sporting rifle available in its price range. You can spend a lot more money before you gain much in accuracy.

Accuracy Results for the CZ 452 American .22 LR with Tasco Mag IV 6-24X Scope

AMMUNITION	GROUP SIZE, INCHES		
	Smallest	Largest	Average
CCI Green Tag	0.60	1.15	0.79
CCI Mini Mag	0.61	0.99	0.91
CCI SGB	0.80	1.09	0.95
CCI Standard Velocity	0.55	1.53	0.94
CCI Velocitor	0.86	1.43	1.13
Eley Target	0.32	0.61	0.51
Federal High Velocity H.P.	0.56	1.12	0.81
Federal Target (711B)	0.90	1.26	1.07
Federal Ultra Match	0.39	0.67	0.54
Lapua Super Club	0.41	0.62	0.57
PMC Match Rifle	0.64	1.14	0.76
PMC Scoremaster	0.77	1.29	0.97
Remington Golden H.P.	0.55	1.02	0.83
Remington Game Load	0.46	0.84	0.66
Remington Target	0.77	1.40	1.08
RWS Rifle Match	0.31	0.94	0.69
Winchester Power Point	0.68	0.94	0.83
Winchester Super-X H.P.	0.62	1.05	0.82
Winchester Supreme	0.51	0.96	0.67
Winchester T-22	0.44	1.00	0.67
Wolf Match Target	0.32	0.68	0.55
		OVERALL AV.	**0.80**

A barrel on the CZ 455 is held in place by two large set screws that push the barrel into the receiver.

CZ 455

The idea of converting a rifle to fire cartridges of different calibers is by no means new. This is possible with some of the modern sporting rifles (referred to as assault rifles in some circles). Rimfire shooters have such an option with the CZ 455. Now, in one stylish bolt action sporting rifle, it is possible to fire .22 LR, .22 WMR, or .17 HMR by making a few simple changes. Although some of the barrels for the CZ 455 do not have sights, those having sights are available.

Two methods for attaching rifle barrels to receivers are either threading them together or press fitting the barrel in the receiver and securing it in place with a transverse pin. Switching barrels is not convenient with either of these techniques. The method utilized by Ruger in the 10/22, which was described earlier in this chapter, involves a block fitting in a notch on the bottom of the barrel that pulls the barrel into the action. CZ has taken a different approach that involves a barrel tenon that has two flat surfaces that are placed at an angle to the axis of the bore. The receiver has two threaded holes that accept set screws with Allen heads. When the barrel is inserted in the action and the set screws are inserted and tightened, the screws impinge on the flat surfaces on the barrel tenon pulling the barrel rigidly into the action.

Changing barrels on the CZ455 is as simple as removing the barreled action from the stock and removing the barrel by loosening the two set screws. A barrel of a different caliber is inserted in the action

As a replacement for the CZ 452, the 455 enables shooters to switch barrels to change calibers.

Accuracy Results Obtained With The CZ 455 and BSA 4-12 X 44 AO Scope

AMMUNITION	GROUP SIZE, INCHES		
	Smallest	Largest	Average
SK Jadg Standard Plus	0.51	0.75	0.67
CCI Mini Mag solid	0.73	1.20	0.98
CCI Standard Velocity solid	1.11	1.43	1.28
Federal HVHP	0.75	1.30	1.01
Remington Club Xtra	0.64	1.08	0.79
Remington Game Load HP	0.50	1.06	0.75
OVERALL AV.			**0.91**

and the screws tightened. Both .22 WMR and .17 HMR cartridges utilize the same magazine. However, when the shorter .22 LR ammunition is used, the magazine is too long, but there is no convenient way to alter the magazine well. The CZ solution to this problem is to use a magazine of appropriate length for .22 LR cartridges that has a spacer that butts against the rear edge of the magazine and is held there by a transverse pin. By that means, the magazine well has no gap and the magazine holding .22 LR ammunition fits neatly in the rifle.

By any standard, the CZ 455 is an elegant rifle made of blued steel and fine wood. The receiver of the 455 has grooves along the top for attaching scope mounts but they have a width of 11 mm (0.433 inch) rather than the standard 3/8-inch (0.375 inch, 9.53 mm) on most rimfire rifles produced in the U.S. Moreover, the bolt handle is shaped so that it will not clear the eyepiece bell of a scope that is mounted low. A set of sturdy steel rings is furnished with the 455 and they have sufficient height to give scope clearance in almost any situation.

Operation of the CZ 455 is essentially identical to that of the 452. Consequently, we will progress directly to the results obtained testing this rifle, which are shown in the accompanying table. Testing was carried out with a BSA 4-12 X 44 AO scope attached.

The data shown in the table indicate that the CZ 455 with the .22 LR barrel attached is capable of giving excellent accuracy, but it would be prudent to test several kinds of ammunition. Most types of ammunition gave average group sizes smaller than one inch. However, the Federal HVHP is a high-velocity hunting load that does not always give stellar accuracy so the results were not unexpected. The one anomaly is CCI Standard Velocity, which normally gives target type accuracy in most good rifles. No explanation for this can be offered. For maximum versatility, it would be difficult to beat a CZ 455 with barrels in .22 LR and one of the magnum calibers.

Many other rimfire rifles are available, but it was not possible to test all of them. The results shown

Magazines of different sizes can be utilized with the CZ 455 so that both .22 LR and magnum cartridges can be used when the appropriate barrel is installed.

should give a good indication of what to expect with similar rifles. The tests include several models of different types in order to show how they perform. It should also be mentioned that the tests provide a great deal of information on how different types of .22 LR ammunition perform. Performance does not always correlate with cost so even inexpensive rimfire rifles are adequate for a wide range of shooting activities.

CHAPTER 15

REVIEW OF SOME CURRENT MAGNUM RIMFIRES

IN CHAPTER 14, the characteristics of several current models of popular .22 LR rimfire rifles were described. Given the current status of magnum rimfire calibers, it is appropriate to devote a chapter to a similar discussion of popular rifles in those calibers. As in the case of the .22 LR rifles, it has not been possible to evaluate the performance of every model offered so once again the discussion will focus on representative versions of the models. Testing consisted of firing five five-shot groups at 50 yards from a bench.

RUGER 77/22M

The outstanding Ruger 77/22 had been in production for several years when Ruger introduced the version chambered for the .22 WMR, the Model 77/22M. This rifle became popular with varmint hunters who wanted more range and a more potent tool than afforded by any .22 LR. Currently, there are four versions of the 77/22M that include blued metal and walnut stock, stainless steel and synthetic stock and a low glare stainless steel and laminated stock. Mechanical features and operation of the rifles are identical to those described in detail for the 77/22 that was discussed in Chapter 14 so that information will not be repeated here. However, information from Ruger indicates that the V-block barrel attachment system has been replaced. That system was utilized until Nov. 13, 2009, but barrels of 77/22 rifles are now threaded into the receiver. One slight difference between the magnum rifles and those in .22 LR is that the rotary magazine holds nine rounds of .22 WMR whereas that for the .22 LR rifles holds 10 rounds.

The author's 77/22M was tested with a scope that is a true classic. It is one of the old steel-tube Weaver scopes made in El Paso, TX. This scope, known as the Model V-12, is a 3-12X variable that has the AO feature. If

Magnum rimfires are (left to right) the .17 HMR, .17 WSM, 5mm Remington, and .22 WMR.

Ruger's 77/22M is an outstanding rifle chambered for the .22 WMR cartridge. The author's rifle wears an old Weaver V-12 scope.

memory serves correctly, the scope was purchased many years ago for $40 in a gun shop in Bismarck, ND. Because the rifle/scope combination has been used for several years, it was with some degree of anticipation that accuracy testing of the Ruger 77/22M was undertaken that led to the data shown in the accompanying table.

The data shown in the table indicate that with several types of ammunition the Ruger 77/22M produces groups of about three-quarters of an inch or less. The smallest groups using .22 WMR ammunition were those given by CCI Maxi Mags with 40-grain hollow point bullets with the average group size being 0.65 inch. In this rifle, the Winchester Supreme usually gave four shots almost in one hole, but the groups always seemed to have one flyer. Both of the identical Federal and CCI TNT loads gave very good accuracy with groups in the 0.72-0.77 inch range. Because of the wide variety of loads that includes both .22 WMR and .22 WRF, a composite group size is virtually meaningless so it is not included.

If you have read Chapter 9 dealing with external ballistics, it should have become apparent as to why the Federal 50-grain load is quite suitable for use on larger varmints when the range is 100 yards or less. It

Accuracy Results for the Ruger 77/22M with Weaver V-12 Scope

AMMUNITION	GROUP SIZE, INCHES		
	Smallest	Largest	Average
CCI Maxi Mag G.D. (50 gr)	0.71	1.40	1.08
CCI Maxi Mag H.P.	0.57	0.72	0.65
CCI TNT	0.63	1.01	0.77
CCI .22 WRF	0.37	0.78	0.63
Federal JHP (50 gr)	0.70	1.31	0.99
Federal TNT (30 gr.)	0.48	1.03	0.72
PMC Predator PSP	1.26	2.75	1.41
Remington Premier (V-Max)	0.62	0.81	0.73
Winchester Dynapoint	0.72	1.55	1.07
Winchester Super-X H.P.	0.57	0.89	0.78
Winchester Supreme	0.88	1.53	1.21

has excellent retained energy because the heavy bullet has a higher ballistic coefficient. The CCI 50-grain Gold Dot load that was available in the past has long since been discontinued, but it did not give highest accuracy in the rifle used in the tests. There have been reports that bullets as heavy as 50 grains are not stabilized by a 1:16 twist because of the lower velocity to which they can be driven. That seems strange in view of the fact that the velocity is even lower when this ammunition is fired from a handgun. No evidence of a lack of stability was seen, but the fact remains that neither of the 50-grain loads produces best accuracy in the Ruger 77/22M tested.

Perhaps the biggest surprise was how well the CCI ammunition in .22 WRF caliber performed in the 77/22M. Logic would dictate that this shorter cartridge might be less accurate because the bullet has to "jump" to engage the rifling just as when a .22 Short is fired in a .22 LR chamber. If you check the data, you will find that the .22 WRF load is just as accurate as anything else in the 77/22M tested! However, the point of impact was almost six inches below where the 40-grain .22 WMR bullets hit, so do not go hunting using .22 WRF ammunition without sighting in first. Also, the 50-grain bullets hit the target about three inches below where the 40-grain bullets hit.

One load that should be immensely popular in the .22 WMR is the Remington Premier that utilizes a 33-grain Hornady V-Max polymer-tipped bullet. Although the advertised velocity for this load is 2,000 ft/sec, my chronograph indicated that the actual velocity is slightly higher. The bullet has a ballistic coefficient of 0.137, which is higher than the value of 0.125 for the highly-praised 17-grain V-Max bullet used in the .17 HMR. Calculations show that the Remington Premier load shoots flat and retains its velocity and energy much better than the 30-grain hollow points used in some .22 WMR ammunition. Although the muzzle velocity is lower, the 33-grain V-Max bullet from a .22 WMR has considerably more energy than any .17 HMR load at all ranges (about 25% more at 150 yards). However, the Remington Premier sells for about $20 per box (which is even higher than the price of the "premium" .17 HMR ammunition).

For most of my shooting with the .22 WMR, the 40-grain hollow points of the CCI Maxi Mag or Winchester Super-X type are used. They give good accuracy, and the bullets have reasonably high ballistic coefficients.

If you have read articles that deal with the .17 HMR, you have probably seen a lot of hype about

Ruger's magnum rimfires utilize a rotary magazine that holds nine rounds.

The Majestic Arms AlumaLite barrel consists of a Lothar Walther barrel surrounded by an aluminum sleeve to give a diameter of 0.920 inch.

how much more accurate the .17 HMR is than the .22 WMR. Although the results of testing .17 HMR rifles will follow this discussion, it is appropriate to make some observations here in relation to the .22 WMR. Some people who write articles about the .17 HMR seem to have forgotten that all currently available .17 HMR ammunition is manufactured to the same specifications, and that it is all "premium" ammunition that makes use of premium bullets. The price of the .17 HMR ammunition reflects that situation. Of course, it should be more uniform than most .22 WMR ammunition, which is made by numerous companies using components that in many instances are by no means "premium." It may also be that manufacturing tolerances are held slightly closer in the case of .17 HMR firearms. Please do not misunderstand. My Ruger 77/17 is slightly more accurate than my 77/22M, but it is a comparison of apples with oranges with the obvious differences that exist in ammunition.

A Ruger 77/22M has been one of the author's favorite rifles for many years. Therefore, it was manufactured before Ruger began to thread barrels into the receivers of these models. With a desire to carry out additional experiments with the 77/22M, the author installed a Majestic Arms AlumaLite barrel. That barrel measures 18 inches in length and has a diameter of 0.920 inch throughout its entire length. A beautiful walnut stock was obtained that had been modified to accept a barrel of this diameter. With the rifle assembled, three five-shot groups were fired with several types of ammunition. The following average group sizes (in inches) were obtained: CCI Maxi Mag, 0.57; CCI V-Max (30 gr), 0.53; Federal Classic 50 gr, 0.43; Remington JHP, 0.69; Remington Premier, 0.49; Winchester Super-X, 0.70; and Winchester Varmint HV (30 gr), 0.45. Although the

These excellent groups were obtained at 50 yards using the Ruger 77/22M with a Majestic Arms barrel.

77/22M with the factory barrel gave good accuracy, adding the Majestic Arms barrel resulted in a clear and significant improvement in accuracy. Even the 50-grain Federal load performed in a superb manner. The Majestic Arms barrel is now permanently installed on the Ruger 77/22M, and the author feels no need for a more accurate .22 WMR rifle.

In an extensive comparison test published several years ago by a careful experimenter using identical .17 HMR and .22 WMR rifles made by Cooper, it was reported that there was almost no difference in accuracy. The author does not believe that there is a great deal of difference in inherent accuracy of the two cartridges, but there may be a difference in quality of ammunition in several instances. With its heavier bullets of larger diameter, the .22 WMR is a better choice when dealing with larger varmints. With its small bullets at higher velocity, the .17 HMR is a better choice for small varmints at extended ranges. If you have a Ruger 77 made before 2009 in one of the calibers, you can add an aftermarket barrel and change to the other because the actions and magazines are identical. Because current Ruger 77 rimfires have barrels threaded into the receivers, it impossible for most shooters to interchange barrels.

The Savage 93 G has classic style, but it is relatively inexpensive.

SAVAGE 93 G

Savage bolt action rifles in .22 WMR caliber carry the model number 93, but variants are numerous. Similar rifles in .17 HMR caliber are designated as the 93R17 or simply the 17 Series. There are no less than 11 versions of the .22 WMR rifles. In both series, different versions are indicated by letters after the model numbers. For example, the 93 FSS is a .22 WMR that has a polymer stock and a stainless steel barrel and action. The 93 BTVSS has a heavy stainless steel barrel and action and a laminated thumbhole target stock.

The Savage Model 93R17 BSEV is a .17 HMR that has a heavy stainless steel barrel with spiral flutes and a laminated stock that contains a large cutout and a "barracuda" style fore arm. Of more conventional style is the 93R17 GV that has a checkered hardwood stock and a heavy barrel (perhaps a "varmint" weight would be an appropriate name for it). Within the 93 Magnum and 93R17 Series approximately 20 variants are listed so a shooter should be able to find a rifle with the desired appearance.

All of the bolt action Savage rifles in .17 HMR and .22 WMR calibers share most features in common, especially with regard to operation. They feature a box type magazine that holds five rounds, a thumb operated safety on the right hand side of the receiver,

The Savage 93 G incorporates the AccuTrigger® assembly.

Two scope bases are utilized when mounting a scope on the Savage 93 G.

Checkering on the grip and forearm add a nice touch on the Savage 93 G.

A box magazine is employed on the Savage 93 G, but the release protrudes slightly too far from the bottom of the rifle.

Magazine capacity of the Savage 93 G is five rounds.

The thumb-operated safety is located on the right hand side of the receiver.

and the famous Savage AccuTrigger®. Receivers are drilled and tapped to accommodate two Weaver No. 16 scope bases that permit the attachment of Weaver-type rings. Two models, the 93 G and 93 GL, are also provided with open sights. For the author, that made the choice of the Savage magnum rifle to order a simple matter. The author's rifle had to be one with wood stock and sights so the 93 G was chosen, and the order was placed with a local dealer. The discussion of the operation of that rifle can serve as an overview of all of the .22 WMR and .17 HMR models.

The Savage 93 G has a nicely shaped hardwood stock that has simple but attractive checkering on the grip and forearm. The stock has a raised comb that makes it convenient to shoot the rifle with either iron sights or a scope. Metal parts have a uniform black matte finish, and the rifle is very traditional in appearance. If there is any unsightly attribute of the 93 G it is that the magazine release and magazine protrude from the bottom of the stock. Other shooters

have different preferences, but the author has always preferred the "clean" look with no projections from the bottom of a rifle.

The detachable box-type magazine holds five rounds in either .22 WMR or .17 HMR caliber rifles and the same magazine is utilized in both. All versions of the 93 and 93R17 rifles function in a similar manner. Although the author purchased the 93 G for testing, it is to be expected that other versions of the 93 and 93R17 rifles might perform somewhat differently, especially heavy barreled models. Also, one can never be sure that a different specimen of the same rifle might show better or worse performance. As this is written, testing of the 93 G to date has shown that it is a reliable rifle that performs well.

The MSRP of Savage Model 93 rifles varies rather widely depending on the features chosen, but the 93 G lists for $285. It can often be found for a somewhat lower price, which makes it an excellent entry-level rifle for hunting small game and pests.

RUGER 77/17

If there is one cartridge that took the rimfire shooting world by storm when it was introduced, it is the .17 HMR. The bottlenecked cartridge utilizes a .22 WMR case necked down to hold a .17-caliber bullet. Initial loads featured a 17-grain Hornady V-Max bullet, and with the polymer tip it is a very attractive cartridge. With a generous charge of slow burning powder (for a rimfire), a muzzle velocity of 2,550 ft/sec could be reached. There are several loads in .17 HMR currently available, and extensive testing has been conducted with six of them that utilize both 17- and 20-grain bullets.

Ruger has produced rifles in .17 HMR caliber since its introduction. One reason is that Ruger already produced rifles in .22 WMR so all it took was a .17-caliber barrel. As a result, Ruger offers the bolt action Model 77/17, and previously offered the lever action Model 96/17, which are the "tiny" bore companions to the "small" bore .22 WMR rifles. The 77/17 tested has a synthetic stock with blued barrel and action. Because the action and mechanical features of the 77/17 are identical to those of the 77/22 and 77/22M, we will progress directly to the test results, which are shown in the accompanying table. The rifle was equipped with a 4-16X Weaver Classic V-16 scope with AO and a

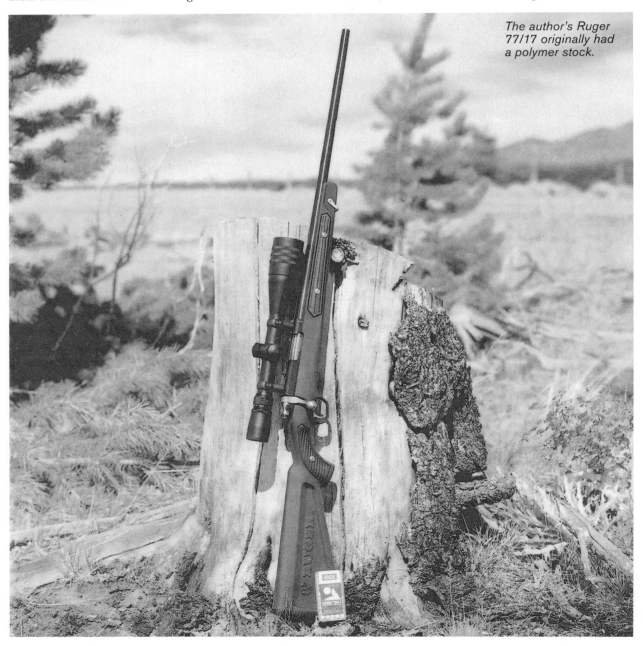

The author's Ruger 77/17 originally had a polymer stock.

Reliable feeding has always been a hallmark of the Ruger magazine.

Accuracy Results for the Ruger 77/17 with Weaver V-16 Classic Scope

AMMUNITION	GROUP SIZE, INCHES		
	Smallest	Largest	Average
CCI Game Point (20 gr.)	0.65	0.85	0.72
CCI TNT	0.38	0.90	0.67
Federal V-Shok	0.33	0.75	0.57
Hornady V-Max	0.49	0.63	0.53
Hornady XTP (20 gr.)	0.42	1.01	0.75
Remington Premier	0.50	0.84	0.63
OVERALL AV.			**0.65**

fine crosshair reticule. This is not a book about scopes, but this one is superb!

Before discussing the results obtained in the accuracy tests, it should be mentioned that this particular rifle was very sensitive to the tension on the two screws that hold the barreled action to the stock. Initially, it was found that some groups tended to be strung out vertically with one or more flyers increasing the size of the groups to 0.7-0.8 inch. Tweaking the tension on the screws reduced this tendency somewhat so that smaller groups were generally obtained. Whether or not this tendency is present in Ruger 77/17 rifles having walnut stocks is unknown.

Several conclusions can be drawn from the data shown in the table. First, there is no great difference in accuracy shown by the different types of ammunition. What a surprise considering that all of the types are loaded to the same specifications! Although the author has seen results reported that show phenomenal groups attributed to .17 HMR rifles, and some such groups were obtained, it seems that an aggregate group size of a little over one-half inch at 50 yards is not too bad considering that all firing was conducted outdoors with a substantial breeze during some shooting sessions. Second, as expected, there was no measurable difference in point of impact regardless of which type of ammunition was being used. There is a difference of only 3 grains in bullet weight, the muzzle velocities differ by only 200 ft/sec, and the bullets all have almost identical ballistic coefficients. This rifle has the accuracy to be a 150-yard pest rifle and the high velocity necessary to give a sufficiently flat trajectory to that distance.

Being of an experimental frame of mind, the author simply had to switch barrels on the 77/17. The aftermarket barrel chosen is a 22-inch tapered octagonal barrel from Green Mountain Rifle Barrel Company. Because rifles of the classic style have always been favored by the author, it seemed appropriate to replace the synthetic factory stock, but a walnut stock was needed to substitute for it. After consulting with almost everyone who sells aftermarket stocks, it was found that most sell aftermarket stocks for almost everything except the Ruger bolt action rimfires or else such stocks are very expensive. Where was one to be found but on eBay. Someone had taken the checkered walnut stock off a 77/22M (probably to replace it with something ugly), and it was purchased. However, the polymer stock has the trigger guard as an integral part in the molding so it was necessary to buy a trigger guard assembly.

With my special 77/17 complete, the accuracy was tested with CCI 20-grain Game Point and 17-grain Federal V-Shok ammunition. The average group sizes were 0.54 and 0.48 inch, respectively. Groups were tight clusters because the tendency to experience flyers was eliminated. Although the accuracy obtained was slightly better with the Green Mountain barrel, the improvement is slight. Was the new barrel worth it? From the point of view of cost, probably not, but as mentioned earlier the author is an experimentalist. If you have a 77/17 that does not group the way you think it should, try changing the tension on the stock screws before you give up.

The Ruger 77/17 is a trim, attractive, sturdy rifle. It has become a frequent companion when searching for pests to eliminate, but it will never accompany the author when hunting small game. The bullets are simply too destructive. Do I like the .17 HMR? Absolutely, but it should be used where its tiny bullets at high velocity are most appropriate, on small varmints.

This CZ 452 in .17 HMR caliber is superbly accurate.

CZ 452 AMERICAN (17 HMR)

As part of its rimfire product line, CZ produces several rifles chambered for the .17 HMR. In general, the variations described in the section in Chapter 14 dealing with the CZ 452 in .22 LR caliber are also available in .17 HMR. As with the .22 LR version, the .17 HMR has the barrel threaded into the action, has a beautiful checkered walnut stock, and excellent polishing and bluing of metal parts. It is truly a beautiful sporter, but one could wish that the magazine did not protrude quite so far from the bottom of the stock. Having discussed the operation of the .22 LR version of this rifle in Chapter 14, we will proceed directly to the results obtained during accuracy testing.

As in the case of the results from the Ruger 77/17, all types of ammunition gave overall group sizes that differ very little, which is expected because they are all so similar. Any variance is likely due to small differences that result from different manufacturing lots. The aggregate average group size of only 0.59 inch at 50 yards represents a high degree of accuracy by this fine rifle. It is likely that someone will want to compare the results from the Ruger with those from the CZ, but the aggregate average from the CZ being 0.06 inch smaller than that obtained with the Ruger 77/17 is totally insignificant. One flyer expanding a group by about 0.2 inch could account for this difference. For all practical purposes, the Ruger 77/17 and CZ 452 give equal accuracy. The CZ sells for slightly less, but the Ruger comes with a set of rings for scope mounting. A choice between the two rifles might come down to what you want to do with it after you have used it for some time. If you want to tinker with it, the older Ruger 77/17 is more versatile because older versions made it possible to interchange barrels, but this is not a factor for recently produced rifles. The CZ is a fine rifle that is usually found at retail for around $500. There are less expensive .17 HMR caliber rifles available and they may match the accuracy of the CZ. However, probably no other rifle in its price range can match both the accuracy and looks of the CZ 452 American.

Accuracy Results for the CZ 452 American with Redfield 3-12X Scope

AMMUNITION	GROUP SIZE, INCHES		
	Smallest	Largest	Average
CCI Game Point (20 gr.)	0.23	0.84	0.61
CCI TNT	0.54	0.72	0.62
Federal V-Shok	0.35	0.56	0.48
Hornady V-Max	0.39	0.66	0.56
Hornady XTP (20 gr.)	0.27	0.78	0.61
Remington Premier	0.54	0.72	0.68
		OVERALL AV.	**0.59**

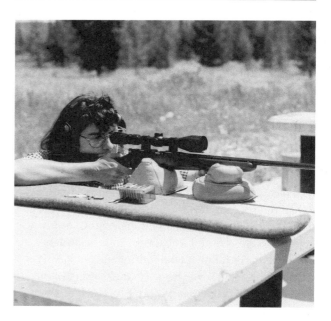

Firing from a bench, the author's wife, Kathy, routinely got groups of one-half inch or less at 50 yards.

For hunting pests or small game, the CZ 455 is an excellent choice and by changing barrels it can be used in many ways.

CZ 455 (17 HMR AND .22 WMR)

The CZ 455 is a popular rifle that can be configured to fire .22 LR, .22 WMR, or .17 HMR ammunition. The details of construction and operation of the CZ 455 were presented in Chapter 14 and need not be repeated here. Consequently, we will progress directly to showing the results obtained during testing the CZ 455 in the magnum calibers. The rifle was tested with a BSA 4-12 X 40 AO scope attached and gave the results shown in the accompanying table.

The results obtained with the .17 HMR barrel on the CZ 455 were uniformly good in keeping with the production of .17 HMR ammunition (see Chapter 7). With the four types of ammunition tested the average group size was well under an inch.

The results with .22 WMR ammunition are worthy of additional comment. First, four types of ammunition gave an average group size of only 0.80 inch, which is perfectly adequate. The two loads that did not perform well were the Federal 50-grain hollow point and the 30-grain CCI TNT Green loads. In the first case, a 50-grain bullet at a muzzle velocity of approximately 1,500 ft/sec may not be stabilized in a 16-inch twist to an optimum degree. As a result, the Federal load has not given the highest accuracy in any of the .22 WMR rifles tested by the author. Second, the very light "green" bullets have proven to be "temperamental" in other rifles tested by the author. If a varmint hunter chooses .22 WMR loads appropriately, the CZ 455 will perform up to expectations.

Accuracy Results Obtained With The CZ 455 and BSA 4-12 X 44 AO Scope

	AMMUNITION	GROUP SIZE, INCHES		
		Smallest	Largest	Average
17 HMR	Federal 17 gr V-Max	0.46	0.61	0.53
	CCI 17 gr TNT	0.37	0.84	0.55
	CCI 20 gr FMJ	0.52	0.85	0.63
	Hornady 20 gr XTP	0.41	0.80	0.68
22 HMR	Fiocchi 40 gr JHP	0.90	0.93	0.92
	Federal 50 gr HP	0.87	1.41	1.14
	CCI Maxi Mag HP	0.48	0.90	0.63
	CCI TNT Green	0.88	1.17	1.04
	Hornady 30 gr V-Max	0.66	0.98	0.77
	Winchester 40 gr JHP	0.80	1.02	0.90

The CZ 455 rifles are classic rimfire sporters. (photo courtesy CZ USA)

When fired from a bench, the stock of the Ruger American fit well.

RUGER AMERICAN

In Chapter 14, the features and operation of the Ruger American in .22 LR were described. It is not necessary to repeat that information here, but it should be mentioned that the specimen bought by the author is beautifully finished. Metal surfaces are highly polished and have a deep blue finish. The rifle is as attractive as many that are far more costly.

For testing, a 2-7X Leupold VX-II was attached. The rifle was tested by firing five-shot groups at 50 yards. An average group size of 0.76 inch, which is typical of many relatively inexpensive .22 WMR rifles, was obtained. With the 50-grain Federal load, an average group size of 1.13 inches resulted, but this load has not shown exceptional accuracy in other .22 WMR rifles. A new load from Hornady is in the Critical Defense line and it utilizes a 45-grain bullet that is advertised to give 1,700 ft/sec from a rifle. However, the chronograph indicated 1,800 ft/sec at 10 feet from the muzzle. The average size of the groups with that load was 0.72 inch. The Critical Defense load was developed for use in short barreled revolvers as a defense load, but with its accuracy and

Although it has a polymer stock, the Ruger American has classic lines.

power it should be an outstanding varmint load.

The Ruger American in .22 WMR is a sturdy, accurate rifle that would be an excellent choice for an entry-level varmint rifle. Although not tested, the American is also available in .17 HMR caliber. Given the MSRP of $979 for the superb Ruger 77/22 series, the American is indeed an attractive option that gives up very little in performance to the more expensive model.

For autoloader fans, the Savage A17 or A22 (in .22 WMR) should be perfect. (photo courtesy Savage Arms)

SAVAGE A17

Although the .17 HMR is based on a .22 WMR case necked to hold bullets having 0.172-inch diameter, the two cartridges are quite different. As powder burns in a cartridge case, pressure is generated that pushes the bullet down the bore. In a semiautomatic rifle, the pressure drives the bolt to the rear to cycle the action. It sounds simple, but there are some critical factors involved.

To prevent damage to the action, the velocity with which the bolt is driven to the rear must not be excessive. If the bolt velocity exceeds some threshold value there will be damage to the action. The velocity of the bolt depends on several factors including its mass, the maximum pressure, and how the pressure varies with time (known as the pressure curve). If the pressure remains high for a longer period of time, the total force on the bolt will be greater and pressure will act on the bolt for a longer period of time. In other words, the pressure-time relationship becomes important. With smaller diameter of the case neck comes the result that gas escapes more slowly and the pressure inside the case remains high for a longer period. Therefore, a semiautomatic action that operates by a simple blowback principle may operate satisfactorily for a .22 WMR, but not with the .17 HMR.

When the .17 HMR was quite new, some companies were quick to release or at least advertise semiautomatic rifles in .17 HMR that were based on unaltered .22 WMR actions. Some of them were never produced, but others, such as the Remington 597, were sold and then recalled. In other cases, rifles utilized heavier bolts, stronger recoil springs, or heavier bolt handles to control bolt velocity during firing.

In 2015, Savage Arms introduced a new rifle known as the A17 chambered for the .17 HMR round. It utilizes a bolt that incorporates a delayed opening feature that allows the bolt to remain locked for a short time until the pressure drops. As a result, the action can handle the .17 HMR cartridge without damage to the action. The bolt is made of hardened chromed steel, but the action is also quite different from those of other rimfires. It utilizes a lug that fits

CCI introduced the A17 load in .17 HMR specifically for use in the Savage A17, but it can also be used in bolt action rifles.

laterally across the top of the bolt. When the bolt is fully forward, the lug engages a recess in the top of the receiver. Surfaces on the top of the lug and the recess in the receiver are cut at an angle, which allows the lug to be withdrawn from the recess easily. This happens as a result of the rearward motion of the carrier. Thus, the breech is essentially locked at the time of firing, but only for a very short time. Before the bolt moves significantly, the pressure is reduced to a safe level.

The Savage A17 measures 42 inches in length and has a 22-inch barrel, but the rifle weighs only about 5.5 pounds. The action features dual controlled feed of cartridges and the bolt is case hardened. A rotary magazine is utilized in the Savage A17 and the barrel has a 1-in-9-inch twist. In early 2016, Savage announced that the same rifle was being introduced in .22 WMR as the A22.

To accompany the Savage A17, a new .17 HMR load appropriately called the A-17 was introduced by CCI. It features a 17-grain polymer tipped bullet that has an advertised muzzle velocity of 2,650 ft/sec, which is 100 ft/sec faster than other loads with 17-grain bullets. CCI states that this new load can also be used in bolt action rifles. Also, other types of .17 HMR ammunition can be fired in the Savage A17. No opportunity to test the A17 was available as of this writing, but working with this handsome rifle is on the agenda.

Savage was first in producing rifles in .17 WSM and this model with a heavy stainless steel barrel is an excellent varmint rifle.

SAVAGE 17 B.MAG

With the introduction of the .17 Winchester Super Magnum (WSM) cartridge, Savage introduced the first firearm to fire that round. Known as the Savage B.Mag, it is essentially a new rifle. Often, a firearm manufacturer will take an existing model, make a few minor changes, add a digit or letter to the name and introduce a "new" model. That is not the case with the Savage B.Mag.

The .17 WSM is a potent rimfire cartridge that pushes a 20-grain bullet at 3,000 ft/sec or a 25-grain bullet at 2,600 ft/sec. With its dual locking lug bolt action, the Ruger 77 series is a natural for chambering to the .17 WSM. That rifle comes in versions that are chambered for centerfire calibers such as the .22 Hornet, .357 Magnum, and .44 Magnum. Of course the rotary magazine would have to be modified, but the action is certainly strong enough for the .17 WSM. In 2015, Ruger announced just such a rifle, but the Savage B.Mag was the first .17 WSM to be produced.

A great many rimfire rifles chambered for .22 LR, .22 WMR, and .17 HMR use no other locking feature

Dual locking lugs are utilized on the Savage B.Mag to provide the strength needed to handle the powerful .17 WSM cartridge.

The bolt release protrudes from the left hand side of the receiver.

It is obvious why this is referred to as the heavy barrel version of the Savage B.Mag.

Trigger pull on the Savage B.Mag is adjusted by means of a rotating wheel located directly behind the trigger blade.

A rotary magazine is employed in the Savage B.Mag.

than the root of the bolt handle mating against the cutout in the receiver. To handle the .17 WSM, Savage developed an entirely new action that has a number of unusual features. First, the B.Mag action utilizes dual locking lugs that are located at the rear end of the bolt on the rotating cocking piece. The forward section of the bolt does not rotate. Second, the rifle is cocked as the bolt is closed rather than on the much more common opening motion. This makes closing the bolt more difficult, but it snaps open easily as the bolt handle is lifted. The B.Mag utilizes a bolt stop that is activated by pressing inward on a small knob that projects from the receiver on the left hand side.

Cocking a bolt action rifle, either on the opening or closing motion, involves pushing the firing pin to the rear to engage the sear, which holds it in that position until the time of firing. Moving the firing pin against the force of a strong spring is accomplished as the bolt is rotated by means of the cam action produced by an angular cut in the bolt sleeve that mates with a protrusion on the firing pin. The Savage B.Mag utilizes dual cam surfaces, which is unusual in an action used on a rimfire rifle. The safety is a sliding tab located on the top of the grip just behind the rear end of the bolt.

Savage developed the AccuTrigger® for use on its centerfire rifles, but has more recently marketed some rimfire rifles with a trigger of that type. The AccuTrigger has some unusual features. First, there is a blade that is positioned in the trigger lever itself. This blade acts as a safety because if the trigger is pulled from the side rather than directly to the rear, the firing pin is blocked. The sear will not be released, but the cocking motion must be repeated before firing can take place.

Second, the AccuTrigger can be adjusted by the user for a let off with a pull between 2.5 and 4 pounds. The pull weight can be changed by rotating a wheel or dial that is located just behind the trigger blade,

but the trigger guard must be removed to gain access to the wheel. The B.Mag utilizes a polymer stock that has a separate section that surrounds the magazine well and forms the trigger guard. It is held in place at the rear by a small tab that fits in a slot in the pistol grip of the stock. The front end is held in place by a plastic locking tab having a ridge that snaps in place in an internal recess. To remove the trigger guard, the magazine must be removed and a blade screwdriver inserted in a slot at the front of the magazine well. That slot gives access to the locking tab. Pushing forward on the screwdriver puts pressure on the locking tab causing the ridge that functions as a lock to be unlatched. Pulling gently downward on the front of the trigger guard causes the front end to be unlatched. After it is unlatched, pulling forward on the trigger guard causes the rear tab to be released from the recess in which it is held.

After the trigger guard is removed, the trigger adjustment dial or wheel can be turned without the barrel and action being removed from the stock. Turning the adjustment wheel changes the pressure on the trigger spring. It is done by placing the rifle on a support with the barrel pointing to the right. The trigger pull can be decreased by turning the adjustment screw counterclockwise. Turning the adjustment screw clockwise increases the trigger pull. Savage literature indicates that the range of pull is from approximately 2.5 to 4 pounds.

The original version of the Savage B.Mag has a slender barrel with a black matte finish and a stock of sporter contour giving a trim rifle weighing only 4.5 pounds. Subsequently, a second version was produced that has a heavy barrel of stainless steel. This version has a weight of approximately 6 pounds, and is the model utilized in this project. Both versions employ a rotary magazine that holds eight rounds. The light weight version has the MSRP of $379 whereas the heavy barrel model lists for $425. However, at the time of this writing early 2016, the lightweight version was seen on sale for $250-275.

The owner or potential buyer of a Savage B.Mag should be aware of some issues. These rifles come with no sights so the use of a scope is necessary, and the receiver is drilled and tapped for attaching scope mounts. Two scope bases are required and the rifle comes with them attached. However, the receiver and the barrel have about the same diameter so the scope is not placed on the receiver in a high position relative to the barrel. As a result, rather high rings must be selected. Moreover, the shape of the bolt handle is such that the scope must be placed high in order for the bolt handle to clear the rear bell as the bolt is cycled. Finally, as a result of working with a considerable number of scopes, it was noted that the placement of the bases on the receiver is such that the turret on some scopes will interfere with placement of the front ring. The Leupold rimfire scopes have eyepiece bells that are of slightly smaller diameter than most others so the excellent 3-9 X 32 EFR AO scope was placed on the B.Mag. Do not buy a Savage B.Mag rifle thinking that virtually any mount and scope can be attached. There are plenty of good options, but if you buy a Savage B.Mag, give some thought to the scope and mount to be used.

The Savage B.Mag needs a stock that is not so flexible, and the rifle is being configured in that way before extensive tests are performed. However, it appears that the B.Mag is a worthy rifle with which to head to the woods or to use on varmints. Although the B.Mag was purchased too late for an extensive series of tests, groups of around an inch were obtained at 100 yards.

In 2015, Savage issued a recall on the B.Mag. On some rifles, it was possible for the rear shroud on the

A scope can be attached to the Savage B.Mag by means of two scope bases that accept Weaver-type rings.

A wider range of ammunition is available for the varmint hunter who uses a .22 WMR rather than one of the .17 calibers.

bolt to make contact with the sliding safety. As the bolt was moved forward, the safety was placed in the "fire" position. Savage made available a free kit that consists of a new shroud and bolt handle. Installation of the parts is a simple process.

In this chapter, the results of a great deal of work with some of the current models of rimfire magnum rifles have been presented. No attempt was made to include all of the models available nor would it have been possible to complete such a comprehensive task in one lifetime. However, the rifles selected for study include some of the inexpensive bolt action models as well as some of the higher priced models. In that way, the selection is broad enough to show what to expect in terms of performance from many of the fine rimfire rifles produced by several manufacturers. Not only do the results of the study show the performance of the rifles, but also the characteristics of numerous types of ammunition are clearly seen. If you have not conducted extensive accuracy tests with your magnum rimfire rifle, study the tables shown in this chapter to see just how important the selection of ammunition is. With some different types of ammunition, your favorite rimfire rifle may perform much better than you thought possible.

CHAPTER 16

SHOOTING VINTAGE AND DISCONTINUED RIMFIRE RIFLES

BECAUSE RIMFIRE RIFLES utilize ammunition that is relatively low in power, firing a large number of shots does not produce a lot of wear and tear on the equipment. The majority of rimfire rifles have parts that are robust in view of the size and power of the cartridges they fire. As a result, a good rimfire rifle will literally last for generations if it is given reasonable care. Some models that are no longer available were produced in enormous numbers, and they are widely encountered as used rifles from a variety of markets. Many of them are by no means worn out, and they are often available at very reasonable prices. In producing this book, it became apparent that although there is an excellent selection of current rimfire models, some attention should be given to some of the models that have been out of production for a time to see how they perform.

In using the term vintage, we mean any rimfire rifle that has not been produced for a few years rather than those that are old enough to be officially called antiques. By so doing, the range of models that could be included is exceedingly large because there have been literally hundreds of different rimfire models produced. This chapter is in no way meant to be encyclopedic in its coverage. The rifles tested are those that are readily available to the author from private sources. No attempt was made to obtain rifles from museums or other collections for testing. As a result, the selection of rifles is of necessity limited, but several types of rifles are included. The idea is simply to take several representative rimfire rifles that are in regular service and to present information for some of them that may be useful to a prospective buyer who is searching for a used rifle. The results will provide a basis for comparing some older models to those in current production. It is appropriate to begin the presentation with a discussion of the rifle that started the rimfire experience of the author.

WINCHESTER 90

A large percentage of rimfire shooters have some special rifle with which they identify in a personal way. It may have been their first rifle, one that was a special gift, or one that commemorates some special occasion. For others, it may be the rifle that they grew up with. In my case, it is a rifle that came into the family when I was but a young lad. A great uncle who was a dentist gave the rifle, a Winchester Model 90 pump chambered for the .22 Short, to my father. However, my grandfather thought that his brother must have meant the rifle for him because it went to his house rather than ours. I cannot remember ever seeing my grandfather fire that rifle or any other. I never heard the story of how my great uncle came to have the rifle. He may have had it since his younger days or it may have come to him as payment from a patient who could not pay his dental bill.

By the mid-1940s, the rifle had made its way to our house but my father, being a shotgun man, almost never fired the rifle. My brothers and I made up for that. For some reason, the old pump sort of became my rifle in terms of use. From the age of 10 or 12, I

There are rifles and there are special rifles. To the author, the Winchester Model 90 was a true companion many years ago.

The Model 90 inherited by the author is chambered for the .22 Short only.

carried that rifle an incredible number of miles and hours. After school, the rifle accompanied me to the large tracts of timber that forested the area along a sizeable river not far from home. Sometimes, it was with me when I went to the woods to build a little fire and wait for dusk while watching the leaves fall from the trees. Because we lived in a rural (almost remote) area, the meat for the winter was home processed. I became the designated shooter and many hogs were dropped with a single .22 Short to the forehead.

After leaving home and graduating from college, the rifle spent several years with me as my only .22. Eventually, I got another rifle and took the old Winchester pump back to my father. About a dozen years ago as this is written in 2016, Dad passed on and eventually it came time to make arrangements for distribution of some of his property. By drawing lots, my oldest brother got the first pick and he took the 20 gauge double gun that had belonged to Dad and another brother took the Smith & Wesson 32 hand ejector. I got the third pick, and without hesitation I picked up the Winchester pump. The Winchester is essentially worn out, but I spent so much time with that rifle in my younger days that I wanted to have it around to pass on to my son sometime in the future.

If this story sounds familiar, you are among the very large number of shooters who have a special relationship with some rimfire rifle. If this introduction seems somewhat long, it is because my relationship with this rifle spans 70 years.

Introduced in 1890, the Winchester pump was produced until 1941 by which time approximately 750,000 had been made. If not the most famous pump rimfire rifle of all time, it is certainly one of the most famous. The serial number on my rifle indicates that it was made in 1920. There were three variants of the Model 90 over the 50 years of its manufacture. The first variant was a solid frame model, but the second and third variants were take down models. Receivers of the three models differ in the nature of the breech bolt. The first variant had solid sidewalls with the breech bolt moving back and forth between the walls. The second model had the same type of breech bolt, but it was a take down model. The third variant had a breech bolt with forward lugs that locked into recesses at the top edges of the receiver side walls. Eventually, the Model 90 gave way to the Model 62, which has a similar appearance except for having a round barrel. The Model 62 was produced from 1932 to 1958.

This section is actually about two Winchester Model 90 rifles. The second is one belonging to my brother that is chambered for the .22 Winchester Rim Fire cartridge, which was introduced in 1890 along with the rifle chambering it. Serial number correlation for this rifle indicates that it was made in 1910.

As in the case of other pump action rimfire rifles, the Model 90 has a tubular magazine and an external hammer. Operating the slide action moves a cartridge from the magazine as the hammer is being cocked by the rearward movement of the bolt. Forcing the slide forward moves the cartridge into the chamber. There is no safety except for a safety notch that is

The takedown screw and the notched receiver identify this as a Third Variant of the Winchester Model 90.

engaged by drawing the hammer back slightly. Sights on the Model 90 consist of an open rear sight with a notch and a bead front sight. There is no provision for mounting a scope because the breech bolt rises out of the receiver as it moves backward.

Shooting these vintage Winchesters did not involve a complete set of accuracy tests. Emphasis was on the functioning of the rifles and just plinking at a few targets from a range of 25 yards. Ammunition tested in .22 Short consisted of CCI, Remington, and Winchester solid high velocity rounds. In .22 WRF, ammunition included the CCI and Winchester loads. These rifles still work and would be suitable for fun and games. Taurus has produced Model 62 pump rifles that are similar to the Winchester Model 62, and Henry also produces a pump with a visible hammer. Taurus also produces the Model 72 pump that is available in .22 WMR and .17 HMR calibers. The point is, the visible hammer pump action rifle has been an enduring design, and rifles of this type are still available as new guns.

Working with the old Winchester Model 90 that belonged to my father brought back a lot of memories. It was really getting reacquainted with an old friend.

WINCHESTER 9422

The production of lever action rifles bearing the Winchester name is well into its second century. One model, the Model 94, was in continuous production for well over a century. Not only is the rimfire lever action being described here a Winchester, but it also has the distinction of being the only rimfire rifle produced by that famous company for many years. Gone are the pump, semiautomatic, and bolt action models that were produced throughout the 1900s. Perhaps one reason for their passing is that in 1972 Winchester introduced the Model 9422, and the rifle was very successful, not that it should be much of a surprise given the popularity of the legendary Model 94 centerfire rifle. However, about the time the first edition of this book was being produced, Winchester announced that production of the Model 9422 was being terminated in early 2005.

The most recent offerings in the Model 9422 included two basic models, the Traditional with a straight grip and the Legacy with a curved grip. On the Legacy, the fore end extends an inch or so farther in front of the barrel band than it does on the Traditional version. Barrel length on the Traditional is 20.5 inches whereas that on the Legacy is 22.5 inches. The

For the shooter who preferred a lever action, the Winchester 9422 Legacy represented elegance and performance.

under-the-barrel tubular magazine is utilized on both rifles so the 15-round capacity of .22 LR ammunition is common to both. Of course, the functions and controls are identical as well. Both the Traditional and Legacy versions were available in .22 WMR caliber and were available for a short time in .17 HMR as the Model 9417 for which the magazine capacity is only 11 rounds.

If there is one word that describes the Winchester Model 9422 that word has to be either classic or elegant. Come to think of it, both descriptors are appropriate. Unlike many rimfire rifles, the receivers are made from forged steel that is highly polished and brightly blued. The receivers incorporate the grooves that are now almost universal for attaching scope mounts on rimfire rifles. Barrels and magazine tubes are also very well finished. Stocks on most of the recently produced rifles examined by the author are made of very good walnut, and the cut checkering is done with a high level of technique. The end result is that the appearance of the Model 9422 is the equal of many (if not most) centerfire rifles. Such elegance comes at a price, and the last manufacturer's suggested price for either the Traditional or Legacy versions was over $500 when they were discontinued. The rifles are highly prized for shooting or collecting so it is not uncommon to see used models with tags of approximately $1,000.

Sights on the Model 9422 are conventional. The front sight is a hooded bead on a ramp whereas the rear sight is the familiar notched blade that can be adjusted for elevation by means of a stepped ramp and for windage by drifting the sight laterally in its dovetail retaining notch. Other than the usual safety notch that is common to many firearms with exposed hammers, there is no safety on the Model 9422.

For accuracy testing, a Leupold Vari-X II 2.5-7X

Accuracy Results for the Winchester 9422 Legacy with a Leupold 2.5-7X Scope

AMMUNITION	GROUP SIZE, INCHES		
	Smallest	Largest	Average
CCI Standard Velocity	0.52	0.79	0.69
CCI SGB	0.85	1.46	1.22
Federal High Velocity H.P.	0.53	1.42	1.03
Lapua Super Club	0.59	1.33	0.94
Remington Game Load	0.89	1.52	1.17
Winchester Power Point	0.68	1.54	1.12
		OVERALL AV.	1.03

scope was mounted on the Winchester 9422. Because the receiver is so short on the lever action, there is little latitude in positioning a scope. The small Leupold fit better than any other scope that was available at the time. The results obtained are shown in the accompanying table.

In testing the Winchester 9422, the intent was to use ammunition that ranges from target loads to some of the popular types used for hunting. The Winchester 9422 handled all of the types of ammunition well. It is particularly gratifying to see that with CCI Standard Velocity and Lapua Super Club the average group sizes were smaller than one inch. Such performance should dispel the wide spread rumor that lever action rifles are capable of only mediocre accuracy. Moreover, the composite group size for all six types of ammunition is just slightly over an inch. If you like lever action rifles but have heard that they may not be accurate, the data show that if you are willing to experiment with several types of ammunition, you should be able to find a couple of types that will give good accuracy. For general use, it would be hard to imagine a finer rimfire rifle for the person who stalks the woods.

Not coincidentally, the resemblance of the Model 9422 to the legendary Model 94 is unmistakable. But this rimfire is more than just a classic in terms of its appearance. Made of high quality materials, this is a durable and functional rifle that is right at home in the woods or fields. It is a superb hunting rifle, especially for the hunter who uses a lever action centerfire for hunting large game. The cost of a Model 9422 is not trivial, but many of the better bolt action rimfire rifles are in a comparable price range. The author may have somehow avoided owning a lever action rimfire for most of his life, but that deficiency is corrected now.

As the manuscript for the first edition this book was being finished in early 2005, Winchester announced that the Model 9422 lever action was being discontinued. Undoubtedly, any rimfire lever actions that were on the shelves at that time were rapidly snatched up by collectors. Now, as the second edition of this book is being prepared, such rifles have become highly desirable and they are frequently seen for prices as high as $1,000, especially if original boxes are also included. In production for over 30 years, the Model 9422 provided a superb alternative for those rimfire shooters who wanted an elegant rifle but did not want it to be a bolt action.

BROWNING SA-22

One of the most enduring designs in rimfire rifles is the little semiautomatic invented by John M. Browning. Known as the Browning Semi Automatic .22 (or simply the SA-22), it may well be the most slender, streamlined rifle made. There is no tube under the barrel and no magazine that sticks out of the bottom of the action. The SA-22 does make use of a tubular magazine, but it is located in the stock. Other semiautomatic .22s including the Winchester Models 74, 03, and 63 had similar cartridge reservoirs. For many years, the SA-22 was offered in both .22 Short and .22 LR calibers, but only the .22 LR version is currently available. In addition, the SA-22 is a take down model with the barrel being held to the receiver by means of a large knurled ring located at the junction of the barrel and action. Although the Browning SA-22 is currently produced by Miroku in Japan, the rifle tested in this work is an older model that was made in Belgium where this model was manufactured by Fabrique Nationale from 1914 to 1976. It clearly merits vintage status even though there is an equivalent model currently produced.

These are two of the fine Browning Semi Automatic rifles that were made in Belgium.

Cartridges are loaded through the port in the side of the stock of the SA-22.

The magazine tube in the SA-22 is contained in the stock. The latch is turned which unlocks the tube so it can be drawn out.

Elegant touches such as the engraved receiver made the Browning SA-22 one of the most sought after rimfire autoloaders of all time.

Unique to the Browning SA-22 is the fact that empty cases are ejected from the bottom of the action. There are no openings on the sides of the receiver. Moving the breech bolt to the rear to load the first cartridge is accomplished by pushing backward on the ridged tab located on the bottom of the bolt. A port on the right hand side of the stock allows cartridges to be inserted into the magazine. The magazine tube is unlatched by turning the flanged end that is located in a recess in the butt plate. The magazine tube can then be drawn from the butt plate so that the loading port in the right hand side of the stock is open. Magazine capacity of the SA-22 is 11 rounds. The version that is chambered for .22 Shorts holds 16 rounds. Weight of the SA-22 is 5 pounds 3 ounces and it measures 37 inches in length. These dimensions make it one of the most portable rimfire rifles around.

Operation of the SA-22 is straightforward. After loading, the bolt is pulled back to the rear and re-leased, which moves a cartridge from the magazine

to the breech. A cross bolt safety is located in the rear part of the trigger guard.

Characteristic of other Browning firearms, the SA-22 is offered in several grades that vary in the extent of engraving and gold inlay work. The suggested price of the SA-22 in Grade I is $700 whereas the highly ornate Grade VI lists for $1,500. Sights on current production rifles consist of a bead front sight and a folding leaf rear. For many years, the SA-22 has been produced with a grooved receiver for attaching a scope. However, this rifle was primarily intended to be a compact companion in the woods while wearing the sights that came on it. Even the stock design is really more compatible with the use of iron sights.

Shooting the little Browning SA-22 made it clear why this rifle has been considered to be a classic for many years. It is so compact and weighs so little that it is a superb choice for the shooter who wants a .22 for those precious times while traveling light in the woods. Moreover, the fact that it is a takedown model makes it an appropriate choice for travel as long as all regulations are obeyed.

With fit and finish that are truly outstanding, the Browning SA-22 is a compact, attractive rifle that bespeaks of days gone by. It would not seriously challenge the accuracy of most of the rifles described in previous chapters, but it doesn't have to. The shooter who selects the SA-22 is going to make the selection based on other criteria. It is in these other areas that the SA-22 is a true classic.

THOMPSON/CENTER CLASSIC

As the first edition of this book was being written, the author thought that the Thompson/Center (T/C) Classic autoloader and the bolt action Remington 504 were perhaps indicative of the health of the market for elegant rimfire rifles. The T/C autoloader retailed for around $400 whereas the Remington 504 that listed for $710 normally sold about $600. Presumably, these rifles were introduced to meet a demand for high quality sporting rifles that were sought by serious rimfire shooters. Neither fits in the category of plinking rifles although either would be eminently suitable for that use. No, these rifles were intended for use by rimfire shooters who take their sport seriously. However, after brief periods of production, both the T/C Classic and Remington 504 are long gone.

The T/C Classic is a true sporting rifle albeit a semi-automatic. High quality rimfire sporting rifles have

A superb autoloader produced by Thompson Center was the Classic.

One reason for the outstanding accuracy of the T/C Classic is that the barrel is threaded into the steel receiver. (photo courtesy Thompson/Center)

traditionally had bolt actions although this is by no means a requirement. The T/C is a rather robust rifle that has a solid feel when it is handled. One reason is that, unlike most autoloaders that have receivers made of an aluminum alloy, the T/C Classic has a steel receiver. Moreover, the 20-inch match-grade barrel is of generous weight, and it is threaded into the receiver in the way traditionally used for centerfire rifles. Such construction is unusual in a rimfire rifle, but it gives a rigid barrel/action unit, and that is partially responsible for the fine accuracy of the T/C Classic.

The T/C Classic has a very well shaped walnut stock, but it is not checkered. Another version of the Classic, known as the Silver Lynx, was available and it had a composite stock and stainless steel barrel and action. Sights on the Classic were unusual at that time because they make use of fiber optic inserts. The front sight has a green fiber optic insert that rides along the top of the post and the square-notched rear sight has fiber optic inserts on either side of the notch. The inserts appear as glowing dots when viewed from the rear, and aligning the dots supposedly aids in getting the front and rear sights in proper relationship. Frankly, such sights do not appeal to the author and he would prefer simply a square-topped post front and square notch in the rear sight, but it is a matter of taste. He never fires at targets when the light is so dim that these optical gimmicks are needed. In dim

Accuracy Results for the Thompson/Center Classic with 3-12X Redfield Scope

AMMUNITION	GROUP SIZE, INCHES		
	Smallest	Largest	Average
CCI Green Tag	0.66	1.08	0.88
CCI SGB	0.54	1.20	0.81
CCI Velocitor	0.70	1.24	0.93
Federal Target (711B)	0.75	1.06	0.87
Remington/Eley Club Extra	0.41	0.74	0.62
Remington Golden Bullet	0.87	1.18	1.03
Remington Target	0.76	1.75	1.33
SK Jagd Standard Plus	0.34	0.85	0.63
Winchester Power Point	0.70	0.95	0.81
Winchester T-22	0.77	1.25	1.05
Wolf Match Target	0.41	1.10	0.86
		OVERALL AV.	**0.89**

light a scope would be a better choice. The receiver of the Classic is drilled and tapped to attach Weaver-type bases so the receiver is not grooved as are many on rimfire rifles. A detachable 5-shot magazine is standard. The safety is a lever located on the right hand side of the receiver with red and green indicators on the top edge of the stock.

In addition to the Classic and Silver Lynx, T/C also produced a target model known as the Benchmark, which had an 18-inch heavy barrel and a laminated target style stock. A 10-round magazine was supplied with this version.

Because the T/C Classic is at home in a variety of situations where a rimfire rifle is used, it was tested with a wide variety of ammunition types. The accompanying table shows the results of the accuracy testing.

Overall accuracy of the T/C Classic is outstanding for an autoloading sporting rifle. With a match grade barrel that has a chamber with match dimensions, it is not surprising that this rifle delivers fine accuracy with target ammunition. Especially fine accuracy was delivered by Remington/Eley Club Extra and SK Jagd Standard Plus loads. However, Winchester Power Points gave an average group size of only 0.81 inch, and the largest average group size (only 1.33 inches) was obtained with Remington Target. The composite group size of 0.89 inch indicates accuracy that is comparable to that produced by many bolt action sporters. If the averages for two Remington loads and the Winchester T-22 are not included, the overall average group size is only 0.80 inch.

It is especially noteworthy that even with the wide variety of ammunition types employed, none of the types performed poorly in the T/C. This is due in part to the fact that because of its rigidity, the barrel and action assembly simply is not affected by minor differences in ammunition.

Numerous jams occurred during the test firing. Ejection was positive, but as the bolt moved forward it frequently took the top round in the magazine forward into the bottom of the barrel breech or into the top edge at the front of the magazine. The nose of the cartridge did not come up at the correct angle. It was found that the spring in this particular magazine seemed not to have sufficient force to raise the nose of the cartridge upward enough for it to move into the chamber. A call to T/C to explain the problem led quickly to a new magazine, and it is clearly constructed in a different manner and incorporates a much stiffer spring. Apparently, the magazines produced later were somewhat different from those made early in the production of this fine rifle. There is no defect in the design, and it is an outstanding rifle.

For shooters who want a fine sporting rifle but who do not choose a bolt action, the T/C Classic is a superb choice. Although not strictly a target rifle, it would be quite at home in the woods hunting squirrels or on the prairie shooting pests. It was not produced in large numbers so finding a good used specimen may not be easy.

RUGER 10/22 RIFLE

Since its introduction in 1964, a seemingly endless number of variants of the Ruger 10/22 have appeared. These have differed primarily in the type of barrel steel and in the stock material and configuration. In 2004, Ruger introduced the Model 10/22 Rifle that has a 20-inch barrel and a smooth hardwood stock that does not have the barrel band that is familiar on the Carbine. With a stock that is slimmer than that on the 10/22 Carbine and has a better-shaped comb, the 10/22 Rifle has a very pleasing appearance. It is amazing how much difference in appearance an inch and a half in barrel length and a slimmer stock makes. The cover of the first edition this book was graced with a photo of the Ruger 10/22 Rifle. One departure of the Rifle from the Carbine deals with the open sights. On the 10/22 Rifle, the front sight is a square-topped post and the rear sight has a matching square notch. The sight picture is much better than that given by a round bead in a notch. In fact, it is possible with the factory sights on the 10/22 Rifle to achieve a rather high level of accuracy.

Mechanical features and function of the 10/22 Rifle are exactly like those of the Carbine and Target models discussed in Chapter 14. Therefore, they do not

With the excellent Simmons 3-9x AO scope attached, the Ruger 10/22 Rifle gave better performance than the Carbine and is more attractive.

Accuracy Results for the Ruger 10/22 Rifle with Simmons 3-9X AO Rimfire Scope

AMMUNITION	GROUP SIZE, INCHES		
	Smallest	Largest	Average
CCI Green Tag	0.49	1.00	0.83
CCI Standard Velocity	0.55	1.48	0.99
Remington Game Load	0.55	1.30	1.00
Remington/Eley Target	0.54	0.86	0.68
Wolf Match Target	0.78	1.26	0.99
		OVERALL AV.	0.90

One of the most popular autoloaders a generation ago was the Winchester Model 190. It is still a fine rifle for many uses.

need to be reviewed, and we can progress directly to the results of accuracy testing, which yielded the data that are shown in the accompanying table.

The accuracy demonstrated by the Ruger 10/22 Rifle is excellent. For the five types of ammunition tested, not one gave an average group size of over one inch. For all of the groups with these five types of ammunition, 67% measured under one inch. Although this does not mean that the 10/22 Rifle is as accurate as a high priced sporting rifle, it does mean that this rifle is a good choice for a wide range of activities that could include hunting small game and varmints as well as plinking.

With a suggested price of around $300, the 10/22 Rifle was often found at retail at a price slightly over $200. To the author, the 10/22 Rifle had all of the desirable features of the 10/22 Carbine in a considerably more handsome firearm. It would have been a nice touch if the rifle had been produced with sling swivel studs. The model known as the Ruger 10/22 Sporter has a checkered walnut stock, but the fore end is squared off and the barrel is the same 18.5-inch unit that is available on the Carbine. As a real eye-catching sporter, the 20-inch barreled 10/22 Rifle could have been offered with a checkered walnut stock shaped just like the hardwood stock that is standard on the rifle. Such a version would be, in the opinion of the author, the most attractive format ever offered for the 10/22. Even without these characteristics, the Ruger 10/22 Rifle is a handsome rifle that is also very capable. Finding a 10/22 Rifle in good condition would be very difficult, and the author has never seen one in a rack of used guns.

WINCHESTER 190

The Winchester Model 190, an autoloader with a tubular magazine under the barrel, was introduced in 1967 and discontinued in 1980. A deluxe model produced with a stock of higher grade of wood with pressed checkering was known as the Model 290. It was produced from 1963 to 1977. The models 190 and 290 were basically identical except for stock and sights. Accordingly, the Model 190 was basically a plain model introduced after the Model 290 had been in production for a few years. The 200 series of rifles also included a lever action Model 250 and a slide action Model 270, but they were never as popular as the autoloader models. A lever action Model 255 was chambered for the .22 WMR. Total production of the 200 series was well over 2 million units, the majority of them being the Model 190 and 290 .22 LR autoloaders. Because of the sheer number of rifles produced, the Model 190 and 290 are frequently encountered as used rifles. Prices tend to be in the $150-175 range depending on condition. The author always wanted a

Accuracy Results for the Winchester 190 with a Weaver 2.5-7X Rimfire Scope

AMMUNITION	GROUP SIZE, INCHES		
	Smallest	Largest	Average
CCI Standard Velocity	0.36	1.22	0.97
Federal High Velocity H.P.	0.92	1.68	1.31
PMC Scoremaster	0.55	1.48	1.21
Remington Game Load	1.00	1.59	1.23
Wolf Match Target	1.10	2.24	1.75

The barrel of this Winchester 190 shows that it could be used with Short, Long, or Long Rifle ammunition.

Model 190 or 290 in the early 1970s but never got one until much later. For some reason, this rifle has always had pleasing lines, but of course this is a subjective judgment.

Operation of the Winchester 190 requires the bolt to be pulled back to the rear and allowed to move forward to load a cartridge in the chamber. The safety is of the cross bolt type, and it is located in the front of the trigger guard. When the bolt is drawn to the rear, pushing the bolt handle inward locks the bolt open although the bolt does not remain open after the last shot. Cleaning a Winchester 190 is facilitated by cocking the rifle and allowing the bolt to go forward. Driving the large plastic pin located above the trigger out of the receiver allows the complete trigger/hammer group to be removed from the bottom of the receiver. If desired, the breech bolt can be removed (carefully! because of the tension of the recoil spring), but be aware that threading the long recoil spring back onto its guide is not always easy to do.

Although the Winchester 190 is a competent, dependable rifle, it and others of its general configuration are not known as tack driving machines. In order to get an idea of its accuracy potential, a limited series of tests was performed in which five five-shot groups were fired at 50 yards with a Weaver 2.5-7X Rimfire scope mounted on the rifle. The results are summarized in the accompanying table.

Accuracy of the Winchester 190 is adequate for the uses to which a rifle of this type is likely to be put. It has sufficient accuracy for plinking and for hunting small game or pests to ranges of 50 yards or so. It is interesting to note that with the CCI Standard Velocity ammunition, the average group size was less than one inch, which is quite good for an inexpensive rimfire autoloader. The data shown in the table also point to the importance of trying several brands and types of ammunition in your rifle if you want to bring out its best accuracy. The author's tests with many rifles have shown that there seems to be a greater difference in accuracy produced by ammunition of different types when in fired autoloaders than when the same types are tested in bolt action rifles. It is interesting to note that the accuracy displayed by the Winchester 190 when using Wolf Match Target ammunition was not as good as with other types. That load has given outstanding accuracy in several other rifles, but for some reason this autoloader did not seem to shoot well with it. On the other hand, the Thompson/Center Classic discussed earlier performs very well with the Wolf ammunition.

The accuracy of the Winchester Model 190 is comparable to that of other light weight autoloaders, lever actions, and slide actions. In all of the firing, the rifle proved to be reliable and no malfunctions occurred. Even though performance of the Model 190 was not spectacular, it is a competent rifle that can sometimes be found at low prices. There does not seem to be much of a demand for the 190 and 290 rifles (or many other older autoloaders), and part of the reason is the enormous popularity of the Ruger 10/22 with all of its after market possibilities for customization. The low priced Marlin Model 60 and the Remington Model 597 are also available as new rifles for a price not much greater than that of a used Winchester 190 or 290 in good condition. Although the Winchester 190 is not my most accurate rifle (or even my most accurate autoloader), I have always had a fondness for this model. Its sleek appearance and the fact that it is a Winchester .22 have made it a favorite plinking rifle for me. If you want to obtain a Winchester 190 or 290, it should not difficult because with over 2 million produced they are often seen in racks of used guns.

The magazine release on the 69A was a recessed button on the left hand side of the stock. The flush fitting magazine gave the rifle clean lines.

WINCHESTER 69A

The idea of a bolt action rifle that offers a high level of performance at a reasonable price has been an attractive one for many years, and numerous models were introduced over the years to meet the demand. One of the most successful of these was the Winchester 69 and 69A. The Model 69 cocked on closing the bolt whereas the 69A cocked as the bolt was opened. The action of the 69A is superb. The fit and finish of the bolt are very good. In fact, the action was identical to that used on the Model 75 Sporting and Target rifles. The Model 69 remained in the Winchester catalogs from 1935-1963 with a total of 355,363 rifles being produced. Good used Model 69s are becoming hard to find, but although the author bought one new in the 1950s for about $35, used specimens now sell for around $300 and up. The reason is simple. The Winchester 69A offered and still offers outstanding accuracy. In terms of performance, a 69A can hold its own with the majority of .22s produced today.

In addition to the open-sighted model, target and match versions of the Winchester 69A were produced that had a hooded ramp front sight and a peep sight. They were budget priced target rifles for beginning shooters or club use. Rifles produced late in the production period had grooved receivers for mounting a scope.

The Winchester Model 69A made use of a 5-shot detachable box magazine that was released by pushing inward on a recessed metal button on the left hand side of the stock. Optional 10-round magazines were also available. Barrel length on the Model 69A was 25 inches and the weight was approximately six pounds. The walnut stock was generally of good quality with

This Winchester 69A Target model is a beautiful rifle with classic styling. It was and is an outstanding performer.

full-size dimensions.

Although the author no longer has a Winchester 69A in the cabinet, a brother does. This rifle is a beautiful target specimen that has a Lyman peep sight attached. For testing, a BSA 3-12X 40 AO scope was mounted on the rifle. The temperature was around the 30 degree F mark with a rather stiff breeze at 10 o'clock. Only limited testing of the Winchester Model 69A was conducted because the conditions were hardly ideal for shooting groups. In spite of the weather, when Wolf Match Target ammunition was used, five 5-shot groups measured in the range 0.53 to 0.78 inch with an average size of 0.63 inch. With Federal Gold Medal Target, the average group size was slightly more than an inch, and it was around that with other types of ammunition. What would the 69A give on an ideal day using the most compatible ammunition? That is not known, but this rifle can

Lever action fans will appreciate the styling and capability of the Ithaca Saddle Gun. This rifle is known for its extremely slick action.

definitely hold its own with the majority of bolt action sporters produced today except perhaps for some of the very expensive models. It would be very nice if Winchester would once again see fit to produce a rifle to replace the 69A and the Model 320 described later in this chapter. Because of the current emphasis on rate of fire and tactical appearance, it is not likely to happen.

ITHACA SADDLE GUN

The .22 LR caliber rifle having the longest time of production is the lever action Marlin Model 39A and its predecessor. Probably the most famous name in lever action rifles is that of Winchester. The newcomer among the producers of lever action rimfires is Henry whose factory is located in Bayonne, NJ. With all these other players in the game, you may be surprised to find that one of the slickest lever action rimfires was marketed by none other than Ithaca, the famous maker of shotguns, although the rifle was actually produced by Erma Werke in Germany.

A lever action look alike was known as the Ithaca Model 49, but it was actually a single shot rifle with a falling block action. A fake magazine tube under the barrel was merely a cosmetic feature. The lever behind the trigger actually operated a falling block that allowed a single round to be loaded in the chamber (this is known as a Martini-type action). Produced from 1961-1978, the Model 49 had a visible hammer and the appearance of a lever action repeater, but looks can be deceiving.

Produced from 1973 to 1978, the Ithaca Model 72 Saddle Gun has an 18.5-inch barrel and a tubular magazine below the barrel. The rifles were available in both .22 LR and .22 WMR calibers. A deluxe version having an octagon barrel and a silver colored receiver was produced for a couple of years in the mid-1970s.

Most of the features of the Ithaca Model 72 are characteristic of other lever actions. It has a full-length tubular magazine under the barrel and a hammer with a safety notch but no other safety. Operation is simply a down-then-up swing of the lever to eject an empty case, cock the hammer, and move a cartridge into the chamber. That operation with the Ithaca 72 is unbelievably smooth and positive. In the tests, the rifle operated flawlessly. It is a pleasant rifle to shoot and would make a nearly ideal rifle for plinking and hunting small game for the shooter who prefers a lever action rifle.

Although the Ithaca 72 has been out of production for many years, the currently produced Henry Lever Action is a very similar rifle. If you examine a collectible Ithaca that isn't for sale or the price of this collectible is too steep, get a Henry. It is also a fine rifle (see Chapter 14).

WINCHESTER 320

Although the Winchester 69A offered excellent performance in an inexpensive sporting rifle in a bygone era, the demand for bolt action rifles was decreasing. Autoloaders had become the hot tickets as rate of fire and can rolling became more common than tucking a rifle under the arm and heading out to the woods to collect a couple of squirrels. The result of this change was that not many new bolt action rimfire rifles were introduced in the turbulent times of the 1960s and 1970s and most were none too successful. One rifle that was introduced was a real gem known as the Winchester Model 320. The Model 320 has a walnut stock that is very well shaped and has pressed checkering and sling swivels. This slick bolt action rifle made use of a five-shot magazine having a magazine release located behind the magazine itself. A grooved receiver made attaching a scope a simple proposition. The highly

The Winchester 320 is a beautifully finished rifle that has a magazine that fits almost flush with the bottom of the stock.

polished and blued finish on the Model 320 is excellent for a rifle that was a relatively inexpensive model. The trigger guard assembly is especially beautifully shaped and polished. The factory sights consist of an adjustable rear sight and a bead front sight on a ramp.

Produced only from 1971 to 1974, the total production was very small for a rimfire rifle. A single shot Model 310 was also available. In the early 1970s, the Model 320 was available for $57.95 and it was a bargain. Used rifles are now seen priced in the $300-500 range. When one considers that a new Ruger or CZ bolt action of comparable quality retails for $500-700, it does not seem that the price of a Model 320 is too outrageous.

It was only as the enormous amount of testing was being done in preparation for developing this book that a serious evaluation of the author's Winchester 320 was carried out. In order to see what this rifle was capable of, a 6-20 X 40 AO Cabela's Outfitter scope was mounted, and the scope was adjusted so that the shots hit near the point of aim at 50 yards.

At the time of testing the Model 320, approximately 35-40 types of ammunition were on hand. There simply wasn't time to test every type of ammunition in all of the rifles so some selection had to be made. The Winchester 320 was not tested with some of the very low end ammunition with which it probably would not perform quite as well. It should be noted that the ammunition tested does include some of the high velocity hunting types.

After selecting the ammunition to be fired, the initial firing was carried out with Wolf Match Target. With the high magnification of the Cabela's scope, it was possible to see the holes as they appeared in the target and even watch some of the bullets in flight. As usual, five five-

Accuracy Results for the Winchester 320 with 6-20X Cabela's Outfitter Scope

AMMUNITION	GROUP SIZE, INCHES		
	Smallest	Largest	Average
CCI Green Tag	0.50	0.82	0.68
CCI SGB	0.70	1.02	0.85
CCI Standard Velocity	0.48	0.80	0.72
CCI Velocitor	0.79	2.21	1.39
Eley Target	0.44	1.19	0.88
Federal Target (711B)	0.62	0.84	0.76
Federal Ultra Match	0.58	0.88	0.76
Lapua Super Club	0.36	0.84	0.67
Remington Target	0.61	1.04	0.85
Winchester Power Point	0.63	0.95	0.81
Winchester Super-X H.P.	0.51	0.90	0.81
Winchester Supreme	0.55	1.17	0.82
Winchester T-22	0.64	1.37	1.00
Wolf Match Target	0.48	0.95	0.73
		OVERALL AV.	**0.84**

Fitted with a scope like the 4X Nikon ProStaff, the Winchester Model 320 is an excellent rifle for the small game hunter.

shot groups were fired. What do I see? My, the groups look small! When the groups were measured, it was found that they were 0.87, 0.48, 0.76, 0.95, and 0.58 inch with an average group size of only 0.73 inch! And now you see why the Winchester Model 320 is still a very desirable rifle. It follows in the tradition of the Model 69A and Model 75 sporters that are well known for their accuracy. A summary of the accuracy data obtained using several types of ammunition in the Model 320 is shown in the accompanying table.

As the data show, the Winchester Model 320 that went out of production in 1974 is an extremely accurate rifle. If the data for CCI Velocitor is omitted, the overall average group size is only 0.80 inch. As can be seen from the data, the Winchester 320 gives accuracy that is on a par with several fine rifles described earlier in this chapter and in Chapter 14. In fact, the Winchester 320 will match the accuracy of the Remington 504 that was a highly rated but short-lived sporting rifle. It should also be mentioned that the performance of the Winchester 320 almost exactly duplicates that of my Ruger 77/22 and that of my wife's CZ 452. All of these bolt action models offer outstanding performance and appearance. However, if you already have one of these models, don't rush out to get one of the others thinking that you are going to obtain a quantum leap in accuracy.

It is the opinion of the author that there has been an increase in interest in high performance rimfire rifles. The fine Ruger 77/22 has been available since 1984. Although some very accurate autoloaders are available, the production of fine bolt action rifles by such makers as Anschütz, Sako, and others has diminished. It is to be hoped that Winchester will once again produce a bolt action model to join these elite manufacturers, and this wish has been expressed to the appropri-

ate personnel. A brief reintroduction of the classic Winchester 52 Sporting Rifle was made in 1993 with a copy made in Japan, but the desire is for a model that would compare to the Model 75 Sporter or the Model 320 described here. Such a rifle would probably have to sell for $500-700. With some of the moderately priced rifles from Savage, Marlin, and Ruger, a true sporting rimfire rifle would face stiff competition. The bottom line is that the Winchester 320 showed that it can hold its own with most other rimfire sporting rifles produced today.

DAISY 2201, 2202, AND 2203

The Daisy name is one of the most widely recognized names in the shooting sports. The only problem is, it is primarily associated with airguns. However, it has not always been so. Daisy Manufacturing Company (now known as Daisy Outdoor Products) entered the field of firearm production in 1968 with the introduction of the VL system that used caseless ammunition. A small cylinder of solid propellant was attached to the base of the bullet, and it was ignited upon firing by a blast of compressed air. Although the rifles firing caseless ammunition were discontinued quickly, the air compression system developed for it became the basis for the Daisy PowerLine 880 air rifle that was introduced in 1972. That model was Daisy's first multi-pump air rifle. However, it is neither the VL system nor air rifle that is of interest here.

In 1987, Daisy bought parts for a small single shot bolt action .22 rimfire from Iver Johnson. The assembled rifle was known as the Daisy Model '08, and it was sold through Walmart stores. About 30,000 units were marketed. In 1988, Daisy reentered the firearm field with the introduction of three models known as the

Although better known for airguns, Daisy also produced rimfire rifles for a short time. Shown here is a Daisy 2201 single shot with a Bushnell 4X compact Varmint scope.

A flange that is threaded into the receiver pulls the barrel into the action.

When disassembled, the Daisy 2201 consists of three major parts. The front swivel stud attaches the forearm to the barrel.

Legacy series, which included a bolt action single shot, a bolt action repeater using a rotary magazine holding 10 rounds, and a semiautomatic that uses a detachable magazine that holds seven rounds stacked vertically. There were, in fact, two versions of each of the models that differed in the type of stock material. The Models 2201 and 2211 were the single shot rifles with polymer and hardwood stocks, respectively. The Models 2202 and 2212 were the bolt action repeaters, and the 2203 and 2213 were the autoloaders with stock materials designated as in the case of the single shot models. All of the models have two-piece stocks that have studs for attaching sling swivels, and all of the models were discontinued in 1991.

The Daisy Legacy rifles have a number of unique features. For example, the barrels consisted of a steel inner barrel encased in a black composite material that has an octagonal surface. The barrels are held to the receiver by means of a knurled locking nut that engages a flange on the breech end of the barrel. The locking nut, which screws into the receiver, has four holes in the knurled surface of its outside edge that allow a special wrench to be used to turn the locking ring. On the bolt action models, the forearm is held to the barrel by means of the front swivel stud.

The Daisy Legacy autoloader models have no bolt handle for cycling the action. A rod that is attached to the bolt protrudes from the front end of the forearm. Pushing the rod backward forces the action open. A similar arrangement has been used over the years on a number of autoloaders, both rimfire and centerfire. For example, the actions on the Winchester Models 03 and 63 were cycled in this way.

As mentioned earlier, a choice of hardwood or plastic stock models was offered for the Daisy rimfires.

One unique feature of the plastic stocked versions is that the stock length can be changed by pressing inward on a large button on the right hand side of the stock and pulling the butt plate outward. The front sight is molded as part of the composite barrel shroud. The rear sight is fully adjustable in a unique way. Elevation is adjusted by loosening a screw and sliding the rear sight forward or backward on a stepless inclined ramp. The sight blade can be moved laterally to adjust windage after a locking screw is loosened. The receiver is made of die cast metal and has grooves for attaching scope mounts. Although many of these features themselves are unique, there is more. The entire trigger assembly can be removed by pressing upward on a button located just behind the trigger guard and sliding the trigger assembly down and backward out of the action. The sear serves as the bolt stop so the bolt can be slid out after the trigger assembly is removed.

In order to see what a Daisy Legacy would produce in terms of accuracy, I mounted a BSA 3-12X airgun scope on a Daisy 2202. Firing was conducted at 50 yards with Wolf Match Target ammunition, which has shown outstanding accuracy in a variety of other rifles. The little Daisy gave groups that averaged 1.25 inches! Other types of ammunition gave groups in the 1.5-2.0 inch range, which is not bad considering that this very light weight, small rifle is a take-down model. Daisy rimfire rifles were intended for use as plinking rifles, and the adjustable stock length made them suitable for youth rifles. If one were to restrict shots to 40-50 yards, the Daisy could also be used for hunting and pest shooting. Prices for used Daisy Legacy rifles have escalated dramatically in recent years, as they have become collectibles.

The Remington 541 is a beautiful sporter that is also well known for accuracy.

REMINGTON 541S

So much was written about the short lived Remington 504 bolt action sporter that it might be possible to overlook some of the other fine sporting rifles that Remington produced over the years. To the author, one of the most elegant was the Model 541, which was available as the 541S sporter and the 541T target models. The major difference between the two versions is in the stock. The stock on the 541T was made with a target styling and without some of the embellishments found on the sporter. For example, the 541S has a forearm tip and grip cap made of dark colored rosewood. It also has a beautiful checkering pattern on the grip and forearm.

Mechanical features of the target and sporter models are identical. Most notable are the multiple lug lockup at the middle of the bolt and the outstanding trigger. A crisp, light let off characterizes the trigger action that initiates a very fast lock time. This makes for controllable, predictable firing. A 5-shot detachable box magazine was employed that sometimes drew condemnation because it was made of plastic. The fact that it did not fit flush with the bottom of the stock did not endear it to many critics. Barrel length is 24 inches on either model. Both versions of the Remington 541 are drilled and tapped to accept scope bases, but the receivers are not grooved.

During the firing tests, the chamber was loaded in single shot fashion. It was noted that some types of ammunition were difficult to load because of the very tight chamber, which has the tight dimensions of a target rifle. It was particularly difficult to single load CCI Green Tag rounds in the rifle.

The rifle tested belongs to a nephew of the author and was purchased as a new rifle. It is clearly marked 541T on the barrel but has the elegant stock of the 541S sporter. A call to Remington showed that the serial number of the rifle corresponds to a 541T, but the stock is not of the target type. The sporter models are normally marked 541S. Several possible scenarios were given as to how the barrel marking and the stock style are at variance, but the actual reason is not known. However, it is not a major issue because the barrel and action of the 541T and 541S are identical, and it is only

The plastic magazine that protrudes from the bottom of the stock is one feature that many lovers of the Model 541 could do without.

the stock that makes one the target version whereas the other is a sporter. The rifle being discussed is clearly the sporter and will be called a 541S regardless of which model number is on the barrel.

Fit and finish of the Remington 541S are outstanding. Highly polished and deeply blued, the barrel and action are beautifully finished. The stock has the high gloss finish similar to that found on centerfire models such as those in the Remington 700 BDL series. No sights adorn the barrel because the rifle is intended to be used with a scope attached.

Firing of the Remington 541S was conducted with a 3-9X Leupold Vari-X II scope attached. The temperature was approximately 30 degrees F and there was a 5-10 mph wind blowing from 10 o'clock. The weather offered very difficult conditions under which to test accuracy, but some 5-shot groups were obtained on targets at a range of 50 yards. It was found that Wolf Match Target, CCI Green Tag, and Federal Gold Medal Target gave average group sizes of around an inch, but these results probably do not indicate the true capability of this fine rifle. With the most compatible ammunition, the Remington 541S should produce groups of about half that size.

Produced from 1986 until 1999, the Remington 541S has long been one of my favorite sporting rifles. Although the author never tested a Remington 504, several specimens were examined, and the 541S seems to be a more elegant rifle. It would be even more elegant in appearance if the plastic magazine did not protrude from the bottom of the stock. If the author had a choice between a Remington 504 and a 541S, he would choose the 541S. It is that good.

Ordered from J. C. Penney in 1964, this Anschütz 141 with the 6-24X AO Cabela's scope will match the performance of almost any rimfire produced today.

Long known for rifles having outstanding fit and finish, the gleaming trigger guard and floor plate of this Model 141 reflect traditional Anschütz quality.

ANSCHÜTZ 141

In the 1960s, an agreement was reached between Anschütz GmbH of Ulm, Germany and the Savage Arms Corporation under which Savage would market Anschütz rifles in the U.S. In 1964, it was possible to order the Anschütz Model 141 from J. C. Penney. The rifle, a small-tube scope, and a padded case constituted a package for which the price was $87.00. Having only a very inexpensive bolt action rifle at that time that did not shoot at all well, the author ordered an Anschütz 141. Several Anschütz sporters and target rifles still utilize the Model 64 action that was used on the Model 141 rifle.

The Anschütz 141 is a bolt action rifle that makes use of a five round detachable magazine. It has a folding leaf rear sight and a hooded ramp front sight. The receiver is grooved for easy attachment of scope mounts. An adjustable trigger with an excellent, crisp let off is another desirable feature. The stock is of some type of European walnut and has a skip line checkering pattern on the grip and forearm, and the tip of the forearm is made of a contrasting dark wood. An Anschütz 141 is a handsome sporting rifle in all respects.

The Model 141 was available for only a few years before it was replaced by the Model 1416. Of course, the Gun Control Act of 1968 meant the end of ordering firearms from Sears, J. C. Penney, or Montgomery Ward, and the changing socioeconomic climate led to the termination of firearm sales by such stores. Gone are

The Model 64 action is still employed on several Anschütz sporting and target rifles.

the store brands such as J. C. Higgins and Ted Williams from Sears and the Western Field brand from Montgomery Ward. In fact, also gone is Montgomery Ward.

As the author was growing up, the Winchester Model 52 was the finest target rifle available for rimfire competition. It was with a Model 52D that the author competed as a member of an Air Force ROTC team that established an enviable record. However, inroads were being made into the Model 52's dominance, and those inroads were being made by Anschütz among others. The Winchester Model 52 has been out of production since about 1979. Now, Anschütz is a dominant force in the production of rimfire rifles for formal competition at the highest levels. All this is meant simply to point out that the Anschütz name on any rifle carries with it the connotation of high performance.

The author was always impressed with how a bullet from the Anschütz 141 always went where it was supposed to when he did his part. Strange as it may seem, comprehensive accuracy tests were never conducted with the rifle until it became necessary to assemble data for this book. At that point, a Cabela's Outfitter 6-20X scope was mounted on the rifle. With several types of target and match ammunition, the Anschütz put five bullets into ragged holes measuring about one half inch. This rifle will hold its own against almost any of the sporting rifles produced

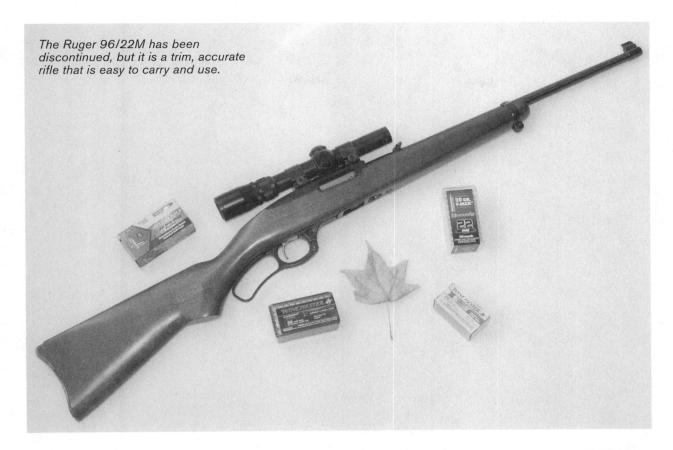

The Ruger 96/22M has been discontinued, but it is a trim, accurate rifle that is easy to carry and use.

today and will give better accuracy than some that carry high price tags.

RUGER 96/22M

Lever action rifles have been popular for over 140 years. Introduced in 1862, the Henry lever action fired a .44 caliber rimfire cartridge loaded with black powder. Following the Winchester 73 in .44-40 caliber came the Winchester Model 1886 in .45-70 caliber. Concurrently with the Winchester Model 1894 came the various Marlin models. With tubular magazines and external hammers, all of these rifles were of the same basic design.

But there was another lever action rifle that was introduced by Savage in 1899 and discontinued only in recent years. That rifle, the Savage Model 99, represented a radical departure in lever action rifles because it had no external hammer, and it utilized a rotary magazine to hold cartridges. A somewhat similar design was employed in the Winchester Model 88, which was also hammerless but used a box type magazine.

William B. Ruger (1916-2002) was a fan of the Savage Model 99, and one of his first feats of engineering was to convert a Model 99 into a semiautomatic.

One of the nice aspects of the Ruger 96/22M is that there is no protruding magazine or release.

He was so enamored with the Savage 99 that he later designed a lever action rifle, the Model 96, that almost too closely copied design features of the Savage 99. It is not difficult to see the similarity in overall configuration. The rounded receiver and curved lever that follows the curved grip of the stock are common to both. Second, both rifles utilize rotary magazines to hold the cartridges.

The Ruger 96 was first produced in .22 LR (discontinued in 2004), but it was also produced in .22 WMR and a very few were chambered for .17 HMR. Maga-

For use on varmints called in to short range, the Ruger 96/22M is very effective.

zines for these calibers hold 10 .22 LR or 9 cartridges in the magnum calibers, respectively.

One day, the author picked up a rimfire Ruger 96M in .22 WMR caliber and, having always liked lever action rifles, was immediately hooked. The Model 96 is 38-5/8 inches long and weighs only 5-1/4 pounds. With its aluminum receiver and 18.5-inch barrel, this rifle is compact and handles extremely well.

The Ruger 96 has many of the features that are found on other Ruger rifles. It was produced only with a carbine style stock, which has a curved butt plate and a barrel band around the fore end. A cross bolt safety is located behind the trigger. Open sights on the Model 96 consist of an adjustable folding rear sight and a front sight that is a bead on a post. Like the Ruger 10/22, the barrel of the 96 is attached to the receiver by means of block that fits in a transverse cut in the bottom of the barrel and is drawn to the receiver by two large screws. This system makes changing barrels a simple matter.

The plastic butt plate is far too slick to be held in one place against the shoulder. That problem was solved by removing the butt plate and spraying it with an abrasive designed to be used on slick surfaces around swimming pools. Two or three coats of the

adhesive gave the butt plate a light color, but it really stays where it is put on fabric.

Mounting a scope is simple because Ruger supplied a scope base that can accommodate either tip-off or Weaver-type rings. The scope chosen was a Cabela's Pine Ridge 3-9X rimfire model. This compact scope measures only about 10 inches in length and has a fine crosshair reticule. The author's Model 96 sometimes wears the even more compact Nikon Monarch 1.5-4.5X scope.

The arc through which the lever must be moved to cycle the action of the Ruger 96 is small (only 54 degrees), and the action operates smoothly. As with the Savage 99, when the lever is pulled away from the grip, the bolt drops down at the rear to unlock it. A steel block runs transversely through the aluminum receiver to provide the sturdy locking surface for the rear of the bolt. Lock up is solid and reliable, and case extraction is provided by dual extractors that are located on either side of the bolt. Because there is no bolt handle protruding from the side of the action, the Model 96 is thinner than the 10/22 autoloaders. Trigger action on the author's Model 96 can best be described as rather heavy and slightly rough. A Lyman trigger pull gauge indicates that let off requires slightly more than six pounds of force, but it is crisp and it improved somewhat with use. Having no visible hammer or cocking piece, it is still immediately obvious when the rifle is cocked because a brass pin protrudes from the top of the receiver when the rifle is cocked then drops just below the surface when the rifle is fired.

For testing, a few shots were fired with Winchester 40-grain .22 WMR hollow points to get the scope adjusted. The first 5-shot groups at 50 yards seemed to have some shots clustered but with one or two fliers. Even so, the first six five-shot groups averaged 0.90 inch. When the stock was removed, it became apparent that at the forward end of the barrel channel, the wood was not rounded to match the shape of the barrel. That was remedied by a piece of fine sandpaper wrapped around a metal tube. After making the barrel channel smooth and putting the stock back on, groups averaged 0.66 inch. Remington Premier with the 33-grain V-Max gave groups that averaged 0.57 inch. Interestingly, all groups were nice clusters with no fliers. The excellent accuracy of the Ruger 96/22M, which is about as good as some bolt action sporters, makes it a superb varmint rifle.

The Ruger 96/22M could not replace a hot centerfire, but it represented one of the best choices available in a rimfire for use on varmints at modest ranges. As in many other situations, an item is not appreciated until it is no longer available, and that is the case of the Ruger 96/22 and 96/22M. Now collectible, the prices of these rifles have soared to the $600-700 range even though they sold for only half that amount when new.

WINCHESTER 9422 MAGNUM

For many years, the lever action Winchester 9422 represented one of the most elegant rimfire rifles available, and it was the only rimfire from Winchester for several years. The Winchester 9422 rifles were beautifully designed and finished. Fortunately, the author acquired a 9422M not long before production ceased. The 9422M was tested for this project and the results obtained are shown in the accompanying table.

Results of Accuracy Testing With the Winchester 9422M with a Scheels 4-12X rimfire scope

AMMUNITION	GROUP SIZE, INCHES		
	Smallest	Largest	Average
CCI Maxi Mag HP	0.50	1.08	0.85
Federal 50 gr HP	0.62	0.98	0.84
Remington Premier	0.59	0.88	0.76
Remington PSP	0.55	0.97	0.72
Winchester HP	0.46	0.87	0.76
Winchester Supreme	0.52	1.03	0.85
		OVERALL AV.	0.80

The data shown in the table should dispel the persistent rumor that lever action rifles are not accurate. The accuracy given by the Winchester 9422M is equal to that shown by most bolt action .22 WMR rifles. It would be hard to imagine a varmint rifle that is more convenient to carry and elegant in appearance.

RUGER 10/22 MAGNUM

With the enormous popularity of the Ruger 10/22, it was natural that there should eventually a magnum version. Although the magnum is very similar in appearance to the .22 LR version, they are quite different rifles. The more powerful magnum cartridge made it necessary for it to have a receiver made of steel. With such a receiver, raised sections were incorporated that had the curved notches milled in them so that proprietary Ruger rings could be utilized. Because of its robust construction, the 10/22M was much more expensive and heavier than the .22 LR version. The factory rifle had a trigger pull that measured almost 12

Although the Ruger 10/22 Magnum looks a lot like the Carbine, it has a steel receiver and is a quite different rifle.

Note the raised sections in the steel receiver that contain the notches for attaching Ruger scope rings.

Accuracy Results for the Ruger 10/22M with a Sightron 3-9 X 36 AO

AMMUNITION	GROUP SIZE, INCHES		
	Smallest	Largest	Average
CCI Maxi Mag HP	0.49	0.76	0.69
CCI Maxi Mag TMJ	0.48	1.04	0.73
Federal 50 gr HP	0.61	1.01	0.89
Remington Premier	0.69	1.53	1.08
Remington 40 gr PSP	0.50	1.02	0.88
Winchester 40 gr HP	0.47	1.16	0.84
Winchester Supreme	0.93	1.35	1.14
		OVERALL AV.	**0.89**

pounds, but let off was crisp. The trigger unit was sent to Herman Tom of Hornet Products, and the trigger pull was adjusted to about four pounds with a crisp let off. Operation of the magnum rifle is the same as the .22 LR version, and it was tested utilizing several types of .22 WMR ammunition, which gave the results shown in the accompanying table.

During testing, the Ruger 10/22M performed flawlessly. With almost all types of ammunition, some groups measuring 0.5-0.6 inch were obtained, except with the Winchester Supreme load. An overall average of 0.89 inch is excellent for a rifle of this type. The 10/22M rifles were discontinued in 2006, and they are seldom seen as used items, and they are priced accordingly.

Although it would have been interesting to test a larger number of rimfire rifles from the past, one must work with the tools and time available. Hopefully, this chapter will give some appreciation of the level of accuracy of a variety of rifles as well as their features and operating procedures. If you have an older rimfire rifle that you would like to shoot, make sure that it is safe and that everything works as it should. Try several types of ammunition, and you may find that the performance you desire from a rimfire rifle has been in the gun cabinet all along.

CHAPTER 17

EVALUATION OF CURRENT RIMFIRE HANDGUNS

SOME RIMFIRE HANDGUNS are among the most popular firearms in existence. There are many reasons for this popularity, but one of the most important reasons is that shooting a rimfire handgun is just plain fun. Another is that one can use a rimfire handgun to build skill that transfers to a different firearm that may be used for hunting or protection. The versatility of a rimfire handgun has been explored in other chapters of this book. However, an additional factor to consider is that it is possible to do a great deal of shooting for a modest amount of money after the handgun has been purchased.

As has been explained elsewhere in this book, the global term "handgun" applies to any short firearm that can be operated with one hand. When such firearms were single shot muzzle loading pieces, the term

A rimfire autoloader such as the Smith & Wesson 2206 (left) enables a shooter to practice with a firearm of the same general type as a centerfire such as the Smith & Wesson 4506 (right).

pistol seems to have been applied, but it was later applied to double barreled handguns and eventually to those with multiple chambers. It is not inappropriate to use the term pistol in a general way rather than just applying it to semiautomatic or single shot handguns. The issue is rather like applying the term "long gun" only to shotguns as a result of the traditional use of the word "gun" as being applied only to one having a smooth bore. Moreover, the term "gun control" is now applied in some circles to *all* types of firearms and even to airguns, which are not even firearms!

The number of types of rimfire handguns available from all of the manufacturers is very large. The total number of variants of all these models is enormous. In any project of reasonable size that is to be completed in one lifetime, the number of pieces studied must of necessity be limited. A phrase often used by coaches is "going with what got us here" and in this case it means using handguns that have been readily available to the author. As a result, a somewhat limited number of handguns were evaluated but with the notion that these models are representative of the available models.

Accuracy

Someone has said that it is not necessary to eat a whole pie in order to tell if is delicious. In the same way, it is not necessary to fire a large number of groups each consisting of many shots in order to assess the overall performance of a handgun. One of the reasons is that the accuracy obtained from any handgun is dependent on the ability of the shooter to a far greater degree than it is with a rifle. The author has had only one eye that performed anywhere near normal throughout his lifetime. In the recent past, the onset of cataracts and other problems with the good eye has resulted in blurring in certain areas of vision. This can be compensated for when testing rifles by making use of a scope of high magnification and a steady rest, but it really hampers accurate shooting of a handgun.

Vision is only one factor in firing a handgun with the ultimate accuracy as a goal. The size of the shooter's hands, the size and shape of the grip, and the quality of the trigger action all enter into the picture. In this work, it was deemed appropriate to fire each handgun with several types of ammunition in order to test the functioning and general handling characteristics of each gun. To determine the true accuracy potential, it is necessary to use a machine rest or mount a scope on the handgun. The inherent accuracy of many handguns is impressive, but most shooters cannot approach this level of accuracy without the use of a scope. Perhaps this is why an increasing number of handguns wear scopes and some models are sold with rails permanently attached for mounting a scope or other optical sight. Because a handgun moves at the moment the sear is released, trigger action is vital to obtaining consistent accuracy. For the pistols tested, the trigger pull was measured by means of a Lyman Digital Trigger Pull gauge.

When a handgun is fired, even one with recoil as light as that produced by a rimfire cartridge, the muzzle jumps. To allow for this movement of the gun as the bullet is moving down the bore, the line formed by correctly aligned sights does not lie along the same line as the axis of the bore, especially for centerfire handguns. In fact, the bore points slightly below the line of sight so that when the muzzle rises during recoil the bullet path will meet the line of sight at the target. Consequently, how the handgun is gripped will affect how much the muzzle jumps and where the bullet strikes on the target. Uniformity in gripping the pistol is essential to consistent shooting. The author once demonstrated this in the following way while shooting a Smith & Wesson K-38 Masterpiece target revolver. After firing several sighting shots with hands propped across a rest, a couple of shots were fired with the square butt of the grip resting firmly on the top of the bench. This prevented the muzzle from rising in a normal way, and the shots hit two or three inches lower than the previous group, which has nothing to do with the outstanding accuracy of this fine handgun. A consistent hold is essential when trying to produce small groups with a handgun.

To begin the tests, several groups were fired at 25 yards with a Browning Buck Mark that is approximately 30 years old. Firing with my hands propped across a rest, the groups measured about 2-2.5 inches

For all of the handguns, the trigger pull was measured by a Lyman digital trigger pull gauge.

with the smallest being 1.19 inches when Winchester T22 ammunition was used. It is impossible for the author to shoot any handgun with better accuracy than that because he can't see any better. Similar results were obtained with a Smith & Wesson 22A. Are the handguns capable of better accuracy? Most assuredly!

To demonstrate these principles, a Weaver 1.5-4X Classic handgun scope was mounted on the scope rail of a Smith & Wesson 22A using Weaver Quad Lock rings. The process took all of a minute or so because the S&W 22A has a permanently attached scope rail. It took a few shots to get the points of aim and impact close together, but the process was simple because the adjustments on the scope worked perfectly. After sighting in, the first 5-shot group at 25 yards with Winchester T22 ammunition measured 0.68 inch! Immediately it became apparent that in order for this shooter to do accurate shooting with any handgun it must be fitted with a scope. It is such a realization that shows why the sizes of groups reported in published handgun tests are relatively meaningless in many cases. Consider taking a rifle that is incredibly accurate and testing ammunition by firing groups at 50 yards using open sights. In such a case, what is being tested is the sighting ability (vision) of the shooter, not the true accuracy of the rifle. Knowing this, the author elected not to fire groups with each of the handguns described and then to report group sizes as some sort of indication of the accuracy potential of these guns. Only if the sighting error is minimized with a scope and a solid rest is used would such data be meaningful, and that was done with a small number of guns. The discussion will be more directly concerned with other characteristics of the guns.

Having made that decision, let us return to describing the true accuracy potential of two handguns. The

Testing the accuracy of a handgun requires better sights than the usual open sights. In this case, a Weaver 1.5-4X handgun scope was mounted on a Smith & Wesson 22A.

With a Weaver 1.5-4X handgun scope attached, the Browning Buck Mark delivered outstanding accuracy.

first is the Smith & Wesson 22A described above. During an extended period of testing, it became apparent that applying a firm, uniform grip for such a long period of time caused my hand to become fatigued and shaky. In general, the groups showed an increase in size the longer the shooting continued even with the same type of ammunition. By looking through the scope and trying to keep the crosshairs in place on the target, the increase in hand shake was obvious. Even with this problem, the average size of 5-shot groups using Wolf Match Target ammunition was only 0.69 inch at a range of 25 yards. With CCI Standard Velocity, the groups averaged almost exactly one inch in size and with Federal Match Target the average was slightly over an inch. Interestingly, the groups were fired in that order, and the increase in group size is due to fatigue in the shooting hand. My wife took the S&W 22A and fired three 5-shot groups with Federal High Velocity hollow points with the first measuring only 0.39 inch. As she continued firing, there was a general increase in group size.

What is the ultimate accuracy of the Smith & Wesson 22A? With one group measuring only 0.39 inch and the average of three others being only 0.69 inch (before hand fatigue became a problem) it must surely be around half an inch or less at 25 yards with some types of ammunition. Even by testing in this way the ultimate accuracy has not been determined, but this is a very accurate pistol. Although the author has never cared for scopes on handguns, it was now clear that one would be required if he ever wanted to do really accurate shooting with a handgun.

The next experiments were conducted with a Browning Buck Mark after mounting the Weaver 1.5-4X scope on it. In order to mount a scope on the Buck Mark it is first necessary to attach a scope rail. The rail

used was one produced by B-Square, and it can be attached after removing the rear sight and top strap on the action. The rail mounts along the top of the frame and is attached by removing two large screws, one that holds the top of the barrel to the front end of the frame and the other that is located at the rear of the frame. With the scope rail placed on top of the frame, the screws are replaced to attach it.

Firing a few shots allowed the scope to be sighted in and testing was initiated. Groups with Federal Gold Medal Target measured approximately one inch for five shots at 25 yards. Groups obtained using CCI Green Tag were similar in size. Switching to Wolf Match Target produced groups measuring 0.79 and 0.91 inch. The Buck Mark is capable of even better accuracy, but shooting conditions were not ideal at the time of the tests. Once again it was demonstrated that the accuracy shown by any handgun is dependent on the ability to achieve a steady, consistent rest and grip. The Browning Buck Mark demonstrated a level of accuracy that would make it a superb choice for the hunter of small game or pests who goes afield with a handgun. Based on later tests, additional information on the accuracy of this fine pistol will be given in the next section.

The accuracy demonstrated by scoped rimfire handguns is truly remarkable when compared to the limited accuracy indicated by firing them with conventional open sights. A Ruger Mark II 22/45 with a 5.5-inch bull barrel belonging to the author's brother has a 2X Bushnell scope mounted. With it he has produced 7/8-inch 10-shot groups at 25 yards using the bulk pack Federal High Velocity hollow points. When 5-shot groups are fired, even smaller groups are regularly obtained. This combination has become his choice when hunting squirrels with a handgun.

With scopes attached, the three handguns described

will regularly give groups that measure well under an inch at 25 yards. Does this level of accuracy show the ultimate capability of these models? Not at all. They were fired while being hand held and as the pull on the trigger approaches three or four pounds, the movement of the crosshairs on the target shows the shaking clearly. After conducting the tests described in this section, it is the opinion of the author that most of the handguns described in this chapter are capable of groups that measure no more than 3/4-inch or so at 25 yards. That is why the usual procedure of shooting several groups and reporting average group sizes was not followed to determine a level of accuracy that does not represent anything but a vision and hand test.

BROWNING BUCK MARK

Introduced in 1985, a Browning Buck Mark has been in regular use by the author since soon after that time. The Buck Mark is the culmination of a series of Browning semiautomatic pistols that included the Nomad and Challenger models from the 1960s and 1970s. The Challenger went through several versions designated as Challenger I, II, and III. With the introduction of the Buck Mark in 1985, the Challenger III was discontinued.

The Buck Mark Standard originally had black composite grips that gave way to grips made of rubber in 1991. In 1987, the Buck Mark Plus version with smooth grips of laminated wood was introduced. It is this model that the author's wife selected after some experience with his older Buck Mark. Several versions of the Buck Mark have been produced in the intervening years. The standard Buck Mark has a 5.5-inch heavy barrel with a recessed crown. One of the unique features of the Buck Mark is that the slide operates within the frame so that the top of the frame does not move during firing. As a result, the rear sight remains stationary, and the action is open on both sides when

Both sides of the receiver are open when the slide is drawn back which makes it easier to clean and inspect.

the slide is drawn to the rear. The front sight is a square-topped blade of generous width whereas the rear sight is fully adjustable.

There are approximately 30 variants of the Buck Mark. In addition to the standard model with an MSRP of $469, there is the Buck Mark Plus that has checkered wood grips and an MSRP of $579. Other variants are available in a wide variety of finishes and with grips of various types. Some models, such as the Hunter, are available with fitted rails for mounting a scope or optical sight. The Buck Mark Challenge (suggested price $549) is distinguished by its round, lightweight barrel and checkered walnut grip panels. The result is a 25-ounce pistol with many of the desirable features of the Buck Mark. The Buck Mark Camper has a round tapered barrel with a matte finish and, with a suggested price of $389, it is the least expensive Buck Mark.

As if the few variants described above were not enough, there are three Buck Mark pistols in the series that are intended for more serious target pursuits. The variant known as the Field Target has a 5.5-inch fluted bull barrel and weighs 38 ounces. It can be had with cocobola grips (suggested price $579) or laminated rosewood grips. These pistols are capable of rifle-like accuracy.

The two Buck Mark pistols tested were a standard model of early production and a more recent vintage Buck Mark Plus. Controls on all versions of the Buck Mark are identical. The release for the 10-round magazine is a button located behind the trigger on the left hand side of the frame. Also, on the left hand side near the rear is found the lever type safety, and just ahead of it is the slide release button. A hold open device on the Buck Mark keeps the slide in the rear position after the last shot is fired. The barrel has flat sides that are highly polished and the top of the barrel has a matte finish.

Sights are adjustable and provide an excellent sight picture. The rear sight on current Buck Mark pistols is adjusted differently than are those on early models. Windage on early specimens was adjusted by means of two tiny screws, one on either side of the rear sight base. The rear sight is held tightly in place between the two screws. Loosening the screw on one side and tightening the one on the other moves the rear sight in the direction of the screw that was loosened. Invariably, the rear sight works loose on the author's older Buck Mark during extended shooting. On newer pistols, the windage adjustment is a single screw with click stops.

Trigger action on the Buck Mark pistols tested is

The safety locks the slide on the Buck Mark and it cannot be placed "on" unless the pistol is cocked.

The rear sight on the Buck Mark is fully adjustable and allows an excellent sight picture to be established.

The recessed muzzle on the Buck Mark (left) is quite different from that on the much older Colt Huntsman (right).

outstanding. The author's older version has a crisp release with a pull of 2.75 pounds with absolutely no creep. The Buck Mark Plus belonging to the author's wife has a somewhat stiffer trigger with let off requiring a pull of 3.5 pounds but also without noticeable creep. The trigger action of these pistols is as good as on any pistol that is not a full-fledged target model. Although it has a listed weight of 34 ounces, the older Buck Mark actually weighs only 31.9 ounces on a postal scale. With the slightly heavier wood grips, the Buck Mark belonging to the author's wife weighs 32.7 ounces.

With a 5.5-inch bull barrel, good sights, and excellent trigger action, the Buck Mark is capable of outstanding accuracy. There was only one failure to cycle with either of the Buck Mark pistols during the testing. A 10-round magazine is standard, and it is the easiest magazine to load for any autoloading pistol owned by the author. Some of the results of accuracy testing the Buck Mark with a Weaver 1.5-4X scope attached were discussed earlier in this chapter. However, the Buck Mark was tested extensively at 25 yards to show the level of accuracy that one can expect from a fine handgun that is fitted with the high quality Weaver handgun scope. The data obtained are shown in the accompanying table.

The data summarized in the table indicate that the Browning Buck Mark is a very accurate handgun. Of course, tested under similar conditions, so are several others. When fired from a steady rest with a scope attached, rimfire handguns are about as accurate as are some rifles. This should come as no surprise because accuracy is not determined by barrel length. The scope removes the necessity for trying to align simultaneously the rear sight, front sight, and target that are at different distances from the shooter's eye. When that problem is overcome, handguns can be extremely accurate. As with all other types of rimfire firearms, the Buck Mark showed preferences in ammunition. Perhaps even more so than a rifle

Accuracy Results for the Browning Buck Mark with a Weaver 1.5-4X Scope

AMMUNITION	GROUP SIZE, INCHES		
	Smallest	Largest	Average
CCI Pistol Match	0.63	1.75	1.01
Federal High Velocity HP	0.52	0.98	0.79
PMC Pistol Match	0.55	0.82	0.72
PMC Scoremaster	0.88	1.46	1.15
Remington Golden HP	1.57	2.02	1.73
Winchester T22	1.75	2.61	2.04
Wolf Match Target	0.73	1.03	0.87

OVERALL AV. 1.19
at 25 yards

Magazines for autoloaders have a button to help move the magazine follower during loading. Guess which of these three magazines is easiest to load.

shooter, the handgun hunter should test several types of ammunition to find types that give best accuracy because bullet placement is more important than is a small increment in velocity. Suffice it to say, the Buck Mark has accuracy that will match the shooting ability of almost anyone.

The grip on the Buck Mark is of comfortable size and contour. The trigger is correctly placed and its shape is comfortable for the finger. Overall, it is a pleasant piece without some of the annoying little nuances that plague some models. Outstanding in fit and finish, accurate, and reliable, the Browning Buck Mark is a superb handgun. It would be difficult to find a more capable pistol in the same price range. Moreover, there are enough variants available to satisfy the esthetic taste of almost any shooter.

RUGER MARK III

Ruger initiated manufacture of rimfire handguns with the Standard model in the late 1940s. It was a very sturdy model made of steel and having a 4.75-inch barrel. When introduced, that pistol had a price of $37.50. Not long after, a target version having a heavy barrel that measured 5 7/8-inches in length and an adjustable rear sight was introduced. It was priced at $57.50.

The Ruger Mark III represents the latest iteration that began with the Standard model that gave way to the Mark II version along the way. The Mark III has some important differences from the Mark II. These include the magazine release, which on the Mark III is located on the left hand side of the frame behind the trigger rather than a latch located on the bottom of the grip as is the case with the Mark II. The Mark III also features a loaded chamber indicator, which is a pivoted bar on the left hand side of the receiver. When a cartridge is in the chamber, the lever is pushed out of the frame slightly and a red dot appears. Also, the Mark III pistols have receivers that are drilled and tapped for attaching the scope rail that is provided

The Ruger Mark series pistols are some of the most successful rimfire handguns of all time. (photo courtesy Ruger)

Accuracy Results for the Ruger Mark III Target with 4X Scope

CARTRIDGE	AVERAGE GROUP SIZE inches*
CCI Mini Mag HP	0.85
CCI Standard Vel.	0.80
Eley Pistol	0.64
Remington Club Xtra	0.77
Remington Golden	0.73
Winchester HV HP	1.04

OVERALL AV. 0.81
*Average of three 5-shot groups at 25 yards from bench rest.

On the Ruger Mark II and III, the safety is located on the left hand side of the frame below the receiver. The bolt can be pulled back with the safety on.

With a scope attached, the Ruger Mark III Target gives accuracy equal to that of some rifles.

with the pistols. The rail is designed to attach in front of the rear sight so only removing three filler screws is required to attach the rail. It is recognized that an increasing number of handgun shooters will add either a scope or some sort of optical sight to their guns. With a 5.5-inch barrel, the Mark III weighs 42 ounces but measures only 9.75 inches in length.

The Mark III Target was tested at a range of 25 yards with a 4X scope attached. Firing was done from a bench rest with the pistol supported. The accompanying table shows the results obtained.

The accuracy exhibited by the Ruger Mark III Target is excellent. It is sufficient to make the Mark III Target an effective tool for hunting at ranges up to at least 50 yards. The pistol functions reliably with virtually any type of ammunition and it is constructed to withstand a lot of firing. With an MSRP of $499, it is also reasonably priced.

KIMBER RIMFIRE TARGET

For some time the author has been infatuated with a Kimber Custom II .45 auto of the 1911 pattern. The pistol has been utilized as the test vehicle for projects dealing with reloading .45 Auto ammunition as well as for general shooting. With the decision to update and expand this book with a second edition, it became apparent that a Kimber rimfire should be featured. Rather than buying a complete new pistol in .22 LR caliber, it was decided that the Kimber on hand would be employed by adding a Rimfire Conversion Unit®. That is done by simply removing the barrel and slide assembly from the .45 Auto and installing the slide and barrel assembly included in the Rimfire Conver-

sion Unit.

Conversion units for converting a .45 Auto 1911 pistols into a rimfire have been available for many years. Colt produced such units as far back as the 1930s and eventually produced a .22 LR version of the famous 1911 known as the Colt Ace. It was intended primarily as a training tool, and as expected, the Ace is now a highly collectable item. The last specimen seen by the author in mid-2015 had a price tag well over $2,000.

Converting a 1911 pattern .45 Auto to a rimfire has numerous benefits. Perhaps the most important is that the shooter can practice with a firearm that has the same grip, trigger action, and safety as the .45 Auto caliber firearm utilized for defense or in other ways.

Although other brands of .22 LR conversion kits are available to fit 1911 pistols, the intent was to keep the pistol "all Kimber" so that route was taken. The Kimber Rimfire Conversion Unit is available in either black or polished finish, and it will fit most 1911 style pistols. Because the author's Custom II has a matte black finish, the black unit was ordered.

Installation of the Kimber Rimfire Conversion Unit requires disassembly of the .45 Auto pistol. That process is carried out starting with the pistol unloaded, cocked, and the magazine removed. Disassembly of a 1911 pistol begins with removal of the nose plug by pressing the guide rod inward and turning the barrel bushing toward the right hand side of the pistol. With the nose plug removed, the bushing and plug that fits over the recoil spring can be removed. Moving the slide to the correct position makes it possible to push the slide locking pin out of the frame and to lift out the recoil spring. Next, the slide is removed from the grip frame by moving it forward. The conversion unit is installed on the grip frame by sliding it on from the front. After the hole in the guide rod base is aligned

A Kimber .45 Auto can be converted to a .22 LR with the Rimfire Conversion Unit®.

Removal of the slide from a 1911-style autoloader requires the slide retaining pin to be withdrawn from the left hand side of the frame.

with that in the frame, the slide stop pin is inserted.

The Kimber .22 Rimfire Conversion Unit has a weight of 13.2 ounces and when mounted on the Custom II frame the result is a .22 LR pistol that weighs 31.3 ounces. Weight of the Kimber Custom II .45 Auto is 38 ounces. The converted Kimber is a superb rimfire pistol that has the look, feel, and function of the legendary .45 Auto. Installation of the Rimfire Conversion Unit was simple and rapid. In very short order, the .45 Auto Kimber Custom II was converted to a .22 LR Target Kimber.

Both the Kimber catalog and instruction manual for the Rimfire Conversion Unit state that high velocity .22 LR should be used. Although the slide is made of aluminum and the recoil spring is not nearly as strong as that in the .45 Auto, the slide needs to cycle smartly in order for the pistol to function reliably. The .45 Auto is a powerful cartridge so autoloaders in that caliber are designed so that the slide and barrel are locked together at the time of firing. The .22 LR version operates on a simple blowback principle with no locking between the barrel and slide.

Using the Kimber as a rimfire pistol is somewhat different than using it as a .45 Auto. First, a magazine is required that will hold .22 LR cartridges rather than .45 Auto rounds. The Rimfire Conversion Unit comes with such a magazine and it is made of a hard polymer material. Second, because the top of the magazine activates the device that holds the slide back after the last shot, the rimfire magazine does not function in that way. Consequently there is no "hold open" after the last shot.

Sights on handguns are normally regulated so that the point of impact coincides with the point of aim while taking into account the degree to which recoil moves the muzzle upward. The .45 Auto caliber Kimber Custom II has fixed sights that accomplish this very well. However, given the difference in power of .22 LR and .45 Auto cartridges, the Kimber Rimfire Conversion Unit is fitted with a fully adjustable, target-type rear sight. The correct direction to turn the elevation and windage adjustment screws is clearly indicated to make sighting in a simple process. The front sight is a square topped post whereas the rear

The slide utilized with the .22 conversion unit is that of the Kimber Rimfire Target.

The conversion unit includes a magazine that holds 10 rounds of .22 LR.

A look at the muzzle makes it obvious that this Kimber is no longer a .45 Auto.

The Kimber Rimfire Conversion Unit is provided with excellent adjustable sights.

sight has a blade with a square notch that mates with the front sight to give an excellent sight picture.

After reading several items posted on the internet about failure of other conversion units to feed, fire, or eject reliably, it was with some apprehension that range testing was begun. The apprehension was totally misplaced with the Kimber. It functioned perfectly with Winchester, Remington, and CCI high velocity ammunition. However, two instances of failure to feed were encountered when firing a "low end" or bulk type of ammunition. The Kimber unit is an elegant piece of machinery and functioning was completely reliable except for those two cases. In addition to conversion units that feature five-inch barrels and stainless or blue slides, units are also available from Kimber in a shorter version for use on more compact 1911 style .45 Auto pistols.

The slide of the Conversion Unit is labeled "RIM-FIRE TARGET" so it was with some eagerness that testing of the pistol was commenced. Firing was done from a standing position using a two-hand hold. The Kimber performed extremely well. It was easy to obtain small five-shot groups when firing at a target placed 10-15 yards away. The pistol was not fired from a machine rest nor was a scope mounted so accuracy is a somewhat subjective issue, and it is possible that the converted pistol may not be suitable for competitive shooting at a high level. However, the Kimber left no doubt that it is certainly accurate enough for informal target shooting, training, or hunting small game at short range. The Kimber Rimfire Conversion Unit has the MSRP of $339 but can often be found at retail for slightly lower than $300.

The author is so impressed with the Kimber ".45 converted to .22" that the pistol will probably remain in that configuration, which has necessitated getting another Kimber to leave as a .45 Auto.

Feeding and ejection were flawless with the Kimber .22 conversion unit.

RUGER SUPER SINGLE SIX CONVERTIBLE

The Ruger Single Six was first offered in 1953 with 4 5/8 or 5 1/2-inch barrel options. The original model had a loading gate that was a flat disk with a thumbnail notch for opening. The author had one of these early versions (now collectible of course), but before long some other firearm needed to have part of its price covered by a trade in. Later, another Single Six came to the author in December 1958 so the author's experience with the Ruger Single Six goes back over half a century. From 1960-1972 the convertible version of the Single Six Convertible was offered with both .22 LR and .22 WMR cylinders.

In 1973, the so-called New Single Six resulted from Ruger's modernization of the single action revolver. The loading gate was connected to the cylinder bolt so that when the loading gate was opened the cylinder could be rotated for loading without the hammer being drawn back to the "half-cock" notch. Also, a transfer bar mechanism was included that prevented the hammer blow from being transmitted to the firing pin unless the transfer bar was moved into its upward position behind the firing pin, which occurs only when the trigger is pulled to the rear. As has been discussed earlier in this book, this was a great safety measure. Many options have been available in barrel lengths, type of steel, and sights over the years.

Single action revolvers represent the ultimate simplicity in terms of operation. The loading gate is opened, the cylinder is rotated to load each chamber, and the loading gate is closed. Drawing the hammer back cocks the revolver and causes the cylinder to turn to index the next chamber for firing. After pulling the trigger and firing a shot, cocking the hammer rotates the cylinder to align the next chamber. When all shots have been fired, the loading gate is opened and empty cases are ejected one at a time by pushing back on the ejector rod and rotating the cylinder to align the next chamber.

The Super Single Six Convertible used in this testing is the stainless steel version that has a 5.5-inch barrel and the adjustable rear sight common to this model. With the square-topped post on a ramp and the square notched rear sight, the sight picture afforded is about as good as with any rimfire handgun. Loading and functioning are predictable and reliable.

With considerable experience with both rimfire and centerfire autoloaders, the author has found them to be extremely reliable, especially the centerfire

With an interchangeable cylinder chambered for the .22 WMR, the Single Six Convertible is a versatile, reliable handgun.

Having a cylinder that chambers all .22 WMR ammunition makes the Single Six Convertible extremely versatile.

The Ruger single action revolvers employ a transfer bar that is raised as the trigger is pulled.

models. However, some (if not most) rimfire autoloaders are somewhat finicky about feeding certain types of ammunition. This was experienced in testing some of the pistols described in this chapter and the next. When it comes to a revolver, if the round goes into the cylinder, it will fire. Only a faulty round (several of which were found in conducting the tests with rifles) will cause a misfire. In keeping with this, no misfires were experienced with the Single Six nor were they expected. It is this type of reliability and the safety that results from the visible hammer that make a revolver so appealing and comforting. In this regard, the Ruger Single Six is unsurpassed.

How accurate is a Ruger Single Six? It is accurate enough to meet or exceed any requirement of this author. To determine the ultimate accuracy, a scope would have to be mounted on the gun and that the author refuses to do. A classic single action revolver is going to remain that way because that is how the gun is going to be carried and used. Some shooters seem to shoot better with an autoloader than with a revolver,

but the author has never found much difference. It is probably more a matter of hand shake and vision in my case although competitors at a high level virtually always use an autoloader in rimfire competition. The Ruger Single Six remains a superb choice for plinking and comfort in remote areas.

When it comes to versatility, it is hard to imagine any rimfire handgun being more versatile than the Ruger Single Six Convertible. The cylinder that holds .22 LR will also accommodate .22 Short, .22 Long, CB, and shot cartridges. The .22 WMR cylinder can be used with all forms of the magnum cartridge as well as the .22 WRF and .22 WMR shot cartridges. As a result, one can do some shooting as long as any type of .22 rimfire ammunition is available.

RUGER MARK 22/45

As popular as the Ruger Mark I and II pistols have been, there are still those who would like something different. One objection voiced by many handgun shooters is that the grip angle on some guns does not match some preconceived notion of what it ought to be. It is the opinion of the author that except in unusual cases, the shooter will adjust to any reasonable grip angle. Many shooters, the author not necessarily being one of them, feel that the grip angle of the Colt Model 1911 represents perfection. Accordingly, Ruger produced a version of its famous semiautomatic known as the 22/45 in which the grip matches the size and angle of the famous Colt 1911 .45 Auto. Introduced in 1992, the Model 22/45 has a polymer grip frame, and the push button magazine release functions in a manner similar to that of the Colt 1911.

Four variants of the Model 22/45 are listed in the 2016 Ruger catalog. These pistols are now referred to as the 22/45 Lite models and they feature barrels that

Ruger's 22/45 features reliability and accuracy in a pistol with a grip that has the feel of the Colt 1911 auto. (photo courtesy Ruger)

The Ruger 22/45 with a heavy barrel gives a pistol that is accurate but lighter in weight than the Mark III. (photo courtesy Ruger)

The latest version of the Ruger 22/45 has a polymer frame and is known as the Lite version. It is available in several colors. (photo courtesy Ruger)

are slender steel tubes inside an aluminum sleeve that also serves as the receiver. Grip frames are made of Zytel® polymer and the aluminum barrel sleeves have cut out sections along the sides. The rather cosmic looking 22/45 models have the MSRP of $549. The variants of the Ruger 22/45 have much in common with the Mark II (described earlier) and current Mark III models, but weigh less because of having a polymer frame. However, the 22/45 pistols are provided with adjustable sights as well as a scope rail.

With a 2X Bushnell scope attached, an older Ruger 22/45 has been used regularly by the author's brother to hunt small game. It is utterly reliable and the accuracy is outstanding. If one is addicted to the grip design of the Colt 1911 .45 ACP autoloader, the Ruger 22/45 might be the rimfire pistol of choice. It has been so pleasing to the author's brother that several rimfire handguns have come and gone over the years, but the 22/45 has remained in his collection. That should tell you where it ranks in the estimation of a serious shooter.

SMITH & WESSON MODEL 22A

As discussed in Chapter 1, the Smith & Wesson name has been associated with rimfire firearms since the earliest days of .22 rimfire history. In the mid-1900s, the reputation of Smith & Wesson was carried on by the medium and larger frame revolvers in calibers such as .357 Magnum, .44 Magnum, and .45 Colt. Later, the introduction of a novel 9mm double action pistol, the Model 39, came about as the general interest in semiautomatic handguns was growing. This led to the present lineup of pistols, which includes many that are designed for law enforcement and defensive uses. However, the Smith & Wesson name appears on a series of popular rimfire pistols as well as on the legendary Model 41 target pistol. There are actually two series of .22 pistols that share most characteristics of design except the metal used in the frame. The two series are the 22A that was introduced in 1996 and the 22S, which was introduced in the following year. The 22S series is made of stainless steel whereas the 22A pistols have frames made of aluminum alloy. Contrasted with pistols having the classic Colt and High Standard appearance, the Smith & Wesson pistols have a modern look, but not as radically so as do the offerings from some other manufacturers. Although Smith & Wesson has just introduced the SW22 Victory as a replacement for the 22A and 22S, they are still seen as new pistols.

In designing the 22A and 22S series, Smith & Wesson kept the top of the frame and the rear sight from moving back with the slide by having a sight rib that serves as the top of the action. Therefore, the rear sight is stationary with the slide moving below it in much the same way as in the Browning Buck Mark. However, the Smith & Wesson pistols have a full-length sight rib permanently mounted on the barrel and action. The rear sight rests in a cut out area at the end of the rib. The sight rib has four lateral notches in it where Weaver-type scope rings can be attached. Although all 22A and 22S pistols have adjustable sights, they are also set up for easily attaching a complete array of aftermarket sights.

The Smith & Wesson 22A is a versatile handgun that is capable of fine accuracy. Optional sighting equipment can easily be mounted on the permanently attached rail.

With a 7-inch barrel, the Smith & Wesson 22S is a good choice when accuracy is needed. With a weight of 42 ounces without a magazine, it might not be the choice of backpackers.

The pistol used in this evaluation is the Model 22A with a 5.5-inch barrel although other variants have 4- or 7-inch barrels. With a 5.5-inch barrel, the 22A is 9.5 inches long and weighs 32 ounces (without magazine) so it is not a compact model. Being made of stainless steel, the 22S models average almost 10 ounces heavier. The alloy frame of the 22A is finished with a black coating, and the pistol has composite grips with rubber inserts along the front and back edges of the grip frame. The grip is hand filling, but not too large, and the grip has an excellent feel. For a period of time, a version of the 22A was available with full coverage camo finish, and wood grips were available on one variant. Pistols in the 22S series were available having 5.5-inch or 7-inch barrels with choices of grips. Smith & Wesson offered grips for the 22A and 22S that were made of hard plastic with or without the rubber inserts, a plastic grip with thumb rest, and a large target grip of laminated wood. As aftermarket items, barrels in 4, 5.5, and 7-inch lengths and grips of different style were available.

Sights on the S&W 22A are standard in that the front sight is a square-topped post and the rear is a blade with a square notch. The rear sight is fully adjustable for windage and elevation by means of slotted screws. The sights permit a good sight picture to be established. Other controls are standard with the safety and slide release levers located on the left hand side of the frame. One feature that is different from most rimfire auto pistols is the magazine release, which is located in a recess along the front edge of the grip frame. This is a holdover from the design of the earlier 2206, 422, and 622 models, which had a similar magazine release. This allows the grip to have a clean appearance with the bottom of the magazine flush with the bottom of the grip. Although the S&W 22A looks a little unusual with a rather large sight rail installed along its top edge, the pistol handles well and has good weight distribution.

The rear sight on the S&W 22A is fully adjustable and gives a good sight picture with the square topped post front sight.

Pressing inward on the checkered button in front of the trigger initiates takedown.

Trigger action on the author's 22A requires a soft take up motion after which the let off occurs with a pull that measures 4.1 pounds. It is very similar to a two-stage trigger in its operation except that during the first stage the pull gets heavier and the trigger moves backward slightly. Overall trigger action is good, but the pull should be about a pound lighter. The rather small trigger has a sharp front edge at the bottom that digs into the trigger finger, and it became uncomfortable during extended shooting sessions. Although the magazine of the 22A has a protruding knob to help in moving the magazine follower downward while loading, it still requires considerable effort to compress the magazine spring. It is not the easiest magazine to load. Two or three failures to feed were experienced during testing with standard velocity ammunition. High velocity ammunition cycled regularly, and this behavior is in accord with the experience of other shooters with many rimfire pistols. Some rimfire autoloaders function better with high velocity ammunition.

Although the accuracy of the S&W 22A was described earlier, it was decided that the pistol should be tested at a distance greater than 25 yards. A Leupold FX-II 4 X 28 scope was mounted using Weaver Quad-Lock rings. From a stable rest supported on a concrete bench, five-shot groups were fired at 50 yards using four types of ammunition. The results obtained are shown in the accompanying table.

Results of testing accuracy of the S&W 22A at 50 yards with a Leupold 4X scope

AMMUNITION	GROUP SIZE, INCHES		
	Smallest	Largest	Average
CCI Standard Velocity	0.84	2.27	1.52
Federal High Velocity HP	1.89	2.05	2.00
Remington Club Xtra	1.22	1.57	1.40
Winchester Super X HP	1.16	2.22	1.79
		OVERALL AV.	1.68

As can be seen from the data, the S&W 22A gives accuracy that is comparable to that obtained with some rimfire rifles. This level of performance indicates that if the shooter does his or her part, the pistol would be suitable for hunting small game pests at ranges up to

Smith & Wesson is in the process of replacing the 22A series pistols with the SW22 Victory. (photo courtesy Smith & Wesson)

at least 50 yards. In discussing the accuracy of the 22A with a representative at Smith & Wesson, the author expressed his surprise. The representative replied that one should not be surprised because barrels for the 22A are made on the same machines that produce those for the legendary Model 41, one of the most accurate rimfire target pistols.

One minor irritation with the Model 22A involved the sight rail. Some of the popular optical sights come with a mounting base attached. In the case of one red dot sight, the base has two Weaver-style cross bolts with one of them being movable in a slot so the spacing between the cross bolts can be varied somewhat. In spite of this latitude, it was not possible to mount the sight on the rail of the S&W 22A because of the spacing between the lateral grooves in the scope rail. This is no more a fault of the 22A than it is of the mounting base on the red dot sight.

Overall, the Smith & Wesson 22A is a substantial pistol that gives excellent performance. As this is written in early 2016, this model is being phased out in favor of the new SW22 Victory, but new 22A pistols are still to be been seen in display cases. With the 5.5-inch barrel or an optional one of 7 inches, the 22A or the stainless 22S would be a good choice for the hunter with small game and varmints in mind. The newly introduced SW22 Victory has most of the features of the 22A series.

WALTHER P22

Two of the most recognizable pistols of all time are the Walther P-38 of World War II fame and the Walther PPK, which is nearly 85 years old. The firm of Carl Walther also has produced some elegant rimfire sporting rifles in the past. Target rifles for the competitive shooter have also carried the Walther name. Although the PPK and PPK/S models live on, Walther is probably best known at this time for the famous

P99 centerfire pistol that is intended primarily for law enforcement and military use. The P99 exhibits numerous innovative features one of which is that the rear portion of the grip is removable so that inserts of different thickness can be attached to change the grip profile. Another novel feature is that the decocking lever is flush with the top of the action near the rear sight and is activated by pushing it downward into the receiver. The P99 is offered with many options in 9mm and .40 S&W calibers.

The P99 also serves as the design model for the CO_2-powered .177 caliber pellet pistol known as the CP99. Another offspring of the centerfire P99 is the rimfire P22, which is the subject of this evaluation. Although outwardly resembling the P99, the P22 has some important differences. First, it has a visible hammer and functions in the way that is customary for double action pistols. When the safety is off, the first shot can be fired in the double action mode whereas succeeding shots are fired single action, or the pistol can be cocked manually and all shots

fired single action. Second, the P22 has dual safety levers that are located on either side at the rear of the receiver. Third, the magazine release consists of a lever that is contoured to match the trigger guard, and it is located along the sides at the rear part of the trigger guard. Pulling downward on either portion of the lever releases the 10-round magazine. The P22 also has a key lock that is located on the right hand side of the frame just above the trigger. Integrated locks of this type are appearing on an increasing number of handguns including the Bersa Thunder 22, Walther PPK, and the new Ruger Mark III. The Walther P22 also has a loaded chamber indicator.

Although the general features of the Walther P22 have been listed above, there is still more to describe. Barrels having lengths of 3.4 and 5 inches are available with the longer barreled models designated as "target" models and those with shorter barrels called "standard" models. However, as a result of the lightweight polymer frame, both models weigh 20 ounces or less. The target pistols have a nonfunctioning "compensator" that

Even with a 5-inch barrel, the Walther P22 is a compact, lightweight pistol with several novel features.

The insert on the back of the grip can be interchanged on the Walther P22 so the grip shape can be altered.

With increased safety in mind, the Walther P22 has a key lock on the right hand side of the receiver. A slotted key is necessary to turn the lock.

As on the Walther P99, the magazine release on the P22 is a lever that forms an integral part of the trigger guard. Pulling down on the lever releases the magazine.

serves as a barrel weight. Sights on both models consist of a post with a white dot insert and a rear blade with white dots on either side of the notch giving the "three dot" type of sight that is popular on modern pistols. Walther offers a bridge-type mount that clamps around the barrel to the sight rail, which constitutes an integral part of the frame in front of the trigger guard. Also offered is a laser sight that clamps to the sight rail so it fits nicely under the barrel ahead of the trigger guard. As a really unique feature, the short and long barrels are readily interchangeable so one is not permanently linked to a standard or target model.

There are six versions of the Walther P22 Pistols that result from there being two barrel lengths. The first is an all black finish. Other options include a black polymer frame with a silver-gray slide and a black slide with an olive drab grip frame. The latter is known as the "military" version in keeping with the designations applied to the P99 pistols.

The Walther P22 can be fired either single or double action. As a result, the trigger action of the P22 is not quite as good as that of the Browning Buck Mark, but it

Dual safety levers are provided on the Walther P22. However, they do not function as decocking levers.

By loosening the two Allen headed screws, the barrel and muzzle weight can be removed so that the shorter barrel can be installed.

is acceptable nonetheless. In single action mode, the let off was crisp at a pull measured as 5.0 pounds. The owner's manual states that the trigger pull in single action firing is 4.85 pounds so it is quite close to the specified value. It is the double action pull for the P22 that is impressive. To fire in the double action mode, a smooth pull of only 9.5 pounds was required. Overall, trigger action is quite good for a small double action model.

One could wish that the designers of the P22 had made the safety levers also function as decocking levers as is the case on many centerfire autoloaders. The only way in which the P22 can be decocked is by carefully holding the hammer while pulling the trigger to the rear and letting the hammer down slowly.

Compact but capable, the Walther P22 is a rimfire pistol with many innovative features. The 3.4-inch barreled pistols are so small and light that they are comparable to many of the so-called pocket pistols that have been produced over the years. Although the short barreled version would make a good hiking piece, even the 5-inch barreled pistol is small and weighs only about 20 ounces. It would also be very convenient to carry, and the longer barrel would give slightly higher velocity, and it could also be fired a little more accurately as a result of the longer sight radius. In firing, the Walther P22 functioned reliably and gave good accuracy for a pistol of this type. With a barrel of either length, the P22 is an effective handgun for plinking, camping, and trail wear.

Carrying the legendary Walther name and formerly marketed by means of an alliance between Walther and Smith & Wesson, the P22 is an interesting piece. Retail prices are in the $300-400 range depending on barrel length and other options.

SIG MOSQUITO

For many years, Sig Sauer has marketed a small .22 LR semiautomatic known as the Mosquito. As this is written in early 2016, the Mosquito no longer appears in Sig's catalog or website. However, new Mosquito pistols are still seen in numerous showcases so it will be described briefly.

The author has had a decade of experience with a Sig Mosquito. Beauty of any object depends on the artistic tastes of the observer, but the Mosquito is an attractive handgun from the author's point of view. It bears a strong resemblance to other classic Sig models such as the P226, and the controls are located similarly. The Mosquito has a number of interesting features and is shipped with two recoil springs of

Although recently discontinued, the Sig Mosquito is a durable, compact pistol.

different strengths so the user can sort of tailor the tension to the ammunition being used. Supposedly, the lighter spring is for use with lower powered loads and the stronger spring with high velocity loads. However, most owners of a Mosquito seem to find that the lighter spring gives more reliable feeding with most types of ammunition. Also, the pistol is provided with three front sights of different heights.

Sights on the Mosquito are of the three dot type with a dot on the rear face of the front sight and one on either side of the rear sight notch. The rear sight is adjustable for windage but not elevation, which can be "adjusted" by changing the front sight. Removing the slide exposes the under side of the front sight. It fits in a slot with hooked retainers that can be compressed so the front sight can be removed from the top of the slide and a different blade inserted. Thus, the pistol has adjustable sights, albeit not by the conventional means of moving only the rear sight. Disassembly of the Mosquito requires the takedown lever to be rotated to unlock the slide from the barrel and frame. The slide is then brought fully to the rear and the rear end of the slide lifted upward to free it from the retaining grooves. The slide is removed by allowing it to move forward.

Although the action was initially gritty, it smoothed considerably with use. As in the case of some other types of .22 LR autoloaders, the Mosquito gave several stoppages with some types of ammunition. However, it functioned reliably with Winchester Power Point and three Remington loads, the Thunderbolt, Golden, and Game Loads. The least desirable feature of the Mosquito is the action of the trigger, which requires a pull of almost seven pounds to fire in single action

shooting. Given these limitations and the skill of the shooter, the accuracy of the Mosquito is on a par with other small pistols.

Early specimens of the Sig Mosquito seem to have been plagued with feeding issues, but these were later corrected to some extent. The Mosquito belonging to the author still fails to feed some types of ammunition so they are simply avoided. Even though new Mosquito models are to be found, the author would see little use to select one given the success of the Ruger SR22 and Walther P22.

RUGER SR22

As is so well stated by E. Kreps in *Camp and Trail Methods* (A. R. Harding, Columbus, OH 1950, p. 64), "There are times when one cannot be burdened with a rifle, and does not care to go entirely unarmed." That statement describes a lot of situations, and a small handgun may be the solution.

A small handgun is a very useful device. It may be used for protection, food acquisition, or fun. Although a rimfire handgun would ordinarily not be the first or best choice for protection, it is far better than bare hands. This was recognized long ago and led to the development of small rimfire revolvers that could easily be carried in a pocket, purse, or kit bag. There is currently an epidemic with regard to defense and the showcases of firearm dealers are filled with small guns suitable for concealed carry and self defense. In fact, some manufacturers have shifted much of their production to such guns. Most are either small semi-automatics chambered for .380 Auto or 9mm Luger or revolvers chambered for .38 Special. However, rimfire shooters have not been neglected.

One of the most recently introduced .22 LR autoloaders is the Ruger SR22. It is a straight blow back (the barrel and slide are not locked together at the time of firing) so only the slide moves to the rear during firing. The barrel is firmly attached to the frame so it does not move. The SR22 incorporates the slide stop feature that causes the slide to remain in the rear position after the last shot is fired and the magazine is empty. Inserting a loaded magazine and pulling the slide to the rear causes the slide to be unlatched so it will move forward when released taking a cartridge from the magazine to the chamber. An accessory rail is located on the forward section of the frame to permit attachment of accessories.

This small pistol has many good features. First, it has an external hammer and can be fired in either

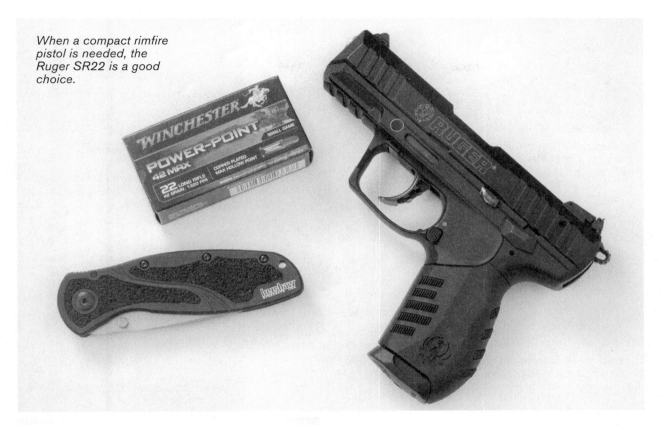

When a compact rimfire pistol is needed, the Ruger SR22 is a good choice.

Although it is a compact pistol, the Ruger SR22 is provided with an accessory rail.

Dual safety levers that also function as decocking levers are provided on the Ruger SR22.

double (pull the trigger) or single action (cock the hammer for the first shot) mode. Right up front, the author confesses to favoring this type of pistol rather than the internal hammer (with an external safety) or the striker fired pistol (with or without an external safety). The external hammer provides the shooter with an instant assessment of the condition of the firearm. Moreover, placing the safety "on" when the pistol is cocked serves as the decocking feature on the SR22. Dual safety levers are provided.

In keeping with the increased interest in firearm safety, Ruger has provided for a loaded chamber indicator. In the case of the SR22, there is a small port where the rear portion of the barrel meets the slide. Peering into that port will allow the shooter to see if a cartridge is in the chamber.

Many rimfire firearms should not be dry fired because the firing pin can impinge on the rear edge of the chamber if nothing is there to deaden the blow. Ruger has designed the SR22 so this does not occur making dry firing possible with no damage to either the firing pin or the chamber *as long as an empty magazine is in place.*

Although the Ruger SR22 is a compact pistol with a 3.5-inch barrel, it is provided with a fully adjustable rear sight, which enables the shooter to sight in the

The Ruger SR22 is provided with adjustable sights that make use of white dots to increase visibility.

Disassembly of the Ruger SR22 is simple and begins with pulling the disassembly lever downward.

In order to disassemble the gun, the slide is drawn to the rear and lifted up to disengage the rails.

Allowing the slide to move forward permits removal of the slide, recoil spring, and guide rod.

Disassembly beyond the level shown is not recommended.

pistol when using a particular type of ammunition. This makes it possible for the shooter to place shots more accurately and that in turn makes the firearm more versatile. Turning the windage adjustment screw in a clockwise direction moves the point of impact to the right and turning the screw counterclockwise causes the point of impact to move to the left. Turning the elevation screw clockwise moves the point of impact down whereas turning it in the opposite direction raises the point of impact. The rear face of the front sight has a white dot in the center whereas the rear sight has a white dot on either side of the square notch. This arrangement of handgun sights, known as a "three-dot system" is quite popular, and the sights on the SR22 are excellent.

The Ruger SR22 is furnished with two rubberized grip adapters that slide over the grip frame making it possible to alter the grip size. These sleeves are held securely in place by a detent at the top of the grip frame and a firm pull is required for their removal. The pistol is also shipped with two 10-round magazines.

Disassembly of the Ruger SR22 is accomplished by placing the pistol on "safe" and removing the magazine. Next the slide is pulled to the rear and locked in that position by moving the slide stop upward so that

the chamber can be inspected. Moving the slide forward allows the take down lever (located at the upper front end of the trigger guard) to be pulled downward away from the underside of the frame. Next the slide is pulled fully to the rear and the rear end lifted upward freeing the slide from the rails. While holding the slide in this position, it is moved forward slowly to free it from the barrel. The guide rod and recoil spring can now be lifted out of the slide. At this point, the pistol is separated into the grip frame with the barrel attached, the slide, and the recoil spring and guide rod.

Reassembly of the SR22 is essentially the reverse of this process, but it is necessary to place the recoil spring on the guide rod with the smaller end of the spring to the rear. The flanged end of the guide rod is placed in a retaining hole in the frame under the barrel. The end of the recoil spring having larger diameter is placed in a recess in the bottom of the slide. The slide containing the guide rod and recoil spring is moved fully to the rear while keeping the rear portion of the slide lifted upward away from the frame. Lowering the slide to the frame requires the hammer to be depressed slightly. The slide is pressed downward to the frame and allowed to move forward slowly so that the slide is mated to the guide rails. Moving the slide fully forward makes it possible to

Even though it is a light, compact pistol, the Ruger SR22 is sufficiently accurate for most purposes.

rotate the takedown lever upward to the locked position inside the trigger guard.

On the range, it was found that the SR22 performed well. Shooting offhand at seven yards produced five-shot clusters that measured less than two inches. However, the clusters were located slightly to the right of center, but the rear sight was easily adjusted with a small screwdriver to place the groups at the point of aim. From that time, groups measuring 1.5-2.0 inches were easily obtained, but this little pack gun was not tested at longer range. Functioning with both Winchester Super-X and CCI Mini Mag ammunition was flawless.

As this is written in early 2016, Ruger has just announced the introduction of a version of the SR22 having a 4.5-inch barrel. The 3.5-inch version weighs only 17.5 ounces and it measures 6.4 inches in overall length. The SR22 having a black finished slide has an MSRP of $415 and that with a slide of silver finish is priced at $429. A third version has a threaded barrel and lists for $449.

The Ruger SR22 functions well and is sufficiently accurate for the purposes to which a compact rimfire pistol is likely to be put. It is an accessory that is easy to carry on those walks in the woods or when engag-

ing in various types of outdoor activities.

It takes little imagination to see that the Walther P22 and Ruger SR22 are very similar. The takedown levers are located in different positions, but the procedure is similar. The Walther has a slide made of a zinc alloy whereas that of the Ruger is made of aluminum. Both pistols permit the grip to be altered with inserts that are provided. The Ruger has a fully adjustable rear sight but that of the Walther is adjustable only for windage. The author owns a Ruger SR22 and his son has a Walther P22 so both pistols have been evaluated. Frankly, it is the opinion of the author that they are equivalent and either would be a very nice companion on the trail or in the camp. As mentioned at the beginning of this section, "There are times when one cannot be burdened with a rifle, and does not care to go entirely unarmed." (E. Kreps, *op cit*.).

Of necessity, a limited number of handguns have been described in this chapter. In most cases, the guns selected are representative of an extensive number of similar models. Therefore, this chapter gives an overview of a larger number of the available rimfire handguns. From compact autoloader to long barreled single action revolver, there is a rimfire handgun to suite almost any taste and budget.

CHAPTER 18

SHOOTING SOME VINTAGE RIMFIRE HANDGUNS

ACCORDING TO HISTORY, the first rimfire firearm was a small handgun chambered for the original .22 Short cartridge. The number of handgun models produced in the intervening century and a half is staggering. Companies that came on the scene and flourished for a time were many, and most of them have been defunct for many years. To try to produce a review of all the rimfire handguns ever produced or even a sizeable fraction of that number would be a prodigious task that would result in a book (make that a *large* book!) on the subject. However, in order to provide some basis for comparison with current models and to give some guidance to the prospective buyer of a vintage rimfire handgun, it is necessary to evaluate a few representative models. This chapter is devoted to some rimfire handguns that are not in current production, but this in no way is meant to indicate that they are necessarily antique firearms, which is a different subject altogether. Along with the discussion of some of these handguns, historical information and notes will be given that relate to other models that are similar. In terms of the enormous range of vintage handguns that have been produced, the sampling here is of necessity quite limited.

As was explained in the last chapter, the accuracy of a handgun is much more a function of who is shooting it than in the case of a rifle. Resting a rifle across sandbags on a sturdy bench and aligning the reticule of a scope of high magnification on a target removes much of the human element. Therefore, presenting the results of thorough testing of several rifles to establish their accuracy capability and to test ammunition is justified. In testing the vintage handguns, it was felt that there was no need for an extensive series of accuracy tests. The idea behind the work was not to try to establish a baseline of accuracy for comparisons between models, but rather to show that these models are still functional, capable pistols. Accordingly, each pistol was fired with several types of ammunition to check function and in collecting data on velocity (see Chapter 8). It was deemed sufficient for the purposes intended to examine each gun with regard to handling characteristics and function and to conduct limited firing. Keep in mind that some models are discontinued and replaced by another so both models may be found for sale for a period of time.

RUGER MARK II

In 1949, Sturm, Ruger, & Co. introduced a semi-automatic pistol that has become one of the most successful rimfire pistols of all time. The initial version was known as the Standard Model and it had a retail price of $37.50 at the time. The author owned one of those early pistols in his late teen years, but before long it was traded for something that had a special interest at the time. It is impossible now to remember what is was. A couple of years later, a target version of the Ruger having a 6 7/8-inch barrel and adjustable sights was introduced. In 1982, an improved pistol known as the Mark II was produced. It differed only slightly from the original model, most notably in changes to the safety that allowed the bolt to be drawn back with the safety "on" and a slight change in the rear of the receiver that allowed the shooter to get a better grip on the grooved areas of the bolt. Production of over 3 million pistols indicates something of the popularity of the Ruger line, which includes many variants that differ in barrel length, sights, and type of steel. Finally, in November 2004 production was shifted to the Mark III series. A more complete discussion of the Mark II variants and the new Mark III was given in Chapter 4.

The Ruger Mark II is one of the most successful rimfire pistols of all time.

The Ruger Mark II tested was the stainless steel Standard model with a 4 5/8-inch barrel and fixed sights. In some ways, this variant has the most pleasing looks of all Ruger rimfire autoloaders in the opinion of this author. Operating the pistol is straight-forward for anyone who is somewhat knowledgeable about .22 semiautomatic pistols. Like many older rimfire pistols, the magazine release on the Mark II is located on the bottom of the grip. Pushing the catch backward releases the 10-round magazine. The magazine release on the new Mark III pistols is a button on the left hand side of the frame just behind the trigger. Loading the magazine with cartridges requires some degree of hand strength because the Ruger makes use of a strong spring, and the button for depressing the magazine is small. Inserting the magazine into the grip and pushing it upward causes it to be latched in position. The bolt remains open after the last shot is fired, and bolt release is located on the left hand side of the frame as is the safety. Drawing the bolt to the rear and releasing it allows it to move forward taking the top round in the magazine into the chamber. Trigger pull on the Mark II was measured as 3.5 pounds with almost no creep.

During testing, the Ruger Mark II performed flaw-lessly, which came as no surprise because that has been the reputation of this pistol for many years. It feeds, fires, and ejects regularly with any type of ammunition. The Browning Buck Mark is a substantial, sturdy hand-gun in all regards, but in comparison the Ruger Mark II seems as if it is built like a tank. This is not meant to imply that the Buck Mark is in any way flimsy because it definitely is not. It is just that with its heavy tubular steel receiver, the Ruger Mark II (or the newer Mark III) is very robust. Long life and reliability have been the trademarks of the Ruger autoloaders for many years. The author did not find the Ruger quite as steady on target as was the Buck Mark because of the difference in weight distribution. However, that a subjective issue that might strike other shooters differently.

Outwardly, the Ruger Mark II and Mark III have some resemblance to the famous Luger. To the author, there is no more attractive rimfire autoloader available. For most shooting, the models with fixed sights are adequate, but many shooters will opt for one of the variants with adjustable sights. As a general "carry" gun, the author would select the fixed sight model with a short barrel, but for hunting small game and pests, he would prefer one of the versions that can readily have a scope attached. The current Mark III Hunter or Target would meet the expectations of any handgun hunter and will last almost forever in the process.

COLT HUNTSMAN

Colt introduced a .22 autoloader in 1915 that was to become one of the premier pistols of that type. With approximately 700,000 pistols produced over a period of 62 years, this pistol underwent a great many improvements and alterations. The pistol was known as the Colt Woodsman although the initial model was known as the .22 Caliber Colt Automatic Pistol, Target Model. The Woodsman name began to be used around 1927, and it lasted for about 50 years. The 4.5-inch barrel length was introduced in 1933. A heavy barrel version introduced in 1938 was known as the Match Target Woodsman, and 4.5- and 6-inch barrels were available. Throughout the early years of the author's shooting experience, the Colt Woodsman was one of the most highly regarded rimfire pistols for target shooting. However, the Woodsman and the later Match Target Woodsman were quite expensive for that time period. They are highly collectible and are even expensive now.

Responding to the demand for a lower priced pistol for general use, Colt introduced the Challenger in 1950. Unlike the Woodsman that had outstanding adjustable sights, the Challenger was a fixed-sight model. After a few years in production, the Challenger gave way to the Huntsman. This model was offered with 4.5- and 6-inch barrels and fixed sights. Approximately 100,000 Huntsman pistols were produced between 1955 and 1977. Early variants had black plastic grips but later pistols like the one described here were produced with checkered walnut grips. As in the case of the Challenger, the Huntsman did not have a device to hold the bolt open after the last shot was fired.

Although the Colt Huntsman was regarded as a sort of budget priced Woodsman, it was a fine handgun with many desirable features. The checkered walnut grips were comfortable and attractive. The traditional

Of classic design, the Colt Huntsman offers the rimfire shooter many of the advantages of the legendary Colt Woodsman.

high polish and exquisite bluing were unmistakably Colt. With the 4.5-inch barrel, a Huntsman weighs only about 29.3 ounces. The 10-round magazine unlatches at the bottom of the grip. Trigger action on the Huntsman is reminiscent of that found on many older semiautomatic pistols. The trigger broke cleanly and reproducibly at 3.0 pounds with no creep and overall trigger action was about as good as that for any of the semiautomatic pistols tested, modern or vintage. One feature of the Huntsman and many other older semiautomatic rimfire pistols that makes one cringe a bit is that the safety must be taken "off" in order to pull back the slide. This means that the shooter may be

As on the Colt Woodsman, the safety on the Huntsman locks the slide. The safety must be off before the slide can be withdrawn.

A large button allows the magazine follower to be drawn downward for easy loading of the Colt Huntsman's magazine.

The magazine release on the Colt Huntsman is located on the bottom of the grip.

holding a loaded pistol in the "ready" condition as the slide is drawn back, and special care is advised.

During the firing tests, the Huntsman performed just as it did when it was new. It fed reliably with all types of ammunition and gave good accuracy even though the sights are not adjustable. Colt no longer produces a rimfire semiautomatic, so older models have risen in value. A Huntsman in good condition will cost as much or more than a new Ruger or Smith & Wesson model, but it would be a good choice for most rimfire shooting. Even though the Huntsman is not the equal of the Woodsman, it is nonetheless a fine pistol.

SMITH & WESSON 2206

Manufactured from 1957 until the present time, the Smith & Wesson Model 41 is one of the premier rimfire target pistols. Although there is always a steady, small demand for such pistols, models for more general use (and having lower price because the list price of the Model 41 is $1,369) are much more popular. In 1987, Smith & Wesson introduced a new model that was designated as the Model 422, and this was followed by the Model 622 in 1990. Both models were offered with 4.5 and 6-inch barrels with either fixed or adjustable sights. The adjustable sight versions were called Target models. The difference between the 422 and 622 models is in the finish. Both were made with aluminum frames and steel slides, but the 422 has a blued finish whereas the 622 has a satin finish resembling stainless steel. Weights of the 422/622 pistols are 21.5 and 23.5 ounces, respectively, for the 4½ and 6-inch barreled pistols. Later, 3-inch barreled versions known as the Sportsman were introduced.

Based on the success and performance of the 422/622 pistols, the all steel Model 2206 was introduced in 1990. Versions were available that had barrel lengths of 4.5 and 6 inches. Weights were 35 and 39 ounces, respectively, so these are hefty, durable handguns. As in the case of the 422 and 622, the 2206 with adjustable sights is designated as a Target model. The 2206 uses a simple blow back principle with only the rear portion of the slide moving. However, one radical point of departure that separates the 2206 from most other autoloaders is the fact that it uses a barrel that is mounted as low as possible in the frame. The idea behind this procedure is that the focus of the recoil is as close to top of the hand as possible, which helps reduce the effect of recoil to give less muzzle jump. The barrel is retained in the frame by a slotted, recessed sleeve and is easily removed.

Made of stainless steel, the Smith & Wesson 2206 is a durable but heavy pistol. Alloy frame models of the same period were the 422 (blue) and 622 (bright).

The Model 2206 makes use of the same 10-round magazine that is used in the S&W Model 41. Unlike most autoloading pistols, the 2206 has a magazine release that is located in a recess on the front of the grip. It might seem that one could inadvertently press the latch and drop the magazine, but that has never happened to the author. The hand simply wraps around the grip without making much contact with the latch, which requires a substantial force to release. The safety lever is located on the left hand side of the frame at the rear. A stop is provided that holds the slide open after the last shot. One attractive feature of the 2206 is that the pistol will not fire with the magazine removed. This is a valuable safety feature because if the magazine is removed, a forgotten round in the chamber can not be fired.

On the Smith & Wesson 2206, the barrel is placed low in its housing. The slotted retaining ring can be removed which allows the barrel to be taken out.

On the Smith & Wesson 2206, the magazine release is a lever recessed into the front of the grip.

The safety lever on the Smith & Wesson 2206 is conveniently located on the left hand side of the frame and operates independently of the slide.

The front edge of the trigger guard is curved to assist when a two-hand hold is applied. An adjustable trigger stop is provided for controlling overtravel. It is a set screw with an Allen head located in the bottom of the rear portion of the trigger guard. The Lyman trigger pull gauge showed that the trigger broke cleanly with a pull of 4.7 pounds on the 2206 tested.

The S&W 2206 digested all types of ammunition without hesitation or stoppage as it always has. Discontinued in 1996, a Model 2206 can sometimes be found for an attractive price. Although the models having adjustable sights are generally preferable, the pistol tested shot very close to the point of aim. Other shooters may need a rimfire handgun with better accuracy, but the author has found the 2206 to shoot quite well. With some eye problems, the author would have to use a handgun with a scope to shoot much better. For the intended uses of the Model 2206, it would be difficult to find a current model that would be more appropriate. It has been a trusted and faithful companion for many years in many places. As described in Chapter 12, it has been a frequent choice for a rimfire for tough times. The characteristics of the 2206 also apply to the 422 and 622 except for latter models having aluminum frames.

HIGH STANDARD H-B

Founded in 1926, the High Standard Manufacturing Company in New Haven, CT, produced rimfire handguns for many years. In 1932, High Standard purchased the Hartford Arms and Equipment Company. Over the years, High Standard, which was first located in New Haven, moved to Hamden, CT then to East Hartford. In 1984, High Standard ceased production of handguns due in no small measure to the enormous popularity of lower priced models such as the Ruger Standard Mark I and the later Mark II and some of the lower priced models from Smith & Wesson, Browning and Colt. But there were many fans of High Standard pistols that mourned their passing, and as will be explained later, it is hard to keep a good product out of the marketplace.

Over the years, High Standard autoloaders were produced in an enormous range of variants. Some of the early models were designated as the Models B, C, A, D, and E. Almost concurrently, other models were designated as the HD, HE, HA, and HB with the letter H denoting that the model has a visible hammer. The most popular barrel lengths were 4.5 and 6.75 inches, but not all models had the same barrel diameter.

With its slender barrel, this High Standard Model H-B is light in weight, but it gives high velocities.

There were also other differences between the models in details such as sights, grips, etc. Eventually, High Standard produced pistols for the U.S. government for military training. Some of these pistols had the letters "US" after the model designation. One model, the HD Military, was also sold to the civilian market. Over half a century ago, a friend of the author had an HD Military model with a 6.75-inch barrel that he could shoot with great skill. His use of that handgun to hunt squirrels demonstrated just how effective a handgun could be in the hands of a careful hunter.

As strange as it may seem at this time, some of the models that had visible hammers did not have an external safety. The hammer functions as it does on a revolver or double action autoloader, which also have no external safety. In 1949-1954, the High Standard Model HB Second Model was produced, which is the pistol described in this section. As with almost all of the other models, it has a magazine that holds 10 rounds and checkered grips made of black hard rubber. The Model HB exhibited the outstanding trigger pull that is sometimes found on older semiautomatics.

Only limited firing tests were conducted with the Model HB, but the 6¾-inch barrel produced high velocities (see Chapter 8). This particular specimen failed to feed a few times because the cartridge was not forced into the chamber fully. The pistol seemed to have a weak recoil spring and/or a tight chamber so only limited testing was conducted. Although highly prized by collectors, many of the older High Standard pistols are still capable of fine performance. Later models such as the Sport King were trim, versatile handguns that would make excellent companions for today's outdoors enthusiasts.

In 1993, High Standard Manufacturing Co., Inc., of Houston, TX began producing handguns that emulate to a high degree some of the earlier models. Three of the new versions are the High Standard Trophy, Supermatic, and the Victor. These are target pistols that can be obtained with sights or scope rails in place. However, the currently produced High Standard pistols are rather expensive. Although not one of the largest producers of rimfire handguns, pistols carrying the High Standard name are once again available.

SMITH & WESSON K-22

In 1899, Smith & Wesson introduced a double action revolver that was destined to become one of the most successful firearms of all time. Known as the S&W First Model, it was chambered for the then-new .38 Special cartridge, and the mid-sized frame was of an appropriate size for that cartridge. The S&W revolver frame of that size is now known as the K-frame. For about 100 years, Smith & Wesson produced revolvers with frames of three sizes. The smallest is the J-frame, the midsize is the K-frame, and the large frame used for magnum calibers is the N-frame. In more recent years, the L-frame was introduced for calibers such as the .357 magnum. The recently introduced .500 S&W is produced on an even larger size frame known as the X-frame.

In a long evolutionary process, the initial .38 Special revolver came to be known as the Military and Police model, and when Smith & Wesson began to designate models numerically in 1958, the highly successful revolver became known as the Model 10.

A true classic, the Smith & Wesson Model 17 (also known as the K22 Masterpiece) is a wonderful handgun for any time period.

The K-frame became the basis for many other models such as the Model 15 Combat Masterpiece, which has a 4-inch barrel and target sights. Although some of the other K-frame models are interesting and important, it is the target revolvers, known as the Masterpiece series, that are relevant here. The K-38 Masterpiece (.38 Special caliber) was known as the Model 14 whereas the K-22 Masterpiece (.22 LR caliber) was known as the Model 17. The Model 18 was a .22 LR version having a 4-inch barrel that was a companion piece to the Model 15 Combat Masterpiece. Some of these models underwent evolutionary changes, but they were eventually discontinued. Currently, Smith & Wesson produces the Model 617, which is built on the K-frame, but it is made of stainless steel and has a full-length lug under the barrel. The current Model 617 is a fine handgun that is considerably heavier than the K-22.

Over the years, the K-22 was available with 4-, 6-, and 8 3/8-inch barrels with the 6-inch length being the most popular. Many options were available including target grips as well as target hammers and triggers. Realizing that most target shooters would cock the gun for each shot, one version was offered as a single action only gun. Needless to say, the revolvers in the Masterpiece series were highly regarded arms that were widely used in target competition. The square-topped post and fully adjustable rear sights are the equal of those on any currently produced handgun. As autoloaders became more popular, the demand for these fine revolvers decreased and most of the options were no longer offered. Another group of shooters who became interested in the K-22 were the small game hunters who chose to hunt with handguns. A K-22 was and still is one of the best choices for this type of activity. Trigger pull on the K-22 is crisp and predictable, which is fully consistent with the intended use of these fine guns.

As Smith & Wesson makes changes in a particular model, the new variants are indicated by a number following the basic model number. For example, the 10-8 designation indicates the eighth variant of a Model 10 Military & Police. The designation can be found by opening the cylinder and looking at the yoke where the serial number and model designation appear. The K-22 evaluated belongs to the author's brother, and it is old enough that it does not have this type of designation. A call to Smith & Wesson allowed a check of the serial number to be made, which showed that this gun was produced in 1951, several years before models were designated numerically. However, in spite of its

age, the K-22 performed admirably. It is completely dependable and displayed excellent accuracy. With the addition of a good holster, the old S&W K-22 would be a superb choice for the outdoorsman who needs a reliable rimfire handgun, and being several ounces lighter than the current Model 617 would make it even more desirable. A safer, more dependable, better performing .22 revolver than the Smith & Wesson K-22 has never been made in the opinion of the author.

SMITH & WESSON MODEL 34 KIT GUN

For many years, rimfire autoloaders have been much more popular than are revolvers, but it has not always been so. Although each type of action has its advantages and disadvantages, one of the most useful rimfire handguns is a compact, sturdy revolver with target sights and good trigger action. There are several reasons for this. First, a revolver can be loaded with the Short, Long, or Long Rifle cartridges, and it is ideal for making use of shot cartridges. Semiautomatics will not feed all of these types of ammunition. Second, it is the belief of the author that revolvers are inherently more safe than semiautomatic pistols. Whether a revolver is loaded or not can be ascertained instantly. Third, when carried in a holster, there is much less chance of the hammer on a revolver being moved back accidentally than there is for the small safety lever on a semiautomatic being moved from the "safe" position. In fact, the author almost never carries a holstered autoloader that has no external hammer with a round in the chamber, because it is unsafe to do so. With modern revolvers, a transfer bar is employed to transmit the blow of the hammer to the firing pin. However, the transfer bar is not moved upward in line with the firing pin until the trigger is pulled back at the time of firing. With all of these factors considered, what is the ideal rimfire handgun for general use?

There are many shooters who believe that the Smith & Wesson Model 34, also known as the Kit Gun, is about as close as one can get to the ultimate in a rimfire utility handgun. It was referred to as the Kit Gun because it was appropriate to include with the camping kit, fishing kit, or hunting kit, not because it was purchased as parts and assembled later. Introduced in 1935, the original model was known as the 22/32 Kit Gun because it utilized the small J-frame of the 32 Hand Ejector model. In 1953, the later version of the Kit Gun, which later became known as the Model 34 when model numbers were assigned, was available with a barrel of 2- or 4-inch length and a weight of

As a handgun for the backpacker, camper, and woods roamer, the Smith & Wesson Model 34 Kit Gun is among the most highly regarded (and sorely missed) choices.

about 22 ounces. The front sight is a serrated ramp of 0.10-inch thickness, and the rear sight has a square notch in a blade that can be adjusted for windage and elevation. Over the years, both round and square butt models were available in blue or nickel finish. From 1955-1974, a variant with a weight of 14.5 ounces was produced with an aluminum frame and cylinder and a 3.5-inch barrel.

Although the Kit Guns of early manufacture (1935-1953) are highly prized as collectibles, the later versions are also highly prized as shooters. This is still one of the most practical rimfire handguns ever made for the hiker, camper, or outdoorsman. As part of the testing program reported here, the near mint nickel-plated specimen belonging to the author's brother was made available for testing (unfortunately it was not made available for purchasing).

Superb in fit and finish, the Kit Gun performed with excellence. It must be admitted, however, that the author was not able to fire it as accurately as he can a Browning Buck Mark autoloader that weighs about 10 ounces more and has a heavy barrel. But in every other aspect, the performance of the Kit Gun would be difficult to improve on. Being a revolver, it can readily accept any .22 LR ammunition from shot cartridges to CCI Stingers with no question as to whether feeding will be reliable. There is no more versatile rimfire handgun than a good revolver. This and many other S&W revolvers perform flawlessly now just as they have for many years.

In spite of its many desirable attributes, the Kit Gun in the form tested is no longer available. What is currently available is the Smith & Wesson Model 317 that has an alloy frame and cylinder. It is an 8-shot revolver that is available with a 3-inch barrel and adjustable HVIZ® (fiber optic) sights. Weighing only 11.9 ounces, it should be a fine backpacker's or camper's gun, but there is one problem. It has a manufacturer's suggested price of $759, which even at retail amounts to approximately $675 according to my dealer. This is approximately twice as much as several autoloader models cost. Therein lies one of the reasons why rimfire autoloaders are currently much more popular than revolvers. Given a choice at a comparable price, the author would select the Kit Gun over most rimfire autoloaders as a trail gun.

RUGER SINGLE SIX

Sturm, Ruger and Company produced its first handgun model in 1949. That handgun was the original autoloader that continues in production today in a highly evolved form known as the Mark III. In 1953, Ruger introduced the single action revolver known as the Single Six. It was very similar in many respects to the original Colt Peacemaker (Single Action Army) that was introduced in 1873. Unlike the Colt, which had a rounded loading gate, the loading gate of the Ruger Single Six was a flat piece of metal with a curved notch to be engaged by the thumb nail during opening the gate. The author bought one of those early models with the flat loading gate and used it until something else caught his youthful fancy (the identity of which can not even be remembered at this time). As in the case of many other items, the early models, which were traded off without regret at the time, have become collectibles and command a premium in price. These become the

This three screw or "old model" Ruger Single Six and the author became companions in 1958. They are still close friends.

pieces known as "I wish I had that one back", a malady that afflicts many shooters. But wisdom comes to those who think so another Single Six with the rounded loading gate was obtained in 1958. Recounting my experiences associated with this handgun over so many years would fill a small volume.

In 1957, the loading gate was redesigned to resemble the rounded loading gate of the Colt single action revolvers. However, the Ruger single action revolvers suffered from some of the same deficiencies as the early Colt models. Most important of these flaws is that when the hammer is down, it rests against the firing pin, which rests against a cartridge that is in alignment with it (the chamber at the "top" of the cylinder). An accidental blow to the hammer could cause the revolver to fire. Drawing the hammer back slightly allows it to engage a safety notch. However, even the safety notch on the hammer that was designed to hold the hammer back slightly away from the firing pin could not be relied upon to prevent accidental discharge when a heavy blow struck the hammer. To circumvent this problem, it was common practice to carry the piece with only five rounds loaded in the cylinder with the empty chamber being directly below the hammer. Another problem was that the hammer had to be drawn

back to half cock to release the cylinder lock so that the cylinder could be rotated during the loading process. After loading, the hammer had to be drawn back to full cock and held with the thumb as the trigger was pulled and held back so that the hammer could be let down slowly. The result was that during the loading process, the shooter was dealing with a cocked, loaded revolver. These aspects applied to both Colt and Ruger single action revolvers in addition to those produced by other makers. Ruger revolvers with this older type of action have three screws visible on the right hand side of the frame. Accordingly, they are known as "three screw" models, but Ruger refers to them as "old model" single action revolvers.

In 1973, Ruger introduced a redesigned single action revolver that circumvented the problems described above. The "new model" revolvers make use of a transfer bar to transmit the blow of the hammer to the firing pin. The transfer bar is raised to be positioned between the hammer and firing pin only as the trigger is pulled. Therefore, unless the trigger is pulled to the rear, a blow to the hammer merely forces it forward against the frame and cannot cause the piece to discharge. Moreover, the loading gate is linked to the cylinder in such a way that opening the gate

The Colt Frontier Scout (left) and the old model Ruger Single Six (right) function in similar ways.

To access the chambers of the old model Single Six, the hammer must be drawn to the half cock position and the loading gate swung out to the right.

releases the cylinder lock and allows the cylinder to be rotated. In that way, the cylinder can be loaded with the hammer in the "down" position. The new model revolvers can be carried with all six chambers loaded, and they can be loaded without having to go through the process of moving the hammer in any way. Clearly, the new model Ruger single action revolvers are much safer than the older models. For many years, Sturm, Ruger & Co. has offered a free upgrade for the three screw revolvers. It requires that the gun be sent to the factory for fitting the new parts, but the old parts are returned with the modified gun so nothing is lost in terms of the collector value of the gun. For the purposes of this project, the pre-1973 three screw models are considered vintage revolvers.

Ruger single action revolvers have an enviable reputation for durability and reliability. Although some versions have fixed sights, excellent adjustable sights are standard on most of the new Ruger single actions, and they provide a good sight picture. On the old

Empty cases are ejected one at a time from the Ruger Single Six by pushing back on the ejector rod.

model tested, the front sight is the familiar semicircle with a square top and serrations on the back edge. The rear sight has a square notch of suitable size. There is no provision for elevation adjustment, but windage can be adjusted by moving the rear sight laterally in its retaining dovetail notch. With virtually any type of ammunition, this handgun has always shot as nearly to the point of aim as the author can discern. The sights have never been found lacking for my purposes, and they have never been adjusted.

Trigger action on my old Ruger Single Action is unbelievably good with absolutely no creep and a let off measured with a digital scale at 2.8 pounds. Of all the handguns tested, only the trigger action of the author's Browning Buck Mark is this good. One rarely finds a trigger with these characteristics today except on target models. In his younger days, the author disassembled the Single Six revolver and internal surfaces were polished with crocus cloth. The action is as smooth as that of any single action revolver produced today and far smoother than most.

When the hammer is drawn back and the trigger is pulled, the Single Six fires every time no matter what type of ammunition resides in the chambers. It is this kind of behavior that makes a single action revolver so reliable. It is also the reason why single action revolvers are still chosen for carry in remote areas by many knowledgeable people. True, the single action is an outmoded design for uses such as military and law enforcement work. But as a handgun for tough times, hunting, or plinking, the single action is still a viable option. Elsewhere in this book is pictured an old Single Six that belongs to a cowboy in Wyoming. It has been carried on foot, on horse, and on an ATV countless hours and miles. It is a working gun, and it still works even though it has very little blue left on it and the grip panels are chipped. One could seriously doubt that the owner of that gun would be interested in trading it for almost any of the modern autoloaders.

The old Single Six described and pictured here had not been used much in recent years as other models had become infatuating. In order to collect some thoughts on the gun, it was carefully examined and tested. There is something special about the look, feel, and pointing qualities of a single action revolver. It was like getting reacquainted with an old friend. For many years, the Single Six described here was the author's only handgun, and it always performed well. It would still meet virtually any need one could have for a rimfire handgun.

With a barrel that measures almost 10 inches in length, this Colt Frontier Scout Buntline is an interesting piece.

COLT FRONTIER SCOUT

With the most recognizable revolver ever made being the Colt Single Action Army model of 1873, there has always been an interest in single action revolvers. The legendary Colt has such an aura of romance and respect that it generates interest in a similar gun chambered for rimfire calibers. This interest led to the introduction of the Ruger Single Six in 1953 and introduction of the Colt Frontier Scout in 1957. In later years, both models were produced with an optional cylinder that was chambered for the .22 WMR. The Frontier Scout was produced with several barrel lengths that included 4.75 and 9.5 inches. Currently, Ruger produces several single action rimfire models, and Heritage Manufacturing produces revolvers with interchangeable cylinders in .22 LR and .22 WMR calibers in both blue and stainless steel.

The Frontier Scout, which has an aluminum alloy frame, was produced in several variants over the years of its production. In 1970, another rimfire single action known as the Peacemaker was produced by Colt, and it remained in production until 1977. It had a steel frame that was case hardened, and the Peacemaker was marketed with an additional cylinder in .22 WMR. The cylinders chambered for the .22 LR were fluted, but those chambered for the .22 WMR were not. A later version known as the New Frontier had a steel frame and adjustable sights. Barrel lengths on the Peace-

Colt produced some elegant versions of the Frontier Scout. This nickel-plated specimen has interchangeable cylinders for .22 LR and .22 WMR caliber cartridges.

maker and New Frontier models were 4 3/8, 6 and 7.5 inches. When taken as a series, the various Colt single action rimfire models have been offered in a wide variety of barrel lengths and sight options. Numerous commemorative models have also been produced. Some were offered with nickel finish, gold accents, and ornate wooden cases, which made them beautiful collectibles.

Operation of a Frontier Scout follows that of the famous Single Action Army. Drawing the hammer back to the half cock position unlocks the cylinder so it can be rotated. Opening the loading gate exposes

Many commemorative Colt Frontier Scout models were produced.

A Colt Frontier Scout such as this one chambered for the .22 WMR is still a fine working gun for the outdoorsman. A single action revolver always looks appropriate in a western style holster.

a chamber into which a cartridge can be inserted. Rotating the cylinder one-sixth of a revolution exposes another chamber, and so on, until all of the chambers are loaded. As discussed earlier revolvers of this type can fire if the hammer is struck. Ruger's solution to this problem was to modify its single action revolvers, which was done in 1973, to incorporate a transfer bar that is in position to allow a blow from the hammer to be transmitted to the cartridge only when the trigger is pulled to the rear.

The two Frontier Scouts tested have barrels measuring 4.75 and 9.5 inches. Sights consist of a rear sight that is simply a groove in the top of the frame and a curved blade front sight. The 4.75-inch barreled specimen is a solid old gun with a close fit between the cylinder and barrel. In the velocity tests, the short barreled gun routinely gave velocities that were about the same as those given by the Frontier Scout that has a barrel nearly five inches longer (see Chapter 8). Performance of both of the Frontier Scouts is just as good as was when the guns were new. This is characteristic of revolvers because there are no problems with feeding cartridges that can plague some older semiautomatics when chamber edges get rough, magazine lips get bent, recoil springs weaken with age, etc. However, revolvers can be plagued with problems related to the hand that rotates the cylinder as the hammer is cocked or the bolt that locks the cylinder in alignment with the barrel.

The crude sights on the Frontier Scouts made accurate shooting impossible, but for short-range work these handguns perform admirably. Moreover, with an aluminum alloy frame, a Frontier Scout is a lightweight handgun that carries easily, and like

other single action handguns points very well. If one is searching for a single action rimfire to carry as a trail gun, the Frontier Scout would be a good choice. Unfortunately, these models are also quite collectible so prices have risen in recent years. A Frontier Scout in good condition is often found for about $500 or so, which can exceed the retail price of a new Ruger Single Six or Bearcat model.

Evaluating the vintage handguns described in this chapter made it clear that these models can perform just as well as current models, but some current models have additional safety features in keeping with the increased concern with safety. Should you select a vintage rimfire handgun for general use? If a specimen is found in good condition at a reasonable price, there is no reason not to select it for a variety of uses. However, the prospective buyer of a rimfire handgun should examine current models along with the older ones to make sure that the handgun chosen has the required feel and handling characteristics. Remember also that new firearms come with a warranty whereas the assurance program for used firearms (if any) usually depends on the dealer. Although models such as the Colt Woodsman and Frontier Scout and the Smith & Wesson K-22 and Kit Gun are no longer produced, they are not difficult to find if you should decide you must own one. However, there are also many choices at comparable or lower prices among the current models for the rimfire handgunner.

SUGGESTIONS FOR FURTHER READING

IN THE PROCESS of dealing with firearms and the shooting sports, many people develop a thirst for additional information. This interest may be directed toward some narrow aspect of the shooting sports or may simply reflect the desire for a broader appreciation of the field. The following bibliography lists references that may prove useful as you seek to improve your knowledge of rimfire firearms and ammunition. The literature dealing with the shooting sports is extensive so some selection was required. For example, even though they contain information on shooting, there is no need to list books that deal specifically with double barreled shotguns, so the books described are some of those that the rimfire shooter will find most helpful.

Barber, John L., *The Rimfire Cartridge in the United States and Canada,* Thomas Publications, Gettysburg, PA (2000). A history of rimfire cartridges.

Crossman, E. C., *Small Bore Rifle Shooting,* Small Arms Technical Publishing Company, Marshallton, DE (1927). One of the classics on rimfire sports.

Cunningham, Grant, *Gun Digest Shooter's Guide to Handguns*, Krause Publications, Iola, WI (2012). A valuable resource for users of all types of handguns, including rimfires.

Datig, Fred A., *Cartridges for Collectors, Vol. 2*, Pioneer Press, Union, TN (1999). Illustrated dictionary of rimfire cartridges. Out of print but sometimes available through dealers who specialize in hard to find books.

Fadala, Sam, *The Book of the Twenty-Two: The All-American Caliber,* Stoeger Publishing Company, South Hackensack, NJ (1989). A general reference work on the 22 caliber that covers both rimfire and small centerfire calibers.

Fears, J. Wayne, *The Complete Book of Outdoor Survival,* Krause Publications, Iola, WI (2000). A complete guide to the skills necessary for survival and safety in outdoor situations.

Forker, Bob, *Ammo & Ballistics 5,* Safari Press, Long Beach, CA (2014). A comprehensive book devoted to ammunition and ballistics.

Geiger, D. F., *.22 Caliber Handguns: A Shooter's Guide,* Andrew Mowbray, Inc., Lincoln, RI (2003). A general introduction to the use of rimfire handguns.

Hatcher, Julian S., *Hatcher's Notebook,* Stackpole Books, Harrisburg, PA (1992). This book is an essential reference on ballistics and a wide range of subjects dealing with arms and ammunition.

House, James E and House, Kathleen A., *Customize the Ruger 10/22, 2nd edition*, Krause Publications, Iola, WI (2016). A comprehensive guide to the Ruger 10/22 and its modification.

Houze, Herbert G., *The Winchester 52: Perfection in Design*, Krause Publications, Iola, WI (1997). The Winchester Model 52 target rifle is probably the most famous small bore target rifle ever made. This book covers the evolution of the Model 52 throughout its period of production.

James, C. Rodney, *The Gun Digest book of the .22 Rifle,* Krause Publications, Iola, WI (2010).

Lachuk, John, *The Gun Digest Book of the .22 Rimfire,* DBI Books, Northfield, IL (1978). A book dealing with all aspects of rimfire shooting by a highly regarded author in the field. As with all such books, the models change although there is a wealth of information presented that is not related to specific models. Long out of print, it still can be found by some dealers in hard to get books. Digest Books are now published by Krause Publications, Iola, WI.

Landis, C. S., *.22 Caliber Rifle Shooting*, The Firearms Classics Library, Palladium Press, Birmingham, AL (1999). A reprint edition of a classic.

Landis, Charles, *Hunting with the Twenty-Two,* Small Arms Technical Publishing Company, Georgetown, South Carolina (1950). Although somewhat out of date, this book has a lot of information on many types of hunting.

Lee, Jerry, *Gun Digest 2016*, Krause Publications, Iola, WI (2016). Billed as "the world's greatest gun book" it has 558 pages to back up that claim. The 70th edition of a classic, it contains numerous articles on a plethora of subjects in addition to a complete catalog section. Also included is a huge section on periodicals and books dealing with guns and shooting. A highly recommended resource.

Lee, Jerry, *Standard Catalog of Firearms*, Krause Publications, Iola, WI (2016).

Long, Duncan, *The Ruger .22 Automatic Pistols, Standard/Mark I/Mark II Series*, Paladin Press, Boulder, CO (1989). A reference work on the ever-popular Ruger pistols.

Long, Duncan, *The Sturm, Ruger 10/22 Rifle and .44 Magnum Carbine,* Paladin Press, Boulder, CO (1988). A small book devoted to the Ruger semiautomatic rifles.

Madis, George, *Winchester Dates of Manufacture,* Art and Reference House, Brownsboro, TX (1984). This little book contains a lot of information on Winchester firearms, serial numbers, and dates of manufacture.

Matunas, Edward, *.22 Rimfire,* Peterson Publishing Company, Los Angeles, CA (1984). This is a special publication that was part of the Guns & Ammo Action Series. An excellent reference that deals with all aspects of rimfire firearms and ammunition. It contains a large amount of information, but many of the firearms discussed are no longer available.

McCoy, Robert L, *Modern Exterior Ballistics,* Schiffer Publishing Co., Atglen, PA (1999). A valuable resource for shooters who want to develop their expertise in ballistics.

Muramatsu, Kevin, *The Gun Digest Book of Rimfire Rifles Assembly/Disassembly,* Krause Publications (1994). A highly respected gunsmith gives step by step instructions for taking apart and putting together a large number of rimfire rifles. Many of the techniques described are useful for working on firearms other than those specifically covered.

Nonte, George C., and Jurras, L. E., *Handgun Hunting*, Winchester Press, New York, NY (1975). The emphasis is on hunting with handguns, and there is a great deal of information that would be useful to the small game hunter using a rimfire handgun.

Quest for Rimfire Accuracy http://members.com.net/benchrest/rimfire_notes.html This website is devoted to information for serious rimfire shooters. Topics posted by experts include equipment, ammunition, and techniques. Highly recommended for the shooter who wants to learn.

Rees, Clair, *Optics Digest,* Safari Press, Huntington Beach, CA (2005). A complete book devoted scopes, binoculars, rangefinders, and spotting scopes.

Schwing, Ned, *Winchester Slide Action Rifles*, Krause Publications, Iola, WI (2004). A reference work on the Models 1890, 1906, 61, and 62 Winchester rimfire rifles. For serious collectors of rimfire Winchester rifles, this book gives an enormous amount of information.

Serven, James E., *Colt Firearms 1836-1960,* Wolfe Publishing Company, Prescott, AZ (1991). A historical book that contains a lot of information on older models of Colt handguns, both black powder and cartridge.

Stebens, Henry M., Shay, Albert J. E., and Hammond, Oscar R., *Pistols: A Modern Encyclopedia,* The Stackpole Company, Harrisburg, PA (1961). Although many of the models discussed are no longer in production, this book is a worthwhile reference on all subjects related to handguns.

Traister, John E., *Gunsmithing at Home: Lock, Stock, & Barrel, 2nd ed.*, Stoeger Publishing Company, Accokeek, MD (1996). Although this book deals with gunsmith work, it also contains a wealth of information on maintenance, tools, finishing, etc.

White, Mark, *The Ultimate Ruger 10/22 Manual and User's Guide,* Paladin Press, Boulder, CO (2000). www.paladin-press.com This book presents a great deal of information on the performance and modification of the most popular autoloader in 22 LR caliber, the Ruger 10/22.

Wilson, R. L., *Ruger and His Guns,* Simon & Schuster, New York, NY (1996). In addition to chronicling the Ruger Company, this lavishly illustrated book contains a great deal on the design and development of Ruger firearms as well as historical information and serial numbers.

Wilson, R. L., *Winchester: An American Legend,* Random House, New York, NY (1991). A noted author provides a history of Winchester firearms in this beautifully illustrated "coffee table" book. A valuable resource for anyone interested in Winchester firearms.

Woodard, W. Todd., *Cartridges of the World, 14th Edition*, Krause Publications, Iola, WI (2014). www.krause.com The standard reference on both current and obsolete metallic cartridges.

Workman, W. E., *The Ruger 10/22*, Krause Publications, Iola, WI (1994). A complete reference work that covers variations, markings, and advertising material from the introduction of the Ruger 10/22 in 1964 to the time of publication. A must for serious 10/22 buffs.

Workman, W. E., *Know Your Ruger 10/22 Carbine,* Blacksmith Corp., Chino Valley, CA (1991). Reference data on the Ruger 10/22.

SOURCES FOR THE RIMFIRE SHOPPER

AcuSport Corporation
730 Hemlock Road
Suite 100
Morgantown, PA 19543-9744
(610) 913.7492
www.acusport.com
A firearms distributor that carries a large number of exclusive versions of many firearms.

Aguila Ammunition, Centurion Ordnance, Inc.
11614 Rainbow Ridge
Helotes, TX 78023
(210) 695-4602
www.aguilaammo.com
Produces an extensive line of ammunition including that in rimfire calibers.

Aimtech Mount Systems
P.O. Box 223
Thomasville, GA 31799
(229) 226-4313
www.aimtech-mounts.com
Sells scope mounts for a wide variety of firearms.

J. G. Anschütz GmbH & Co. KG
Anschütz North America
7661 Commerce Lane
P.O. Box 129
Trussville, AL 35173-2837
(205) 655-7500
http://jga.anschuetz-sport.com
Manufacturers of an extensive line of high quality rimfire rifles.

Alpen Optics
10329 Dorset Street
Rancho Cucamonga, CA 91730
(877) 987-8370
www.alpenoptics.com
A supplier of scopes and other optics.

Altamont Stocks
901 North Church Street
Thomasboro, IL 61878
(800) 626-5774
www.altamontco.com
Manufacturer of stocks and grips for many types of firearms.

Bell & Carlson
101 Allen Road
Dodge City, KS 67801
(620) 225-6688
www.bellandcarlson.com
A manufacturer of stocks.

Beretta USA Corp.
17601 Beretta Drive
Accokeek, MD 20607
(800) 237- 3882
www.berettausa.com
Manufacturer of a complete line of handguns including several rimfire models.

Bersa
Eagle Imports
1750 Brielle Ave, Unit B-1
Wanamassa, NJ 07712
(732) 493-0333
www.bersa.eagleimportsinc.com
Manufacturer of the Bersa Thunder 22.

Bianchi International
Safariland Group
13386 International Parkway
Jacksonville, FL 32218
(800) 347-1200
www.safariland.com
A part of the Safariland Group. Producer of an extensive line of holsters.

Birchwood Laboratories, Inc.
7887 Fuller Road, Suite 100
Eden Prairie, MN 55344
(800) 746-6862
www.birchwoodcasey.com
A supplier for an extensive line of
targets, gun cases, and gun care
and refinishing supplies.

Bob's Gun Shop
P. O. Box 200
Royal, AR 71968
(501) 767-1970
www.gun-parts.com
A supplier of gun parts.

Bo-Mar Tool & Mfg. Co.
6136 State Hwy. 300
Longview, TX 75604
(903) 759-4784
One of the leading producers of
handgun sights.

Boyds' Gunstock Industries
25376 403rd Avenue
Mitchell, SD 57301
(605) 996-5011
www.boydsgunstocks.com
The producer of many types of
laminated and walnut stocks
for rifles.

Brownell's
200 South Front St.
Montezuma, IA 50171
(800) 741-0015
www.brownells.com
Supplier of tools, accessories,
and parts in a bewildering array for
all types of firearms. Has a retail
store at 3006 Brownell's Parkway,
Grinnell, IA.

Browning Arms
One Browning Place
Morgan, UT 84050
(800) 333-3288
www.browning.com
Producers of lever action and
semiautomatic rimfire rifles and
pistols.

BSA Corporation
3911 SW 47 Avenue, Suite 914
Ft. Lauderdale, FL 33314
(954) 581-2144
www.bsaoptics.com
Marketer of an extensive line of
scopes and other optical sights.

B Square
Safariland Group
13386 International Parkway
Jacksonville, FL 32218
(800) 347-1200
www.safariland.com
A part of the Safariland Group.
Manufacturer of B Square scope
mounts.

Burris Company
920 54th Avenue
Greeley, CO 80634
(970) 356-1670
www.burrisoptics.com
The manufacturer of a
comprehensive line of high quality
scopes and other optics.

Bushnell
9200 Cody
Overland Park, KS 66214
(800) 423-3537
www.bushnell.com
A Division of Vista Outdoors
(formerly ATK Sporting Group).
Manufacturer of a broad range
of scopes and other optical
equipment for the shooter.

Butler Creek
Bushnell Outdoor Products
9200 Cody
Overland Park, KS 66214
(800) 221-9035
www.butlercreek.com
A Division of Vista Outdoors
(formerly ATK Sporting Group).
A source for products for general
firearm accessories.

Cabela's
One Cabela Drive
Sidney, NE 69160
(800) 237-4444
www.cabelas.com
A supplier of an enormous range of
supplies for shooters both through
catalog and retail sales.

Carl Zeiss, Inc.
711 Moorefield Park Drive
N. Chester, VA 23236
(800) 441-3005
www.zeiss.com
A manufacturer of elegant scopes
and other high quality optics.

CCI/Speer Ammunition
2299 Snake River Avenue
Lewiston, ID 83501
(800) 379-1732
www.cci-ammunition.com
A division of Vista Outdoors
(formerly ATK Sporting Group).
One of the largest manufacturers
of ammunition including a very
extensive line of rimfire cartridges.

Champion Traps & Targets
1 Vista Way
Anoka, MN 55303
(800) 379-1732
www.championtarget.com
A division of Vista Outdoors
(formerly ATK Sporting Group). A
source for targets, bipods, shooting
rests, rifle stocks for the Ruger
10/22, and other shooting supplies.

Charter Arms
18 Brewster Lane
Shelton, CT 06484
(203) 922-1652
www.charterarms.com
Manufacturer of a revolver in 22 lr
and 22 WMR calibers.

**Cheaper Than Dirt Outdoor
Adventures**
P.O. Box 162087
Fort Worth, TX 76161
(800) 421-8047 (orders)
www.cheaperthandirt.com
A large on-line retailer of product
for shooters that also has retail
stores in Round Rock and
McKinney, Texas.

Chiappa Firearms
1415 Stanley Avenue
Dayton, OH 45404
(937) 835-5000
www.chiappafirearms.com
Manufacturer of replica firearms
including many in rimfire calibers.

Clark Custom Guns, Inc.
336 Shootout Lane
Princeton, LA 71067
(318) 949-9884
clarkcustomguns.com
Producer of products and services
for enhanced accuracy.

Colt's Manufacturing Company
P.O. Box 1868
Hartford, CT 06144-1868
(800) 962-2658
www.colt.com
A source of information and
service for Colt handguns. Colt M4
and 1911 models in rimfire calibers
are produced by Walther.

Competition Electronics
3469 Precision Drive
Rockford, IL 61109
(815) 874-8001
www.competitionelectronics.com
One of the manufacturers of
chronographs.

Cooper Firearms of Montana
3662 Highway 93 North
Stevensville, MT 59870
(406) 777-0373
cooperfirearms.com
Manufacturer of elegant
sporting rifles.

CZ USA
P. O. Box 171073
Kansas City, KS 66117-0073
(800) 955-4486
www.cz-usa.com
Marketer of the outstanding CZ
rimfire rifles produced in the Czech
Republic.

Davidson's, Inc.
GalleryOfGuns.com
6100 Wilkinson Drive
Prescott, AZ 86301
(800) 537-2565
www.davidsonsinc.com
Gallery of Guns is the consumer
website for Davidson's Inc., a
huge distributor that carries many
distributor exclusive firearms.

E. Arthur Brown Company
4088 County Road 40 NW
Garfield, MN 56332
(800) 950-9088
www.eabco.com
On-line retailer of barrels, stocks,
and other accessories.

Electronic Shooters Protection
15290 Gadsden Court
Brighton, CO 80603
(303) 659-8844
espamerica.com
One of the manufacturers of
hearing protectors.

Eley Limited
Selco Way
Minworth Industrial Estate
B76 1BA
West Midlands
England
www.eley.co.uk
A producer of an extensive line of
rimfire ammunition including high
quality target ammunition.

Excel Industries
4510 Carter Court
Chino, CA 91710
www.excelarms.com
Maker of the Accelerator
semiautomatic pistols and rifles.

Federal Cartridge Company
900 Ehlen Drive
Anoka, MN 55303
(800) 379-1732
www.federalpremium.com
A division of Vista Outdoors
(formerly ATK Sporting Group).
One of the largest producers of
ammunition including many types
of rimfire ammunition.

Fiocchi Ammunition
6930 Fremont Road
Ozark, MO 65721
(417) 725-4118
www.fiocchiusa.com
A producer of many types of rimfire
ammunition.

Forster Precision Products
310 E. Lanark Avenue
Lanark, IL 61046
(815) 493-6360
www.forsterproducts.com
Manufacturers of a .22 LR
headspace gauge and other types
of gunsmithing tools.

Freedom Arms, Inc.
314 Highway 239
Freedom, WY 83120 (307) 883-
2468
www.freedomarms.com
Producer of single action
handguns including small rimfire
models.

G-96 Products, Inc.
85-Fifth Avenue, Building No. 6
Paterson, NJ 07524-1112
(877) 332-0035
www.g96.com
Producer of numerous gun care
products.

GALCO International Ltd.
2019 W. Quail Ave.
Phoenix, AZ 85027
(800) 874-2526
www.usgalco.com
One of the large producers of
handgun holsters.

Graf & Sons, Inc.
4050 S. Clark Street
Mexico, MO 65265
(800) 531-2666
www.grafs.com
Retailer of ammunition,
gunsmithing tools, gun care
products, scopes, and stocks,
magazines, barrels, and many
other products for the Ruger
10/22 and 10/22 Magnum.

Green Mountain Rifle Barrels
P. O. Box 2670
Conway, NH 03818
(603) 447-1095
www.gmriflebarrel.com
A large manufacturer of barrels for
both cartridge and muzzle loading
firearms including the Ruger
10/22.

Gunslick
1 Vista Way
Anoka, MN 55303
(800) 379-1732
www.gunslick.com
A division of Vista Outdoors
(formerly ATK Sporting Group).
Manufacturer of a line of gun care
products.

**Henry Repeating Arms
Company**
59 East 1st Street
Bayonne, NJ 07002
(201) 858-4400
www.henryrepeating.com
Maker of several models of
rimfire rifles.

Heritage Manufacturing, Inc.
16175 N. W. 49th Avenue
Miami Lakes, FL 33014
(305) 685-5966
www.heritagemfg.com
Manufacturer of single action revolvers with 22 LR and 22 WMR cylinders.

High Standard Mfg. Co.
5151 Mitchelldale, B14
Houston, TX 77092-7222
(713) 462-4200
www.highstandard.com
Manufacturer of High Standard and AMT semiautomatic pistols.

Hogue
P. O. 1138
Paso Robles, CA 93447
(800) 438-4747
www.hogueinc.com
Producer of a wide range of handgun grips and stocks including the rubber OverMolded models.

Hoppe's
Bushnell Outdoor Products
9200 Cody
Overland Park, KS 66214
(800) 423-3537
www.hoppes.com
A division of Vista Outdoors (formerly ATK Sporting Group). Manufacturer of gun care products, targets, and shooting bags along with other gun accessories

Hornady Mfg. Co.
3625 West Old Potash Hwy
Grand Island, NE 68803
(800) 338-3220
www.hornady.com
Manufacturer of reloading equipment, ammunition, and supplies. Developer of the 17 HMR and 17 Mach 2 calibers.

Hornet Products
P. O. Box 1664
Sarasota, FL 34230-1664
(941) 359-1319
www.hornetproducts.com
Supplier of a wide range of aftermarket products for the Ruger 10/22 and 77/22 rifles and Mark II pistols. Products include Green Mountain, Lothar Walther, and Volquartsen barrels.

Hunter Co., Inc.
3300 W. 71st Avenue
Westminster, CO 80030
(303) 427-4626
www.huntercompany.com
Producer of leather goods and holsters.

J. A. Ciener
8700 Commerce St.
Cape Canaveral, FL 32920
(321) 868-2200
www.22lrconversions.com
Produces 22 LR conversion units for several popular models of handguns and rifles.

Jard, Inc.
3149 Nest Avenue
Sheldon, IA 51201
(712) 324-7409
www.jardinc.com
Producer of aftermarket triggers for many rifles including Ruger 77/22 and 10/22.

Jarvis, Inc.
1123 Cherry Orchard Loop
Hamilton, MT 59840
(406) 961-4392
www.jarvis-custom.com
Maker of high quality aftermarket custom barrels.

Kahles USA - HPS
2170 Carney Drive, Suite F
Orofino, ID 83544
(208)476-0600
www.kahlesoptik.com
A manufacturer of a line of high quality scopes and other optics.

Keystone Sporting Arms, Inc.
155 Sodom Road
Milton, PA 17847
(800) 742-0455
www.cricket.com
Maker of the Cricket and Chipmunk lines of youth rifles.

Kimber Mfg. Inc.
555 Taxter Road, Suite 235
Elmsford, NY 10523
One Lawton Street, Yonkers, NY
10705 (800) 243-4522
www.kimberamerica.com
Maker of high quality pistols and
bolt action sporting rifles.

Klean-Bore, Inc.
Safariland Group
13386 International Parkway
Jacksonville, FL 32218
(800) 347-1200
www.safariland.com
A part of the Safariland Group. A
marketer of an extensive line of gun
care products.

Kramer Handgun Leather
P. O. Box 112154
Tacoma, WA 98411
(800) 510-2666
www.kramerleather.com
A supplier of an extensive line of
holsters and other leather goods.

Lapua Ammunition
Nammo AS
P. O. Box 142
NO-2831 Raufoss, Norway
+47 61 15 36 00
www.lapua.com
The European manufacturer of
many types of rimfire ammunition
including brands such as Lapua
and SK Jagd.

LaserMax
3495 Winton Place
Rochester, NY 14623
(800) 527-3703
www.lasermax.com
Producer of laser sights for a wide
variety of firearms.

Leica Camera, Inc.
1 Pearl Court, Unit A
Allendale, NJ 07401
(800) 222-0118
www.leica-camera.com
Legendary producer of superb
cameras and other optical devices
of the highest quality.

Leupold & Stevens, Inc.
14400 NW Greenbrier Parkway
Beaverton, OR 97006-5790
(800) 538-7653
www.leupold.com
One of the largest manufacturers
of scopes of all types and other
optics. Models available include
those for any type of shooting.

**Lilja Precision Rifle Barrels,
Inc.**
P. O. Box 372
81 Lower Lynch Creek Road
Plains, MT 59859
(406) 826-3084
www.riflebarrels.com
A manufacturer of high quality rifle
barrels.

Lipsey's Guns
www.lipseysguns.com
A huge firearms distributor that
carries numerous versions of the
Ruger 10/22 that are exclusive to
Lipsey's.

**Lothar Walther Precision
Tools, Inc.**
3425 Hutchinson Road
Cumming, GA 30040
(770) 889-9998
www.lothar-walther.com
Manufacturer of match grade
barrel blanks that are used by
many custom barrel makers and
gunsmiths.

Lyman Products Corporation
475 Smith Street
Middletown, CT 06457
(800) 225-9626
www.lymanproducts.com
Marketer of a digital trigger pull
gauge and many gunsmithing tools
and supplies.

Magnum Research, Inc.
12602 33rd Avenue SW
Pillager, MN 56473
(508) 635-4273
www.magnumresearch.com
Manufacturer of complete rifles
and ultra light graphite-sleeved
barrels for the Ruger 10/22 and
10/22 Magnum.

Majestic Arms, LTD.
101-A Ellis Street
Staten Island, NY 10307
(718) 356-6765
www.majesticarms.com
Producer of the Aluma-Lite barrels
designed by Dino Longueira with a
steel insert in an aluminum sleeve.
Also produces many upgrade parts
for Ruger pistols.

Marlin Firearms
100 Kenna Drive
P.O. Box 248
North Haven, CT 06473-5621
(800) 544-8892
www.marlinfirearms.com
One of the largest manufacturers
of rimfire rifles.

Midsouth Shooters Supply
770 Economy Drive
Clarksville, TN 37043
(800) 272-3000
www.midsouthshooterssupply.com
Retailer of many gun accessories
including barrels, stocks, and
sights. Their website has an
extensive list of vendor links.

Midway USA
5885 W. Van Horn Tavern Road
Columbia, MO 65203
(800) 243-3220
www.midwayusa.com
One of the largest catalog
companies that offers a wide range
of aftermarket item, scopes, grips,
etc.

Millett Sights
9200 Cody
Overland Park, KS 66214
(888) 276-5945
www.millettsights.com
A division of Vista Outdoors
(formerly ATK Sporting Group).
Marketer of a well-known line of
scopes, mounts, and other items
for many firearms.

**Montana X-Treme Gun Care
Products**
Western Powders, Inc.
P. O. Box 158
Miles City, MT 59301
(406) 234-0422
www.montanaxtreme.com
Marketer of a line of gun care
products.

**Mossberg (O. F. Mossberg
& Sons, Inc.)**
7 Grasso Avenue
North Haven, CT 06473
(800) 363-3555
www.mossberg.com
Manufacturer of a full line of rimfire
rifles.

MTM Molded Products Co.
3370 Obco Court
Dayton, OH 45413
(937) 890-7461
www.mtmcase-gard.com
A producer of shooting benches,
shooting rests, gun vises, target
stands and dry boxes.

**Natchez Shooters Supplies,
Inc.**
P. O. Box 182212
Chattanooga, TN 37422
(800) 251-7839
www.natchezss.com
Catalog and on-line retailer with
a complete range of items related
to the shooting sports. Products
offered cover all phases of the
shooting sports.

National Rifle Association
11250 Waples Mill Road
Fairfax, VA 22030-9400
(800) 672-3888
www.nra.org
The source of an incredible amount
of information on shooting sports
and the organization most visible
in supporting Second Amendment
rights.

Nightforce Optics
336 Hazen Lane
Orofino, ID 83544
(208) 476-9814
www.NightforceOptics.com
Producer of scopes and other
optical equipment for shooters.

Nikon
1300 Walt Whitman Road
Melville, NY 11747-3064
(800) 645-6687
www.nikonsportoptics.com
A well-known manufacturer of
cameras, scopes and other optical
devices that includes rangefinders
and scopes for rimfires.

North American Arms, Inc.
2150 S. 950 East
Provo, UT 84606
(800) 821-5783
www.northamericanarms.com
Maker of small revolvers in rimfire
calibers.

Numrich Gun Parts Corp.
226 Williams Lane
Kingston, NY 12401
(866) 686-7424
www.e-gunparts.com
A large supplier of factory parts for
many firearms.

Oehler Research, Inc.
P. O. Box 9135
Austin, TX 78766
(800) 531-5125
www.oehler-research.com
One of the premier manufacturers
of chronographs.

Outers Guncare
1 Vista Way
Anoka, MN 55303
(800) 379-1732
www.outers-guncare.com
A division of Vista Outdoors
(formerly ATK Sporting Group).
Marketer of an extensive line of gun
care products.

Pachmayr
475 Smith Street
Middletown, CT 06457
(800) 423-9704
www.pachmayr.com
A division of Lyman. Maker of an
extensive line of aftermarket grips
for handguns.

Pentax U. S. A., Inc.
Ricoh Imaging Americas
Corporation
633 17th Street, Suite 2600
Denver, CO 80202
(800) 877-0155
www.us.ricoh-imaging.com
A company well-known for high
quality scopes and other optics.

Plano Molding Company
431 E. South Street
Plano, IL 60545
(800) 226-9868
www.planomolding.com
A producer of many products for
shooting sports including polymer
gun cases.

PMC Ammunition
Boulder City, NV 89005
(702) 294-0025
www.pmcammo.com
Supplier of an extensive line of
rimfire ammunition.

Pro Ears
Altus Brands
6893 Sullivan Road
Grawn, MI 49637
(800) 891-3660
www.proears.com
A manufacturer of hearing
protectors.

Pro-Shot Products
311 S. Baughman Road
Taylorville, IL 62568
(217) 824-9133
www.proshotproducts.com
Marketer of an extensive line of gun
care products.

RCBS
605 Oro Dam Boulevard East
Oroville, CA 95965
(800) 379-1732
www.rcbs.com
A division of Vista Outdoors
(formerly ATK Sporting Group).
Manufacturer of reloading
equipment, a trigger pull gauge,
and gunsmithing tools.

Redfield USA
14400 NW Greenbrier Parkway
Beaverton, OR 97006-5790
(877) 798-9686
www.redfield.com
A division of Leopold & Stevens.
Manufacturer of scopes and other
optics.

Remington Arms Company
P. O. Box 700
870 Remington Drive
Madison, NC 27025
(800) 243-9700
www.remington.com
One of the oldest and most
respected firearms companies.
Markets many types of rimfire
ammunition.

Rifle Basix
P. O. Box 49064
Charlotte, NC 28227
(704) 499-3087
www.riflebasix.com
Manufacturer of triggers for a
variety of rifles including rimfires.

Rimfire Sports & Custom
20280 Rosedale Court
Ashburn, VA 20147-3317
www.rimfiresports.com
On-line retailer of barrels, stocks,
and other accessories for the
Ruger 10/22 and 10/22 Magnum.

Rossi
16175 NW 49 Avenue
Miami Lakes, FL 33014
(800) 948-8029
www.rossiusa.com
A division of Braztech International.
Manufacturer of several convertible
rifles and handguns in shotgun/
rimfire or centerfire/rimfire
combinations.

RUAG Ammotec GmbH
Kronacher Strasse 63
90765 Furth Deutschland
www.ruag.com
Manufacturer of RWS ammunition
that includes many types of rimfire
loads.

Sack-Ups
1611 Jamestown Road
Morganton, NC 28655
(877) 213-6333
www.sackups.com
Producer of gun sleeves for
storage and transporting firearms.

Safariland Group
13386 International Parkway
Jacksonville, FL 32218
(800) 347-1200
www.safariland.com
A manufacturer of a variety of gun
products including holsters, Break
Free and Kleen Bore cleaning
products and B Square scope
mounts.

Sako Limited
P. O. Box 149
FI-11101 Riimimaki
Finland
(358) 10-830-5200
www.sako.fi
Manufacturer of the elegant Sako
Quad, a switch-barrel rifle available
in 17 HM2, 17 HMR, 22 lr, and 22
WMR calibers

Savage Arms, Inc.
100 Springdale Road
Westfield, MA 01085
(800) 370-0708
www.savagearms.com
Manufacturer of an extensive line
of bolt action, semiautomatic, and
single shot rimfire rifles.

Scheels All Sports
2101 W. 41st Street
Sioux Falls, SD 57105-6140
(605)334-7767
www.scheels.com
A chain of retail stores that
markets an extensive line of items
for shooting. Also markets a line
of proprietary scopes, including
rimfire models, made to Scheels
specifications and carrying the
Scheels label.

Schmidt & Bender, Inc.
741 Main Street
Claremont, NH 03743
(603) 287-4830
www.schmidt-bender.com
A manufacturer of high quality
scopes and other optics.

Shilen Rifles, Inc.
P. O. Box 1300
Ennis, TX 75120
(972) 875-5318
www.shilen.com
One of the highly respected names
in aftermarket barrels. The Shilen
name frequently appears in the list
of equipment used by winners in
competitive events.

Shooter's Choice
Ventco, Inc.
15050 Berkshire Industrial
Parkway
Middlefield, OH 44062
(440) 834-8888
www.shooters-choice.com
A producer of a line of gun care
products.

Shooting Chrony, Inc.
3840 E. Robinson Road
PMB 298
Amherst, NY 14228
(800) 385-3161
www.shootingchrony.com
A manufacturer of well known
chronographs.

Sightron, Inc.
100 Jeffrey Way, Suite A
Youngsville, NC 27596
(919) 562-3000
www.sightron.com
Marketer of an extensive line of
scopes, red dot sights, and other
optical equipment. The scope line
ranges from competitively priced
low-end models to truly outstanding
upper end scopes, and includes
models for rimfire rifles.

Sig Sauer
72 Pease Blvd.
Newington, NH 03801
(603)610-3000
www.sigarms.com
Producer of the P226 classic 22
and Centerfire X-change kit.

**Simmons Outdoors
Corporation**
9200 Cody
Overland Park, KS 66214
(888) 276-5945
www.simmonsoptics.com
A division of Vista Outdoors
(formerly ATK Sporting Group). A
large marketer of scopes and other
optical equipment.

Sinclair International, Inc.
200 South Front St.
Montezuma, IA 50171
(800) 717-8211
www.sinclairintl.com
A division of Brownells. A catalog
retailer of an enormous range
of products for shooters with
emphasis on products for use in
competition.

Smith & Wesson
2100 Roosevelt Avenue
Springfield, MA 01104
(800) 331-0852
www.smith-wesson.com
Manufacturer of a wide variety of
handguns for sporting, military, and
law enforcement uses. Originator
of the 22 rimfire cartridge.

Sports South
(800) 388-3845
www.internetguncatalog.com
A huge distributor of many dealer
exclusive models of firearms.

Steiner Optik
331 East 8th Street
Greeley, CO 80631
(888) 228-7747
www.steiner-optics.com
Manufacturer of high quality
scopes and other optics.

Sturm, Ruger, & Co., Inc.
Customer Service Department
411 Sunapee Street
Newport, NH 03773
(603) 865-2442
www.ruger.com
One of the largest firearm
manufacturers in the U.S.

Superior Products
SPS Marketing
(888) 243-6725
www.slip2000.com
The marketer of a line of gun care
products.

**Swarovski Optik North
America, Ltd.**
2 Slater Road
Cranston, RI 02920
(800) 426-3089
www.swarovskioptik.com
A manufacturer that is famous
for producing scopes and other
optical devices of the highest
quality.

Swift Optics
4975 Miller Street, Unit B
Wheat Ridge, CO 80033
(877) 697-9438
www.swift-sportoptics.com
A producer of scopes and other
optics.

Tactical Solutions
2772 S. Victory View Way
Boise, ID 83709
(866) 333-9901
www.tacticalsol.com
The manufacturer of several types
of outstanding light-weight rifles,
barrels and accessories.

TALO Dristributors, Inc.
www.taloinc.com
Distributor of dealer exclusive
models of the Ruger 10/22.

Tasco
9200 Cody
Overland Park, KS 66214
(800) 423-3537
www.tasco.com
A well-known manufacturer of
moderately priced scopes and
other optics.

Taurus International Manufacturing, Inc.
16175 NW 49 Avenue
Miami Lakes, FL 33014
(800) 327-3776
www.taurususa.com
Manufacturer of handguns
including several in rimfire calibers.

Tetra Products
FTI, Inc.
8 Vreeland Road
Florham Park, NJ 07932
(973) 443-0004
www.tetraproducts.com
A marketer of a line of gun care
products.

The Woodchuck Den, Inc.
11220 Hilltop Road SW
Baltic, OH 43804
(330) 897-0614
www.woodchuckden.com
A retailer of a variety of shooting
accessories.

Thompson/Center
2100 Roosevelt Ave.
Springfield, MA 01104
(866)730.1614
www.tcarms.com
A division of Smith & Wesson.
Manufacturer of the G2 Contender
rifle and pistol in numerous
calibers including 22 lr and 17
HMR.

Timney Triggers
2020 West Quail Avenue
Phoenix, AZ 85027
(866) 484-6639
www.timneytriggers.com
Manufacturer of replacement
trigger assemblies for many rifles.

Trijicon, Inc.
P. O. Box 930059
49385 Shafer Avenue
Wixom, MI 48393-0059
(800)338-0563
www.trijicon.com
The manufacturer of a broad range
of products that includes sights,
scopes, and other optics.

Triple-K Mfg. Co., Inc.
2222 Commercial St.
San Diego, CA 92113
(619) 232-2066
www.triplek.com
Manufacturer of holsters,
especially for single action
revolvers.

Uberti
Stoeger Industries
901 Eighth Street
Pocomoke, MD 21851
(800) 264-4962
www.uberti.com
Manufacturer of rifles and revolvers
in the style of the old west.

Uncle Mike's
Bushnell Outdoor Products
9200 Cody
Overland Park, KS 66214
(800) 423-3537
www.unclemikes.com
A division of Vista Outdoors
(formerly ATK Sporting Group).
Marketer of a wide range of
shooting accessories that
includes sling swivels, studs, gun
cases, slings, holsters, and other
accessories.

United States Rimfire Association
IR50/50 Inc.
2241 Weaver Pike
Bristol, TN 37620
(423) 341-1891
www.ir5050.com
The association devoted to rimfire
shooting sports.

USA Rifle Stocks
Xsalta, LLC
State College, PA 16801
(800) 814-0985
www.usariflestocks.com
A retailer of stocks and barrels.

Volquartsen Custom, Ltd.
P. O. Box 397
24276 240th Street
Carroll, IA 51401
(712) 792-4238
www.volquartsen.com
One of the premier manufacturers
of aftermarket barrels, triggers, and
other items as well as complete
rifles, especially autoloaders
in rimfire calibers. Volquartsen
products are also available from
large suppliers such as Brownell's,
Cabela's, and Midway USA.

Walker's Game Ear, Inc.
P. O. Box 535189
Grand Prairie, TX 75053
(877) 269-8490
www.gsmoutdoors.com/walkers
A manufacturer of hearing
protectors.

Walther Arms, Inc.
7700 Chad Colley Blvd.
Fort Smith, AR 72916
(479) 242-8500
www.waltherarms.com
Manufacturer of several 22 lr
caliber handguns including the
Colt M4 and 1911 A1 produced
under license from Colt.

Weaver
1 Vista Way
Anoka, MN 55303
(800) 379-1732
www.weaveroptics.com
A division of the Vista Outdoors
(formerly ATK Sporting Group).
Manufacturer of optics and many
types of scope rings and Ruger
10/22 bases.

**Widener's Reloading &
Shooting Supply, Inc.**
P. O. Box 3009 CRS
Johnson City, TN 37602
(800) 615-3006
www.wideners.com
Retailer of gunsmithing tools and a
wide range of products related to
the shooting sports.

**Williams Gun Sight
Company, Inc.**
P.O. Box 329
7389 Lapeer Road
Davison, MI 48423
(800) 530-9028
www.williamsgunsight.com
The manufacturer of Williams
Firesights® and peep sights.

Winchester Ammunition
600 Powder Mill Road
East Alton, IL 62024-1273
(800) 356-2666
www.winchester.com
A famous ammunition manufacturer
whose products include many
types of rimfire ammunition.

Winchester Repeating Arms
275 Winchester Avenue
Morgan, UT 84050
(800) 333-3288
www.winchesterguns.com
Winchester does not currently
produce rifles in any rimfire
calibers.

**Wolf Performance
Ammunition**
P.O. Box 757
Placentia, CA 92871
(888) 757-9653
www.wolfammo.com
Importer of the Wolf ammunition
line that includes target types of
rimfire ammunition.

SOURCES FOR HUNTING INFORMATION

Alabama Department of Conservation and Natural Resources
64 N. Union Street #551
Montgomery, AL 36130
(334) 242-3471
www.outdooralabama.com

Alaska Department of Fish and Game
333 Raspberry Road
Anchorage, AK 99518
(907) 267-2532
www.adfg.alaska.gov

Arizona Game and Fish Department
5000 W. Carefree Highway
Phoenix, AZ 85086-5000
(602) 942-3000
www.azgfdportal.az.gov

Arkansas Game and Fish Commission
2 Natural Resources Drive
Little Rock, AR 72205
(501) 223-6300
www.agfc.com

California Department of Fish and Wildlife
1416 9th Street, 12th Floor
Sacramento, CA 95814
(916) 445-0411
https://www.wildlife.ca.gov

Colorado Parks and Wildlife
6060 Broadway
Denver, CO 80216
(303) 291-7227
http://cpw.state.co.us

Connecticut Department of Energy and Environmental Protection
79 Elm Street
Hartford, CT 06106
(860) 424-3000
www.ct.gov/deep/site/default.asp

Delaware Division of Fish and Wildlife
89 Kings Highway
Dover, DE 19901
(302) 739-9910
www.dnrec.delaware.gov/fw/Pages/DFW-Portal.aspx

Florida Fish and Wildlife Conservation Commission
620 S. Meridian Street
Tallahassee, FL 32399
(850) 488-4676
myfwc.com

Georgia Department of Natural Resources
2 M.L.K. Jr Drive NW
Atlanta, GA 30334
(404) 656-3500
www.gadnr.org

Hawaii Department of Land and Natural Resources
Kalanimoku Building
1151 Punchbowl Street
Honolulu, HI 96813
(808) 587-0400
http://dlnr.hawaii.gov

Idaho Fish and Game
600 S. Walnut
Boise, ID 83712
(208) 334-3700
http://fishandgame.idaho.gov

Illinois Department of Natural Resources
One Natural Resources Way
Springfield, IL 62702
(217) 782-6302
www.dnr.illinois.gov

Indiana Department of Natural Resources
402 West Washington Street
Indianapolis, IN 46204
(877) 463-6367
www.in.gov/dnr

Iowa Department of Natural Resources
Wallace State Office Building
502 East 9th Street
Des Moines, IA 50319
(515) 725-8200
www.iowadnr.gov

**Kansas Department
of Wildlife and Parks**
512 SE 25th Avenue
Pratt, KS 67124
(620) 672-5911
http://ksoutdoors.com

**Kentucky Department of Fish
and Wildlife Resources**
#1 Sportsman's Lane
Frankfort, KY 40601
(800) 858-1549
http://fw.ky.gov/

**Louisiana Department of
Wildlife and Fisheries**
P.O. Box 98000
2000 Quail Drive
Baton Rouge, LA 70898
(800) 256-2749
www.wlf.louisiana.gov

**Maine Department of Inland
Fisheries and Wildlife**
41 State House Station
Augusta, ME 04333-0041
(207) 287-8000
www.maine.gov/ifw/

**Maryland Department of
Natural Resources**
580 Taylor Avenue
Tawes State Office Building
Annapolis, MD 21401
(410) 260-8367
http://dnr2.maryland.gov

**Massachusetts Department of
Fish and Game**
251 Causeway Street, Suite 400
Boston, MA 02114-2152
(617) 626-2152
www.mass.gov/eea/agencies/dfg/

**Michigan Department of
Natural Resources**
P.O. Box 30028
Lansing, MI 48909
(517) 284-5815
www.michigan.gov/dnr/

**Minnesota Department
of Natural Resources**
500 Lafayette Road
St. Paul, MN 55155-4040
(651) 296-6157
(888) 646-6367
www.dnr.state.mn.us

**Mississippi Department
of Wildlife, Fisheries,
and Parks**
1505 Eastover Drive
Jackson, MS 39211
(601) 432-2400
http://mdc.mo.gov

**Missouri Department
of Conservation**
2901 W. Truman Blvd.
Jefferson City, MO 65109
(573) 751-4115
http://mdc.mo.gov

**Montana Fish, Wildlife,
and Parks**
1420 East Sixth Avenue
Helena, MT 59620
(406) 444-2535
http://fwp.mt.gov

Nebraska Game and Parks
2200 N. 33rd Street
Lincoln, NE 68503
(402)471-0641
http://outdoornebraska.ne.gov

**Nevada Department
of Wildlife**
6980 Sierra Center Parkway #120
Reno, NV 89511
(775) 688-1500
www.ndow.org

**New Hampshire Fish
and Game Department**
11 Hazen Drive
Concord, NH 03301
(603) 271-3421
www.wildlife.state.nh.us

**New Jersey Division
of Fish and Wildlife**
P.O. Box 420
Trenton, NJ 08625-0420
(609) 292-2965
www.njfishandwildlife.com

**New Mexico Department
of Game and Fish**
1 Wildlife Way
Santa Fe, NM 87507
(888) 248-6866
www.wildlife.state.nm.us

**New York State Department of
Environmental Conservations**
Division of Fish, Wildlife, and
Marine Resources
625 Broadway
Albany, NY 12233
(518) 402-8995
www.dec.ny.gov

**North Carolina Wildlife
Resources Commission**
1751 Varsity Drive
Raleigh, NC 27606
(919) 707-0010
www.ncwildlife.org

**North Dakota Game
and Fish Department**
100 N. Bismarck Expressway
Bismarck, ND 58501
(701) 328-6300
http://gf.nd.gov

**Ohio Department
of Natural Resources**
2045 Morse Road
Columbus, OH 43229
(614) 265-6565
http://ohiodnr.gov

**Oklahoma Department
of Wildlife Conservation**
2145 NE 36th Street
Oklahoma City, OK 73111
(405) 521-3851
www.wildlifedepartment.com

**Oregon Department
of Fish and Wildlife**
4034 Fairview Industrial Drive SE
Salem, OR 97302
(503) 947-6000
www.dfw.state.or.us

**Pennsylvania Department
of Conservation and
Natural Resources**
Bureau of Recreation and
Conservation
400 Market Street
Harrisburg, PA 17101
(800)326-7734
www.dcnr.state.pa.us

**Rhode Island Department of
Environmental Management**
Bureau of Natural Resources
235 Promenade Street
Providence, RI 02908
(401) 222-3162
www.dem.ri.gov

**South Carolina Department
of Natural Resources**
1000 Assembly Street
Columbia, SC 29201
(803) 734-3886
www.dnr.sc.gov

**South Dakota
Department of Environment
and Natural Resources**
523 East Capitol
Pierre, SD 57501
(605) 773-3151
http://denr.sd.gov

**Tennessee Wildlife
Resources Agency**
440 Hogan Road
Nashville, TN 37220
(615) 781-6500
https://tn.gov.twra

**Texas Parks and
Wildlife Department**
4200 Smith School Road
Austin, TX 78744
(512) 389-4800
https://tpwd.texas.gov

**Utah Department
of Natural Resources**
P.O. Box 145610
1594 W. North Temple
Salt Lake City, UT 84114
(801) 538-7200
http://naturalresources.utah.gov

**Vermont Agency
of Natural Resources**
1 National Life Drive
Montpelier, VT 05620
(802) 828-1294
http://anr.vermont.gov

**Virginia Department
of Game and Inland Fisheries**
P.O. Box 90778
Henrico, VA 23228
(804) 367-1000
www.dgif.virginia.gov

**Washington Department
of Natural Resources**
1111 Washington Street SE
Olympia, WA 98504
(360) 902-1000
www.dnr.wa.gov

**West Virginia Division
of Natural Resouces**
324 Fourth Avenue
South Charleston, WV 25303
(304) 558-3315
www.wvdnr.gov

**Wisconsin Department
of Natural Resources**
101 South Webster Street
Madison, WI 53707
(888) 936-7463
http://dnr.wi.gov

**Wyoming Game and Fish
Department**
5400 Bishop Blvd.
Cheyenne, WY 82006
(307) 777-4600
https://wgfd.wyo.gov

About the Author

James E. House has been an active participant in shooting sports for about 70 years. Although he began shooting airguns, he was a member of the Air Force ROTC rifle team while a student at Southern Illinois University in Carbondale where he received B.S. and M.A. degrees. After receiving a Ph.D. in chemistry from the University of Illinois, he spent 32 years as a faculty member and administrator at Illinois State University.

Since becoming an Emeritus Professor, House has been an Adjunct Professor of Chemistry at Illinois Wesleyan University and has been a productive author. His books include titles on chemical kinetics, quantum mechanics, inorganic chemistry, and a book on descriptive inorganic chemistry that was co-authored with his wife, Kathleen A. House. He is also the author of *American Air Rifles* (Krause Publications, 2001), *CO_2 Pistols & Rifles (*Krause Publications, 2003), and with his wife, *Customize The Ruger 10/22* (Krause Publications, 2015). Approximately 400 of his articles have appeared in publications such as *Gun World, American Survival Guide, Modern Pioneer, The Backwoodsman, The Varmint Hunter, The Illinois Shooter,* and other magazines that deal with shooting and outdoor sports. He and his wife have traveled extensively in the mountain states where they engage in photography, camping, and shooting activities.